THE RELIGIOUS ORDER

*A study of virtuoso religion and its
legitimation in the nineteenth-century
Church of England*

The Religious Order

*A study of virtuoso religion and its
legitimation in the nineteenth-century
Church of England*

Michael Hill

Distributed in the United States by
]CRANE, RUSSAK & COMPANY, INC.   BOOKS
347 Madison Avenue
New York, New York 10017

Heinemann Educational Books Ltd

LONDON EDINBURGH MELBOURNE AUCKLAND TORONTO
HONG KONG SINGAPORE KUALA LUMPUR
IBADAN NAIROBI JOHANNESBURG NEW DELHI

ISBN 0 435 82412 0

Published by Heinemann Educational Books Ltd
48 Charles Street, London W1X 8AH
Printed in Great Britain by
Richard Clay (The Chaucer Press) Ltd
Bungay, Suffolk

Contents

To Lyn

Acknowledgements

This book originated as a doctoral thesis under the supervision of Dr B. R. Wilson, to whom I am deeply indebted for his patient advice and perceptive criticism. I am extremely fortunate in having had the benefit of his keen scholarship and intellectual precision, since I have learned to distinguish these qualities from the mediocre pedantry which occasionally passes for sociology in our older universities. I also count myself very lucky indeed to have had the enthusiastic help and encouragement of Father A. M. Allchin from an early stage in the research. He showed me how to treat the subject with humanity and above all to enjoy what I was doing.

Professor D. A. Martin was a source of many insights in the research and was a constant guide when the going got rough. He has spent a great deal of time on this book and has suggested many ways of improving it. Finally, the part played by Professor D. G. MacRae in keeping me on course and eventually in seeing the book through to its completion deserves my unstinting thanks. Six years is long enough to be involved in one book, but at least it has not been an eremitic experience.

Dr A. H. Halsey deserves a word of thanks for occasionally correcting my English.

To those I have named, and to all my colleagues and students at the London School of Economics who have helped to sustain me in my research, I am deeply grateful. For the final result I alone must be held responsible.

A particular word of thanks is due to Miss Pat Walsh, who arrived on the scene at a very bleak point in the research and managed, by her sheer good humour and faultless typing, to prod me into completing the first draft. The final draft was impressively typed by Miss Valerie Campling.

For my wife, the publication of this book must seem like the departure of a familiar lodger. She has seen it go through various stages and the odd minor crisis and she must be glad to see it on its way. For her help—in simply being there but also in bibliographical and proof-reading chores—the book is dedicated to her.

London School of Economics, October 1973

I

The Religious Order in the Sociology of Religion

THIS BOOK IS an attempt to explore several areas in the sociology of religion which have already been broadly mapped out but which have so far received little detailed analysis. Weber and Troeltsch were the first in sociology to point to the importance for a large institutional body such as the Roman Catholic Church of affiliated monastic groups with a highly rigorous ethic. The idea that such communities represent a 'leaven within the lump' which is somehow able to revive and stimulate the larger organization is familiar to theologians, historians and sociologists alike. It is also apparent that similar forms of 'ginger group' play a parallel role in political parties. My purpose in this book will be to take this general notion—which was the rather crude idea from which my research initially took shape—and to construct from it a sociological model in the form of an ideal type of the religious order. This will make possible comparisons with other types of organization as well as the application of sociological techniques in a detailed case study. The first half of this book is concerned with establishing and comparing basic categories and the second half with applying these in a restricted historical context.

The book has three major themes. Firstly, I am interested in the construction of organizational typologies in the analysis of groups within Christianity. There is a vast amount of theoretical and empirical literature on the use of such typologies which I have evaluated elsewhere and which forms a background to the point at which this treatment starts. [1] The religious order has been very largely ignored in typologies but I hope to show that it can be fitted substantially and significantly into the existing frameworks, often with very important consequences. This will be the purpose of the first three chapters.

Secondly, I am concerned to explore, by means of historical

data, Weber's concept of the religious *virtuoso*, which he sees most characteristically embodied in monastic asceticism. Virtuoso religion may be analytically distinguished from two other types, mass religion and the religion of charismatic figures. Weber himself contrasted the relaxed style of mass religion, which was closely in tune with the life of average humanity, with the ethical rigorism of virtuoso religion. This would seem an obvious distinction between the religious order and the church of which it forms part, though I shall be especially interested in the problem posed by the incorporation of virtuoso elements *within* the structure of a mass religion. The distinction between the virtuoso religion of small face-to-face groups, and the charismatic religious movement which is usually thought of as originating in the tightly-knit group of leader and disciples, is a central theme of this book. On the face of it, virtuosi and charismatics seem indistinguishable, but although they may be related empirically, there is a clear analytical distinction between them.

The religious virtuoso follows what he takes to be a pure and rigorous interpretation of normative obligations which already exist in a religious tradition. He is an extremist, and the monastic ideal of perfection has always been seen in terms of religious extremism, whether it be expressed as the *ne plus ultra* (there is nothing beyond) of the Carthusians, or as the 'recluse fanatics' of Gibbon's history. It is interesting that Weber should have noticed this category of religious response, because he imposed a similar standard on his own research when he claimed that its purpose was 'to see how much I can stand'. In contrast with this rigorous restatement of an existing religious tradition, charisma represents a shattering of what exists already and the articulation of an entirely new basis of normative obligation. It aims *not* at pursuing ethical ideals 'to the letter'—which is a characteristic claim of monastic groups—since to the member of a charismatic movement 'the letter' has been effectively destroyed. While the typical statement of a charismatic leader can be given as 'It is written, but I say unto you . . .', the characteristic statement of a virtuoso is 'It is written, and I insist . . .'. Charismatics proclaim a message: virtuosi proclaim a method.

The third theme of this book follows directly from the second. If, as is being suggested, the strong virtuoso component in Christianity can be distinguished from both mass religion and from its charismatic origin and pedigree, how has this component been legitimated historically? The explanation seems to lie in an analysis of the different ways in which *traditional* legitimations may be used within the same religious institution. Virtuoso religion typically refers back to a strongly-valued source of tradition which it restates in its pristine purity and seeks to emulate by means of ethical rigorism. Thus tradition is the basis on which virtuosi claim legitimacy. However, the way in which the traditional referent is used—though it can be seen as corresponding with Weber's concept of traditional authority—involves a specific version of historical change. Virtuosi take as their central point of reference a period in the early history of their religion which can be seen as particularly authentic. They then compare this pristine model with their perception of the contemporary reality, and are impressed by the extent to which this comparison indicates a *decline*. Their response is to practise a style of religious observance which aims at *reinstating* the valued tradition. Although in the limited historical context in which this occurs the activities of virtuosi may resemble innovation, they do not claim to be following a novel religious style, and this has important implications for the study of traditional authority. Since tradition may provide the leverage needed for social change, we must view this apparently most static type of authority as containing a dynamic potential: it is possible to speak of a 'revolution by tradition'.

Very often, though by no means necessarily, such 'revolutions by tradition' have formed part of a cyclical process of change. The significance of this emerges most clearly in the history of monasticism, which is punctuated by strict observances, their gradual relaxation, and the reinstatement of reformed observances. In all of these episodes, immense importance has been attached to the model of primitive Christianity and to the purity of the original Rule of the order: the normative tradition provided by these two sources has given the leverage for change. The intention in drawing out the implications for a study of change of traditional legitimacy has not been to obscure the significance of charismatic authority; indeed, it is hoped that the concept of a charismatic breakthrough will be thrown into even clearer relief by the contrast with traditional leverage. Certainly, it would be difficult to ignore the role of reformers such as St Bernard and St Francis, and the latter is explicitly treated in the context of charismatic authority. It might also be objected that the term 'revolution by tradition' is unduly paradoxical: on the contrary, it is almost a tautology. Revolution is too often regarded in the restricted perspective of linear progression, as a steep slope or a 'step' on an inclined plane leading from tradition to modernity. But its other meaning, that of a 'turning round', is equally important, and it is this aspect which will be explored here. The emphasis will therefore, in the dictionary phrases, be on 'cyclic recurrence' rather than on 'fundamental change'.

The present approach to the study of change fits, with some adaptation, into the framework of Weber's categories of legitimate authority. The value of this framework in the study of religious organizations and movements has been discussed elsewhere, [2] but the fundamental concerns of the present treatment can briefly be introduced. It seems beyond dispute that what one writer has called the 'current fashionable use' [3] of the concept of charisma has diluted it almost beyond recognition. This dilution has occurred through a blurring of the analytical distinctions between the three types of legitimate authority, especially by interpreting charisma as the only way in which Weber accounted for change on both a societal and an organizational level. At the same time the concept of charisma and its routinization—originally adapted from the vocabulary of early Christianity—has been especially useful in the sociology of religion, and it is in this area that the dilution of the concept might be expected to raise the most problems. To change slightly an analogy used by Peter Worsley, charisma is not so much a 'sponge' concept [4] as a 'soap' concept —intrinsically useful, slippery if passed around too much, and perhaps in danger of disappearing with the bathwater of discarded ideas.

It is important to recognize that all *three* types of legitimate authority incorporate potentially dynamic features. Rational-legal authority may be regarded as resting on a fundamental contradiction, as Weber indicated in his distinction between formal and substantive conceptions of law, and in his observation that bureaucracy and democracy are in important respects conflicting political imperatives. Charismatic authority, with its articulation of new ideas and new obligations which are gradually institutionalized, is clearly a dynamic concept. The same is also true, however, of traditional authority, which carries the possibility of historical leverage and change. The implications of change within an institution which claims some degree of traditional legitimacy will be considered in detail in the history of the Benedictines and in competing groups within the Church of England. To give an immediate example of this use of tradition, we might look at the disappearance of religious orders from Protestantism after the Reformation. The Reformers believed that they were reinstating the ideals of primitive Christianity as a requirement for all Christians, who must therefore strive to practise a virtuoso ethic in their daily lives. In this context, where the pristine tradition was being reinstated, how could there be room for select and segregated groups claiming that they alone represented the full embodiment of the pristine model? In an entirely similar way there can be no room in the post-millennial society of the Soviet Union for a body like the Jehovah's Witnesses, whose basic message is that the millennium has yet to arrive.

On the level of detailed interpretation, the emphasis on tradition as an important characteristic of religious orders differs somewhat from the emphasis on charismatic qualifications which Weber gave to monasticism. [5] A brief explanation of these differences should suffice to show that they are not at all fundamental. Firstly, I do not deny that charismatic qualifications have been claimed by, and attributed to, members of religious orders and monastic communities. In chapter 5 there is an analysis of the charismatic basis of the Franciscan Order, where the 'hierocratic ambivalance toward asceticism and monasticism' is specifically indicated. It is also indisputable that the origins of Christian monasticism in fourth-century Egypt contained a large charismatic component—this too I have tried to bring out in the historical summary. However, I contend that claims to traditional legitimacy have been an important means of reconciling the institutional church to monastic communities, and of accommodating these and religious orders within its universal framework. Secondly, I am almost exclusively concerned with the development of religious *orders* within Western Christianity. The fact that the development of such formal organizations of virtuosi—one of which, the Dominican Order, has been widely seen as an early form of representative democracy—should have occurred in Western Christianity rather than in Eastern Orthodoxy or in Middle Eastern and Eastern religions seems to point to distinctive features in their development, one of which, I would argue, is their capacity to embody tradition. Weber's treatment of monasticism is broadly comparative and many of his examples of monastic charisma are taken from a non-Christian context. Thirdly, Weber is most concerned to show how the ascetic and charismatic elements of early Christian and other forms of monasticism were re-interpreted by the wider church and rationalized so that they became a most powerful and useful channel of ecclesiastical policy. My argument is simply that claims to traditional legitimacy played an important part in this accommodation.

In short, I have tried in this book to adopt a restricted and more manageable perspective than one in which 'monasticism' is discussed as a general category. I am concerned exclusively with the development of the specific organizational type of religious orders in Western Christianity and with the way in which a model of this organization can be applied to groups in the nineteenth-century Church of England. This has involved constructing fairly precise analytical models which can then be used to throw into clear relief the complex historical patterns which are encountered. The use of ideal types is predicated on the need to adopt a limited frame of reference, but I hope this has not led me too far from history's rights of way. A brief summary of the structure of this book will show the direction it takes, and following this summary the chapter will conclude with a review and critique of sociological interpretations of the religious order.

In chapter 2 an ideal type of the religious order is constructed, which draws attention to what are seen as its most significant sociological features. Thus the order only exists as part of a church, although it has a certain degree of moral and organizational autonomy. While in the main tradition of Christianity it cannot reject the world as totally evil and beyond redemption, the order rejects any compromise of its conception of the Gospel ethic and it isolates or insulates itself against normal contact with the world. Total commitment is demanded of the members of an order, and considerably more obedience is required than in the church at large. An order will be locally community-based, and its origin as a movement of laity in the early church, though eroded in the course of its historical development, remains as an ideal which may be represented by considerable lay participation in ritual. The ethic practised by members of an order is not put forward as necessary for all the members of a church, and thus the elaboration of some form of dual morality accompanies the formal recognition of the order as a distinct group within the church. Each member of the order is basically seeking personal perfection, although an order may define perfection in different ways—for instance, in terms of an active or contemplative vocation. Finally, membership of an order may only be gained and maintained by proof of special merit. The features of the ideal type are elaborated with material from the history of religious orders within early and later Western Christianity.

In the light of this ideal type, it is possible to compare religious orders with other types of organization, both religious and secular. In chapter 3 a comparison is made between the religious order and the sect, using a recent characterization of the latter. There are many parallels, especially in the area of high commitment and perfectionism. However, since orders are offshoots of a more universalistic church, they do not involve the same rejection of church compromise with the world or the same hostility to the rest of society. Above all, the sect internalizes its own authority, while religious orders derive their authority ultimately from the parent church. Goffman's concept of the total institution has been applied to monastic and conventual institutions, and the ideal type can be compared with this type of organization. There are indeed certain superficial features which orders share with other examples of total institutions, such as prisons and mental hospitals, and these are mainly concerned with the way that orders centre their daily activity on a strict timetable and insist on their members performing many functions in community. The fundamental distinction is that orders are *voluntary* organizations whose members have consciously chosen to adopt the particular way of life involved, whereas the other examples given by Goffman are typically non-voluntary. In addition, religious orders have in the last analysis non-instrumental goals. This crucial feature can be explored further by considering the religious order as a limiting case within Etzioni's concept of normative compliance, the basis of which is that rules and administrative requirements are legitimated by reference to symbolic rather than pragmatic dictates. Even in a religious order which has an active vocation, non-instrumental goals will be found to have prime importance.

In chapter 4, Weber's concept of traditional authority is explored as a means of expressing in sociological terms one of the most commonly found sources of change and 'innovation' in religious orders, namely reference back to a pristine state either within the order or in the church at large. The argument is particularly directed at the need to use concepts precisely, because there is a tendency for a whole range of radical social and organizational changes to be attributed to the influence of charisma. This is not altogether appropriate in the case of religious orders, which often have a strong sense of tradition deriving from their early history. The Order of St Benedict is cited as one order which had a very explicit concept of tradition as laid down in the Holy Rule: this was the basis for periodic upsurges of strict observance. The Order of St Francis also had an important basis in tradition, but contained a distinct and in some ways disruptive claim to a charismatic origin.

In the following chapter the concept of change through tradition is applied to the English church of the eighteenth and nineteenth centuries in order to provide an interpretation of two important reform movements—the Methodist movement and the Tractarian revival. Two major versions of Christian tradition are outlined: the Protestant episodic theory, in which the Reformation is seen as a crucial event, and the Catholic continuity theory, in which the course of church history is seen more as the continual creation of tradition. In the Church of England the various schools of churchmanship can be defined partly in terms of their perception of church tradition. The High Church party had a strong conception of the tradition of the early church (the church of the first few centuries); the Low Church divines of the eighteenth century and the Evangelicals of the later nineteenth century had a strong notion of the Biblical tradition of the Church of England, though this was sometimes replaced by the idea of a Reformation tradition. The Middle Ages provided a traditional referent for a fairly marginal group of later Tractarians. There is evidence to suggest that the earliest phase of the Wesleyan movement adopted the concept of an early church tradition, just as did the later Tractarian movement, but the Wesleyan interpretation of the early church contained the idea of fluidity and free-floating personal charisma, while the Tractarian variant was centred more on the basis for routinized charismatic roles in the early church, especially as represented in the doctrine of Apostolic Succession.

Against the background of the Church of England's 'mixed tradition', the legitimation of Anglican religious orders in the nineteenth century is seen as an originally High Church attempt to reinstate one of the organizational features of the early church. Since other groups in the church held different conceptions of what was the proper traditional model of church organization, the sisterhoods and brotherhoods had to compete with alternative conceptions of legitimacy. In particular, the Evangelicals had a strong commitment to the office of deaconess as found in the New Testament church. High Church apologists for the sisterhoods found it necessary to acknowledge this feature of the earliest period of church history, but they developed an argument to show how sisterhoods gradually became the most important form of women's work in the church. The medieval church was important in a few styles of legitimation, mainly in the case of Romantics like Father Ignatius, or as a parallel case of the need for brotherhoods in large towns on the model of the early friars. The post-Reformation Church of England provided some important sources of legitimacy, for instance through the example of Nicholas Ferrar, who founded a quasi-monastic family community in the early seventeenth century. But one of the commonest and most widely received means of legitimation in the nineteenth century was the demonstration of the pragmatic and utilitarian characteristics of any apparently new institution, and this was very much the case with religious orders, which were frequently interpreted as useful means towards empirically derived ends: sisterhoods were associated with nursing and charitable work, brotherhoods with the provision of cheap supplementary help in urban parishes.

In chapter 7 the nineteenth-century Anglican orders are analysed in terms of the first feature of the ideal type of religious orders set out in chapter 3, namely the order's existence as part of a church. The relationship between the Anglican orders and the church seems to have been problematical, because these groups originated as private, unsanctioned enterprises which were often gravely suspect. They were typically seen as disruptive of ecclesiastical authority, and they tended to evolve their own conceptions of where the authority of the Church of England really lay. Gradually, however, a relationship between the church and the orders was articulated and a consensus evolved from two directions: on the part of the church authorities, it was acknowledged that the sisterhoods and brotherhoods could perform valuable services for the whole of the church; and on the part of the orders, it was recognized that one way of preventing interference from outside was by seeking the protection of the church. In this way a bargain was struck in which the orders were allowed a considerable degree of freedom, even to the extent of taking vows, in return for their co-operation with the church authorities. Despite these developments, at the end of the nineteenth century the authority links were still somewhat tenuous.

The remaining features of the ideal type, which are dealt with in the following chapter, throw into clear relief the overall conformity of the Anglican orders to the basic pattern, but they indicate significant deviations attributable to the particular historical setting. For example, the moral and organizational autonomy which has usually been sought by religious orders was especially strong in Pusey's model of the organization which ought to be adopted by sisterhoods. He was insistent that sisterhoods should be centralized so that interference from the parochial clergy could be minimized; and this was made necessary by the fact that only a minority of the parochial clergy was in sympathy with the movement. The order's emphasis on the sinfulness of 'the world' is very strong in the case of those nineteenth-century communities which were founded by Anglicans from an originally Evangelical background (with its strong conception of individual sin), and R. M. Benson of the Society of St John the Evangelist exemplifies this characteristic. One of the most basic features of the order, its expression of total commitment by means of vows, was the subject of immense controversy in the nineteenth-century Church of England, but was eventually admitted as legitimate because it was feared that if vows were not permitted some of the best potential recruits to the brotherhoods might seek their vocation in another religious body. Obedience too was a problematical aspect of the order's development, since it was difficult to enforce sanctions when the source of authority (which in the order's case is the parent church) was tenuous. The lay emphasis of religious orders was certainly found in the Anglican communities, perhaps in response to the re-emphasized distinctiveness of the priestly role.

In chapter 9 the wider social influences are analysed, and it is suggested that the choice of sisterhoods or deaconesses as the major form of women's work in the church was very closely related to different conceptions of the status of women: sisterhoods in this sense are the first signs of incipient feminism among women of the middle class. One of the most frequent Protestant accusations against sisterhoods, and especially against their founders, was that they were exerting a subversive influence on familial authority. The immense importance of Victorian conceptions of the family was clearly recognized by those who supported sisterhoods, since they always found it necessary to deny any disparagement of the family. There were, at the same time, widely perceived demographic factors which made some form of autonomous role for women an urgent necessity: the surplus of women over men in the population of Great Britain during the nineteenth century was noted at the time and had considerable impact on church work for women. The relationship between sisterhoods and secular female occupations is one of mutual reinforcement. Florence Nightingale found personnel for her nursing expedition to the Crimea among the sisterhoods, and this raised the status of nursing generally, but subsequently the sisterhoods seem to have gained prestige because of Miss Nightingale's popularity. Secular agencies gradually took over the work that sisterhoods had undertaken, which is one explanation of their increasing tendency to adopt the contemplative life.

The brotherhoods which arose towards the end of the nineteenth century were very much connected with the need to deal with the social problems of cities. One of the most interesting features of their introduction to the Church of England was the explicit political legitimation they were given, as representatives of a national church which was concerned to reach rich and poor alike. An understanding of the secular context of religious orders —which emerges with great clarity in the study of Anglican sisterhoods and brotherhoods—is crucial to our explanation of why such organizations have adopted their specific historical form, and this is the point on which the book ends. For the moment, however, we must try to establish a sociological model for the analysis of religious orders.

This is all the more necessary because there has been relatively little specific sociological treatment of the religious order, although there is a wealth of historical and theological material. Apart from a handful of articles which are centred on a discussion of the place of religious orders in a typology of organizations, a book on the social organization of the Benedictines, and a voluminous literature on the demographic characteristics of recent and contemporary orders and congregations, [6] there is not much detailed analysis of the order as an organizational type. However, there are references to it in several places, most of them fairly oblique, and it will be helpful to place these in a broad perspective before proceeding to a detailed analysis.

The basic notion with which we are concerned is that the religious order is a parallel, or analogue, within the context of Catholic Christianity of the sect: a shorthand way of expressing this is to call the order a 'sect within a church'. Throughout sociological discussion this is a frequently encountered concept and it will be the purpose of the first part of this book to expand the idea into a clearly formulated ideal type. In common with other models of Christian organization, we are indebted for the original statement of this relationship to Max Weber and Ernst Troeltsch, who refers to the '. . . two sociological forms of the sect-type, the Religious Order and the voluntary association . . .' [7] Following his earlier elaboration of the church–sect dichotomy, Troeltsch gave several examples of sectarian movements. Prominent among these was the Franciscan Order, of which he says: 'The Franciscan movement belonged originally to the sect-type of lay religion.' [8] He went on to describe an important feature of both sects and religious orders, their strong lay emphasis, and he also distinguished a feature specific to religious orders, their lines of control to the church.

Weber was similarly interested in this affinity of sect and order and he drew an analytical distinction between 'virtuoso' and 'mass' religions. Sects and communities of monks were firmly placed in the former category. [9] He saw an incipient tension between these two religious styles and he postulated a resulting mutual compromise, though he did not specify what form this compromise took in the historical example of Christian monastic communities. In his essay, 'The Protestant Sects and the Spirit of Capitalism' he noted another similarity between sects and religious orders: both of them have what we might best describe as a 'hierarchy of spiritual status'. Weber stated:

> The discipline of the asceticist sect was, in fact, far more rigorous than the discipline of any church. In this respect, the sect resembles the monastic order. The sect discipline is also analogous to monastic discipline in that it established the principle of the novitiate. [10]

At this point he inserts a footnote suggesting that in all probability there existed a period of probation in every sect, and the Methodist example of a six-month probationary period is given.

O'Dea uses those two sources to indicate the 'two important "choices" confronting sectarian groups'. [11] They can opt to remain within the general body of the church, and in doing so they will often become important reforming agencies. In this sense, monasticism was such a protest movement. Or they may decide to secede from the church and form sects, which has been the most evident pattern from the late Middle Ages onwards. Such groups will normally be persecuted by the dominant church, and this will enhance their spirit of austerity.

In much the same way Stark refers to protest movements—or what he calls the 'revolutionary aspects' of the universal church—which are initially '. . . anonymous, inchoate, inarticulate, a kind of groundswell, one might say, felt rather than seen'. [12] The outcome of such groups will either be secession and sect-formation or to remain within the church and form an order. In the latter case, withdrawal from the universal church will never be as total as the withdrawal of the sect from the established church. At this juncture it is important to stress that what is crucial for the sociologist in these ideas of protest group 'choice' are the ways in which the choice is limited by the particular social setting in which these types of movement emerge. For Stark, the choice will be made according to whether the church is universal or established: if universal, an order will form; if established, there will be sectarian schism. It will obviously be part of the task in this thesis to try and isolate some of the factors which appear to be significant in the case of those movements which do begin within churches and eventually develop a separate organization.

The difficulty with both the O'Dea formulation and the Stark version is their acceptance of the church's orientation as a basis for the sociological analysis of sectarian movements. In the first place, the idea of a 'choice' facing protest movements is rather misleading. Not all sects begin within churches and those that do not cannot be thought of as having a 'choice' at all. It also overlooks another frequently encountered process of sect emergence, namely the rejection of church organization as the first stage in the formation of a protest movement and hence the *a priori* elimination of one of the two 'choices'. Stark also neglects the dissenting and sectarian movements which appeared within the context of pre-Reformation Catholicism. It is relevant to point out that the term 'choice' in itself carries the notion of conscious, goal-directed behaviour, and this may not necessarily be the best way of seeing the process.

A useful typology of the various forms of organization which may be adopted by protest movements as long as they remain within a more universalistic church organization is given by Wach, who refers to 'protest within' as a form of *ecclesiola in ecclesia*. [13] The first kind of protest, in which the groups involved do not identify themselves with the ideal community, do not attempt to set themselves up as a separate unit, and which see themselves chiefly as the 'leaven of the gospel', is called the *collegium pietatis*. Among the examples given of such loosely organized groups are the early Puritans, the Oxford Movement of the nineteenth century and early Methodism. At a more formal level of organization is the second type of protest group, the *fraternitas*, which Wach sees as a logical progression out of the 'like-mindedness' of the *collegium pietatis*. In groups of this kind, a minimum of organization is seen as existing alongside an egalitarian concept of fellowship, but stratification and specialization of function usually bring the *fraternitas* to a more developed stage of organization. Examples given are the Pietist and Methodist groups. Finally, the monastic order represents the most fully developed form of minority group protest within a wider church organization and is characterized by its permanence and by its rejection of secular concerns. Examples are given of 'orders', 'congregations' and 'societies' in Roman Catholicism, and monasticism in other religious traditions is also discussed.

Wach's typology is constructed by taking three ideal-typical stages on a continuum extending from minimal to extensive separate organization on the part of the protest movement. The distinctions between the different levels of organization are clearly flexible, as is shown by the inclusion of Methodism in both the *collegium pietatis* and the *fraternitas* categories. Tractarianism likewise seems to overflow these categories: in an ideological sense, the Oxford Movement had obvious elements of the *collegium pietatis*, but it showed a tendency to develop towards the *fraternitas*, for instance with the Society of the Holy Cross, and the Anglican religious orders of the nineteenth century were very central elements in the movement as a whole. Wach's categories are useful in indicating the empirical range of 'protest within' but less useful in the sense that they provide no analytical criteria on which different types of protest movement may be distinguished.

The importance of the ideological context is indicated by Martin. [14] From his interest in the origins of the major denominations as *ecclesiolae in ecclesia* he makes a radical distinction between Catholic and Protestant cultures. In Catholic cultures one of these groups, he argues, would normally join or form an order. But this implies a dual standard of morality for it asserts, in effect, that it is as compatible for the church to be permissive within its own sphere of activity as it is for the virtuoso member of a religious order to be uncompromising in his sphere. Protestantism has rejected the conception of the dual standard, and although perfection for all is only maintained in principle there is no recourse to compromise by elaborating a dual set of standards for Christians. Thus the Protestant solution:

> ... is to take the order out of the cloister and set it in the world. Whereas in Catholic cultures the average man is within the Church and the man of exceptional vocation within the order, in Protestant cultures all men are called to be tertiaries. [15]

For Martin, the conceptual distinction between the sect and the order is based on the latter's recognition that its standards are not capable of being realized universally. The order is 'an analogue, within the inclusive church, of the spiritual élitism which finds expression in the sect' [16], and it serves to channel some of the tensions which emerge as extreme sectarianism.

A different approach to the setting up of a typology for the study of religious orders is presented by Francis. [17] Working from Toennies' contrasted types of *Gemeinschaft* and *Gesellschaft*, he draws a distinction between the monastic community, the ideal type of which is a small, personalized, psychological group, and the religious order, which is a more complex form of organization of the 'associational' type. Hence the *community* of religiosi is an intimate face-to-face group which is quasi-familial and whose members are bound by the typically monastic *stabilitas loci* (each monk ideally remains in the community he has joined until death); the order, on the other hand, tends to substitute more impersonal, segmental, abstract and instrumental relationships among the members of local establishments, which are properly called convents ('meeting-places'). The best example of the first is the Benedictine abbey and of the second, the Society of Jesus.

Francis in effect compares two distinct levels of organization. In describing the Benedictine abbey as a *Gemeinschaft*, he is neglecting the existence of a wider federal structure, and he certainly ignores the wider institutional importance of the Rule of St Benedict. Similarly, local confraternities of Jesuits will always have *gemeinschaftlich* characteristics. Support for this view can be found in the work of Moulin who, after discussing the constitutional arrangements of groups of religious including the Jesuits, Franciscans and Cistercians, concludes: 'Pour le religieux, l'Ordre est une *Gemeinschaft* . . .' [18]

In the course of his study of member commitment in religious orders, Vollmer makes a related assertion. [19] He is concerned less with an analysis of the religious order in a typology of religious organizations than with the application of general organization theory, but his argument bears central relevance to some aspects of the present discussion. Vollmer asks: '. . . in what ways are the characteristic competences of organizations related to the types of commitment which they develop in their members?' [20] The two social processes which determine the type of commitment are socialization and control. Religious orders are a particularly fruitful field because they require that their members should be socialized in such a way that they develop a total commitment exclusive of all other organizations. The development of commitment is seen as involving mysticism, the goal of which is to indoctrinate the novice into the ways of life of the organization so that the member comes to accept the tasks and the structure of the order as legitimated by the presence of divine authority. The process of detachment involved in asceticism is interpreted as a means of concentrating all the member's interests on life within the religious order. Private property and private thoughts are ideally eradicated, but this is not achieved easily. Mysticism is the positive aspect of socialization and asceticism performs the negative function of alienation, by means of which commitment to the organization is made total.

The mechanisms of social control are seen to be: (1) the inculcation of an *ideology* so that members make decisions in terms of organizational objectives; (2) the imposition of decisions made elsewhere in the organization through legitimate channels of *authority*. Both mechanisms are employed in all religious orders but with differential emphasis. The Benedictines are an example of an order making the most extensive use of ideological control while the Society of Jesus uses mainly authoritarian control. While the Benedictines are based on decentralized authority and familial control by the abbot (whose authority, we must add, is strictly subordinate to the ideological precepts of the order as formally expressed in the Rule of St Benedict), the Jesuit organization is centralized and authority is maintained through hierarchical offices. Vollmer thinks the Jesuit organization and type of authority are favourable to a forward-looking, innovatory ethos, while that of the Benedictines is more concerned with pristine monasticism and is distinctly conservative. This distinction is based on a valuable insight but the form in which it is expressed is misleading. To anticipate somewhat, one of the central arguments of this book will be that a concern with pristine ideology is often a potent source of innovation.

NOTES

1 M. Hill, *A Sociology of Religion* (London, Heinemann, 1973), chaps 3 and 4.
2 ibid., chaps 7 and 8.
3 P. Worsley, *The Trumpet Shall Sound* (London, MacGibbon and Kee, 1968) (second edition), p. x.
4 ibid., p. liii.
5 Max Weber, *Economy and Society* (3 vols) (New York, Bedminster Press, 1968), pp. 1166–73.
6 For the bibliography which includes this demographic data, see the *5e Conference International de Sociologie Religieuse: 'Vocation de la Sociologie Religieuse. Sociologie des Vocations* (Tournai, Editions Casterman, 1958).
7 Ernst Troetsch, *The Social Teaching of the Christian Churches*, transl. Olive Wyon (London, Allen and Unwin, 1931), p. 723.
8 ibid., p. 355.
9 H. H. Gerth and C. Wright Mills (eds), *From Max Weber: Essays in Sociology* (London, Routledge and Kegan Paul, 1948), pp. 287–8.
10 ibid., pp. 316–17.
11 Thomas F. O'Dea, *The Sociology of Religion* (Englewood Cliffs, Prentice-Hall, 1966), pp. 68–9.
12 Werner Stark, *The Sociology of Religion*, vol. III, 'The universal church' (London, Routledge and Kegan Paul, 1967), p. 250.
13 Joachim Wach, *Sociology of Religion* (Chicago, The University Press, 1962), pp. 173–93.
14 D. A. Martin, *Pacifism* (London, Routledge and Kegan Paul, 1965) p. 163 and pp. 191–3.
15 ibid., p. 163.
16 ibid., p. 4.
17 E. K. Francis, 'Towards a typology of religious orders', *American Journal of Sociology*, vol. 55, no. 5, March 1950, pp. 437–9. Another article which is not mentioned in the present review of the literature because it largely follows Francis is H. P. M. Goddijn, 'The sociology of religious orders and congregations', *Social Compass*, vol. VII, nos. 5–6, 1960, pp. 431–47.

18 L. Moulin, 'Pour une sociologie des ordres religieux', *Social Compass*, vol. X, no. 2, 1960, pp. 145–70. It has been pointed out in discussions I have had on this point that almost all forms of local Christian organization have *gemeinschaftlich* characteristics, the only exceptions being such things as holy places and shrines which tend to have a fast turnover of devotees.

19 Howard M. Vollmer, 'Member Commitment and Organizational Competence in Religious Orders', *Berkeley Publications in Society and Institutions*, vol. 3, no. 1, Spring 1957, pp. 13–26.

20 ibid., p. 13.

2

An Ideal Type of the Religious Order

ONE OF THE most characteristic features of virtuoso religion, Weber noted, was asceticism. Asceticism is the individual observance of rigorous physical and mental methods in pursuit of the goal of perfection, which may be defined as non-involvement with the world, or as a catalytic impingement with, and transformation of, the world. Asceticism has always existed in Christianity and in its different manifestations it has been sanctioned by most Christian groups, though in its monastic form it has not typically been encouraged by Protestantism. Asceticism is a major component of monasticism and its presence in an extreme and individualistic form is clearly evident among the desert monks of fourth-century Egypt. They practised a rigorous, largely unstructured type of asceticism, even to the extent of calling each other 'athletes'. The competitive spirit was very apparent and was encouraged. An excellent instance of this is provided by Macarius of Egypt, who appears to have been a model of 'monkmanship'. Waddell points out the main features of his asceticism in a concise passage:

> The great Macarius, indeed, seems to have been moved for a while by the ill spirit of competition. Did he hear that one Father ate only a pound of bread, himself was content to nibble a handful of crusts: did another eat no cooked food for the forty days of Lent, raw herbs became his diet for seven years. [1]

The radical individualism of this type of asceticism is well demonstrated in the account of Macarius's visit to the monastery at Tabenna, of which Pachomius was abbot. There, Macarius became the equivalent of Mayo's 'rate-buster', outdoing all the other monks in ascetic practices, and the outcome was characteristic: we are told that the other monks complained to their

19

abbot that Macarius was making them look foolish and warned that either he should be expelled from the monastery or they would all leave, in one body, that same day. After complimenting him on his zeal, Pachomius sent Macarius back to the desert.

Monasticism is a formal and segregated type of Christian asceticism. In this sense, it occurs when unstructured asceticism crystallizes into a definite local or social form, with customs and moral imperatives in addition to those of asceticism by itself.

> The question of the beginning of monasticism only arises when ascetics, either as single individuals or in groups, separate themselves from the churches whose members take a normal share in the life of the world round about; their 'apotaxis', or repudiation of the world, then becomes a matter of geography, and can be seen objectively. [2]

When asceticism is institutionalized in the form of a monastic community, which necessarily has socially structured elements, it is possible to conceive of the community as falling somewhere on an organizational continuum between the individual (eremitic) and the collective (cenobitic) poles of social interaction; but the origin of the monk—signified by the etymology of *monachus*, 'alone'—must be traced to the isolated individualistic asceticism of the hermit seeking his own salvation. It is the Eastern Orthodox Church at the present time which most closely approximates to the original pattern of monasticism. [3] Most theological literature attributes the motivation of all monks to the Gospel exhortation which motivated one of the earliest and hence archetypal monks, St Antony: *'If thou wilt be perfect*, go and sell all thou hast . . .' The eremitic pole has remained an ideal throughout the history of monasticism in both Eastern and Western Christianity (though it is stronger in the Eastern branch). This helps to explain the periodic upsurge of 'primitive' eremitical observance at times of reform [4]—for instance in the eleventh century when the Camaldolese (1012) and the Carthusian (1084) orders were founded—and the ideal of isolation within monastic communities which is exemplified by the Cistercian 'solitude in community'. [5]

There is some variety in the use of the term 'religious order' and the present definition must be made clear. Three classes of definition may be distinguished:

1. *The vocational definition.* The notion of *Ordo Monasticus* is used to describe all those who have accepted a certain way of life and a

reasonable translation of this would be 'monastic estate'. In fact, this is the only possible meaning of 'order' in Eastern Christianity, where distinct formal organizations of monks do not exist.

2. *The Canon Law definition.* Anson gives a brief account of the way in which Canon Law classifies the order:

> There are different categories of societies of men and women bound by the vows of religion. According to Canon Law they are thus classified: (1) *Religious Orders*, whose members take Solemn Vows. These include Canons Regular, Monks, Friars, Clerks Regular, and all Nuns who have the privilege of solemn vows. (2) *Religious Congregations*, whose members take Simple Vows. [6] These include most societies of men and women which have been formed since the Council of Trent. [7]

3. *The constitutional definition.* Although Pachomius and Benedict are frequently credited with the foundation of religious orders, the Cistercian Order founded in 1098 is in this sense the first *Order* with a centralized authority structure and a single abbey or office (in this case the abbey of Cîteaux) at its head. Before then the Benedictines were made up of a collection of technically autonomous abbeys. The extent to which the Benedictine Rule was used varied enormously and although it had considerable prestige there were other Rules and adaptations of the original. Even today

> In the strict sense there is no Benedictine *Order*. Both in theory and in varying degrees in practice, each Benedictine monastery is an independent unit. However in 1215 the Fourth Lateran Council laid down that groups of monasteries were to be formed into Congregations, following the earlier reform movement at Cluny and the example of the Cistercian Order. [8]

The best definition for sociological purposes is one that clearly delimits the field of study but at the same time overlaps theoretical distinctions which are, in any case, not always observed by specialists in other disciplines. Thus we may define the religious order as an organization recognized by the church, either centralized and hierarchically governed, or locally governed but bound to uniformity of Rule and observance, of priests, or laymen, or priests and laymen, or laywomen who have committed themselves to the goals of the organization and who live in segregation and community—the degree of which will vary between different orders—and who accept as binding on themselves more exacting moral injunctions than those propounded for the church at large. This is clearly a broad definition and in order to give it more precision it will be helpful to establish a 'directional index' in the form of an ideal type, compared with which we can study concrete examples.

1. The religious order only exists as part of a church.

If a weighting were to be given to each component of the ideal type, this feature would claim the greatest significance, because many of the other components are directly related to it. At the same time, it cannot be viewed as non-problematic because there is no simple relationship between a religious order and the more inclusive church of which it forms a part. It would be most accurate to see the relationship between the order and the church as one of incipient tension which normally remains latent but which may emerge as overt conflict and even as schism. Indeed, the history of Western Christianity has generally been interpreted in the framework of this Love–Law dialectic, derived from the Gospel ethic, between the church-type organization and smaller groups of Christian virtuosi.

In the earliest, least structured stage of monasticism the lines of control between the church and the desert monks of Egypt seem to have been highly tenuous, after which their gradual imposition can be traced. Initially, retirement from the world entailed also retirement from the body of the church, since the earliest monks were solitaries. There is evidence too of a strong charismatic tendency among these ascetics which on occasion served to by-pass an important aspect of the authority nexus in the primitive church which was located in the dispensing of sacraments. Some of the Egyptian hermits claimed to have received a miraculous distribution of the eucharistic sacraments [9], and this was representative of a more general devaluing of the church's sacramental control which was the logical corollary of, if not the general practice of, the desert solitaries:

A monk had no need of his fellow-men. Strictly speaking, he had no need of either church or sacrament, for his salvation depended entirely on his own moral powers. Nevertheless, service on Sunday was inconceivable without the eucharistic sacrifice and the communion which followed. [10]

The small colony of hermits at Climax, in a remote and inaccess-
ible part of the desert, exemplified the extreme isolation from the
rest of the church which was sought by some solitaries. They were
visited by Palladius, one of the contemporary chroniclers of the
monks, who described them as being in complete isolation from
the 'constant communion of the mysteries' (meaning the sacraments), and the effect on one of their number was that he returned
to the world 'all puffed up with pride', gave himself over to
gluttony and drunkenness and spoke no edifying word to anyone. [11] Palladius uses this as a moral tale to demonstrate the
need for a directing influence over hermits. [12] Similarly, the
incumbents of authority positions in the church (bishops in
particular) were notably distrusted, and several studies of Egyptian
monasticism have noted its original anti-sacerdotal character.
One of the most widely quoted expressions of this attitude is that
of the contemporary Cassian: 'Wherefore this is an old maxim of
the Fathers that is still current . . . that a monk ought by all means
to fly from women and bishops.' [13] The reason for this advice
is that both will distract a monk from the quiet isolation of his
cell and from a single-minded pursuit of perfection. There are
examples also of monks who claimed miraculous ordination as
presbyters by Christ himself [14]—obviously a charismatic
challenge to the church's authority.

Thus we can indicate certain unmistakable tensions and sources
of conflict between the earliest forms of monasticism and the
authority of the church: it is hardly surprising that these monks
were fairly well represented among those labelled as heretics. On
the other hand, there began to develop at a very early phase in
Egyptian monasticism some of the features which made control
by the church easier to achieve. The main characteristics were a
marked individualism and a competitive striving for personal
advance in virtue: voluntarism, it has been argued, was the most
striking feature of the desert Fathers. [15] And it was precisely
this voluntarism which led to the eventual institutionalization of
this form of monasticism, for hermits would often choose to live
in a semi-eremitical environment. This they could do either by
living alone in their cells, usually out of earshot of each other but
meeting as a proto-community for Saturday and Sunday worship,
or by living as companions in the same house, again only meeting
for weekend worship. This is what was referred to above as the
crystallization of asceticism into a distinct local or social form.

Although there would be no formal Rule of life in such a colony, the authority of elders and those who were experienced in the ascetic life would have been a significant feature, not least because the teacher–disciple relationship was widely valued.

Consequently in some parts of the Middle East, notably in Palestine, *lauras* grew up, these being local colonies of hermits voluntarily submitting themselves to the personal authority of a single abbot. St Antony was the leader of just such a village of cells, and we find evidence at this stage of development of rather more formal moral injunctions being incorporated into Rules. With the differentiation of particular individuals (more or less informally at first) as leaders, and with the growth in importance among the ascetics of the notion of obedience to a spiritual superior as a sign of personal virtue, the first lines of control from the church to the monastic groups can be indicated. For although obedience was not explicitly promised directly to the church, the institutionalization of these local groups resulted in a restriction of schismatic tendencies, and at the same time the church was able, through its hierarchy of authority, to encapsulate these groups. This was frequently achieved by contact between bishops and abbots, so that the monks' submission to the personal and often charismatic authority of his superior indirectly became submission to the authority of the more inclusive church. St Antony, for example, was a powerful influence in the Nicene party and a friend of Bishop Athanasius; St Basil, the organizer of Eastern Orthodox monasticism, later became a bishop and was prominent for his refusal to draw a hard and fast line between monks and other Christians. The closest *rapport* between early monasticism and the church was achieved in the Western branch of Christianity, where bishops were repeatedly the founders of monasteries: Eusebius of Vercelli, St Martin of Tours, St Ambrose of Milan, Paulinus of Nola and St Augustine of Hippo are among the most important.

The crucial link between the church and the religious order is the Rule. The Rule of any order is an important nexus of authority because it regulates the internal organization of the group but it derives its legitimacy externally, from the church, which plays an important part in framing the constitutional blueprint. The development of internal Rules is a very early feature, apparently closely linked with the institutionalization process we have described. The first formal Rule is generally acknowledged to be that of Pachomius, who in 315 founded a cenobitic monastery at Tabenna in Egypt, which eventually grew into a large group of monasteries containing some 5,000 inmates. [16] While the Rule itself was based on the code of military discipline which Pachomius had experienced as a soldier in the Roman army, the 'athletic' aspect of asceticism was not firmly controlled and in principle nobody was to be hindered from fasting and other individual ascetic observances [17]: the reason for this lack of detailed regulation was the strong tradition at that time that a perfect monk had no need of a Rule of life. However, the potential social disruption which lay in this provision must have led to norms of ascetic behaviour, albeit informal, and we have evidence of one such incident in the case of Macarius. In this early period of church history the Rule of a monastic group, while to a large extent regulating the behaviour of its members, did not provide a formal link with the church as a source of legitimacy for the regulations contained in it. The growth of more stringent control is particularly evident in Western Catholicism, for not only did bishops found monasteries but they also encouraged the adoption of particular Rules, for example the Rule of St Benedict. Eventually, the degree of control exercised by the centralized authority of the church was such that any new order was required to submit its Rule for approval before it could be officially authorized, and such approval by the papal authorities would normally require the incorporation of suggested modifications to the Rule.

The importance of this control function is nowhere more evident than in the early history of the Franciscan Order. The original Rule, which was later lost, seems to have been no more than a set of guiding ethical principles which Francis derived from a random opening of the Bible at three different places. The 'random searching' procedure is common to many 'enthusiastic' movements: one reason for its importance is the enhanced legitimacy given to the ordinances which are derived from it because of their implied supernatural origin. The three passages which Francis found recommended poverty, healing and preaching to the poor, and a Rule based on these was submitted to Pope Innocent III in 1209. The Pope was somewhat undecided about this Rule for two main reasons. Firstly, there were a great many penitential movements growing up at this time, some of them deeply critical of ecclesiastical authority, so there was some concern that the older monastic orders might be threatened: against this Francis had to defend the active basis of the new movement. Secondly, Pope Innocent was very doubtful whether the goal of absolute poverty was feasible. Francis convinced him of this and the Rule was approved, but the issue of poverty was in fact later to create violent disruption and the eventual schism of one branch of the Franciscan Order. [18] By 1212, Francis had institutionalized the custom of calling all his friars together for an annual chapter, and the Pope's further verbal approval was given to the Rule at the Fourth Lateran Council of 1215. This was the council at which the church's formal control over the religious orders was notably widened in response to the proliferation of lay movements. The foundation of new religious orders which did not observe an already existing Rule was forbidden; men and women who wanted to follow the monastic life were ordered to choose an existing approved Rule; and regulations for a more centralized organization of communities like the Benedictines were carried. This was reflected at the General Chapter of the Franciscan Order in 1217, when it was organized into provinces, with ministers appointed to supervise each one. During his lifetime, Francis commanded his followers to observe the Rule *literally* and never to seek papal authority for modifications to it [19], and he made an explicit statement of this in his *Testament* which was dictated shortly before his death in 1226. However, the exigencies of large-scale organization—which had to be faced by the ministers rather than by Francis himself since he was much more important as a charismatic leader than as an administrator—led to a recasting of the original Rule in 1221 and its approval by Pope Honorius III in 1223: this was known as the 'Regula Bullata'. The latter, while mitigating somewhat the heroism of the original Franciscan brotherhood, is noteworthy for its insistence on complete poverty for the whole order corporately. But further growth led to a gradual mitigation of the ideal of poverty and to an increasing separation of two groups within the order, the 'conventuals' (those who wished to see some modification, a group consisting for the most part of officials in the order) and the 'spirituals' (the remnants of the original charismatic band who wished to observe the Rule *'ad litteram'*). The fact that the latter were to be so important in the 'heresy of the Fraticelli' [20] is very striking evidence of the way in which the Rule of a religious order imposes both internal and external control on its members and forms an important link between the church and its minority virtuoso communities. In most cases the charisma of the original movement (when it exists) and the organizational demands of the church's formal hierarchy will be accommodated within the same Rule. The Franciscan Order is an interesting exception in this respect, because a document attracting support on charismatic grounds, the *Testament*, existed alongside and was to some extent at variance with the Rule and its modifications as approved by the church authorities.

In strong contrast, it has been said of the Dominican Order: 'The popes called it into existence and defined its character and work.' [21] There was a parallel distinction between the respective founders of the two orders: Francis was a layman, keenly aware of the importance of the laity in the face of a notoriously wealthy church, while Dominic was a cleric, formerly a regular canon and attached to the formal institutions of the church. The foundation of the Dominican Order, the purpose of which was officially given as the checking of heresy, was specifically utilitarian. Since there had been no approved Dominican Rule in existence before the Lateran Council of 1215, which Dominic attended, it was necessary to adopt some already existing Rule. This Dominic did without much difficulty, selecting the Rule of St Augustine which he had earlier adopted as a regular canon. It was simple, easily adaptable, did not impose enclosure or stability like the Rule of St Benedict and was moreover highly suitable for an order of preaching friars. There was a particular Dominican promise of obedience to the Holy See. To this pragmatic origin was shortly added a rationally constructed organization which has often been cited as the model of a democratic constitution. Supreme legislative and administrative powers within the order were given to elected boards in order to represent the specialized knowledge of the members, and a centralized but representative international organization was quickly set up. While in the case of the Franciscan Order the chief goal of its charismatic founder, the ideal of poverty, was difficult to institutionalize in a large-scale organization without serious disruption and fragmentation, the growth of this type of legal rational organization for the Dominicans could be achieved more easily by interpreting it as a valuable means towards the prime goal of the order, which was preaching. Perhaps because of this facility for institutionalization of its dominant goal the Dominican Order has never shown the same fissiparous tendencies as some of the other orders.

Troeltsch describes the process by which monasticism became incorporated into the religious life of the church in a manageable form:

> However hard monasticism might struggle for a certain measure of independence, and however undefined had been its relationship with the Early Church, in the Medieval Church it was organized first of all under the bishops, and then, when the Religious Orders came into existence, under the Papacy; every other kind of asceticism either was, or then, became, heretical. [22]

This is a process which is closely related to the idea of the Rule as an instrument of control, and Troeltsch adds another important ideological link. He argues that the church was attracted by monasticism because it discerned in it an incomparable method of renewal and power, though it made clear that salvation was not to be obtained by monasticism and asceticism alone but through the church and its sacraments. But he also suggests that monasticism was drawn to the church because it was only by means of the international power and autonomy of the church that the domination of the monasteries by the civil authorities could be broken. Thus the Catholic organicist theory of the church was elaborated alongside the medieval notion of mutual provision of services between the different social strata. [23]

What this entailed for the religious orders was the possibility of providing a vicarious sacrifice for the whole of Christendom, a relationship which Troeltsch summarized when he spoke of 'the spiritual treasury of the Church, into which those surplus offerings are poured, to be shared out again as indulgences...'.[24] So it became the duty of Christians in 'the world' to preserve and procreate the race, which ascetics cannot do; while in return the ascetics render service for others through intercession, penitence and the acquisition of merit. This concept is of immense importance for any study of religious orders. First of all, it can be interpreted as a further step in the redefinition of the ascetic ideal, which was initially simply defined as the salvation of the individual hermit, then, with the development of cenobitic monasticism, that of the monastic community [25], and finally towards the salvation of the whole of Christendom. Secondly, it helps to explain the absence of religious orders in Protestantism with its insistence on the individual's personal responsibility for his own salvation. And thirdly, it marks a major distinction between the order and the sect because the latter is for its own members only.

2. Though part of a church, the religious order always maintains a certain degree of moral and organizational autonomy.

Since every religious order is by definition part of a wider church-type organization its moral doctrines cannot have unrestricted freedom and must ultimately conform to those of the parent group, but they may diverge at certain points from the more universalistic pronouncements of the wider church. We shall deal with this characteristic in some detail under the next three headings but certain preliminary observations may be made. In particular, church-type organizations are characterized by the formal elaboration of belief systems by a group of professional theologians, and thus divergence from the canon is 'visible'. It is quite valid to define the limiting case of moral autonomy as heresy, and we might well begin by considering the extent to which religious orders have been, or have become heretical.

There is conflicting evidence on the earliest phase of Egyptian monasticism, but Anson finds sufficient evidence to conclude that the two 'intellectual' heresies of Arianism (the denial of the divinity of Christ) and Origenism (which argued the pre-existence of souls and denied any identity between the mortal and resurrection bodies) were strong among the early hermits, in the first case in Lower Egypt and in the second case in Nitria. Of the latter, Anson writes, 'The customary silence of the desert was broken by fierce arguments, sometimes ending in brawls and riots.' [26] In this context attention has already been paid to evidence of anti-sacramentalism among the early monks which could certainly be termed moral autonomy. However, it must be noted that in the church of the patristic period several heresies did not begin as such but were defined as false doctrine by councils of the church only after the beliefs had been adopted. There is consequently some fluidity and less formal distinction between accepted and heretical belief.

But the later heresy of the Spiritual Franciscans, otherwise known as the 'Zealots', was much more clearly a schismatic movement since it rested on a three-stage conception of the millennium in which monks were to usher in the Age of the Spirit. Furthermore, it resulted from the overriding Franciscan goal of poverty which the Spirituals insisted on maintaining despite several attempts by the Holy See to arrive at a workable compromise. This is an excellent example of the moral autonomy of a religious order taking precedence over the group's allegiance to the church.

Far more common than heresy as examples of moral autonomy are the numerous cases of exaggerations or '*ad litteram*' interpretations of particular Christian beliefs and practices which, although they do not qualify as deviations from the dogma and ritual of the church, at least represent particular distortions of it. One of the most obvious instances of this is the frequently encountered idea of 'perpetual' observance. Dom Cuthbert Butler finds that under the influence of Cluny perpetual celebration of the liturgy became a widespread monastic norm, and Anson describes an unsuccessful attempt to introduce this practice among the Carmelites:

> There was such enthusiasm for the purely contemplative life during the seventeenth century that some Italian desert convents were eager to introduce perpetual mental prayer, on the same lines as those medieval monasteries which engaged in perpetual chanting of the Divine Office, or the post-Tridentine communities of women that organized perpetual adoration of the Blessed Sacrament. [27]

It will be evident that practices of this kind can readily be accommodated within the church's scheme of vicarious oblation. At the same time, what we might call the 'spiritual division of labour' may have either an empirical or a non-empirical validation. For instance, a religious order which is mainly committed to preaching and teaching, like the Dominicans or the Jesuits, will be an effective and practical service agency in the hands of the church. One particular example of non-empirical effectiveness is the way in which the Franciscan Order has 'specialized' in the Blessed Virgin Mary. As well as popularizing feasts and devotions to the B.V.M. the order was active in propagating the doctrine of the Immaculate Conception.

Religious orders differ in the extent to which they claim autonomy from the church. The Dominicans and the Jesuits both take a fourth vow of obedience to the Holy See and can be seen very much as proselytizing agents of the papacy. On the other hand, religious orders like the Cistercians and the Trappists apparently have a high degree of autonomy and are at the same time 'for themselves' rather than being instrumental in any empirical sense. And yet there is an interesting paradox in this comparison because the Jesuits have the unique experience (if we ignore the sectarian branch of the Franciscan Order) of having been suppressed by the papacy. This raises the problem of internal and external authority in sharp relief, and some useful observations can be made on the relevant factors in this area.

The Rule of St Benedict which, it will be remembered, was originally designed for autonomous communities of monks rather than for a religious order with a centralized constitution, specifically makes provision for the intervention of the local bishop in the internal affairs of the abbey. In Chapter 64 of the Rule, on the appointment of abbots, it is stated that if an unworthy man is elected to this office the local bishops have the power to intervene. Until the Lateran Council of 1215 the Benedictine abbeys had no formal organizational framework and therefore no strong basis for the exercise of overall internal authority which was founded principally on ideological commitment to the Rule. In the early days of the Cistercian Order such intervention was the right and duty of the bishop and canons of Châlon, near Cîteaux, who were required to watch for disorders and to scrutinize abbatial elections. However, as the Cistercian Order accepted its own constitution, the *Carta Caritatis*, and took on the constitutional government of a General Chapter, exemption from episcopal control was standardized *de jure*. [28] It seems clear that when the internal authority of a religious order is decentralized, then the more centralized hierarchy of the church will be involved at all levels of the order's organization, at least peripherally. When authority within an order becomes formalized and centralized on the other hand, control from within obviates the necessity for control by the church at all levels.

Even so, moral autonomy is still a feature of centralized religious orders, and the Jesuit suppression can be cited in support of this statement. The general features of the events which led up to the action being taken can be largely summarized as the attempts by various nation states (principally France, Spain and Portugal) to curtail the independence of the church on rather similar lines to the Anglican Reformation, with the Society of

Jesus vigorously asserting the autonomy of its own and the church's spiritual authority. Events came to a head in 1767–8 when Spanish, Neapolitan and French representatives all urged Pope Clement XIII to suppress the Jesuits after the latter had already been expelled from these territories. This the Pope refused to do, reasserting the strong line which he had already set out in his Bull *Apostolicum* of 1765: 'Let no one dare be rash enough to set himself against this my present approbative constitution lest he incur the wrath of God.' [29] It is significant that at the time of these events the Catholic monarchs were allowed to exercise a veto over papal elections, and with the explicit threat of a break between these states and the Roman church behind the election of Clement's successor, Cardinal Ganganelli was elected as Clement XIV in the reasonable expectation that he would suppress the Society. [30] This he did after some hesitation, and of the Pope's Brief *Dominus Ac Redemptor* by which the order was suppressed Hollis writes:

> The gravamen of his charge is that wherever the Jesuits have been throughout their history there has always been discord. He does not even advert to the possibility that it may be an explanation that the Pope had been steadily attacked for the last two hundred years and that the Jesuits were attacked because they supported the Pope. [31]

What this example illustrates perfectly is that even when an order ostensibly surrenders its authority to the external representative of the church's hierarchy, to the extent of taking a vow 'that they must immediately, without any shuffling or excuse, undertake whatsoever His Holiness commands . . .' [32] and of forbidding their superior to try to influence the Pope without the permission of the rest of the Society, [33] such an erosion of formal organizational autonomy at no stage approximates to the complete abrogation of moral autonomy, since in the last analysis normative principles will be found to have primacy in the choice of goals. This suggests that when we eventually look at religious orders in terms of Etzioni's typology of compliance it will be inappropriate to characterize religious orders as examples of instrumental compliance. All religious orders, however active their apostolate, and however much they may be seen as service agents of the institutional church, are fundamentally and pre-eminently organized around an intrinsic core of normative compliance.

3. In the main tradition of Christianity the religious order can never be dualistic in the sense of rejecting the world as totally evil (though its theology may occasionally approximate very nearly to a form of dualism) although it both totally rejects any compromise of its conception of the Gospel ethic and isolates or insulates itself against normal social intercourse.

For any religious organization which sees its mission in terms of a universalistic and inclusive impact on the whole of society, which is the ideological position of the church-type of organization, it is not usual to interpret the world as totally evil. On the other hand, this interpretation has frequently been made by small, élitist Christian groups, and it is necessary to consider how far this has been characteristic of religious orders and to what extent the Catholic Church has been able to accommodate this orientation within its overall universalistic ideology.

In the original form of desert monasticism we can in fact detect strong dualistic elements. As Hannay says, 'To the Egyptian monk the power of devils was, except only the power of God, the most practical and pressing question which could be discussed'. [34] One of the most striking images which appears in histories of these desert monks, which were written at the same time, is of the desert being populated with devils, against which a continual struggle had to be waged. The imagery of the desert monks is perhaps best described as the projection of the interior conflict which faces any solitary whose goal is the ethic of perfection, and one of the ways in which this dualistic belief can be reconciled within the church's universalistic scheme of values is by interpreting the monk's struggle as being waged on behalf of the rest of Christendom through what Troeltsch called a 'vicarious oblation'. Expressed this way, the church's religious communities become, as it were, the forward troops in a widely dispersed conflict. This explanation can often be encountered in the literature and a very precise version of it is given by Steinmann:

> As long as the battle against Satan continues on earth, Christian monasticism will continue to establish at the very heart of Christianity those solitary places, the monasteries, where in the silence of the cells apocalyptic struggle against the forces of evil may be resumed. [35]

Nor is this an isolated case from a particular period of the history of religious orders. A remarkably similar statement was made in the journal of an Anglican sisterhood as recently as 1966:

> It is our great joy and privilege to recite the Night Office at 2 am, a time when the powers of darkness are very active and the suffering needs of mankind and the souls departing from this life are specially needing to be held to the Love of God. [36]

Another notable feature of religious orders has been the occasionally very strong millennial tradition, which is closely related to dualism since both emphasize the radical imperfection of society as it exists. Millennialism was a common feature throughout early Christianity, and the urge to make a physical separation from the world was strengthened by the belief in an imminent Parousia (the second coming of Christ to judge mankind and to end the present social order). [37] In this context the epithet quoted by Cassian which advised monks to flee from women and bishops acquires a deeper meaning, for if the world is about to undergo a radical transformation it could be seen as imperative to avoid those who would make the monk love the world and those who would make him serve it. The case of the Spiritual Franciscans, already briefly outlined, demonstrates the potential for millennial reinterpretation of an élite observance which could not be accommodated within the more universalistic and compromising *Weltanschauung* of the church. But it is clear that a more general tendency among religious orders has been to accept a less radical but in some respects more self-legitimating form of millennial belief of the type which Martin describes. [38] While religious orders have shown much less active hostility to the world or to society than have sectarian groups, and have consequently not anticipated the same catastrophic end to society in an immediate future, they have substituted for this an emphasis on the realization of the Kingdom of God within the community itself. Thus 'the order concentrates attention on the eternal as it is realized in every moment of the present' [39] and it is in the present that the self-selecting community restores to perfection primitive ideals which have elsewhere been compromised. This resolution of the dilemma of millennialism facing a small élitist body inside a church is nowhere better exemplified than in the description of the religious life which the church itself uses when it calls it 'the life of angels'. [40]

In rejecting any compromise of its '*ad litteram*' interpretation of the Gospel ethic, a religious order may take several courses of action. In the first place it will normally seek maximum observance of its precepts through meticulously detailed regulation of daily activity. Secondly, it will often attempt to reinforce value commitment by frequent reiteration of its Rule. There may in addition be symbolic reminders of ideological injunctions, an excellent example of which is Cistercian architecture. Thomas Merton has described the frequent use of 'death's head' motives throughout the abbey as a reminder of the basic other-worldliness of the monk's vocation. Having emphasized the physical symbolism of the monks' dualism he also finds it necessary to emphasize that Cistercian abbeys were often built in the middle of swamps to ensure physical isolation (and thus to refute '. . . the mistaken idea that the Cistercian fathers liked to build in marshy and unhealthy places so that the monks would always be ill. This condition would enable them to do penance and would keep death, their last end, inescapably before them . . .'). [41] The architectural form of Cistercian abbeys was likewise strictly governed by ideological prescriptions which have been described as four sets of almost exclusively negative theories that were elaborated to guide the Cistercian architect.

> They consisted first of the Augustinian principle demanding a structure without *affectus*, that is without emotional expression. Secondly, corresponding to Benedict's stipulation that the monastic church should be nothing but an *officina*, the oratories were to be ideal workshops for 'the art of holiness'. [42]

To these were added St Bernard's stipulation that the population of monks should transcend 'a meaningless hull of stone' and an awareness that Cluny had succumbed to what a General Chapter of the Cistercian Order called 'the superfluities which deform the honesty of an old religious order'. [43] Taken together, these features imply a highly pervasive concern with the preservation of uncompromising pristine values and a propagation of these ideals through diffuse symbols.

In an enclosed, contemplative order isolation from the world and from the rest of society is physical and to all intents and purposes total. However, this is by no means typical of all religious orders, particularly those like the friars which have an active apostolate, and other forms of isolation and insulation have been developed so as to minimize the degree of interaction between the members of an order and the rest of society; and even, in some eremitical orders, the degree of interaction between members and fellow members. On the latter point, many observers of the religious life have noted the function of the monastic cowl, which almost completely hides the wearer's face except from immediately in front and serves to limit social interaction to a minimum. Among others, Fermor has noticed the function of this characteristic feature of contemplative orders, [44] and so, in characteristically acid fashion, has Gibbon in his treatment of the Egyptian monks:

> Recluse fanatics have few ideas or sentiments to communicate; a special license of the abbot regulated the time and duration of their familiar visits; and, at their silent meals, they were enveloped in their cowls, inaccessible, and almost invisible, to each other. [45]

The special habit also functions as an important insulating mechanism when the members of a religious order are outside the confines of their community. There is some relationship between the style of the religious habit and the degree of social distance which is implied according to whether an order is active or contemplative. Thus, the dress of an active women's order like the Congregation of Our Lady of Sion or the Little Sisters of the Assumption (both of which are nineteenth-century foundations) is in the practical, 'deaconess' style, while that of a contemplative order like the Bridgettine or Cistercian Nuns is much fuller and more distinctly 'monastic' in style. Similarly, among male religious, the deep-cowled habit of a Carthusian contemplative contrasts with the dress of a Jesuit, which is scarcely distinguishable from that of a secular priest, and at the extreme of involvement in surrounding society, the Little Brothers of Jesus, who perform normal manual work as individuals, wear no special religious dress at all.

Typical of the means by which religious orders seek to isolate or insulate their members against the surrounding society is the provision in the Rule of St Benedict, which acknowledges that a monk may have to leave the confines of the monastery for short periods, but he is forbidden to mention anything he has seen or heard in the world outside. Even in an order which has an active apostolate some form of psychological insulation will be practised, the best example of this being the *Spiritual Exercises* of St Ignatius, which were specifically written for use in periodic Retreats, both of members of the Jesuit Order and of others.

4. The religious order demands total commitment.

Total commitment is an imperative element in religious orders. It involves the detachment of members from all external loyalties (save those which are mediated by the order, for instance obedience to the pope) and an important component of this feature is the process of alienation, by means of which the order tries to ensure the detachment of its members from all other potentially conflicting loyalties. About this the Rule of St Benedict is very specific, and it appears to give this organizational goal primacy: 'Above all, let the vice of private ownership be cut off from the monastery by the roots.' [46] Every religious order in which solemn vows are taken views the initial and sustained detachment of its members from material possessions as an essential prerequisite for the growth of total commitment, and there are many examples in the various Rules of a preliminary 'stripping' process through which the intending member renounces the use of all personal property during the period of his membership and symbolizes this by exchanging his previous dress for the monastic habit. [47] But even at this early stage of membership it is difficult to separate, even analytically, the negative component of alienation from the positive component of indoctrination, because the two processes are simultaneously emphasized. For example, the changing of clothes is accompanied by a ritual which stresses the symbolic significance of the new dress. As the Trappist Usages explicitly state of the clothing ritual: 'The ceremonies which accompany this rite show that the postulant takes a step forward in separation from the world and in being incorporated into the community.' [48] Even the negation of previous personal identity which is sought by discarding the former Christian name is accompanied by the adoption of a new religious name, which symbolizes the probationer's status as member of a new primary group. The emphasis placed on entrance procedures is suggestive of the way in which religious orders interpret their function as a process of resocialization—for example, St Benedict speaks of the *'conversatio morum'*, a lifelong changing of behaviours—and consequently need to lay great stress on the break between the individual's previous life and the life of a new recruit to the religious order. [49] Goffman notes this 'stripping' process in all total institutions which attempt a reform of their inmates, although there do appear to be fundamental differences in the extent to which such institutions attempt to develop positive commitment among their members.

On a very similar pattern to the practice of the early desert monks, the new recruit to one of the major religious orders would be put under the supervision of an older, more experienced member whose duty it was to expound the Rule and to explain the regulations of the religious order: this is what has been termed the positive component of indoctrination and its terminal goal has been well expressed in the case of the Benedictines by Knowles, who calls it 'the monasticism of the soul'. [50] One way of ensuring that only the most highly committed novices reach the stage of taking vows is by constantly holding out the possibility of withdrawing from the order; but that this is only imperfectly achieved is demonstrated by some of the recent evidence cited by Moorhouse [51] of an increasing number of professed members of religious orders who give up their member-ship after having taken solemn vows, and hence in the face of excommunication. An important means whereby orders ensure that only those who are specially committed remain full members is to put no serious barrier in the way of a member who wishes to leave, though the threat of excommunication is certainly a negative sanction and some Rules, notably the Rule of St Benedict, prefer to resocialize deviants—if this is possible—before actually excluding them. Fear of inadequacy after a period of seclusion and sheer inertia are two other sources of lack of commitment among individual members of religious orders, though evidence of the ease with which a member can leave is given by Baldwin:

> The arrangements made by the Church for the dispensation of nuns who, for valid and adequate reasons, desire to leave their convents and return to the world, could hardly be wiser or more practical. (I may add that in my own case, the kindness and consideration which I received throughout, from everyone concerned, could hardly have been surpassed. It almost over-whelmed me.) [52]

What the contemporary decline in vocations and apparent increase in defections do indicate, however, is the degree to which religious orders have always relied on a fairly high level of presocialization, often anticipatory socialization, so that the extent to which they were ever capable of resocialization seems to have been more apparent than real. On this point, Dekkers in Holland carried out an enquiry into the decline in female vocations. This enquiry began in 1954 and covered some 30,000 female religious, or 90 per cent of the total in Holland. Maintaining that the family had been substantially deprived of its religious socializing function, he concluded that the decline in vocations had been a consequence. He described

> . . . le changement de structure du foyer au cours des 50 dernières années. Au lieu du foyer fermé, protégé contre les influences étrangères, où étaient confondus habitation et délassement, nous eûmes un foyer plus ouvert, qui dut céder des rôles qui lui étaient propres comme l'enseignement, la culture, les délassements. De ce fait, l'unité du foyer se désagréges. Suite à cela, il perdit sa fonction d'éducation religieuse . . . Le nombre des vocations religieuses en subit donc sensiblement les conséquences. [53]

In this passage is very clearly implied the function of the family in preparatory socialization before the recruit begins his socialization inside the order. An index of the traditionalistic nature of families which send recruits into religious orders is given by Collard, Dekkers and Dellepoort [54] who all note the relatively large size, even among Catholics, of the families of origin of Religious. Dellepoort found that 70 per cent of vocations in Holland came from families with six or more children, and 17 per cent from families with ten or more. Such families were also more likely to be authoritarian, and as the overall structure of the family becomes democratic, another source of the decline in vocations becomes apparent. Goddijn expresses this succinctly as the attempt of some nineteenth-century foundations to 'stifle the women of the twentieth century into the corsets of the nineteenth . . .' [55] At all events, the available data suggest that the development of total commitment in religious orders is a function of a wider process than simply resocialization within the order and requires a certain level of preliminary socialization which may even include the choice of a religious vocation as such. [56]

Formal commitment expressed in the taking of vows was an innovation of St Benedict, and in fact it was seen as limiting the monastic promise, since originally the search for perfection was unrestricted. Benedict himself recognized the degree to which he had mitigated the original austerities of monasticism, for he called his Rule a 'little rule for beginners'. The growth of formal vows is a similar process to the development of Rules as ecclesiastically approved constitutions and represents an increasing institutionalization of the religious life so that accommodation into, and control by the church were more easily achieved. Having once defined the canonical status of vows it thereby became possible to specify their content, though this did not in itself obviate conflict as the example of the Franciscan vow of poverty well illustrates. Luther and Calvin were opposed to vows only when they related to acts which were not obligatory: the latter because he considered all good acts as obligatory, and the former because the vow to perform a free action was contradictory to the spirit of voluntarism. But both justified vows by the practical reason of strengthening the will. [57]

5. The religious order demands considerably more obedience from its members than the wider church demands from either its lay members or its clergy.

Behind this apparently obvious characteristic lies a rather more complex situation. The way obedience is defined, articulated and formalized in the order is of immense importance. One of the most illuminating statements on this point is that of Calmette, who remarks that the humility demanded by St Bernard from his monks 'rendered them malleable'. [58] The movement from the individualistic asceticism of the Egyptian hermits, which was seen by the monks themselves as personal obedience to God but was criticized by some observers as spiritual pride, to the inculcation of an ethic of humility was partly a response to the increasing importance of cenobitical monasticism—in which individualism could be highly disruptive—but it was also a norm which made coexistence within the church's framework a more readily achieved goal. Though the first detailed provisions on obedience were made under the quasi-military monastic system of Pachomius, Benedict vastly extended the idea and in the Benedictine Rule set up 'obedience without delay' as the first degree of humility. The Rule also introduced the notion of an extra-organizational source of legitimacy because the commands of a superior were to be treated as the commands of God and were to be carried out accordingly. Once again we see demonstrated the primacy of normative over strictly utilitarian organizational goals. Benedict goes further than requiring merely external observance for he proposes the higher goal of interior obedience as the most virtuous. Although seemingly impossible commands may be queried and perhaps mitigated, they must be attempted if ordered by a superior. This is a fairly common feature of Rules, and St Ignatius, for example, makes exactly the same provision.

It is necessary to make the qualification at this point that there are two factors which limit the theoretically limitless scope of the religious vow of obedience. Firstly, there are often very stringent provisions for the election of superiors which are designed to achieve maximum consensus about the source of formal authority in the group. The Benedictine Rule details some of the qualities the abbot is expected to possess and makes the observation that he too is subject to the normative primacy of the Rule. As a symbolic reinforcement of this there is maintained in some Benedictine communities the tradition of the abbot washing the feet of his monks. Secondly, under Canon Law a command to do something evil would be clearly invalid, even under a vow of obedience, and could not be legitimately performed. Obedience is often expressed as a scale: hence both Benedict and Ignatius give a scale of . humility and obedience which begins with external execution of commands and ends with the submission of the will and of personal judgement.

When we compare the level of obedience demanded by a religious order from its members and by the church at large from its members we find a striking difference. The order makes far more widespread and detailed demands on its members than does the church, and this is formally distinguished as the dual morality of Precepts and Counsels. The Catholic doctrine is briefly defined by Barnes and Fanning [59]: the Precepts of the Gospel are those ethical statements which are binding on all, while Counsels are adopted as the vocation of comparatively few Christians; as Fanning puts it, '. . . the former imposes an obligation, while the latter is a persuasion'. [60] The process of differentiating these two ethical levels is described by Barnes in terms which strongly suggest the Weberian concept of routinization:

. . . the danger in the Early Church, and even in Apostolic times, was not that the 'counsels' would be neglected or denied, but that they should be exalted into commands of universal obligation, 'forbidding to marry' (1 Tim., iv, 3), and imposing poverty as a duty on all. [61]

Hence, just as monasticism became the formalized continuation of a more general high level of ascetic practice, so the dual standard of morality, with the most exacting standards of ethical conduct reserved for a small minority with a particular vocation, also evolved and was formalized. The rejection of this dual standard by, in Barnes's account, 'heretics in all ages, especially by many Protestants in the sixteenth and following centuries . . .' is an important aspect of the church's ideological provision for, or rejection of, groups of *virtuosi* within the church.

Moorhouse points out that in the *Codex Iuris Canonici* the three evangelical Counsels of perfection—obedience, poverty and chastity—are stated as obligatory for all Religious but obedience is given priority. [62] His excellent catalogue of the detailed and sometimes absurdly trivial limits to which the goal of obedience may be driven suggests that we should examine exactly how the norm is implemented in practice. We have more evidence of how the norm may operate ineffectively than the reverse, but this nevertheless throws light on the position of obedience in a religious order. Baldwin, for example, explicitly states that her reason for leaving the convent was a failure to understand the meaning of obedience—'Obedience was my stumbling-block' is how she explains her defection—and the account she gives of the meticulous requirements of her community is a good example of observance in the absence of normative legitimation. For instance, she describes the practice of 'custody of the eyes' (another form of social insulation): 'You were obliged to take short, measured steps, head bent just a little forward and eyes invariably cast down. Even had a bomb exploded just behind you, it would have been more perfect not to look up.' [63] In the absence of any internalized sense of obedience which is the goal of several monastic Rules, the detailed regulation comes to be seen as '. . . the complex machinery of another long monastic day.' [64] The necessity for some degree of anticipatory socialization is as apparent in this context as it was for the development of total commitment. This was noted in a recent theological account of the religious life, where it was argued that it was now much more difficult for religious orders to obtain as high a degree of obedience from their

members as they formerly could. [65] The most important cause
of this was seen as the democratization of the modern family and
the greater freedom of thought in modern industrial society
which are to a considerable extent in conflict with the religious
order's goal of total obedience. The effect is exactly the same as
that already given: the religious order is faced with a corres-
pondingly more extensive task of resocialization. One of the
solutions to this dilemma which was suggested was the more
frequent practice of Retreats—already suggested as a psychological insulating mechanism—which, it was argued, would
serve to internalize the member's or potential member's detachment from secular influences.

*6. The religious order is locally community-based and to some degree always
forms a quasi-familial* Gemeinschaft *and a permanent, participating
ritual group.*

There is a vigorous communitarian element in religious orders
in Western Catholicism which has a very early origin. Indeed,
Canon 497 of the *Codex Iuris Canonici*, which defines the 'religious
state', implicitly denies hermits and anchorites the canonical
status of 'religious persons'. [66] The elements characterizing the
religious state are given as 'community of life, constituted by
incorporation of the member into the community, common
dwelling under one roof, and a common rule of life'. [67] Communal living in fact antedates formal monastic groups and several
writers have indicated the communistic features of the very early
church, the blueprint for which was the charismatic group of
Christ and his disciples. The most clear statement of this is made
by Rousseau: 'La vie commune a incontestablement été . . . la
première dans le christianisme'. [68]

However, there is good evidence to show that the earliest form
of monastic collectivity, the Pachomian monastery, was predominantly a *local* rather than a communitarian social form and
did not possess strong *gemeinschaftlich* features. The basic structure
existed: in each settlement there were 1,500 to 2,000 monks
divided into numerous houses of thirty or forty monks, each
subdivided into groups of ten monks under a foreman (the
influence of Roman military organization is apparent here). Each
house had a master, and each monastery had an abbot who was
assisted by a steward. Furthermore, there was a system of centralized supervision of all monasteries on the pattern of the later

religious orders. On the other hand, the face-to-face primary group structure was notably lacking:

> D'autre part, on a remarqué que s'il y avait discipline et order dans le cénobitisme pakhomien, les individus n'y étaient spirituellement que «juxtaposés». La vie de famille, l'harmonieux agencement des esprits et des coeurs centré sur un idéal spirituel élevé et cultivé en commun, la vraie fraternité monastique en un mot, n'existait pas encore dans ce monachisme. Au point de vue spirituel, chacun était laissé a lui-même, ou au père qu'il s'était choisi, comme çela avait été le cas pour l'anachorétisme. *Omnia eorum conversatio*, a écrit Rufin, *ita est in multitudine posita, quasi esset in solitudine.* [69]

The important development which came with the Rule of St Benedict was the formation of the first quasi-familial monastic community. Since the Rule was clearly aiming at a mitigation of some of the pristine austerities of asceticism, the formation of a permanent face-to-face community can be seen as one way of achieving this. [70] In shaping a type of monasticism which contained 'nothing harsh, nothing burdensome', Benedict made the significant innovation of a vow of stability. The effect of this vow was to tie the monk perpetually to the community of his initial profession, and such a goal was only possible in conjunction with the infusion of pervasive communitarian norms, particularly those relating to the treatment of deviants. In the Rule detailed provision is made for the treatment of those who offend against the regulations of the community, and the guiding principle throughout is the attempted reform of the individuals in question. Expulsion is only advocated as a last resort, and even then a member may be received back three times before he is finally abandoned. The key figure in this quasi-familial community is the abbot: in his role are combined two distinct symbols of authority, the representative of Christ and the father of the community, and thus legitimacy is ultimately derived from outside the community by stressing the wider symbolic significance of authority roles. The paternalistic role of the abbot is not a universal feature of religious orders, but it is one of the focal points of the monastic community, as Knowles observes:

> ... there have always been, and are still, some characteristics of abbatial government which are not found in every religious organization. In the first place, the very name 'Abbot', 'Father',

suggests a relationship, suggests that the Abbot cannot exist apart from, or act without a thought for, his monks. [71]

It was important in the development from eremitical to cenobitical monasticism to stress social rather than individual goals of perfection. As a result, the goal of submergence of self in the community becomes paramount, and in the Rule of St Benedict the best monk is the one who does not 'murmur'. The object of this injunction is the prevention of what was laconically expressed in the words of a thirteenth-century friar: 'A community of religious is like a herd of pigs. When one grunts, they all grunt.' [72] The eremitical pole which is apparent in periods of reform within some of the older orders has remained a latent ideal throughout the whole of their history, so that it is best to see even the Benedictine *Gemeinschaft* as resting on an incipient tension between eremitic and cenobitic models. Two reasons for this can be given. In the first place, the community of virtuosi, while strictly being only a means to an end, may by a process of inertia become an end in itself. The process of goal displacement has been well documented in the case of bureaucratic organizations by Merton [73] and a similar process is observable in several of the religious orders: the example of Cluny seems appropriate to this discussion and is studied in chapter 4. Secondly, although a community may serve to mitigate some of the tensions which are apparent in the isolated asceticism of the hermit, it is also in itself a source of various tensions. Warnings about the dangers of 'particular friendships' can be found in the Rule of St Benedict and in most Rules since then, and the kinds of friction which arise from close social contacts in a small, relatively isolated group will be quite obvious. For reasons of this sort, religious orders like the Cistercians have more or less successfully resolved the tensions through a life of 'solitude in community' and the Carthusian life has been described as 'community in solitude'. [74] The function of the cowl and of 'custody of the eyes' is that of minimizing social contact. Silence is another such means, as is the detailed prohibition of physical contact. With such reservations in mind, it is nevertheless accurate to describe the religious order as a *Gemeinschaft*. Though the degree of permanence may differ from one order to another, the local group always forms a participating ritual community, and group ritual is always the framework on which other daily activity is based.

7. The religious order is originally a lay movement with considerable lay participation, and this remains as an ideal though it may be eroded by the church as a means of maintaining control.

Religious orders originated as, and for a long time remained, lay movements. We have already described the early development of monasticism as a systematization of more general lay practice, and there was a strong anti-sacerdotal tendency among the Egyptian monks. It seems likely that the earliest lay ascetics among groups of Christians did not withdraw physically from the world but carried on the ascetic life in their family groups, abstaining from marriage, keeping fasts, and devoting themselves to prayer and good works. [75] The first evidence of a differentiation between monastic groups and the rest of the membership of the church occurred at precisely the time when the priestly hierarchy of the wider church was being institutionalized, and the monastic movement had been widely interpreted as a form of protest by the laity against the curtailment of the old privileges. As one source neatly puts it: 'Monasticism in its origin was the protest of the lay spirit against any conception of religion which excluded the laity from the highest obligations or the supremest attainment.' [76] The importance of the lay status of monks was still borne out in the sixth century Rule of St Benedict, which stated in Chapter 60 that priests were not to be let into the monastery too easily and must be made to obey the Rule like the rest of the monks. However, with the abbot's permission they were to be allowed to perform some of their priestly functions such as giving blessings and saying Mass.

Until the early Middle Ages, in the Western Church, a monk was assumed to be a lay-monk but it very quickly became the established practice that most monks were priests, and priests are in a strong majority in contemporary male religious orders: it is worth noting by contrast that orders of women are of necessity entirely lay. By the eleventh century Canons Regular—ordained priests adopting the Religious Life—were beginning to organize themselves under Rules, usually the Rule of St Augustine. Later religious orders like the Society of Jesus required ordination as a prerequisite for full membership, and there now exists a 'caste system' of religious orders. According to Canon 491 of the *Codex*, Canons Regular take precedence over Benedictine and other monks, monks take precedence over other Regulars like Dominicans, Franciscans and Jesuits, and these take precedence over all other religions, including Redemptorists, Passionists and Oratorians. Similarly, Canon 564 lays down that the novitiate in any order is to be separated as far as possible from the part of the community dwelling occupied by the fully professed members, and novices preparing to be lay brothers are required to be separated even from the other novices. [77] These features of Western Christianity suggest a fairly substantial divergence from the original pattern of monasticism, and at the present time it is the Eastern Orthodox Church which preserves the closest parallel to the primitive lay movement: the Greek equivalent of '*monachus*' has always meant specifically a lay-monk, and in Eastern orthodoxy there is a distinct term for a priest-monk. However, in the same way that the eremitical ideal has remained latent one might perhaps find a similarly latent lay ideal, a hypothesis which is derived from Workman's contention that 'monasticism never forgot that personal holiness is something higher than any succession can bestow'. [78]

Paul Sabatier, the Calvinist scholar whose extensive research on St Francis found a place on the Papal Index, gave precisely this interpretation to the Franciscan movement. His analysis of the conflict between sainthood and priesthood, set in the context of the highly secularized thirteenth-century ecclesiastical establishment, represents the Franciscans as a reformist lay movement. Francis was thus a charismatic lay leader who protested against the wealth of the church, though his movement eventually became routinized as the church extended its control over the religious orders: 'The thoroughly lay creation of St Francis had become, in spite of himself, an ecclesiastical institution. . . . The prophet had abdicated in favour of the priest . . .' [79] There is a good deal of evidence to support Sabatier's contention that Francis was engaged in a lay protest against the personal unworthiness of priests, but it can be maintained, on the other hand, that there was no rejection of the priestly office as such. We are told that on entering a city, Francis would first visit the bishop, and the statements he made about priestly authority were positive, though sometimes with interesting conditional clauses:

. . . the Lord gave me, and gives me, so much faith in priests *who live according to the form of the holy Roman Church*, on account of their order, that if they should persecute me, I would have recourse to them. And if I had as much wisdom as Solomon had, and if I should find *poor* priests of this world, I would not preach against their will in the parishes in which they live. [80] (my emphasis)

By way of reconciling these conflicting views we can perhaps say that the Franciscan movement, though contained within the overall hierarchical framework of the church (either as a result of routinization or as the expressed goal of its founder) was one with a substantial lay component, as is clearly shown in the important innovation of 'secular tertiaries' (laymen holding allegiance to the specific goals of the order but otherwise living 'in the world' like other laymen) and by the later disputes between a section of the order and the authorities of the church.

The growth of a priestly population in the older religious orders had been accompanied by an internal stratification into 'choir' and 'lay' monks. The former were usually priests, or in female orders the better educated recruits, while the latter have been described as the equivalent of 'stewards in an officers' mess'. [81] In the Benedictine Order this began as a custom but ended in the regulation that 'choir' monks must proceed to Holy Orders, and they were freed from manual work by the existence of 'lay' brothers. Similarly, the Cistercian Order was stratified into *monachi* and *conversi*. Very recently there have been indications of a reversion to the more primitive model of full lay participation by the removal of this distinction. The revision was recommended by Vatican II, but even before this there was evidence of a change in some of the older religious orders. In the Mount Saviour abbey of the Benedictines of the Strict Observance, founded by Dom Damasus Winzen at Elmira, New York, in 1950 the change had been initiated. Merton explains the 'innovation' in terms of a reversion to pristine practice: 'Dom Damasus is trying to return to the very early monasticism in which the monk was purely and simply a monk, and not also a priest or cleric. According to his plan, there are to be only a few priests in the monastery, and no laybrothers.' [82] An entirely similar reversion to primitive observance has been taking place in the English Province of the Subiaco Congregation of Benedictines, for example at Prinknash Abbey. This is simply one example of the way in which primitive traditions appear to survive a long period of latency in religious orders, only to re-emerge as 'innovations' at a later stage.

8. The religious order is a collection of religious virtuosi *with an un-compromising interpretation of the Gospel ethic which is sanctioned by the church but is not put forward as necessary for all.*

Attention has already been paid to the frequent appearance of '*ad litteram*' interpretations and the elaboration of Precepts and Counsels. Some further implications of this characteristic remain to be considered.

It has been proposed that in many respects monasticism has followed a primitive ideal within the church, albeit an intensification of more general lay practice. There is much in the original antithesis between the church type and the sect type of organization to suggest that it was at the time when the Christian church finally became the dominant religious institution in the Roman Empire, and was consequently faced with the dilemma of having to compromise with secular institutions, that the 'bold radicalism' [83] of monasticism first became differentiated. This process has frequently been symbolized in terms of the most obvious practical consequence of Christianity's new status as an established religion, the end of persecution. The development is very well summarized in the following passage:

> It is no coincidence that monasticism should have developed immediately after Constantine's conversion at the very time when the persecutions ceased and Christianity became fashionable. The monks with their austerities were martyrs in an age when martyrdom of blood no longer existed; they formed the counterbalance to an established Christendom. [84]

As usual, Gibbon is more terse: 'Prosperity and peace introduced the distinction of the *vulgar* and the *Ascetic Christians*.' [85] The contrast between the heroic simplicity of the religious *virtuoso* and the 'lithomania' [86] of the church is a recurring theme in the literature and lies at the basis of the characterization of the order as a quasi-sect. By means of the theory of vicarious oblation the church has typically granted such virtuoso activity special honour and has accepted it as functional for the rest of the church—the often encountered notion of 'reservoirs of religion' is one expression of this. Butler and Merton accept the view that monasticism is functional for the church but—using an argument which is familiar to sociologists—they deny that the function of an institution is necessarily the reason for its inception: monasteries are basically 'for themselves'. [87] This argument of course is specifically concerned with monastic orders. Many other religious orders have explicit practical goals written into their constitutions, so that in their case function and cause may be very much equated. This leads directly to a consideration of an important *empirical* feature of virtuoso religion.

One of the most typical historical aspects of this virtuoso component of monasticism has been celibacy, and it is important to set this practice in context. In pre-Christian Graeco-Roman thought the growing importance of a dualistic belief in the evil nature of the body was associated with a gradual exaltation of the virgin state. This dualism also emerged in early Christian teaching on celibacy and can be seen in a range of statements in the New Testament. Thus, approval is given to those who are eunuchs for the sake of the kingdom of heaven (Matthew 19:10 ff.); leaving one's wife for the sake of Jesus (Mark 10:29) or for God (Luke 18:29) is commended; and it is affirmed that in the resurrection there will be no marriage (Matthew 22:30; Mark 12:25); this is why the religious life is sometimes called 'the life of angels'. Saint Paul wishes everyone to be in the same state as himself (1 Corinthians 7:7) and he notes that unmarried Christians are single-minded while married ones have divided loyalties (1 Corinthians 7:32 f.). At first the celibate life was not obligatory on clergy as a necessary part of their function, though there was widespread belief that celibacy represented a more perfect level of observance, and dualistic exaggerations of this belief into a universal principle were not uncommon. It was a particularly important aspect of the Manichean heresy which St Augustine first shared and then renounced.

In the early church monasticism certainly increased the appeal of celibacy, but it had no monopoly on it. For the church at large, laws dealing with celibacy can be found as early as the beginning of the fourth century, and it is clear that many priests discontinued marriage relationships after their ordination. An effort to make celibacy a universal law of the church failed at the First Council of Nicaea (325), but Pope Siricius in 385(6?) prescribed absolute celibacy for higher clergy. From the fifth to the seventh centuries promises of continence were often required from candidates for ordination (and their wives); after the sixth century the separation of the couple was demanded, the wife often retiring to a religious community. Celibacy was incorporated into church doctrine as a counsel, which made it a more perfect state than marriage but did not make it obligatory on all members of the church. Thus celibacy has always been a feature of virtuoso communities in Christianity, and these have maintained an uncompromising interpretation of this counsel of perfection. At the same time, it is by no means an exclusive feature of these groups and for a long period it was obligatory on the whole of the clergy. However, in the case of the latter this was partly to prevent the alienation of church property, which might otherwise fall into the hands of the priest's family, and the adoption of celibacy by the clergy at large has never been as uncompromising. Clerical concubinage was rife in the tenth and fifteenth centuries, and popes have had to condone the marriages of priests which had taken place during schisms: Julius III, for example, gave dispensations to English priests who married during the reign of Henry VIII. In short, what virtuoso communities have regarded as an essential basis of their search for perfection, the church at large has tended to regard as a question of ecclesiastical law. [88]

9. The individual member of a religious order is basically seeking personal perfection, whether such perfection is defined in terms of individual or social goals or of an active or contemplative life. [89]

The goal of perfection is common to all religious orders, and is invariably attributed directly to the evangelical Counsel which began the monastic career of the first hermit, St Antony. But this overriding goal has been expressed in many different ways, one of the most important distinctions being that between individualistic perfection and perfection in community. The goal of the Egyptian hermit was to be 'alone with the alone' and the fact that such a goal survived the widespread development of cenobitical monasticism is well illustrated by the version of this which was given by the seventeenth-century Cistercian writer, Cardinal Bona: '. . . no one can find God except he is solitary, for God himself is alone and solitary'. [90] In complete contrast is the organicist theory of the church, very closely related to the medieval structure of feudalism, in which personal perfection and salvation are seen as only attainable through interaction with other members of the whole body of Christians which makes up the church. An excellent statement of this ideal was made by Congreve, a member of the Anglican Society of St John the Evangelist, who said:

Fellowship, brotherhood, is of the essence of the Religious Life, whether of Cenobite or of Solitary. . . . Religious brotherhood is not an imperfection tolerated for the present on account of the incurable weakness of human nature; it is a sacrament of Divine Love, a means towards perfection, a type of all Christian life . . .' [91]

In both of these cases the stated goal is *personal* perfection, and the immense variety among religious orders can therefore be attributed to differences of means in pursuit of this goal. A pattern emerges of the resolution of the tension between the two poles of eremitical and cenobitical monasticism in some form of compromise. The eremitical extreme is unstable because it easily gives way to excesses [92] and is difficult to regulate. On the other hand, as we have already seen, goal displacement is a source of decay in cenobitical religious orders. There is an apparent attempt to reach a 'critical balance' so that the tensions inherent in each pole can be neutralized.

The Carthusian Order is often cited as an example of the relatively successful balancing of these two elements [93] and will serve as a useful case from which to draw hypotheses. In fact, the Carthusian 'fulcrum' comes very close to the eremitical pole of the continuum, since the order was originally formed out of one of the numerous groups of hermits who at the end of the eleventh century established themselves in desolate parts of northern France. The life of a Carthusian monk is spent in the isolation of his cell, which is somewhat similar to a small cottage, and he meets the other members of the monastery only for liturgical celebration and a weekly walk outside the monastery: even meals are normally taken privately. The austere and very much hidden life of this order seems to have contributed to its reputation for stability, for, as Jessopp notes, 'With the single exception of the Carthusians, no monastic order seems to have been able to keep true to its original rule for more than two centuries at the utmost'. [94] The Carthusians have remained obscure by choice and have always refused dignities and marks of favour from the church. One of the reasons given by Merton for their refusal to take steps to have any member of the order canonized is that they prefer to *be* saints rather than to be *called* saints. So remarkable has been the consistency of this order in never having needed reform that it has become proverbial: *Cartusia numquam reformata quia numquam deformata.* Thus some degree of isolation seems to be a prerequisite for the continued stability of a contemplative religious order, though this is open to very different interpretations. An interesting reworking of the 'lonely crowd' theme shows just how closely the cenobitical pole can be approached without completely subverting the eremitical pole:

> St Pachomius discovered another kind of solitude [besides that of the hermit]. In the first great monastery of Egyptian cenobites, at Tabenna, the monk learned how to disappear—not into the desert but into a community of other monks. It is in some ways a far more effective way to disappear; an asceticism that is peculiarly deep and lasting. [95]

The distinction between a contemplative and an active apostolate can be made on similar criteria, though in the case of active orders the group within which personal perfection and salvation must be sought is less rigidly coterminate with the limits of the order and includes the other members of the church and the world at large for whom services are provided. And we have already dealt with the kinds of insulating mechanisms which may be employed by religious orders whose members perform an innerworldly vocation.

10. Membership of a religious order may only be gained and maintained by proof of special merit.

Religious orders always impose rigorous controls (at least formally) on the process by which full membership may be attained, and the probationary periods of postulancy and novitiate are specifically designed to probe the seriousness of the would-be recruit's vocation and to find evidence of humility and psychological stability. This process is best summed up by the advice in Chapter 58 of the Rule of St Benedict, 'Test the spirits, to see whether they come from God.' The Chapter continues:

> If such a one [a new applicant] . . . persevere in his knocking [at the gate], and if it be seen after four or five days that he bears patiently his harsh treatment and the difficulty of admission and persists in his petition, then let admittance be granted to him, and let him stay in the guest house for a few days. [96]

After this the applicant is required to live in the novitiate with the other novices and to be placed under the direction of a senior

monk who will scrutinize his behaviour closely. The qualities
looked for are a genuine and zealous search for God, obedience,
and patience in the face of humiliations. Obedience to a certain
degree of arbitrary authority is a common feature of the probationary period, which includes both postulancy (the preliminary
stage of induction) and novitiate (when temporary vows are taken,
sometimes more than once). Benedict introduced few innovations
in this respect because some kind of rigorous test of entry was
apparently demanded by religious orders from the very earliest
period. Cassian, for instance, described the test of entry to an
Egyptian monastery, which included lying outside the gates for
ten days or more, continually vilified by the taunts of the monks
inside, until there was sufficient evidence of the humility and
patience of the applicant. [97] During the period of squatting outside a Pachomian monastery the liturgy and psalms were given to
the applicant to be learned as a further test of merit, [98] and
having been granted admittance the postulant would be required
to spend another three years as a probationer, during which time
he would have to study reading and writing, the Old Testament
and the Psalms, and only after this would he be allowed to take
the monastic clothing. [99] Such preliminary testing is a universal
feature of religious orders, and contemporary orders require
entirely comparable evidence of merit and of capacity for the life
of varying austerity which members are expected to undergo: the
directories of the religious life often list in some detail the specific
personal qualities which are taken into consideration by the
different orders. There are also characteristic differences in entry
requirements which depend both on the kind of activity performed by the order and on the particular values which different
orders stress: hence, for example, the first Rule of St Francis
contained the direction that postulants were to be received
'kindly'.

Stringent tests of merit before full membership is obtained
perform principally two functions. Firstly, they are one of the
most vital means by which each order can protect itself against a
relaxation of its heroic ethic. This is a significant feature of the
Cistercian reform which grew out of the Cluniac decline. Having
listed three of the reasons for the decline of Cluny—inadequate
probation, growing wealth and lack of leadership—Knowles goes
on to describe the reception into the abbey of 'vast numbers of
new recruits without adequate probation or training'. [100] This

failure was even admitted by Peter the Venerable (Abbot of Cluny 1122–57) when he carried through some necessary reforms. On some occasions a probation of only a few hours had been required. A reform of this aspect of Benedictine observance was made by the Cistercians, who imposed in the novitiate 'a close and careful watch-and-ward upon every thought, emotion and sense-perception, prescribed with an insistence which marked it as no merely temporary measure, but as the discipline of a lifetime'. [101] And yet it is ironic that precisely the same source of decline over-took the Cistercian Order, for less than a century after the death of St Bernard there was an '. . . influx of vocations due to the attraction exercised by the Saint, but which had been insufficiently sifted and tested by superiors'. [102]

The second function of the entrance test of merit, together with the 'stripping' process, is that of a *rite de passage*. This emerges most clearly in the humiliation procedures of some early Rules. For example, according to the Rule of St Fructuosus (eighth century) the porter was obliged to test the applicant's sincerity by 'insults and revilings'. [103] Frequently, when membership of an in-group is generally accepted as providing privileged status and specialized knowledge, the members will seek to symbolize this to new entrants, and at the same time stress their low status in the group, by subjecting them to humiliation. [104]

Finally, membership will only be maintained by proof of special merit because, even though stringent attempts are made to pre-select members and though the formal taking of a vow is often sanctioned as a lifelong commitment, it is indispensable for the viability of such small face-to-face communities that provision should be made for the expulsion of members who show a serious decline in merit. Expulsion is available as a sanction to church-type organizations, but its significance is diminished because the universalistic criteria on the basis of which membership is granted do not permit exacting criteria for expulsion.

The purpose of this chapter has been to delineate the major components in an ideal type of the religious order. For this reason, the historical material on which it is based has been drawn from a broad spread of examples. In the following chapter we will compare this model with other closely related ones before going on to test its implications on a more detailed historical level.

NOTES

1 Helen Waddell, *The Desert Fathers* (London, Collins (Fontana), 1962), p. 21.
2 Hans Lietzmann, 'The era of the Church Fathers', vol. IV, in *A History of the Early Church* (London, Lutterworth, 1949–51), p. 132.
3 Of particular interest is the '*staretz*' of the Russian Orthodox Church, who is a solitary, wandering monk with no formal position in the ecclesiastical hierarchy but is thought to have extraordinary personal holiness and is sought as a counsellor in spiritual matters. Even the *staretz* is usually locally established near his monastery, though he is free from most of the demands of the monastic timetable.
4 This is the subject of chapter 4.
5 Peter F. Anson, *The Religious Orders and Congregations of Great Britain and Ireland* (Worcester, Stanbrook Abbey Press, 1949), p. 77.
6 On the distinction between Solemn and Simple vows see, e.g., Geoffrey Moorhouse, *Against All Reason* (London, Weidenfeld and Nicolson, 1969), p. 153. The difference is described as 'a very fine juridical one that only canon lawyers can appreciate properly'.
7 Anson, op. cit., 1949, p. 13.
8 ibid., p. 25.
9 See, e.g., James O. Hannay, *The Spirit and Origin of Christian Monasticism* (London, Methuen, 1903), chap. 4.
10 Lietzmann, op. cit., 1951, p. 158.
11 Peter F. Anson, *The Call of the Desert* (London, S.P.C.K., 1964), p. 24.
12 Some of the best documentation on this is given by W. H. Mackean, *Christian Monasticism in Egypt to the Close of the Fourth Century* (London, S.P.C.K., 1920) who describes the self-sufficiency of the monk Valens. The latter is reported to have refused the Eucharist with the proud explanation: 'I have no need to become a partaker, for I have seen Christ today' (p. 128).
13 John Cassian, *The Institutes* and *The Conferences* (Oxford, 1894), Select Library of Nicene and Post-Nicene Fathers, vol. IX (transl. Edgar C. S. Gibson), p. 279.
14 e.g. Lietzmann, op. cit., 1951, p. 160.
15 On this see Edward Cuthbert Butler, *The Lausiac History of Palladius* (Cambridge, 1898). Texts and Studies, vol. 6, no. 1, 2, section on Antonian monasticism.
16 David Knowles, *From Pachomius to Ignatius* (Oxford, Clarendon Press, 1966), p. 3.
17 There is a description of the Rule of Pachomius in Robert T. Meyer, *Palladius: The Lausiac History* (London, Longmans, Green, 1965).
18 A more detailed treatment of this important series of events is given in Chapter 4.
19 Decima L. Douie, *The Nature and the Effect of the Heresy of the Fraticelli* (Manchester, University Press, 1932), p. 2.
20 See below, pp. 96–97.

21 John-Baptist Reeves, O.P., *The Dominicans* (London, Sheed and Ward, 1929), p. 15.

22 Troeltsch, op. cit., p. 241.

23 The 'estate' system is very similar to the occupational aspect of the Indian caste system in that it provides for the reciprocal rendering of services in the absence of a money economy.

24 Troeltsch, op. cit., p. 242.

25 Below, pp. 43–45.

26 Anson, op. cit., 1964, p. 27.

27 ibid., p. 120.

28 Knowles, op. cit., 1966, p. 26.

29 Christopher Hollis, *A History of the Jesuits* (London, Weidenfeld and Nicolson, 1968), p. 146.

30 Clement XIII's death in February 1769 has been attributed to the strain of attacks on the Society of Jesus.

31 Hollis, op. cit., pp. 154–5.

32 James Brodrick, S.J., *The Origin of the Jesuits* (London, Longmans, Green, 1940), p. 73.

33 ibid., p. 74.

34 James O. Hannay, *The Wisdom of the Desert* (London, Methuen, 1904), p. 17.

35 J. Steinmann, *St. John the Baptist and the Desert Tradition* (London, Longmans, 1958) p. 157.

36 *F.L.G. Letter*, March 1966, p. 3 (quoted by Moorhouse, op. cit., p. 120.

37 Anson, op. cit., 1964, p. 9.

38 Martin, op. cit., 1965, p. 191.

39 ibid., p. 191.

40 Some sects, particularly millennial sects, also seem to 'realize' their own heavens, especially when the sect persists for a long period. An example of this is provided by the Rappites.

41 Thomas Merton, *Waters of Silence* (London, Hollis and Carter, 1950), p.29.

42 François Bucher, 'Cistercian architectural purism', in *Comparative Studies in Society and History*, vol. III, no. 1, October 1960, p. 93.

43 ibid., p. 93.

44 Patrick Leigh Fermor, *A Time to Keep Silence* (London, John Murray, 1957), p. 20: 'Their hands were invisibly joined, like those of mandarins, in the folds of their sleeves, and the stooped faces, deep in the tunnel of their pointed hoods, were almost completely hidden. A wonderful garb for anonymity.'

45 Edward Gibbon, *The History of the Decline and Fall of the Roman Empire* (J. B. Bury, ed.) (London, Methuen, 1909–14), vol. IV, p. 71.

46 Paul Delatte, *The Rule of St Benedict* (London, Burns, Oates, 1921), p. 245.

47 Bouyer finds that this is the most striking of all the monastic observances. Louis Bouyer, *The Meaning of Monastic Life* (London, Burns, Oates, 1955), p. 118: 'In fact, if we approach monastic life from the external side and the detail of its practice only, it is certainly the detachment, the stripping of self which cannot fail to strike us primarily.'

48 Moorhouse, op. cit., p. 260. The Usages were abandoned shortly after Moorhouse's book was published.

49 This, incidentally, is one of the reasons why it is so difficult (though increasingly less so) to get reliable and detailed socio-demographic data on the membership of religious orders.

50 David Knowles, *The Benedictines* (London, Sheed and Ward, 1929), p. 78.

51 Moorhouse, op. cit., pp. 80–1.

52 Monica Baldwin, *I Leap Over the Wall* (London, Pan Books, 1957), pp. 302–3.

53 H. Dekkers, 'Les vocations religieuses féminines aux Pays-Bas', *5ᵉ Conférence Internationale de Sociologie Religieuse*, op. cit.

54 Dekkers, op. cit.; E. Collard, 'L'étude sociologique des communautés religieuses féminines et de leur recrutement'; J. Dellepoort, 'Analyse sociographique et statistique des vocations sacerdotales aux Pays-Bas' in ibid.

55 H. P. M. Goddijn, 'The monastic community life in our times', *Social Compass*, vol. X, 1–2, 1965, p. 104.

56 There are some interesting contrasts here with Coxon's data, where it was found that contact with the clergy was a more important variable influencing the choice of both 'normal' and 'late' Anglican ordinands than was parental encouragement. Also, Anglican ordinands tended to come from smaller families and there was an over-representation of one-child families. But the importance of family socialization for Catholic ordinands is supported by Coxon's observation that this group of ordinands makes the choice of career on average at an earlier age than the Anglican group. See A. P. M. Coxon, *A Sociological Study of the Social Recruitment, Selection and Professional Socialization of Anglican Ordinands*, unpub. Ph.D. thesis, Leeds, 1965.

57 See A. Vermeersch, 'Vows', in *Catholic Encyclopaedia* (New York, The Encyclopaedia Press Inc., 1913), vol. 15, pp. 511–14.

58 Joseph Calmette, *Saint Bernard*, Paris, F. Brouty, J. Fayard et Cⁱᵉ, 1953.

59 In *Catholic Encyclopaedia* (New York, The Encyclopaedia Press Inc., 1913).

60 ibid., p. 372 (vol. 12).

61 ibid., p. 436 (vol. 4).

62 Moorhouse, op. cit., p. 146.

63 Baldwin, op. cit., p. 14.

64 ibid., p. 23.

65 Gérard Huyghe, *Tensions and Change, The Problems of Religious Orders Today* (London/Dublin, Geoffrey Chapman, 1965). Huyghe welcomed the democratizing tendency of modern society and hoped it would influence the religious orders.

66 Anson, op. cit., 1964, p. xv.

67 ibid., p. xv.

68 Olivier Rousseau, *Monachisme et Vie Religieuse d'Apres l'Ancienne Tradition de l'Eglise*, Paris, 1957, p. 71.

69 ibid., p. 77.

70 It is interesting that the effectiveness of this kind of primary group support should be confirmed by the findings of recent social psychological studies. For example, Himmelweit noticed the emphasis placed on educational success among middle-class families, and hypothesized

that heightened ambition on the part of parents would more frequently result in neurotic symptoms among this group of children. In fact this was not the case, and the explanation given indicated the 'cushioning' effect of the close affective links within the middle-class family.

71 Knowles, op. cit., 1929, p. 56.
72 Quoted by Cyril Beaufort (Bede) Jarrett, *The Religious Life* (London, Burns, Oates, 1939), third edition, p. 128.
73 Robert K. Merton, *Social Theory and Social Structure* (New York, Free Press, 1967), p. 199.
74 Anson, op. cit., 1949, p. 77.
75 Butler, op. cit., 1898.
76 Herbert Brook Workman, *The Evolution of the Monastic Ideal* (London, Charles H. Kelly, 1913), p. 13.
77 There is a valuable account of provisions of this sort in Moorhouse, op. cit., p. 154.
78 Workman, op. cit., p. 343.
79 Paul Sabatier, *Life of St Francis of Assisi*, transl. Louise Seymour Houghton (London, Hodder and Stoughton, 1904), p. 102.
80 Quoted in Paschal Robinson, *The Writings of St Francis of Assisi* (London, J. M. Dent, 1906), p. 82.
81 Moorhouse, op. cit., p. 155.
82 Thomas Merton, *The Silent Life* (London, Burns, Oates, 1957), p. 75.
83 Troeltsch, op. cit., p. 117.
84 Timothy Ware, *The Orthodox Church* (Harmondsworth, Middlesex, Penguin Books, 1964), p. 45.
85 Gibbon, op. cit., p. 57.
86 Meyer, op. cit., 1965, p. 4, giving the background to Palladius's Lausiac History, writes: 'Palladius . . . dedicated his work to Lausus, the royal chamberlain at the court of Emperor Theodosius II. This was at a time when the Church, newly liberated from the catacombs, was in a period of *lithomania*, a madness as it were for great ecclesiastical edifices. Palladius wished to teach Lausus lessons of true edification, the building and formation of character modeled on the lives of the desert saints.'
87 Edward Cuthbert Butler, *Benedictine Monachism* (London, Longmans, Green, 1924), pp. 382-3: 'Yet must we not lose sight of the fundamental principle of monasticism, that the real use of a monastic house lies not in activities and usefulnesses. It lies rather in things that cannot be counted by statistics or estimated by results. A recent Oxford Professor of Church History has said finely that "if society is to be permeated by religion, there must be reservoirs of religion . . .". This is the essential function of monasteries and monks, this their most real contribution to the well-being of the Church and of Society that a monastery be a "reservoir of religion", and its monks men primarily absorbed in "the pursuit of religion". The good works and utilities will surely follow; but they are by-products.' Thomas Merton, op. cit., 1957, p. 8: 'Not even Christians have been exempt from anxiety over this apparent "uselessness" of the monk, and we are familiar with the argument that the monastery is a kind of dynamo which, though it does not "produce"

grace, procures this infinitely precious spiritual commodity for the world.'

88 The data on celibacy are taken from *A Catholic Dictionary of Theology* (London, Nelson, 1967); *A Dictionary of Comparative Religion* (London, Weidenfeld and Nicolson, 1970); *The Oxford Dictionary of the Christian Church* (London, Oxford University Press, 1957); and *Sacramentum Mundi* (London, Burns, Oates, 1968).

89 It will be remembered that even a contemplative vocation may be interpreted in a socially utilitarian way as the source of powerful prayer from which both the church and society at large benefit.

90 Anson, op. cit., 1964, p. 197.

91 George Congreve, *Christian Progress: with Other Papers and Addresses* (London, Longmans, 1910), p. 198. One writer goes as far as to call the monastery a 'cooperative society for the promotion of holiness'. Augustus Jessopp, 'The monastic life and its teachings', in Harry Jones (ed.), *Some Urgent Questions in Christian Lights* (London, Rivingtons, 1889), p. 27.

92 Simeon Stylites and the other 'pillar saints' are good examples.

93 Tudor Edwards, op. cit., calls the Carthusian life the *ne plus ultra* and mystic peak of the monastic life. Knowles makes a valuable comment on its persistence: 'The significance of the Carthusians in the history of Western monasticism is that they domesticated the eremitical life without destroying it.' David Knowles and William Francis Grimes, *Charterhouse* (London, Longmans, Green, 1954), p. 2.

94 Augustus Jessopp, 'Monasticism', in *Companion to English History (Middle Ages)*, F. P. Barnard (ed.) (Oxford, Clarendon Press, 1902), p. 257.

95 Merton, op. cit., 1950, p. 4.

96 Saint Benedict, *The Rule*, transl. Abbot Justin McCann (London, Burns, Oates, 1952), pp. 129–31.

97 Cassian, op. cit., p. 219.

98 H. Leclercq, 'Monachisme', in *Dictionnaire d'Archeologie*, etc., op. cit., p. 1835.

99 Rofail F. Farag, *Sociological and Moral Studies in the Field of Coptic Monasticism*, Leiden, [The Annual of Leeds university oriental society, 1959–], 1964.

100 David Knowles, *Cistercians and Cluniacs, The Controversy Between St Bernard and Peter the Venerable* (London, Oxford University Press, 1955), p. 9.

101 Watkin Williams, *Studies in St Bernard of Clairvaux* (London, S.P.C.K., 1927), p. 105.

102 Albert Plé, *Religious Life, No. 2. Vocation*, being the English version of *Le Discernement des Vocations*, transl. Walter Mitchell (Blackfriars, Oxford, 1952), p. 62.

103 I. Gregory Smith, *Christian Monasticism From the Fourth to the Ninth Centuries of the Christian Era* (London, A. D. Innes, 1892), p. 155.

104 A very similar function is served by the mutilation rituals of some primitive societies which take place at puberty as a mark of newly-acquired adult status.

3

The Religious Order in a Comparative Perspective

THE RELIGIOUS ORDER has sometimes been regarded as an organization having certain features in common with the type of organization which is characteristic of sectarian groups. One way of exploring the similarities is to compare the ideal type of the order with the ideal type of the sect put forward by B. R. Wilson in his 1959 article. [1] This will be done by 'matching' the organization of religious orders against the categories used in Wilson's article.

1. The sect is a voluntary organization.

Voluntary membership is one of the more obvious features of religious orders which, being celibate, cannot bestow birthright membership. In the organicist theory of the church it is part of the reciprocal relationship between the members of orders and the ordinary lay members of the church that the latter continue to provide new members for the orders. Cuthbert Butler argues that the origins of monasticism in Egypt were similarly voluntaristic. However, before pointing out the parallels it is valuable to insert a preface in parenthesis, and to argue that certain historical features in religious orders have curtailed the voluntary element in organization. One such feature was the feudal practice whereby an abbey would be held in fief by a particular family, with a consequent restriction on the freedom of choice of the members in the election of abbots. An interesting example of the effect of such recruitment is the monastery of La Trappe where, in 1664, the first reforms which eventually led to the formation of the Cistercian Order of the Strict Observance (Trappists) were initiated by Abbot de Rancé. La Trappe was initially a particularly decadent Cistercian abbey, mainly as a result of the fact that for the century up to 1664, it had been held *in commendam*. As a direct result the pristine goals of the community had been diluted. De Rancé himself was a commendatory abbot who at first despised what he interpreted as the futility of monks and only became a monk with difficulty but, as often happens as a result of conversion, once in office he became an extremist.

Perhaps we should also note in this context the importance of some kind of pre-socialization process, for this would seem to perform very much the same function as childhood socialization in the case of the ordinary lay members of the church. It has already been suggested that some kind of pre-socialization may have been more important than at first seems likely and it is sometimes more meaningful to describe the process as one of *anticipatory* socialization in which the goal of membership of a religious order is more consciously presented. [2] For instance, in strongly Catholic cultures the practice of 'giving one son to the Church' may well result in the selection and direction of one child in a family towards membership of a religious order. It is reasonable to suppose that a similar form of anticipatory socialization takes place in educational institutions which are administered by religious orders, whether in a directive way or more in the nature of careers advice. Judging from some of the advertising material in directories of the religious life, religious orders use exactly the same format as other agencies that advertise particular careers, and the advertisements are sometimes very like those for the armed forces. The following advertisement for the Society of African Missions appeared in the *1965 Directory of Religious Orders Congregations and Societies of Great Britain and Ireland*: [3]

> An Urgent Message for all Boys and Young Men. WHAT DOES THE FUTURE HOLD FOR YOU? Your School days will soon be over and you will have to decide what you will be when you grow up. HAVE YOU EVER THOUGHT OF BECOMING A PRIEST? If you feel an attraction for the Church and have the right qualities you could not make a nobler or better choice ... WHY NOT WRITE NOW for our Vocations Leaflet ... ?

These are a few examples of the way in which occupational choice may to some extent be channelled towards a voluntary organization like the religious order, but there is a more widely based form of socialization into the norms of the church as a whole which presents the goal of membership of a religious order as especially prestigious: namely the process of canonization. [4] Just as the originally spontaneous development of monasticism was gradually brought under the control of the church, so the virtually uncontrolled emergence of saints from a combination of tradition and popular sentiment gradually became institutionalized in a form that permitted control of group values by the church. Pope Benedict XIV in the mid-eighteenth century gave an important deliverance *de beatificatione et canonization sanctorum* in which it was insisted that no inquiry was to be started into the suitability of a particular candidate for beatification or canonization until the 'natural virtues' of 'prudence, fortitude, or strength of soul, temperance and justice' had been proved to exist in him. Miracles, which were the charismatic and originally the most important component of sainthood, were to be secondary considerations. 'Canonization thus became a most effective instrument for institutionalizing certain types of personality, thereby insuring the perpetuation of group ideals.' [5] Sainthood itself only has meaning as part of a system of spiritual stratification (Mecklin refers to the saint as a 'spiritual aristocrat') and since the potential population eligible for the canonization process contains a disproportionately large number of the members of religious orders, then the religious order is clearly accorded a position of great prestige in the church's overall scheme of values. [6] Hence there is a broad normative pressure in the direction of membership of these groups. We can extend this discussion further. It seems likely that the saint, as a symbol and interpreter of universalized human values, has in recent history been replaced by counterparts drawn from a less traditional sector. Mecklin cites the examples of Abraham Lincoln and Florence Nightingale, and there are also the more recent examples of Ghandi and Martin Luther King. As other than ecclesiastical personifications of the heroic *ne plus ultra* of group values become more prominent, we might hypothesize a concomitant decline in the prestige of heroic religious goals.[7]

We have so far been dealing with necessary qualifications to the broad picture of a voluntary organization, but the latter nevertheless stands. Religious orders place great emphasis on the need for conscious adult choice in membership (not least because their viability rests on this) and Canon Law imposes minimum ages for notiviate and profession (16 for temporary vows, 21 for permanent vows [8]). A comparison of the normal age for taking vows and the normal age of Confirmation (by which full membership of the wider church is gained) indicates how important is the element of conscious choice for the religious order. As we have already noted stringent, though of course imperfect, attempts are made to ensure that no probationer reaches the stage of full membership without good evidence that he is capable of maintaining his commitment. In simple terms, if an élitist religious group like a sect or a religious order fails to retain its voluntary associational characteristic then it becomes something else. There will be a tendency for the sect to show denominational features while the order will decline and either eventually disappear or at some stage give rise to a pristine reform movement. One of the reasons why it is impossible to accept without qualification Goffman's analysis of religious communities as 'total institutions' is that they are voluntary associations while the rest of his illustrations are largely coercive organizations.

2. Membership is by proof to the sect authorities of some special merit.

For sectarian groups, merit is defined as special enlightenment, conversion experience or rigorously tested knowledge of sectarian beliefs, and the different criteria on which membership is granted typify the several varieties of sect. The definition of merit is thus indicative of the central beliefs of a particular sect. In the case of religious orders, as has already been outlined in some detail, special merit is defined chiefly as a higher level of commitment, shown by a serious desire to enter the order, and as a high level of obedience and humility. Although the definition of what constitutes special merit may differ, its indispensability does not. The sect defines its special merit in contrast to the behaviour of the rest of society, while the religious order stands in contrast basically to the rest of the church. It is as a result of the accommodation of a special kind of merit within the universalistic standards of the church that the functional relationship which we have observed between the religious order and the church is able to operate:

There can be no doubt that the distinction [between Precepts and Counsels] saved Christianity. It reconciled every extremist who was prepared to face the facts at all, and so retained within the Church that witness to Christian other-worldliness so greatly needed at a time of acute secularization.[9]

There is special pleading in this quotation, for it implies that sectarian groups who secede from the body of the church have somehow failed to 'face the facts', and thus the statement is very similar to the concept some sociologists use of a 'choice' facing elitist groups but it does very clearly express the functional relationship from the viewpoint of the institutional church.

3. Exclusiveness is emphasized, and there may be expulsion.

Both the sect and the religious order base their exclusiveness on the New Testament exhortation, 'Be ye separate'. [10] The mechanisms of isolation and insulation in religious orders are examples of this exclusiveness. Variations in dress and the regulation of behaviour are apparently associated with the extent to which an order is engaged in other- or inner-worldly activity. There is an interesting variation in the types of isolation and insulation which characterize sectarian groups. Sects which are most exclusive in their ideology or their restriction of social interaction outside the confines of the sect may even seek the same form of organizational and behavioural imperatives as those of religious orders, that is, physical isolation and social insulation by means of special dress. It is significant that those sectarian groups which have demanded highly deviant kinds of social behaviour from their members have also sought to resolve some of the social tensions by living in a segregated community, though not always successfully. Thus the Oneida Community, which practised communism of marriage; the Doukhobors, who practised at various times and places communism of property, pacifism, and refused to register births, marriages and deaths; and the Shakers, who were also pacifist, communistic and celibate—these have all taken their withdrawal from society to the point of establishing segregated communities. While some social tensions may be neutralized (for instance, problems created by marriage with non-members) and communal support provided for members, the mere 'visibility' of a segregated community may create conflicts, as the history of these communitarian sects shows. [11]

Expulsion, like a rigorous entry procedure, is one of the means by which religious orders and sects alike preserve a high level of commitment and observance. The opposite of this position is demonstrated not by the church, which usually has a clearly defined though less exacting belief system, but by the liberalism of the denomination, where formal beliefs are more loosely defined.

4. The self-conception is of an elect gathered remnant with special enlightenment.

On the above characteristic there is a superficial similarity between the sect and the religious order, with a more subtle distinction between their conceptions of an elect group. Special enlightenment in the sense of self-knowledge or supernatural experience will be encouraged in the order and acknowledged by the church, and ascetic achievement is sanctioned by the church as especially prestigious. But the church has been careful to prevent monastic élitism developing into an heretical and schismatic concept of the elect remnant. To this end the church has always maintained the dual standard and has refused to claim that the type of life followed by members of religious orders is necessary for salvation or that all must attempt to embrace it, but has argued instead that it represents a particular vocation of which only a small number are capable. The exponents of the religious life reinforce the church's position: St Benedict stressed humility and obedience in his Rule; St Francis, in a passage already quoted, reiterated his respect for the secular priesthood; and St Ignatius imposed a vow of obedience to the Holy See on his members. However, it is sometimes difficult to distinguish the notion of a special vocation from that of a superior vocation open only to an elect, especially when this is reinforced by selective canonization. There are several instances of élitism reaching the point of heresy and even of schism and two of these—the individualism of the Egyptian monks and the heresy of the Spiritual Franciscans who very definitely saw themselves as a 'remnant'—have already been cited. A very similar process is evident in the account which Knox gives of the badly disciplined convent of Port Royal, of which the Jansenist Singlin was the chaplain:

> The disciples of Port Royal are encouraged to approach God with confidence as being 'de ceux qui, par un heureux sort, se trouvent du petit nombre de vos élus'. I do not mean that they consistently denied the hope of salvation to all those who were not penitents of M. Singlin. But the feeling that you form a very small nucleus within the Church, coupled with the belief that only a very small nucleus within the Church is destined for heaven, easily leads to the unconscious assumption that the two 'remnants' are one. [12]

While sects very consciously see themselves as an elect 'remnant' set apart from the 'massa damnata' of the rest of humanity, the religious order must include among the ranks of the potentially saved the ordinary lay members of the wider church. But that there has existed some kind of covert tendency towards schismatic élitism in historical examples of religious orders seems clear from the evidence cited.

5. Personal perfection is the expected standard of aspiration.

Personal perfection has been interpreted as a fundamental goal of the members of religious orders. Originating as the individual perfectionism of the Egyptian hermits, it became redefined in social terms with the growth of monastic communities, and the historical evidence suggests that organizational stability is best achieved when there is a balance between the individual and social definitions of this basic motivation. Personal perfectionism is characteristic of both active and contemplative orders, and this is made very explicit in theological expositions of the latter when it is argued that monasteries are firstly and pre-eminently schools of holiness for their own members rather than service agencies for anyone else.

6. In the sect there is ideally a priesthood of all believers and always a high level of lay participation.

Religious orders originated as lay movements—and have largely remained as such in the Eastern Church—but in Western Christendom were gradually modified to become organizations of ordained priests. Part of this development consisted in the elaboration of the distinction between 'choir' and 'lay' monks which seems to parallel the stratification of some sects into 'elect' and 'hearers', but with one crucial distinction: in the religious order such a distinction has no eschatological significance. It appears, however, that full lay participation has remained as an ideal throughout the history of religious orders and has been restated in some very recent reforms. Despite the frequently encountered internal stratification of orders, and despite the fact that a doctrine of the 'priesthood of all believers' would be incompatible within the church's doctrinal framework, it has always been a characteristic of religious orders that all their members have participated in ritual to a much greater extent than the ordinary laity. By comparison, the role of the latter (at least until very recently indeed) has been much closer to that of an audience than to a group of co-participants.

7. *The sect is hostile or indifferent to the secular society and the state.*

As part of the church, the religious order is inhibited from condemning either the secular society or the state as beyond redemption, nor can most orders ignore their activities. However, there is a general tendency, when the church has pushed its compromise with the world beyond a certain point, for religious orders to be stimulated into intense agitation and reinforcement of pristine values, sometimes resulting in the formation of new orders. The most notable example of this tendency is the formation of the Franciscan Order, and the suppression of the Jesuits suggests that a lack of compromise in religious orders may sometimes be interpreted as inconvenient by the authorities of the church. Thus it would be accurate to describe the order as accepting the church's alliance with the world only on condition that this alliance does not altogether neutralize the other-worldly ethic of Christianity. It is because of their function in preserving pristine values that religious orders have so often been seen as spiritual 'reservoirs', 'safety-valves', 'ginger groups', or, according to Werner Stark's caricature, as the antithesis to the church's world-compromise (thesis) out of which emerges the universal church (synthesis). [13] The attitude to the world of religious orders can therefore be typified as reformist, either adopting objectively observable (active) or non-empirical (contemplative) means to achieve this goal. This relationship was earlier compressed into the term 'catalytic impingement and transformation' [14] and perhaps the closest sectarian parallel, at least to an order with an active apostolate, is the Salvation Army.

8. *The commitment of the sectarian is always more total and more clearly defined than that of the members of other religious organizations.*

The commitment of a member of a religious order is required to be total since it is designed to exclude all other potentially conflicting loyalties and it will in many cases be lifelong. The meticulous regulation of member activity is possible in a communitarian organization, and an examination of the timetables of different religious orders shows to what extent this is done. [15] Commitment is defined at length in most Rules and Observances and is very clearly symbolized at the stage when the new member formally states his commitment by taking vows.[16] In this respect the sect and the religious order are very similar and contrast most strongly with the church and the denomination.

9. Sects have a totalitarian rather than segmental hold over their members, and their ideology tends to keep the sectarian apart from 'the world'. The ideological orientation to secular society is dictated by the sect, or member behaviour is strictly specified.

The features specified in this characteristic are those which are most fully developed in the 'total institution', though Goffman's concept contains the less applicable idea of coercion. Briefly, it can be said that the religious order and the sect share some but by no means all of the features of total institutions, and that the features they do share are a totalitarian hold over their members and a barrier between members and the secular society which is even more marked in the case of religious orders which impose physical isolation. But the ideological orientation which is dictated by these religious groups is seen as legitimate by their members because these are voluntary organizations with a freely committed membership. This is a vital distinction between the order and the sect on one hand and, say, a prison on the other.

To these various points of comparison between the sect and the religious order we may add two further parallels. Firstly, both the sect and the order are, in relation to other types of religious organization, *Gemeinschaften*, or at any rate a confederation of such whose total association, when it occurs, has *gemeinschaftlich* features. The contrast with other religious organizations is mainly one of degree, because in a fundamental way *all* religious organization is centred on the local community of worshippers, but there is nevertheless a substantial difference between the community of a sect or order and the much more associational nature of the church.

Secondly, both the sect and the order share a tendency which Knox describes as follows:

There is, I would say, a recurrent situation in Church history—using the word 'church' in its widest sense—where an excess of charity threatens unity. You have a clique, an *élite*, of Christian

men and (more importantly) women, who are trying to live a
less worldly life than their neighbours; to be more attentive to
the guidance (directly felt, they would tell you) of the Holy
Spirit. More and more, by a kind of fatality, you see them draw
apart from their co-religionists, a hive ready to swarm. . . .
Then . . . the break comes. . . . Almost always the enthusiastic
movement is denounced as an innovation, yet claims to be preserving, or to be restoring, the primitive discipline of the
Church. . . . Almost always, schism begets schism. [17]

This is an extremely impressionistic statement which needs to be
specified much more clearly, but it does indicate a general process
which is shared by the sect and the order because fragmentation is
endemic in these two organizational types. Orders which have
experienced such fragmentation, usually as a result of a small élite
within the order which has set up a more 'primitive' observance,
and which have later been officially recognized by the church, include the Augustinians (Augustine Recollects), the Benedictines
in particular (Camaldolese Hermits, Cassinese, Cistercians, Trappists), the Carmelites (Discalced Carmelites) and the Franciscans
(Capuchins, Conventuals and Regulars). An important explanation of this phenomenon is that the church, by permitting a certain
amount of fragmentation among its religious orders (there are of
course limits to its permissiveness, as the Spiritual Franciscans
showed), has attempted to institutionalize the kind of conflict over
pristine purity which may completely split a sectarian group.

By now we hope to have established enough parallels to
demonstrate that sectarian groups and religious orders share many
features in common. It now remains to consider some of the most
basic differences between the two types of organization.

Of prime importance is the feature which has been reiterated
throughout this typological discussion, that the religious order
exists only as part of a church and has to be sanctioned by that
church. Thus it is based ultimately on an external source of
authority. The sect, on the other hand, contains its own authority
and sometimes—incipiently or formally—reposes authority in a
democratic polity, at least of males. Despite the formal equality
among members of an order and the common practice of electing
the incumbents of authority positions, the authority system is
always absolute, whereas in the sect it is by no means always so,
and when it is, legitimation is invariably internal. The Rule of an

order, which must by definition be sanctioned by the church before the order can be officially recognized, is a powerful means of control because it limits the extent to which charismatic elements can change the value system of the organization. Even when reinterpretations of the original Rule have been made, these must be sanctioned by the external authority of the church before they can become the foundation documents of new religious orders.

Celibacy is not a common feature of sects, and neither is the order's practice of restricting membership to one sex only, but sectarian groups may impose restrictions on intermarriage and there may be regulation of sexual activity. Interestingly, one of the sects which was most similar to the religious order in this respect, the Shakers, was also communitarian. [18]

The members of a religious order often claim to perform mystical and sometimes practical services for the rest of mankind. This is true of some sects—the Salvation Army is an example—but by no means all sects see themselves as having this sort of relationship with the surrounding society.

This last comment provides a key to the distinction between the two types of Christian *virtuoso* activity, because it typifies the attitudes of sectarians and members of religious orders to the world at large. Here there is a primary divergence of orientation. While the sect always draws a distinction between itself and both the rest of Christendom and the rest of humanity, the order distinguishes only the heathen. This is a corollary of the fundamental distinction that the order only exists as part of the church, albeit as a type of 'sect within a church'.

The comparison of religious orders with an established ideal type of sectarian organization throws light on several important parallels as well as on major points of difference. Perhaps the key characteristic of orders is that they are always legitimated by reference to the institutional church of which they form part. This will emerge with great significance in the study of Anglican orders, which often had fairly tenuous links with the wider Church of England. Comparison with other types of religious organization provides a perspective which is restricted in its context, and in the second half of this chapter attention will be directed at the wider comparative framework available in Goffman's model of the total institution (which is found to have limited use in an analysis of religious orders) and in Etzioni's typology of organizational compliance.

THE RELIGIOUS ORDER AS A TOTAL INSTITUTION

The analytical basis for considering the religious order as an example of a total institution is contained in Goffman's *Asylums*,[19] where he describes 'those establishments designed as retreats from the world even while often serving also as training stations for the religious; examples are abbeys, monasteries, convents, and other cloisters.' [20] Other examples of total institutions are residential homes for the incapable and harmless (the blind, aged and orphaned); segregated institutions for the incapable but potentially harmful, however unintentioned (T.B. sanitoria, mental hospitals); restrictive institutions such as prisons; and institutions which are isolated so as to perform some goal better, such as army barracks, boarding schools and large mansions. All of these institutions stand in contrast to one of the basic social arrangements of modern society, which is that individuals tend to sleep, play and work 'in different places, with different co-participants, under different authorities, and without an overall rational plan. The central feature of total institutions can be described as a breakdown of the barriers ordinarily separating these three spheres of life.' [21] In a total institution all aspects of life are conducted in the same place and under the same single authority. This would certainly apply to those religious orders which impose stability, in particular to enclosed contemplative orders, and to the extent that even the most active order will have some local conventual basis, in general the religious order can be seen as approximating well to this feature.

A second characteristic is that in total institutions each phase of the member's daily activity is performed in the immediate company of many others who are treated very much alike and are required to perform the same activities together. [22] Again, there will be some variety in the degree to which orders conform to this pattern because the member of an active order may frequently be isolated outside his own community, but all orders provide some form of communal support (the main aspects of this being communal meals and group ritual) so that the individual member is to a large extent submerged in the group. In addition to this there are of course stringent restrictions on the possession and use of personal property which are largely designed to ensure detachment from the surrounding society and attachment to the group, and result in an eradication of external criteria of social differentiation as far as possible.

Thirdly, all phases of daily activity are tightly scheduled and the whole sequence is imposed from above by formal rules and a body of officials. There is a strong superficial resemblance here between the detailed daily timetable of a religious order and the other examples which Goffman cites. But there is a crucial difference in the type of legitimacy which such rulings have in the different organizations. In a total institution, such as a prison, the only form of support for rulings is negative and coercive: the threat of sanctions. This is not an example of legitimate authority at all, whereas in a religious order rulings are normatively legitimated, frequently in a highly explicit way. To take a very good example, the 'Usages of the Cistercian Monks of the Strict Observance'[23] are continually punctuated with quotations from the Bible and from the Church Fathers giving the non-instrumental reasons for particular injunctions. For instance, having given very detailed instructions about when, where and how to salute the abbot, the Usages continue in an indented paragraph:

> When we salute the Abbot we salute Christ whose place he holds in the monastery. That is why when Christ is actually present on the altar we no longer salute His representative. 'After I had heard and seen, I fell down to adore before the feet of the angel, who shewed me those things. And he said to me: See thou do it not, for I am thy fellow servant, and of thy brethren. Adore God.' (Apoc. XII, 8–10). [24]

The importance of non-instrumental legitimation can be seen by taking the last of Goffman's characteristics of total institutions, which is that the various enforced activities are brought together into a single rational plan purportedly designed to fulfil the official aims of the institution. Though activities may be 'enforced' in religious orders in the sense that compliance with them is a prerequisite for continued membership, we have already stressed that orders have an important *voluntary* associational basis. As part of this, there are extensive attempts to obtain positive obedience (the 'monasticism of the soul') before the stage of full membership is reached. And the 'single rational plan' of the total institutions on which Goffman bases most of his analysis is identical with the type of rational action to which Weber gave the term *zweckrational* [25] —the orientation to discrete individual ends, when the end, the means and the secondary results are all taken into account and judged. This type of action is exemplified by 'visible' empirical calculations and, although it forms an important part of the orientation of active religious orders, it will even in these cases be secondary to non-instrumental, normative behaviour which Weber calls *wertrational*—the orientation of action in terms of absolute value where the ultimate values governing action are self-consciously formulated. Action of this latter type is most clearly characteristic of enclosed and contemplative religious orders, and the paradox is that it is precisely these orders which conform most closely to the first two features of total institutions, which are seen in purposeful-rational terms. In fact, Goffman explicitly states that it is the purposive calculation of empirical means and goals which is the primary function of total institutions: 'The handling of many human needs by the bureaucratic organization of whole blocks of people . . . is the key fact of total institutions.' [26]

Therefore, while we may expect to find several points of comparison between the concept of a total institution and the organization of religious orders, resulting from the exigencies of regulating small, isolated, residential groups, there is a crucial divergence in that social relationships within the latter are oriented towards non-instrumental goals, and any regulation of member behaviour will be legitimated by reference to these. Expressed in a slightly different way, Goffman's ideal type would be appropriate for those members of religious orders whose commitment has been eroded or lost. While there are certainly examples of this,[27] the weight of the evidence points in a very different direction. To take a single example, one of the functions of the 'stripping' process undergone by new entrants alike in religious communities, prisons and mental hospitals, is to alienate the new recruit from all other loyalties, but in the religious order it is very difficult to distinguish such a process from the simultaneous one of establishing positive normative identification with the new membership group. A penal institution can function quite efficiently without the positive commitment of its members, but the tensions which this would cause in a voluntary association like the religious order would totally subvert its goals.

The inappropriateness of important aspects of Goffman's formulation stems from his central concern with the condition of mental patients, as his examples manifestly indicate, though some of the implications which he draws are relevant to our study of the religious order. However, his treatment of orders is typified by a too rigid reliance on the notion of efficient bureaucratic management as an essential goal, so that any other goals which the organization may establish tend to be dismissed as 'strategies' by means of which the organization hides from its members its 'real' goal of efficiency. An example of this is his treatment of work. Outside the total institution, he argues, work is done for profit. Inside the institution, work is performed according to the bureaucratic requirements of the organization, as in any economic institution, but there is no financial reward. Consequently, alternative motivations have to be provided, such as the notion of 'work therapy' or rehabilitation in mental hospitals. Having quoted a Poor Clare's account of work in a convent as something voluntarily done for God's sake, he interjects with a footnote: 'The application of an alternative meaning to poverty is of course a basic strategy in the religious life.' [28] In the case of the Poor Clares especially, being the Second Order of the Franciscan branch, this explanation is entirely inappropriate, because the foundation of the order was the *result* of an attempt to attain the normative goal of poverty rather than the reverse. But by interpreting this organizational exigency as a primary goal, Goffman is able to find universal confirmation of his hypothesis.

One of his most useful observations is the existence of a staff-inmate division in total institutions which is strictly maintained and allows minimal possibilities for social mobility over the status line of managers and managed. The former are usually integrated into the outside world while the latter spend most of their time in the confines of the institution. A consequence of this division is the growth of antagonism between the two groups and often ritualized expressions of contempt by inmates for staff. In most cases, the members of religious orders are best envisaged as a single group of inmates with minimal differentiation of staff. It is true that there are certain differentiated authority positions, but their scope is often closely circumscribed, both by formal regulation and—as in the case of the Benedictine abbot—by tradition and normative prescriptions. Such positions are often filled by election, are by no means always permanent, and may be surrounded by the kind of ritualized humiliations—like washing the feet of the other members—which serve to symbolize the subordinate status of the official to the normative authority on which the order is based. There is an interesting exception to this principle in those orders which also function as theological seminaries, where a more stratified organization sometimes emerges, and

Coxon [29] finds some points of similarity between Goffman's concept and the Society of the Sacred Mission at Kelham, which is an Anglican community attached to, but distinct from, a theological college.

The probationer at Kelham wears 'civvies' and these serve to mark him as the member of an out-group—indeed, the dress of a probationer at one time included short trousers. Kelham also requires the interesting 'stripping' practice of a photograph of each postulant holding up a number in front of him, which is an interesting parallel to the entrance procedure of prisons. But Coxon points out that since membership of these sorts of total institutions is voluntary, there is not the same resentment and heightened tension between staff and inmates and the most that seems to result is a humorous parodying of staff: for example, impersonations are performed at Christmas concerts (these, incidentally, are a similar source of tension release among junior hospital staff). And even at Kelham there is such a difference in organization from the sort described by Goffman that Coxon goes on to develop the more fruitful notion of normative power in religious groups of this sort. Anson's account of Kelham likewise suggests a significant weakening of the staff-inmate division when he speaks of 'no apparent distinction of persons—all share and share alike in whatever has to be done. For instance, a senior Father will certainly find himself under obedience to a student when it comes to manual work.' [30] In short, the important qualifications which we have had to make with respect to the concept of religious orders as 'total institutions', and our basic contention that normative commitment is their pre-eminent feature, suggests that a more valuable comparative analysis of these organizations is to be found by using the latter criterion.

THE RELIGIOUS ORDER AS A LIMITING CASE OF NORMATIVE COMPLIANCE

Etzioni's analysis of complex organizations [31] is ostensibly concerned with organizations which fit the generic heading of the Weberian concept of 'bureaucracy', but in reality his treatment includes a wider range of organizations. From the initial observation that there is some difficulty involved in combining the specific with the general in the concept of bureaucracy, Etzioni goes on to argue that there is a need for middle range theories. Otherwise, he says, differences between the ideal type and the particular empirical cases will lead to the latter being treated as 'exceptions'; or the feature which is different will be recorded with surprise; or the model will be discarded: all of which are, of course, misuses of the concept—perhaps not the most valid reasons for introducing new concepts. The analysis which Etzioni gives expands the typology of authority in Weber's work by taking as the basic criterion for classification the concept of *compliance*. Compliance is defined as 'a relation in which an actor behaves in accordance with a directive supported by another actor's power, and to the orientation of the subordinated actor to the power applied.' [32] The operative factors in compliance are the behaviouristic notions of rewards and deprivations, and according to the type of power which is manipulated by those in directive positions (physical, material and symbolic) we may speak of three basic types of compliance—coercive, utilitarian and normative. The orientation of the subordinated actor can be characterized as positive (commitment) or negative (alienation) and is partly determined by the degree to which the power applied is considered by the subordinate to be legitimate.

It will be immediately apparent that the analysis is wider than Weber's, since the latter's typology is derived from the concept of *legitimate* authority. Although Weber distinguished between a 'voluntary association' (*Verein*) and a 'compulsory association' (*Anstalt*), the latter was treated mainly as an inclusive group which encompassed all individuals who happened to fall into an objectively defined category (birth and territorial residence being the two most important), and the two groups which were most obviously compulsory associations in this sense were the state and the church (as contrasted with the sect, which was a voluntary association). But the main focus for Weber was how the claim for and receipt of support by those in authority positions was patterned in different 'styles' of legitimacy. Etzioni, on the other hand, treats legitimacy itself as problematic and goes on to argue that the kind of involvement which each type of organization elicits from its members will tend to be congruent with the kind of power exercised in the particular organization. From this it follows that an organization exercizing coercive power will typically contain members with alienative involvement, an organization exercising remunerative or instrumental power will produce calculative involvement, and an organization based on

normative power will be found to have members with moral involvement. The value of the typology is that it provides a wide
comparative basis for analysis yet at the same time makes possible
very detailed hypotheses about aspects of the organization in
question. The importance of this typology for the present discussion is that Etzioni, throughout his exposition, cites the example of religious orders as a very clear-cut case of normative
organization, and it is no exaggeration of his typology to treat
religious orders as a limiting case of normative compliance.

All religious organizations, of course, fall within the category
of normative compliance. Their distinguishing characteristic is the
use of predominantly normative sanctions against members who
fail to meet the requirements of the group: denial of access to
highly valued privileges such as ritual and sacraments is one of the
few means of socialization available to religious organizations and
if these fail there is little else the church can do. This is well
demonstrated by the sanctions against heresy: these usually include excommunication, which is primarily a normative sanction,
though it could be interpreted in a situation of religious conformity as a socially coercive one. Until the twelfth century the
church mainly observed the principle laid down by St Bernard,
'*Fides suadenda, non imponenda*', but this altered when other institutions besides religious ones saw themselves as being threatened
by various heresies. The negative sanctions then ceased to be
purely normative and commonly included death. The church continued to exercise normative sanctions (albeit reinforced by coercive sanctions after the use of torture was approved by the papal
bull '*Ad extirpanda*' of Innocent IV in 1252) and the theoretical
distinction between normative and coercive sanctions was maintained by the practice of handing over obstinate heretics to the
secular arm, which effectively meant death at the stake. This would
seem to be a classic example of Weber's description of the church
as an *Anstalt* or, to set it in Etzioni's terms, the alignment of a
normative organization with a coercive organization (the secular
state).

Etzioni sees coercive compliance as very much a secondary
source of compliance in predominantly normative organizations,
and we can certainly argue that the apparent coercive component
in some of the sanctions used by religious orders—penance and
mortification—is of relatively minor importance compared to the
elaborate normative validation which these sanctions have. How-

ever, many of the ultra-Protestant 'exposures' of religious orders which were common in the nineteenth century contain an image of precisely the kind of coercive organization which Etzioni and Goffman describe, frequently to the extent of calling them 'prisons'. Such images, though often unexpressed and sometimes based on unreliable and scurrilous evidence, form an integral part of the social environment of religious orders and especially of enclosed communities. Without taking them into account it becomes impossible to explain some of the riots, the popular stereotypes and, more important, some of the half-articulated fears which ran through the religious debate on this issue in the nineteenth century, both in regard to Roman Catholic and Anglican communities. [33]

A major difference between coercive organizations, which fit very closely into the notion of 'total institutions', and normative organizations lies in their élite structures. Whereas élites are rigidly differentiated in coercive organizations, with the resulting staff-inmate division, they are almost completely amalgamated in normative organizations. Thus, 'lower participants in normative organizations are much better integrated into the organizational polity than lower participants in coercive organizations, and they are less likely to develop even a partial polity of their own. [34] Etzioni describes the process of co-optation whereby religious organizations typically provide many co-operative roles for their members. The significance of these has been studied in the case of sects [35] and in the case of denominations, [36] and it can be stated on the basis of material already presented that the proliferation of 'lay' roles in religious orders is very marked. Although there are formally differentiated authority positions in all religious orders, these are invariably legitimated by, and in subjection to, normative injunctions. The practice of holding periodic Chapters at which all the members of a community are present is indicative of the ideal of participation in which all members are involved in administration to some extent.

Etzioni distinguishes expressive and instrumental élites as two differentiated groups in normative organizations and argues that religious organizations vary somewhat in the allocation of power between the two types of leaders. The case of the Jesuit Order is given to show that the head of a house, a rector in charge of 'spiritual matters', is clearly superior to a father-minister, who is in charge of 'temporal and external discipline', but research is also cited which suggests that parish priests often spend much of their time on administrative matters. Top-ranking religious functionaries like bishops are similarly thought to neglect their expressive roles and to become engrossed in instrumental activities. But as far as the two different kinds of élite are concerned in religious orders, the Jesuit Order is typical of the general pattern. When administrative offices exist they are either subordinate to more expressive roles or are widely permeated with expressive functions so that it becomes difficult to separate the two aspects of the single office. In particular, the role of abbot is highly expressive, containing symbols of other expressive roles such as those of 'father' and 'representative of Christ'. Likewise, one of the reasons implied in the advice to monks to flee from bishops was that bishops were particularly associated with instrumental goals; and these goals are above all rejected by the members of religious orders.

The degree and type of consensus among members which is required by a normative organization is a good deal more extensive than in other organizations, though Etzioni suggests that considerably less consensus is required than was originally believed, especially in so far as cognitive perspectives are concerned. This is more true of church-type organizations than of sects and religious orders, however, because the latter organizations, as we have seen, *dictate* the beliefs of their members and they also expect a higher degree of more specifically defined commitment than do other Christian groups. While it is easier for a universalistic religious group to permit a degree of latitude in beliefs, religious orders require a highly disciplined personnel and an effective authority structure if normative relaxation and disruptive individualism are to be prevented. This is why religious orders tend to seek a high degree of internalized consensus among their members.

The amount of selectivity in recruitment which is shown by normative organizations is presented by Etzioni in the form of a continuum, in which the cult is most selective, the sect next, followed by the denomination and then the church. Etzioni comments: 'Selectivity seems to be positively associated with the intensity of commitment of the average participant.' [37] There has already been found a similar high degree of selectivity in the sect and the religious order which is equated with the total commitment demanded by both groups. Etzioni's 'impressionistic' comparison of various religious orders, which concludes that the

Jesuits are among the most selective and therefore the most committed, is not particularly helpful. The qualitative differences in the definition of what constitutes commitment between different religious orders make such measurements misleading.

A resolution of the complications surrounding the concept of a 'total institution' is provided by Etzioni's variables of 'scope' and 'pervasiveness'. Scope refers to the range of activities which are under the control of the organization. Organizations whose members share many activities are *broad* in scope and those whose activities include most or all of the participants are *total* organizations. In the limited sense in which Etzioni uses this term, it is valid to refer to religious orders as total organizations, though this should be distinguished from Goffman's term, 'total institution' with its more questionable implications in the case of orders. Pervasiveness refers to the number of activities inside or outside the organization for which the organization sets norms. The normative boundaries of a collectivity (as measured by pervasiveness) and its action boundaries (as measured by scope) do not necessarily coincide. The over-generalized concept of a 'total institution' can now be broken down using these variable. A prison, for example, is an organization whose scope is broad but whose pervasiveness is low because most of its norms are derived from outside the organization. Religious orders are extremely high on pervasiveness since they always require normative 'insulation' [38] on the part of their members. Scope too will often be broad, the limiting case being enclosed contemplative communities, but scope may of necessity be partly restricted when the order is engaged in an active apostolate. In the latter case, pervasiveness in the form of psychological control and support is likely to be very important indeed. As an instance, we might quote the *Spiritual Exercises* of St Ignatius which are designed to educe normative commitment prior to any regulation of activity:

> It will greatly benefit him who receives the Exercises to enter upon them with a courageous heart and with liberality towards his Creator and Lord, offering Him all his will and liberty, in order that His Divine Majesty may make use of his person and of all he possesses according to His most holy will. [39]

Thus a total *organization* may be of two main types: either with broad scope and low pervasiveness, which seems to fit closely the examples of a 'total institution' such as prisons and asylums, or with broad scope and high pervasiveness, which is a more useful conceptualization of the religious order.

NOTES

1 B. R. Wilson, 'An analysis of sect development', *American Sociological Review*, vol. 24, no. 1, February 1959.

2 One result of this pre-selection will be to effectively limit the range of occupational choices open to the intended member. Studies in the sociology of work suggest that even in a complex industrial society occupational choice will be restricted by the expectations and norms of primary socialization, whereas in a pre-industrial society they will be restricted largely by the low level of occupational differentiation. In other words, the limits of occupational choice in pre-industrial societies are largely structural: in industrial societies they are partly structural but mainly ideological.

3 Glasgow, John S. Burns and Sons, 1965, p. iii.

4 John M. Mecklin, 'The passing of the saint', *American Journal of Sociology*. Supplement to vol. LX, May 1955, pp. 34–53.

5 ibid., p. 50.

6 P. A. Sorokin, *Altruistic Love. A Study of American 'Good Neighbours' and Christian Saints* (Boston, The Beacon Press, 1950).

7 We can also examine the 'substitution function' in terms of radical political/religious alternatives. It has been noted by Martin as well as Stark that in Catholic cultures, where religious radicalism can be seen as being largely 'catered for' by religious orders as against the Protestant sectarian variant of religious radicalism, the typical form of sectarian activity is *political*—hence the importance of a secular left-wing proletariat in some European societies. This is a fascinating area for research, but it must regrettably be left untouched in the present book.

8 *Dictionnaire de Droit Canonique* (publié sous la direction de R. Naz), Paris-VI, Libraire Letouzey et Ané, 1959, p. 347: 'Le sujet doit avoir l'âge requis, c.-a.-d. seize ans accomplis pour la profession temporaire, vingt et un ans accomplis pour la profession perpétuelle (can. 573).'

9 Kenneth E. Kirk, *The Vision of God* (London, Longmans, Green, 1934), p. 103.

10 II Corinthians 6, 17. This is a quotation which comes originally from the Old Testament, where the notion of *holiness* as being *separate* is much more characteristic. 'Ye' suggests a community of separatists.

11 I am indebted for the data on utopian communities to John Whitworth, whose thesis, *Religious Utopianism* (D.Phil., Oxford, 1971) is of central interest.

12 Ronald A. Knox, *Enthusiasm. A Chapter in the History of Religion* (Oxford, Clarendon Press, 1950), p. 207.

13 For my caricature of Stark's caricature, see the *British Journal of Sociology*, vol. XIX, no. 1 (March 1968), pp. 97–8.

14 See above, p. 19.

15 For example in Moorhouse, op. cit., pp. 276–80.
16 There is an interesting script of a broadcast from the Dominican Priory, Hawkesyard, which reproduces the service of profession in the Dominican Order together with a commentary. See *The Making of a Friar* (London, Aquin Press, 1955).
17 Knox, op. cit., p. 1.
18 Other sects which imposed similar restrictions were the Rappites and Thomas Lake Harris's Brotherhood of the New Life. There may be, of course, men and women in the same monastic 'family' (Benedictine, Augustinian, etc.) but there is always a formal division so that men form the First Order (of St Benedict, etc.) and women the Second Order.
19 Erving Goffman, *Asylums. Essays on the Social Situation of Mental Patients and Other Inmates* (Harmondsworth, Middlesex, Penguin Books, 1968).
20 ibid., p. 16.
21 ibid., p. 17.
22 At this point Goffman uses the word 'members' to described all those who come within the authority of the institution. This is a much more useful term than 'inmates', because it allows for a wider variety of organizations to be encompassed. The present argument is largely concerned with the appropriateness of 'members' rather than 'inmates' in the case of religious orders.
23 Moorhouse, op. cit., pp. 257–399.
24 ibid., p. 288.
25 See Hill, op. cit., 1973, pp. 214–216.
26 Goffman, op. cit., p. 18.
27 Some of the best evidence of the effects of a failure to obtain commitment is provided by those individuals who have abandoned the religious life. Interestingly, Monica Baldwin (op. cit.) describes her monastery in retrospect very much as a total institution. There is comparable material in Kathryn Hulme, *The Nun's Story* (London, Pan Books, 1959).
28 Goffman, op. cit., p. 87.
29 Coxon, op. cit., chap. 4.
30 Peter F. Anson, *The Call of the Cloister* (London, S.P.C.K., 1964), p. 146.
31 Amitai Etzioni, *A Comparative Analysis of Complex Organizations* (New York, Free Press, 1961).
32 ibid., p. 3.
33 There is sufficient material in the British Museum to provide an extensive list of the nineteenth-century Protestant pamphlets and the Catholic replies. The idea that convents were prisons is found in almost every pamphlet 'exposure'. See also M. Hill, 'Religion and pornography', *Penthouse*, vol. 6, no. 1, April 1971.
34 Etzioni, op. cit., p. 102.
35 We have already considered the sectarian notion of a 'priesthood of all believers'. Studies of sectarian growth in periods of rapid social change also suggest that sects may provide substitute statuses for members. See, for example, Bryan R. Roberts, 'Protestant groups and coping with urban life in Guatemala City', *American Journal of Sociology*, 73.6 (1968), pp. 753–70.

36 Robert Currie, *Methodism Divided* (London, Faber and Faber, 1968) in several places describes the independence of Methodist lay leaders and the recurrent conflict between them and the ministry. Statistical confirmation of the strong lay element is given in Michael Hill and Peter Wakeford, 'Disembodied ecumenicalism: a survey of the members of four Methodist Churches in or near London', in *A Sociological Yearbook of Religion in Britain*—2, David Martin (ed.) (London, S.C.M., 1969), pp. 19–46.

37 Etzioni, op. cit., p. 156.

38 One formulation of this goal has already been cited as 'the monasticism of the soul'.

39 St Ignatius of Loyola, *The Spiritual Exercises*, transl. W. H. Longridge (London, A. R. Mowbray, 1950), p. 11.

4

The Revolution by Tradition

THIS CHAPTER occupies a pivotal position in the overall structure of the book, since it introduces the Weberian category of legitimate authority as an important source of insights on change in religious orders. As outlined at the start of chapter 1, the virtuoso component in Christianity has been closely attached to a model of church history which contains the crucial notion of a pristine, authentic religious tradition. An analysis of attempts to reinstate this tradition and the implications such leverage has for organizational change provides a link between the first part of the book, which was concerned with an exploration of the concept of virtuoso religion in Christianity, and the case study of the Church of England which follows. It will be the purpose of this chapter to examine the ideal type of traditional authority, and especially its hitherto neglected dynamic aspect, and then to apply the concept to some important segments of Benedictine and Franciscan history. The Benedictines, it will be suggested, have experienced several major reforms in which traditional reinstatement has occurred. By contrast, the Franciscans have incorporated a clear and potentially disruptive charismatic component, though a traditional source of legitimacy nevertheless exists in their case. Both examples point to the 'innovatory' nature of tradition. [1]

If we take as a starting-point Weber's typology of legitimate authority, it is clear that traditional authority contains two elements: this type of authority is described as 'resting on an established belief in the sanctity of immemorial traditions and the legitimacy of the status of those exercising authority under them . . .'. [2] A clear distinction is made between a *normative* component, the sanctity of immemorial traditions, and a subordinate *social* component, the individuals who exercise authority under the constraints of these traditions. In his more detailed statement of traditional authority Weber appears to give the social component considerably more weight:

> The person or persons exercising authority are designated according to traditionally transmitted rules. The object of obedience is the personal authority of the individual which he enjoys by virtue of his traditional status . . . Obedience is not owed to enacted rules, but to the person who occupies a position of authority by tradition or who has been chosen for such a position on a traditional basis. [3]

At the same time, the commands of a person in a position of traditional authority may be legitimated in one of two ways: firstly, and in part, in terms of traditions which themselves directly determine the content of the commands and the extent of authority. In this sense, if the traditional leader exceeds the limitations of the tradition this may endanger his traditional status by undermining his legitimacy. This is very clearly an example of the primacy of normative injunctions over the individual exercising authority, and it is clear that reference to these normative elements may result in a challenge to the leader's authority. The second part of legitimation for the leader's commands is derived from his free personal decision, since traditional authority leaves this open to a certain extent. The sphere of traditional prerogative rests on the observation that the obligations of obedience on the basis of personal loyalty are essentially unlimited.

So there are two aspects to traditional authority: there are those actions which are bound by a specific tradition, and there is action which is free from any specific rules. In emphasizing the conservative and stable characteristics of traditional authority, Weber gave extensive consideration to the second of the two sources of legitimate commands. For example, the exercise of authority was seen as being oriented normally to the question of what the traditional leader and his staff would permit and what would be likely to arouse the resistance of the subjects. A general impression is given of the continual creation of precedents within a vaguely defined sphere of traditional competence, and Weber in fact noted that, in the legal provisions of traditional authority, what was actually new would be claimed to have always existed but to have recently become known through the wisdom of the promulgator. An example of this is, of course, the traditional basis of the Roman Catholic Church, in which dogma may be formally defined at a particular point in time but will be seen as having existed throughout the history of the church in its traditions. [4] But Weber took the discussion a stage further and opened up the possibility of a more dynamic interpretation when he argued:

> When resistance occurs, it is directed against the person of the chief or of a member of his staff. The accusation is that he has failed to observe *the traditional limits of his authority*. Opposition is not directed against the system as such. [5]

This last statement leads back to a consideration of the normative primacy of traditional authority, and the observation that in some cases of traditional authority the normative aspect is more significant for the orientation of leaders and their subordinates than the more stable element of social compliance—which is indeed what Weber initially implied when he noted that those exercising authority came 'under' the sanction of immemorial tradition. By concentrating on the 'unwritten' basis of tradition Weber was implicitly highlighting its most stable features, and the image which emerges is very close to the idea of a traditional society which Gellner has put forward. [6] It is equally valid to expand the alternative interpretation which can be derived from Weber and examine the normative element in traditional authority as a potential source of radical change. There is some similarity between the use of traditional referents in the legitimation of contemporary authority and the more diffuse concept of a 'Golden Age', though this aspect of the discussion must necessarily be curtailed.

The use of such traditional sources for the legitimation of radical activity brings them into the sphere of relative deprivation theory. As has been pointed out in relation to millenarian movements, [7] relative deprivation may be generated by: (*a*) comparing the present to the past; (*b*) comparing the present to the future; (*c*) comparing self with others. Hence a comparison of the present with a past which is seen as a highly valued model of social organization, is in these terms a potent source of relative deprivation. When this kind of comparison results in concrete activity, for example by trying to re-establish the social organization on which traditional legitimacy is claimed to be based, this activity will involve at the same time a 'past-orientation' and a 'future-orientation'. In his study of Cargo Cults, Worsley has called this the 'Janus-faced' attitude to time of the members and pointed to the importance of the *evaluation* of time for such social movements. [8] Applying this to the present discussion, a 'revolution by tradition' can be described as the attempt to realize in the present or in the immediate future a basis for authority which has the sanction of precedent. The relevant tradition will be claimed to have 'always existed' but to have been neglected or usurped by those at present in positions of authority with the result that the latter can no longer claim legitimacy.

Traditional authority is often treated as if it were a monolithic concept, with one tradition characterizing a single society or one institution within a society, but the use which has been made of the 'revolution by tradition' implies that different groups within the same society or institution may represent different traditions or interpretations of a tradition; that there may exist, in other words, a mixed tradition. In some contexts this divergence might be expected to result in the overthrow of those in authority, but it is also possible that there may be an interplay between the different versions of the tradition. The difference is between a conflict situation and a competition situation. Where there is a broad overall consensus the variants within the shared tradition will be termed the different *referents* of tradition. In the next chapter it will be argued that this has been a continuing feature of the different schools of churchmanship within the broad framework of the Church of England, and a detailed consideration of the concept can be left until then. For the moment, we will conclude the general historical treatment of religious orders by applying the perspective of traditional reinstatement to the Benedictine and Franciscan Orders. A brief recapitulation will highlight its main features.

To summarize: the Weberian category of traditional authority has been expanded in order to distinguish a normative and a social component in the definition which Weber gives. The former has been interpreted as a series of abstract checks and balances on the otherwise self-determined legitimacy of the traditional leader and his staff, and this model throws light on the way that a restatement of the limits of traditional legitimacy can be used to justify radical activity without any necessary reference to other types of legitimate authority—especially charismatic authority. This was labelled a 'revolution by tradition'—a process which has been of central significance in the historical development of religious orders.

As normative organizations, most religious orders have a very restricted component of bureaucratic authority, and where bureaucratic administrative arrangements do exist they are strictly subordinate to the goal of normative compliance. Instead of considering them in terms of traditional authority, however, it might be contended that religious orders are essentially charismatic in structure. While this may be true of specific examples, the best general approach can be made by treating religious orders as organizations with a particularly strong normative tradition, this tradition being embodied in the Rule of each order, rather than in the specific personal example of the founder. The members of religious orders, we have argued throughout, are in Weberian terms *virtuosi* rather than charismatic personnel. Indeed, it could well be maintained that the wider church has only been prepared to accommodate such groups on condition that they accept a degree of discipline and obedience—internally through the constitutional structure of the order and externally through the control of the church authorities—which is largely incompatible with a central characteristic of charisma, the articulation of new obligations. This does not entirely exclude charisma from the analysis of religious orders, because in any form of Christian organization where routinized charisma is a defining characteristic of formal roles, as in the church type of organization, its influence must be taken into account. It does imply, on the other hand, that a frequently observed source of change in religious orders and in more universalistic religious groups can be explained without recourse to this concept.

Analysis in terms of traditional rather than charismatic authority rests on the observation that a normative tradition rather than the influence of exceptional personnel is the source of organizational change. Some of the best evidence for such a process is the Benedictine Rule and its various reinterpretations. Knowles unequivocally attributes change within the Benedictine family to the Rule itself when he states that, at every rebirth within the order (a term which reinforces the idea of tradition-linked rather than novel change) the Rule has provided the inspiration for reform as against exceptional personnel in a particular governing body initiating changes. [9] He later makes an even more specific reference to the process when he speaks of an 'Appeal to Tradition', meaning an appeal back to the pristine tradition of the Rule. The fact that the normative tradition is the prime cause of change is further confirmed by his observation that *interpreters* of the Rule are highly revered in Benedictine history. The status of an interpreter is obviously secondary to, and his prestige derived from, the high valuation of the tradition he interprets. These remarks, together with some of the material already cited, point to a fruitful empirical example of the Rule of St Benedict.

The two most prominent features of the Rule are its mitigation of austerities: in his Prologue Benedict sets out his goal as *'nihil asperum nihilque grave'*, 'nothing that is harsh or rigorous', [10] and its strong emphasis on a quasi-familial polity. While it was largely because of its perceptive organizational blueprint that Benedictinism became the predominant type of monasticism in western Europe, it also contained an inherent tendency towards goal-displacement, in which the monastic community was substituted as an end-in-itself and its non-empirical legitimation weakened. Groups within the order who interpreted this as decline would always restate the Rule as the normative source of pristine tradition. One reason for the Rule's importance was that, in the earliest phase of Benedictine development, when each separate abbey was a complete unit and when secular social changes had a particularly disruptive effect, the Rule was the unique and distinct norm of monastic life and provided a continuing tradition. Another reason why the Rule should have such salience was the part it played in socialization. It was a universal custom to read a portion of the Rule each day and as a result it acquired a status which was only matched by the psalms and the gospels. [11]

It was with precisely this goal of primitive restatement of the Rule that the monastery of Cluny was founded about the year 910, as Berlière notes:

> Cluny, créé au milieu d'une société profondément troublée et dans un temps de décadence presque générale, apparaît dès son origine comme un centre de restauration monastique. La règle de S. Benoît était tombée en désuétude; il fallait la restaurer en larattachant aux saines traditions du passé. [12]

The important characteristics of Cluny's early history are: the reforming zeal of its abbots; the crucial fact that none of them either proposed or put into effect any material innovation in the observance of the Rule; and the use of exactly the same justification as that of the Cistercians nearly two hundred years later, 'Back to St Benedict'. [13] The second abbot of Cluny, St Odo, became famous for his reforming zeal and was called in to reform many other monasteries, including some in Rome. [14] At first these monasteries retained their independence, but as the influence and the temporal possessions of Cluny increased it became customary for Benedictine abbeys to become dependent on Cluny: this was particularly true during the abbacy of St Odilo (994–1048). A factor favouring the subjection of abbeys to Cluny was the independence it gave them from interference by the local bishops and from the secular authorities. This resulted from Pope Benedict VIII's ruling of 1016, and 'It is with him that the idea of a Cluniac *Order* may be said to begin: a substitution for the Benedictine idea of monastic autonomy of the conception of a congregation of monasteries allowing allegiance to a single abbey, their government all ultimately controlled by its Abbot.' [15] Internal centralization in religious orders is associated with the growth of independence from external control, and Cluny falls into this familiar pattern.

Associated with the growth in Cluny's spiritual influence and privilege was an increase in material prosperity and a movement away from the pristine observance of the Rule. Knowles thinks that Cluny eventually had 'as a body, none of the quasi-eremitical, purely contemplative elements of earlier monasticism, little of the simple, patriarchal family life. . . . It was, in essence, a liturgical life.' [16] There was an increase in the number of psalms and prayers recited daily and an ever-growing elaboration of ceremonial in the performance of the liturgy. By the second half of the eleventh century Cluny was characterized by its 'splendour of ceremonial, tireless activity in performance, and regularity of large masses of monks'. [17] So great were the demands of group ritual at this time that even in the longest days of the year, when according to the Rule of St Benedict sleep should have been shortest, the Cluniac monk had scarcely half an hour of free time at his disposal. The previous balance between spiritual and manual work was altered so that manual labour became little more than a ritual semblance. Thus, as a result of goal-displacement in the direction of more extensive communal activity, there was very little opportunity for the silent, individual pursuit of communion with God which had always been maintained, even in the most cenobitical of orders, and in reaction to this process there was a characteristic reversion to the pristine purity of the Rule.

An attempt at reform had been made around 1075 by a newly

formed Benedictine monastery at Molesme under abbot Robert.
But the attention it attracted soon resulted in the same kind of
decadence as that at Cluny.

> It had property and numbers; the simple day-to-day life under
> the direct command of the abbot was no longer possible; cur-
> rent uses were adopted and a number [of monks] wished to
> interpret them as in other contemporary houses. Thus the
> original aim of simplicity and perfection was endangered... [18]

In 1098, when it became impossible to reconcile the aims of the
two conflicting groups, twenty monks and their abbot seceded
and set up a new foundation in the forest of Cîteaux: this was
the origin of the Cistercian Order. Once again, the purpose of
the reformers was not innovation but a simple restatement of the
Rule of St Benedict in its pristine purity, as is demonstrated by the
authoritative judgement of Knowles:

> The original exodus from Molesme, led by St Robert in 1098,
> was, it is clear, prompted by a desire to get back to a more
> literal observance of the Rule of St Benedict. . . . The changes
> they desired were of three kinds. They wished for a stricter
> life, a more solitary life, and a life in which the work of the
> hands had a place. [19]

The Cistercian foundation was therefore a movement towards
simplicity and austerity and was characterized by what several
writers have referred to as a strong note of puritanism, [20] even
of ferocity. In particular, there was a studied avoidance of all
forms of aesthetic satisfaction which, as well as including the
restrictions on architectural style which we have already described,
also included clothing. Cluny had eventually reached the stage
when no material was too fine for the monastic habit: this the
Cistercians regarded as effeminate and voluptuous, and some
descriptions of them suggest that they practised what amounted
to a cult of uncleanliness. [21] Just as the earlier Cluniac reform,
the origin of the Cistercian Order can be traced to an *ad litteram*
interpretation of the Rule and is thus a reaction rather than an
introduction of new observances, a 'revival and a reaction' as one
writer has neatly summed up the process we have called a 'revolution by tradition'. [22]

The fact that the central concern of the Cistercians was the detailed observance of the Rule is shown by the meticulous criticism they made of the way in which Cluniac practice differed from the specific regulations in the Rule. For example, Chapter 29 of the Rule states that a fugitive monk can only be received back into his monastery three times, but this observance had been relaxed by the Cluniacs. Chapter 41 lays down that from Whitsuntide throughout the summer the monks are to fast, [23] but at Cluny there was considerable relaxation of this provision—perhaps inevitably so, because the amount of energy required for the almost continual chanting of offices could not be sustained on a restricted diet. [24] Chapter 48 emphasizes the importance of daily manual labour—'Idleness is the enemy of the soul' [25]—but the performance of manual labour at Cluny became so attenuated that it was eventually only a vestige of its intended significance. Chapter 58 of the Rule lists in detail the procedures to be followed when admitting new monks, setting out the Benedictine principle of stability in the monastery of profession and imposing a substantial probation on the novices before profession. The Cistercians were able to point to serious abuses of these provisions among the Cluniacs where, as a result of both size and prestige (which attracted many members of the nobility into the monastic life), it was not uncommon for a monk to profess stability in more than one monastery and for the period of novitiate to be very short indeed. All these were points the Cistercians made against the decadence of the Benedictines, and it will be seen that they spring from a meticulous interpretation of the Rule rather than from some charismatic interpretation of origin. St Bernard did, it is true, exercise a great deal of personal influence, and some of his 'reinstatements' of pristine tradition are more properly seen as 'innovations', but to the extent that the *claim* on which Cistercian reform was based was a traditional claim, it is relevant to the discussion.

Cistercian life originated in the stripping of all incidental accretions which had crept into the Benedictine life and was an attempt to bring observance of the Rule of St Benedict back to its primitive zeal. To this end the sanctuary of the abbey church was cleared of useless decorations, following the reasoning that these were of no use to monks who had given up the life of the senses for the life of the spirit, [26] and was turned into a 'workshop'. Initially, Cistercian asceticism consisted of real work, not in artificial or ritual observances, and because the monks did most of their own work the serfs were not exploited as they had been at Cluny.

Merton dates the Cistercian zenith from 1098 to the mid-thirteenth century. After this period there was a re-emergence of the cyclical process of decay and reaction. By the seventeenth century the Cistercians had abandoned much of the original spirituality of St Bernard as over time they had become luxurious, partly as a result of their success as agriculturalists. There seems to be a parallel (at least a superficial parallel) between the development of this group of puritan monks and the later dilution of the Protestant ethic among eighteenth- and nineteenth-century capitalists. Already in the sixteenth century the Cistercian organization was beginning to fragment into smaller, isolated Congregations. A characteristic reaction was the initiation of 'strict observances', for instance at Charmoye and Chantillon, and although the movement spread it did not at first break off from the rest of the order. These were modest reforms, though it appears that Cîteaux disapproved of them. [27] In 1664 the Cistercians of the Strict Observance (Trappists) began their reform at La Trappe, and their Rule was approved in 1678. We have already considered this restatement of pristine monasticism, but certain of its features show that it was a reversion to pre-Benedictine monasticism and not simply a return to the purity of the Benedictine Rule. For example, abbot de Rancé encouraged his monks to compete in their asceticism, and extreme mortification tended to become an end-in-itself, which is of course very much the pattern of early Egyptian monasticism. This prompts the question, how far can the earlier Benedictine reforms be seen as going *beyond* a simple restatement of the Rule of St Benedict?

The Benedictine historian Dom Cuthbert Butler sees some of the 'innovations' of Cluny and Cîteaux as, strictly speaking, developments of St Benedict's Rule rather than pure reinstatements. Most obvious among these novel aspects is the superimposition of a centralized organization on federations of abbeys, which in the case of Cluny tended to weaken the pristine feature of quasi-familial administration. Gasquet too describes the Cluniac reform as 'a deflection from the mere simplicity of St Benedict's ideas'. [28] Similarly, in the *Carta Caritatis* of St Stephen Harding, which in 1119 set up the constitution of the Cistercian Order, the framework of a centralized administration is presented in the same sentence as a reference to the Rule of St

Benedict: 'We will and we order all monks in the confederation to observe the Rule of St Benedict in all things as it is observed at Cîteaux.' [29]

It is indicative of the emphasis placed on tradition in the Roman Catholic Church (and in its religious orders especially) that Butler should identify as a process of 'corruption' any divergence from the primitive type. He cites the statement of Newman, that one of the standards by which 'true developments' are distinguished from 'corruptions' is the fidelity with which they preserve the primitive type. [30] In relation to the concept of a 'revolution by tradition', the degree to which contemporary empirical examples are identical with the pristine form embodied in some tradition is a point of interest, but not an essential part of the concept. What is most significant is the fact of a *claim* to be reinstating some pristine form which then becomes the basis for activity in pursuit of this goal. If such a claim to a pristine tradition becomes legitimate, then this is valid evidence for using the Weberian category of traditional authority. In the case of Cluny and Cîteaux there was just such a claim and activity in support of it.

Changes within the Franciscan Order can be explained partly in terms of a 'revolution by tradition', but the influence of charismatic leadership must also be taken into account. A distinction has been made between the official constitutional basis of the order in the *Rule* and the independent status of the *Testament* of St Francis. Thus there existed the possibility of two different appeals back to pristine purity. One was the appeal to an '*ad litteram*' interpretation of the Rule, which was complicated both by the reinterpretations of the Rule made by the ecclesiastical authorities and by the independent statement of St Francis in the *Testament* that the Rule was to be interpreted literally. The result was that, after the Testament had been formally declared unofficial and not binding on members, any '*ad litteram*' appeal could be censured as being anti-authoritarian. The other was the appeal to the ethic of the original small charismatic group which was sanctioned by the *Testament*. Given this situation, it is hardly surprising that the order underwent fragmentation. The history of the Franciscan upheavals is detailed, complex and polemical, but its basic features can be summarized.

Shortly after the death and canonization of St Francis (died 1226, canonized 1228), the general of the order and other friars concluded that a literal interpretation of the Rule was impossible and they laid the issue before Pope Gregory IX for instruction. The first official ecclesiastical interpretation came in 1230, and said that the *Testament* had no obligatory force because Francis had never sought official confirmation of it, but that the Rule was obligatory. On the issue of poverty, it was argued that although Francis had forbidden the possession of money he had not forbidden the use of it, and as a solution an agent (*nuncius*) could look after the money and hold property in the name of the order. Considerable discontent emerged during the generalship of Elias (1232–9). He was in favour of receiving money for the needs of the order, and collected a large amount with which to build the great church of Assisi, but he failed to call a Chapter-General and it was Pope Gregory IX who called one in 1239 and allowed Elias to be deposed. The two succeeding generals, Albert of Pisa and Haymo of Faversham, seem to have retained the confidence of the Spiritual Franciscans despite some disagreement between these and the Conventuals. In 1244 Crescenzio of Jesi became general and his sympathies were definitely on the side of the Conventuals. Some of the Spirituals complained of increasing laxity in the order and wished to put their case before the pope: in response to this the general exiled them in pairs to different convents in different provinces.

In 1245 Innocent IV issued the Bull *Ordinem vestrum* in which he assumed the ownership rights of all the movable and immovable goods of the order and gave his permission for the brothers to make whatever use they wished of the order's money through their agents. A further decree of 1247, *Quanto studiosus*, gave the order the right of appointing two proctors in each province to manage their financial affairs. However, with the generalship of John of Parma (1247–57) a stricter form of life began in the order. The general was an austere man who was distressed by the abuses which had crept in and aimed to follow the example of St Francis. At the Chapter-General of Genoa in 1251 [31] he pushed through, despite strong opposition, a decree that the proctors should no longer be appointed and that the order should make no use of the modifications allowed by *Ordinem vestrum*.

About this time the split between the two parties in the order became more significant as a result of the doctrine known as Joachimism. The latter was the set of writings by Abbot Joachim de Fiore which can be roughly summarized as follows. The history of the world is divided into three stages—the Age of the Father (Old Testament), the Age of the Son (New Testament) and the Age of the Holy Ghost, when all men would gain spiritual understanding of the Scriptures. The new age was to be preceded by the destruction of Antichrist and would be preached by an order of barefoot monks: the year 1260 was the date fixed for this event. As Douie observes, 'Naturally, the Franciscans believed that they were the bare-footed order prophesied by Joachim and became fervent exponents of his ideas.' [32] Although the Roman hierarchy condemned the trinitarian part of the doctrine at the Lateran Council of 1215, there was little suspicion surrounding it until the mid-thirteenth century, when events in the Franciscan Order brought it to a head. In 1254 a book called the *Eternal Gospel* appeared, written by a Franciscan and consisting of Joachim's three works, together with an introduction and a commentary which gave the Franciscan Order an important role in the prophesied development. The work was condemned and John of Parma was forced to resign because of his association with the doctrine. Thereafter the Spiritual Franciscans lost all hope of controlling the order's policy and relaxations gradually crept in. Furthermore, the continued allegiance of the Spirituals to Joachimism made them all the more open to attack by the Conventuals.

In 1279 the decretal *Exiit qui seminat* of Pope Nicholas III stated that all property left to the friars belonged to the church and that they were allowed to use anything necessary for their life and work. By 1309 the split within the order had reached such proportions that a papal inquiry was instituted at which both parties were present and in 1310 a papal bull exempted the Spirituals from the jurisdiction of their superiors during the period of the inquiry. Although a compromise was suggested in the papal decretal *Exivi de paradiso* of 1312, it failed because the Spirituals were by then more rigid in their attitudes, and for the next few years there was fighting and at times open riot between the two parties. After attacks on the Spirituals by Pope John XXII in 1316 and 1317 and a burning for heresy in 1318, effective resistance on their part within the order seems to have largely ceased, though echoes of their beliefs continued. For example, in 1321 the controversy over the poverty of Christ again threatened to cause schism within the order and the decretals *Ad Conditorem*

Canonum (1322) and *Cum Inter Nonnullos* (1323) were published, the first affirming that complete renunciation of property did not necessarily constitute the perfect life, and the second specifically declaring that the Spirituals' doctrine of the absolute poverty of Christ and his Apostles was heretical.

Drawing out the implications of this extremely complicated century of Franciscan history, it appears that '*ad litteram*' restorations of the pristine purity of the Rule were difficult to accommodate for several related reasons. In the first place, the Rule was neither sufficiently unambiguous, nor did it have the status of an established and institutionalized tradition to make legitimate appeals possible. Secondly, it was because the fluidity of interpretation was due in part to the church's continual redefinition of important observances that any independent appeal on the part of a group within the order was likely to be condemned as antiauthoritarian. Thirdly, the emphasis placed on poverty and a rejection of scholarship by a section of the order were similar to the criticisms of the church which other schismatic, élitist groups were making at the same time. Finally, among the group which was seeking a reversion to pristine observance there was a strong notion of charismatic origin, and this the authorities both in the order and in the wider church interpreted as potentially a highly disruptive source of legitimacy. In short, the 'innovations' which the Spirituals wished to make to the order's observances were too tenuously bound to an established tradition to be capable of firm institutional control by the church.

It is interesting to note that a formal, officially sanctioned division into two Franciscan branches did not occur until 1517, though its origins can be traced as far back as 1334, when in Italy John of Valle received permission from the general of the order to live in a hermitage with four brethren and to observe the Rule in its pristine rigour. This was the origin of the 'Observant' movement. By 1352 four other hermitages had been opened and considerable freedom gained from the general's control. But in 1355 the community was again put under jurisdiction because it had received apostates and heretics, especially Fraticelli. In 1368 a member of this community, Paulo de Trinci, made another attempt with several companions to observe a more rigorous interpretation of the Rule. On this occasion the group of reformers was convinced of the need for obedience and discipline as a result of the failure of other movements, and their discipline was instrumental in gaining the general's permission for expansion. In 1415 the *Friars of the Strict Observance* were constituted by Pope Eugenius IV as a semi-independent body within the order, and it was not until 1517, after several attempts to reconcile the two branches had failed, that the 'Observants' were finally separated from the Conventuals and declared the true Order of St Francis. Eleven years later the *Friars Minor Capuchins* were formed into an independent branch by Pope Clement VII. Of the latter Anson says, 'The object of this reform was to observe the Rule of St Francis to the letter *and in the spirit of the Founder.*' [33]

There had in fact been calls for reform throughout the Observant movement after it became the chief representative of the Franciscan Order, and the Capuchins grew out of this trend. Matteo de Baschio received Pope Clement VII's permission to observe the Rule to the letter, and an account of this which is given by a recent Capuchin writer indicates how important normative primacy is in a religious order, both as a source of change and as a source of disciplined compliance. It also suggests that conflict in the Franciscan Order was due to two factors: (1) insufficiently detailed prescription of observances in the Rule; and (2) as a result, the incorporation of other sources of legitimacy, either charismatic or instrumental, into interpretations of legitimate activity:

> . . . he [Matteo de Baschio] was in his action formulating a principle which a few years later was to bring bitter strife into the Franciscan Order—the principle that the Rule is above the Order and that the Order exists only to effect the full observance of the Rule: a dangerous principle doubtless in the hands of any but the pure lovers of the Rule . . . [34]

The difference between the Benedictine and Franciscan Orders and between their respective processes of change is centred on the importance for each of the Rule. The Benedictine reforms were based on the well-established normative primacy of the Rule, which had crucial functions in the process of socialization within the order and which had also served to unify the order in the early period of its history. As a result, reference to an '*ad litteram*' restatement of the Rule could be made clearly and with persuasive force. The Franciscan Rule, on the other hand, was much more a collection of statements of ideals than a detailed organizational blueprint, [35] and the extensive catalogue of papal glosses on the use of the Rule is fairly substantial evidence of the lack of detailed organizational provision in the original. At the same time there existed alongside the Rule the personal example of the founder of the order which in a similar way detracted from the extent of control exercised by the Rule. If the novelty of the Rule of St Francis was its 'spirit of freedom', [36] this was also the reason why appeals back to it tended to overflow the limits of institutional observances and to combine appeals to other legitimators of radical change, especially the appeals to charismatic origins and the symbolic significance of the order in a particular millennial doctrine. Consequently, other elements besides a normative tradition embodied in the constitutional document of the order were necessarily involved in Franciscan development, and there was not the same clearly distinguishable reference to traditional legitimacy. One way of simplifying the difference between the Benedictine and Franciscan Orders in this respect is to emphasize strongly the distinction between the Rule and the Order in the case of the Franciscans: here there is a striking contrast with the Benedictine Order, where it can be said without distortion that for all practical purposes the Rule and the Order are synonymous. In a Benedictine 'revolution by tradition', therefore, virtually no other reference is necessary except to an 'ad litteram' interpretation of the Rule.

The process of change which results from making a comparison with an earlier state of pristine purity and which may be subsumed under Weber's category of traditional authority has been frequently noted by those who have written about the religious life. A useful summary is the statement of Lavaud, that '. . . no human institution works at its own restoration so spontaneously as a religious order'. [37] In this way the fissiparous tendency of one kind of small élitist group seems to have been institutionalized by the church as a means of accommodating it within a more universalistic framework. Since it is often argued that monasticism itself can be interpreted as the preservation of a primitive form of Christianity, it follows logically that in the more limited context of each religious order there should be an entirely parallel attempt to preserve a pristine interpretation of the Rule. However, this kind of change is not only a feature of religious orders, and there is evidence of the same process in the wider institutional context of the eighteenth- and nineteenth-century English religious organizations.

NOTES

1 The word 'innovatory' has been put in parenthesis to stress that activities for which the sanction of traditional authority is claimed are 'reversions' rather than 'innovations', though they will often *appear* to be innovations in their narrow contemporary context. R. F. Littledale summarized this concept in his lecture—which is highly pertinent to the present argument —on *Innovations* (Oxford, A. R. Mowbray, 1868), pp. 4–5: 'Remember what Innovation means. It is the introduction of a new thing, unknown before. If something which is old, and has been worn out by use, or has been stolen, is replaced, we do not call that replacement Innovation, but Restoration.'

2 Max Weber, *The Theory of Social and Economic Organization* (London, William Hodge, 1947), p. 301.

3 Max Weber, op. cit., 1947, p. 313.

4 Another good example is the English system of Common Law, in which any 'new' legal enactment is deemed to have always existed but merely to have been recognized in recent times. Even here, however, the tradition is not exactly immemorial, since the year 1184 (the death of Henry II) is considered as the 'limit of legal memory'.

5 Max Weber, op. cit., 1947, p. 314, my emphasis.

6 In *Thought and Change* (London, Weidenfeld and Nicholson, 1964), pp. 1–2, Gellner relates an incident which occurred in 1865, when there was a climbing accident on the Matterhorn. Two of the three survivors were local peasants, Taugwalder father and Taugwalder son. In his later years the son began to describe the incident as though he had been Taugwalder the father, which observers put down to senility, but Gellner finds it an illuminating insight into the concept of time in the 'timeless' environment of a mountain village. Since there had always existed a Taugwalder senior (with a beard) and a Taugwalder junior (without a beard) it was natural for the son, when he grew old, to adopt the role of Taugwalder senior. This 'trimming of genealogies' is a feature of some traditionally stereo-typed societies.

7 P. Worsley, *The Trumpet Shall Sound* (London, MacGibbon and Kee), 1968, p. lv.

8 ibid., p. lv.

9 David Knowles, *The Benedictines* (London, Sheed and Ward, 1929), chap. 1.

10 P. Delatte, *The Rule of St Benedict* (London, Burns, Oates, 1921), p. 18.

11 David Knowles, *The Monastic Order in England* (Cambridge, Cambridge University Press, 1963), second edition, pp. 13–14.

12 Ursmer Berlière, *L'Ordre Monastique des Origines au 12e Siècle* (Paris, P. Lethielleux; Desclée et Cie., 1921), p. 192.

13 Watkin Williams, *Monastic Studies* (Manchester, Manchester University Press, 1938), p. 24. See also Georgina Rosalie Galbraith, *The Constitution of the Dominican Order, 1216–1360* (Manchester, Manchester University Press, 1925), p. 11: 'The pious founder of the Abbey of Cluny had nothing further from his mind than to improve or alter St Benedict's scheme. His

cry, as that of every other monastic reformer during the middle ages, was a return to the strict observance of St Benedict's Rule.'

14 Perhaps this was derived from a strong sense of urgency, for it seems that Odo regarded the year 1000 as the Apocalypse (L. M. Smith, *The Early History of the Monastery of Cluny* [London, Oxford University Press, 1920]). Smith also points out that the period as a whole was marked by a spirit of anti-materialism (ibid., p. 56): 'Great as Odo was, he could not have accomplished the work that he did had the times not been ripe. In the beginning of the tenth century a spirit of revolt at the coarse materialism of the day passed over society. As the best way to counteract that materialism, earnest men turned to the encouragement of monastic life. New monasteries were founded, and those that had fallen into disrepute were reformed.'

15 Joan Evans, *Monastic Life at Cluny 910–1157* (London, Oxford University Press, 1931), p. 18.

16 Knowles, op. cit., 1963, p. 30.

17 ibid., p. 148.

18 Knowles, op. cit., 1963, p. 199.

19 David Knowles, *Cistercians and Cluniacs* (London, Oxford University Press, 1955), p. 12.

20 For example, see Jessopp, op. cit., 1902, p. 255: 'The Cistercians were, in the beginning of their history, the rigid precisians, the stern Puritans of the cloisters.'

21 See, for example, George Duckett, *Brief Notes on Monastic and Ecclesiastical Costumes*, Lewes, [1891?]. In this we are reminded of Havelock Ellis's dictum that 'Christianity killed the bath'.

22 Archdale A. King, *Citeaux and her Elder Daughters* (London, Burns, Oates, 1954).

23 Though Benedict characteristically left this to the discretion of the abbot, stating that if work in the fields or excessive heat make it necessary, the time of the meal may be advanced. Benedict adds: 'Let him [the abbot] likewise so temper and arrange all things that souls may be saved and that the brethren may fulfil their tasks without any murmuring.' (Delatte, op. cit., p. 278.)

24 Knowles, op. cit., 1963, p. 150: '. . . we shall not wonder at the anecdote told by the Cluny chronicler of Abbot Hugh and Peter Damian: that when the latter praised all at Cluny save the quantity and quality of the food and drink, which exceeded that allowed by the Rule, he received the reply that before making such a criticism he should himself spend a week in following exactly the daily order of life, and that he would then confess that it could not be executed on such sparing fare.'

25 Delatte, op. cit., p. 304.

26 Thomas Merton, *Waters of Silence* (London, Hollis and Carter, 1950), chap. 1.

27 Merton, op. cit., 1950, chap. 3.

28 Quoted in E. C. Butler, *Benedictine Monachism* (London, Longmans Green, 1924), p. 238.

29 ibid., p. 239.

30 Elsewhere, Butler gives a more dynamic interpretation of change within

the ideology and organization of Christianity which compares rather interestingly with the Weberian concept of routinization: ' . . . whatever processes of growth in Christian or Catholic ideas and institutions may be revealed by history as explicable by sociological or psychological laws, it does not follow that they are corruptions or perversions of the Gospel ideas proclaimed by Christ, so long as these ideas live and work on throughout the course of the development.' (*Religions of Authority and the Religion of the Spirit* [London, Sheed and Ward, 1930], p. 30.)

31 The Chapter-General of Genoa is sometimes dated 1249. See J. R. H. Moorman, *A History of the Franciscan Order . . .*, (London, Oxford University Press, 1968), p. 114, footnote 1.

32 D. L. Douie, *The Nature and the Effect of the Heresy of the Fraticelli* (Manchester, Manchester University Press, 1932), pp. 6–7.

33 Anson, op. cit., 1949, p. 103, my emphasis. Anson's statement is a clear indication that more than a simple '*ad litteram*' restatement was involved in Franciscan reforms.

34 Father Cuthbert [Lawrence Anthony Hess], *The Capuchins* (London, Sheed and Ward, 1928), 2 vols, vol. 1, p. 31.

35 See, for example, the way the Rule deals with the issue which was to cause the most conflict: 'The brothers shall appropriate nothing to themselves, neither a house nor place nor anything.' (Raphael M. Huber, *A Documented History of the Franciscan Order, 1182–1517* [Washington, Catholic University of America, 1944], p. 629.)

36 Knowles, op. cit., 1966, p. 46.

37 Benoît Lavaud, *The Meaning of the Religious Life*, transl. Walter Mitchell (London, Blackfriars Publications, 1955), p. 37.

5

The Revolution by Tradition in the English Church of the Eighteenth and Nineteenth Centuries

THERE IS an intimate link between religious and political legitimation in English society which can be traced at least as far back as the Reformation and which has been particularly close since the late seventeenth century. Even if one only examines this linkage in terms of personnel, the connection can be made, but the relationship goes deeper than this and involves the way in which religious and political legitimations imply an acceptance of secondary rather than ultimate values. [1] The fact that the religious situation in England has for some three centuries involved the pluralistic coexistence of more or less competing religious groups which have for the most part avoided making universalistic claims has, the argument goes, significantly influenced political legitimations, which also rely on the masking of fundamental values. I wish to explore one aspect of this link further. It seems beyond question that claims to traditional legitimacy have played an important part in political and wider social legitimations in English society. Political symbolism is pervaded by it and it is widely diffused in other institutional sectors: one trivial but unmistakable example is the way in which selective secondary schools, however recent their apparent origins, feel the need to trace a pedigree which often runs back to a pre- or immediately post-Reformation foundation. The line of interpretation which begins in this chapter suggests that the Church of England contains within its own framework of authority both the features of competing legitimations and diverse claims to a traditional pedigree, and that these have always been demarcated in terms of schools of 'churchmanship'. Thus the Church of England can be said to have a 'mixed tradition' in

which different *referents* of what constitutes an authentic traditional model of church organization have competed and have for
the most part coexisted. In this chapter the broad outlines of these
different referents of tradition will be drawn, and detailed consideration will be given to the similar tradition of early Methodism
and the origins of the Oxford Movement.

The Methodist revival of the eighteenth century and the
Oxford Movement of the nineteenth both had profound consequences for the English religious environment: indeed, their
influence is still of considerable importance in contemporary
English religion. It is necessary at the outset to state that no
sociological statements on this topic can be fully comprehensive
because both movements have a complex and in places a highly
controversial history, one consequence of which has been a vast
literature. For example, one need only compare the conflicting
views of historians of Methodism, who see it either as a Puritan
or as a High Church movement, to see the extent of the debate—
though this, it appears, is one area for which our interpretation
offers some resolution of conflicting views. Thus, the sociological
treatment given here is not intended to be exhaustive, nor does it
rule out alternative interpretations based on different theoretical
models or historical sources. In a sense, this qualification is an
unwritten clause of any piece of sociological research, since
models derived from empirical data must always be regarded as
conditional. But the present approach is a valuable general
perspective for the simple reason that it does draw together in a
systematic way a substantial part of the historical material, and
at the same time it offers explanations and secondary hypotheses.
This suggests that the attempt to elicit a pattern from the empirical
perplexities is not altogether useless.

Methodism, beginning as a movement within the Church of
England, broke through the latter's institutional boundaries and
is chiefly interpreted as a diffuse social movement throughout the
early industrial society of late eighteenth- and nineteenth-century
England. In contrast, the Tractarians strongly re-emphasized the
historical continuity of a church organized on a traditional basis,
and sought to reform the Church of England in this way. Although
the Tractarians always maintained a strong commitment to charitable work, especially in the new urban areas, they have chiefly
been assessed by historians on the criterion of reform in the
specifically ecclesiastical organization of the Anglican Church.

On the surface, therefore, there appear to be enormous differences in the organization, personnel, beliefs, and areas of influence of Methodism and the Oxford Movement. The contrast has been thrown into clear relief by sociologists. Thus, while the Oxford Movement can be seen as representing a church-type restatement of the Church of England's organization, early Methodism has often been conceptualized as a sect. [2]

While there are substantial differences between the two movements, particularly in the later course of development which each took, there is a frequently encountered comparison of Methodism and Tractarianism. For instance, the leaders of the Oxford Movement, far from depreciating the early Methodists in order to emphasize their own uniqueness as reformers and to depict the eighteenth century as the 'darkness before the dawn', [3] made several comparisons between the reformist zeal of the Wesleyans and their own attempts to revive 'true religion' in the Church of England. One of the best expressions of this attitude was given in 1870 by the Tractarian, George Body (later Canon of Durham):

> I think if John Wesley could rise up in our midst today, that his great and noble heart—and a greater and nobler never beat in England—would beat with exultation and joy as he saw the prelates, the priests, and the laity of the English Church gathered together in solemn conference to consider this question—how the masses of the people may be awakened to the knowledge of the Fatherhood of their God, to the love of their Redeemer, and to the power of the Eternal Spirit. And if this be true, let us remember that John Wesley did in his day, to a great degree, what we want to do today. [4]

We cannot dismiss such statements as attempts to gain enhanced legitimacy for the later movement, for there was little to be gained from a comparison with a movement which eventually separated from the established church. Nor can such statements be attributed entirely to a sense of diplomacy in a party of the Church of England which had as its goal the inclusion of all religious groups in a genuinely catholic Church of England (though diplomacy may well have played some part in this type of statement): if this had been so, there would have been a wider appeal to the whole of Nonconformity rather than to the Methodists in particular. [5]

The main proposition of this chapter is that early Methodism (that is, broadly within the lifetime of John Wesley and especially during his early career) and the Oxford Movement shared a very similar interpretation of the historical basis for traditional legitimacy in the Church of England. An attempt will be made to re-define the theological foundations of Methodism and the Oxford Movement as sociological categories in such a way that their most significant features emerge. Already, in the very terms used to describe these movements, certain questions are implied. The growth of Methodism in the eighteenth century is usually called a revival: of what was it a revival? Similarly, the origin of the Oxford Movement in the nineteenth century was described as putting new life into the 'dry bones' of the church: what form did this revitalization take? Both of these movements were attempts to renew religious organization. It will be argued that there are a limited number of possible forms which such renewal can take, and that the Methodists and the Tractarians based their strategy for organizational reform in the church on very much the same traditional blueprint. The reforms which resulted from these movements were seen by their protagonists, not as innovations in the contemporary Church of England, but as reinstatements of pristine beliefs and practices. Thus they come under the heading of 'revolutions by tradition' and we may apply the theoretical model of the last chapter to an analysis of their influence.

The concept has already been introduced of *referents* of tradition, whereby different groups within a single overall tradition may stress different aspects of that tradition by giving a differential emphasis to particular historical periods. In the overall tradition of Christianity there are basically two distinct concepts of traditional legitimacy. In the first place, there is what may be termed the Catholic 'continuity' theory. Here there is an emphasis on the continual creation of tradition, not by novel innovations but by the cumulative definition of what has 'always existed' but which has gradually become known throughout the course of history. There may be fluctuations, as, for example, in periods of decay and reform, but the general perspective is of a timeless basis for legitimate authority in much the same way that Weber presented his ideal type of traditional authority. A most important means of stressing this theory is the Catholic Church's 'iceberg' self-image, in which the total definition of 'the Church' includes not only the 'visible' church of living participants but also the former members who have become the 'invisible' church.

The other major Christian tradition is what will be termed the Protestant 'step' theory. [6] In this theory, there is a major historical event at the Reformation, when, after a period which is interpreted as one of continual and marked decline, there is a radical reversion to the pristine purity of the Gospel, away from the accretions and abuses of the Roman Church. With the 'step' theory there is a marked lack of continuity and a process of a long period of church history is short-circuited by looking directly back from the Reformation to the Gospels. These are the two major concepts of tradition within Christianity and they should be treated as ideal types which will appear in different combinations when concrete empirical examples are studied. The Church of England is an interesting example, precisely because it combines both the major traditions. An interpretation of the various influences on, and images of, the Church of England is given by Neill, [7] who makes a statement which is common in religious polemics but which is perhaps especially appropriate to our treatment of Anglicanism: 'We cannot begin to understand [Anglicanism] unless we are prepared to accept it as something unique and unlike anything else.' [8] Anglicanism is often described as being 'Catholic but Reformed'—a neat summary of its position.

Of prime importance, therefore, is the *mixed tradition* of Anglicanism. This means that within the Church of England there are distinct groups which regard different periods in the church's history as being of crucial importance, and these groups have always been referred to as schools of 'churchmanship'. Within the inclusive Anglican tradition there are diverse secondary traditions. [9] We can trace four main referents of tradition to which groups within the Church of England could resort in claims of legitimacy. Firstly, there was the notion of an important tradition beginning with the Reformation. Some Anglicans saw their church quite explicitly as part of a wider continental Protestant tradition, and several attempts were made in the eighteenth century to achieve unity of some sort with continental Protestant bodies. One of these schemes involved the bestowal of a valid apostolic episcopal succession on the Lutheran Church. Among those who had a strong notion of a Reformation tradition were a number of eighteenth-century Low Church Whigs, and they were prepared to go a long way in compromising with the Dissenters in their attempt to form a national church.

The second traditional referent was the Middle Ages, and this was to gain great importance in claims to legitimacy in the nineteenth century. [10] The members of the Oxford Movement, especially in the later part of the nineteenth century, looked to the medieval Church of England, which they called the *Ecclesia Anglicana*, for the basis of their pre-Reformation tradition. Allchin expresses this succinctly: 'The Tractarians, in their desire to assert the continuity of the post-Reformation Church of England with the mediaeval Church, possibly overestimated this debt.' [11] During the eighteenth century the Middle Ages were generally devalued, particularly as represented by Gothic architecture. In this respect, Wesley was a good example of his time, for he disliked Gothic buildings. There is evidence too that the white-washing of church interiors in the eighteenth century had an ideological as well as a decorative function, for it symbolized the illumination of religion by the pure light of reason. [12] Carpenter uses the epithet 'neat' to describe the intellectual environment of the eighteenth century, and he illustrates the enormous importance for the Church of England of the cult of Reason. [13] As well as being seen as aesthetically imperfect, Gothic architecture also symbolized the Roman Catholic Church, and in eighteenth-century England 'No Popery' was one of the most universal rallying-cries.

But at the end of the eighteenth and the beginning of the nineteenth century there was a great change in attitudes towards the medieval period. During the first thirty years of the nineteenth century considerable antiquarian research was done into England's medieval churches, and in 1839 the Cambridge Camden Society was founded with an interest in medieval architecture [14]; also, the Romantic atmosphere which the Tractarians found so congenial owed much to the novels of Sir Walter Scott and the Romanticism of Southey. Pusey, for example, paid several visits to Scott and there were various connections between the Lakeland Poets and the main figures of the Oxford Movement. It is possible to over-emphasize the Romanticism of the movement, as Elliott-Binns points out when he says that the Oxford Movement

. . . certainly looked to the past and tried to disinter the remains of Christian antiquity; not merely because it was dissatisfied with the present, and suffering from that nostalgia for the past which is so often the result of an inward conflict of the soul in warfare with its environment, but as containing definite teaching which was being forgotten. The Tractarians were practical and sensible men, even in their attitude to the past; it was only the lesser men who belonged to the school which only sees the Middle Ages by moonlight . . . These most went over to Rome. [15]

But the radical *volte-face* of attitudes towards the medieval period made possible legitimations which were based on this particular traditional referent. In an important passage which substantially bears out the theoretical model used in this chapter, Allchin argues that the novels of Walter Scott 'substituted the middle ages for the ancient world as the golden age of the past in popular imagination'. [16] The growth of this attitude, which has been widely documented, [17] and which is perhaps best epitomized by Hurrell Froude's 'hatred' of the Reformers, eventually brought the Anglo-Catholic movement very near to a Catholic 'continuity' theory in which the church of the Middle Ages achieved considerable salience.

The third traditional referent was the church of the Gospels and the Acts of the Apostles. The Protestant wing of the Church of England saw the Reformation as a return to this pristine model following a period of acute decline in Roman Catholicism during the Middle Ages. This is what we have described as the Protestant 'step' theory of tradition and it was important in providing a pedigree of legitimacy for reforms which might otherwise have appeared to be simply innovations based on no divinely sanctioned model. An illuminating summary of this version of tradition is given by Latourette:

> Their distinctive convictions, Protestants declared, were of the essence of the Gospel and therefore were not new. They insisted that theirs was the primitive and therefore the true Christianity and that it was not they, but the Roman Catholics who were innovators and heretics. [18]

From this Protestant viewpoint the Bible is the sole source of authority, and the one admissible model of pristine purity is the New Testament church. It is essential to make absolutely clear in the present discussion that there was a distinct reference to the

Scriptural church in this school of churchmanship, and that it very explicitly excluded the early Fathers of the church. Sykes has drawn together three substantial extracts from eighteenth-century Low Church divines which demonstrate this point very well indeed. [19] They are too long to give here in their entirety, but one of them—which Sykes calls 'the most unequivocal declaration' of the regius professor of Divinity at Cambridge, Richard Watson (1737–1816)—will serve quite adequately as an illustration:

> I reduced the study of divinity into as narrow a compass as I could, for I determined to study nothing but my Bible, being much unconcerned about the opinions of councils, fathers, churches, bishops and other men as little inspired as myself. . . . I never troubled myself with answering any arguments which the opponents in the divinity-schools brought against the Articles of the Church, nor ever admitted their authority as decisive of a difficulty; but I used on such occasions to say to them, holding the New Testament in my hand, *En sacrum codicem.* Here is the fountain of truth, why do you follow the streams derived from it by the sophistry, or polluted by the passions of man? [20]

It might be argued against an elaboration of the New Testament church as a separate referent of tradition that it is only a particular example of our first category, the Reformation tradition, or that, since all Christian groups must at some point refer to the New Testament for the basis of their legitimacy, it is too universal to be of any analytical value. Against the first argument it may be said that it is extremely useful to distinguish a New Testament tradition, because then it becomes possible to interpret acceptance of the Reformation by certain groups as being *conditional* on the extent to which the latter can be interpreted as a reinstatement of the primary tradition. This is important, for instance, in controversies over whether the Reformation had 'gone far enough' or had 'gone too far'. [21] Hooker seems to exemplify this point, for he strongly opposed the Puritan belief in a 'literal following of the Scriptures as an absolute in the sense that whatever was not expressly commanded in Scripture was unlawful...' [22] Similarly, the Trinitarian controversy of the eighteenth century might be evinced as a case of the Scriptural basis of legitimacy asserting its importance over the majority Reformation position. In the case of the Trinitarian controversy, the major Protestant groups formed at the time of the Reformation had accepted the doctrine of the Trinity which had been formally elaborated by the Creeds and Councils of the post-Gospel church—especially by the Apostles' Creed and the Councils of Nicaea (325) and Constantinople (381) —but it was possible for Protestant groups to refer directly to the New Testament, where the doctrine was less coherently stated, and in doing so they were clearly giving the latter primacy over the Reformation tradition. Against the second argument, that the Scriptural basis is common to all Christian groups and is therefore of no analytical value, it can be argued that as a documentary premiss for all Christian organizations the ethical injunctions of New Testament are by no means uncontroversial, and interpretations of it have very often made use of a tradition located in a certain period of church history. The church of Acts and Epistles is one such period. Statements like that of Richard Watson strongly suggest that we should treat this as a separate tradition. [23]

Finally, the traditional referent around which the discussion is based for the remainder of this chapter was that of the early church. This contained not merely the notion of a basis in New Testament tradition but in the Church of the first four or five centuries—that is down to the Council of Chalcedon in 451. [24] This tradition, it will be argued, was the one on which both the early Wesleyans and the Tractarians legitimated their 'innovations', and it is a similar 'revolution by tradition', using the early church as a basis for claims to legitimacy, which can be seen in both the Methodist and Tractarian reforms. In the early eighteenth century Anglican clergy appear for the most part to have neglected the study and the example of the early church, though the latter had always formed an important part of Anglican legitimations: as a consequence of this, the Wesleyans emerged with a restatement of this tradition. Likewise at the end of the eighteenth and the beginning of the nineteenth century there was a comparable decline in Anglican interest in the early church: then came the Oxford Movement with its firmly-held conviction that the model of the early church was the principal model for Church of England reform. To trace this traditional referent in all its detail would require a treatment which is beyond the scope of this book. However, certain important indicators are available and provide a pedigree for this tradition from the Reformation onwards.

One of the earliest collections of Anglican theological opinion is contained in the sixteenth-century book of Homilies, which was intended to provide alternatives to the Sermon: the Homilies therefore represent a good source of basic Anglican doctrine. The first part of the book of Homilies was published in 1547, Cranmer being one of the authors, and the second part, whose main author was Jewel, was completed in 1563, except for the last homily which was authorized in 1571. There are in all 33 homilies and they vary in length. The account of them given by Lowther Clarke shows quite clearly on which period of church history they base their proof:

> Most of the discourses are made up of the common stock of Christianity. Being addressed to the general body of church-goers, they keep to the high road of doctrine and practice as generally understood. *Against Peril of Idolatry*, however, is enormously long, closely reasoned, and crammed full of references to Scripture, the Fathers, and history generally. *But the double method of proof, from the Bible and the Fathers, is characteristic of nearly all the Homilies.* [25]

Among the Fathers, Augustine's authority is paramount, and the double method of proof explicitly establishes a basis for traditional authority which is wider than the New Testament alone and makes reference to the period of church history which included the early church. It is an interesting comment on our later discussion to note that Newman found substantial support for his opinions in the Homilies. [26]

This theory of the Church of England's tradition was most consistently carried by the High Church school of Laud and his successors. After the Restoration of 1660 this school put the tradition through a process of extension, as Sykes shows:

> The churchmanship of the restored Laudian school was characterized by its wealth of patristic scholarship and learning, and by its interest in the Eastern Orthodox Church . . . From this contact with the Eastern Orthodox Church there resulted a careful study of its history and traditions, a revived zeal for Greek patristic literature, and a natural resolve to cultivate closer and friendly relations with so venerable and apostolic a communion, which rejected uncompromisingly the papal supremacy claimed by the Latin Church. As a corollary of this

interest there ensued a re-emphasis upon the episcopal character
of the English church and upon the points of difference which
separated it from the Protestant dissenters in England. [27]

Among this group the Nonjurors [28] were of particular importance as representatives of the high tradition of Anglicanism.
They were later to be an important formative influence on the
religious thought of John Wesley, but for the moment it is as
transmitters of the early church traditional referent that they are
of interest. Abbey and Overton find that the Nonjurors were so
much in sympathy with the model of the early church [29] that
they evaluated the contemporary organization of the Church of
England by reference to this model:

> All looked back to primitive times as the unalterable model of
> doctrine, order, and government; all were firmly persuaded that
> the English Reformation was wholly based on a restoration of
> the ancient pattern, and had fallen short of its object only so far
> forth as that ideal had as yet been unattained. [30]

The tradition of the early church as a referent for legitimating the
contemporary Church of England was thus well established in the
sixteenth century and was by the end of the seventeenth century
most consistently carried by the High Church party in general,
and especially by the Nonjurors. The extension of this tradition
in the direction of an attempted rapport with the Eastern Orthodox
Church is a logical development which can be explained fairly
easily. A party which emphasized the importance for the Church
of England of a reinstatement of the pristine purity of the early
church found in the Eastern Orthodox Church the contemporary
embodiment of a church free from the accretions of Rome—a
clear approximation to their image of the Golden Age of church
history. [31]

As has been argued, this tradition tended to become eclipsed
in the Church of England around the beginning of the eighteenth
century. Several reasons can be given for this, among which the
four most important are: (1) the departure of the Nonjurors,
many of whom were among the most learned Anglican theologians; (2) the presence among the clergy of a significant number
of ministers who had gained office during the Commonwealth
and who were committed to a more radical Puritan (therefore
Scriptural) interpretation of the Reformation; (3) political pres-

sure, including the preferment of Whig bishops [32]; and (4) related to the political pressure was the suppression of Convocation in 1717, which fragmented the church and made synodical rule impossible. The early church tradition was never completely obscured, but it declined enormously in importance in the Church of England of that period. Lowther Clarke concludes from his detailed historical research that in the eighteenth-century preparation for Holy Orders did not seem to have included any reading of the church Fathers. An important observation is made by Cragg, who interprets the transition from the seventeenth to the eighteenth century in terms of the substitution of reason as the source of authority in place of antiquity—which in Weberian terms means the gradual replacement of legitimations on traditional grounds by rational-legal legitimations:

> For any thoughtful person in the seventeenth century the problem of authority was urgent. It was involved, directly or indirectly, in every controversy of the age. In theology the appeal to antiquity had been considered weighty. The Latitudinarians did not repudiate the authority of classical and patristic authors, but they used their works with caution. The Bible still held its position as the chief and ultimate court of appeal. Scripture was interpreted by reason, of course, and the way in which it was used underwent a subtle but perceptible change. The Latitudinarians stood half way between the unquestioning reliance on authority which was characteristic of the early seventeenth century and the rationalism of the early eighteenth. [33]

Along with the white-washing of church interiors went a similar illumination in the field of ethics, as conscience and private judgement became increasingly relied upon. The outcome of this was 'a marked inclination to resent anything like submission to the dicta of any previous age'. [34] Extensive documentation of the rejection by eighteenth-century churchmen of appeals to antiquity could be given [35] but perhaps one example, that of Archbishop Secker, will suffice to demonstrate the predominant attitude, for Secker made a point of warning his clergy against 'over-great reverence for antiquity'. [36]

To draw together the main features of the Church of England immediately before the Methodist Revival, we have evidence of a traditional referent of legitimacy in the Church of England based on the early church which had been carried in the main by the High Church party, and in particular by the Nonjurors. For various reasons this tradition had declined at the end of the seventeenth and beginning of the eighteenth centuries. The overall picture of the early eighteenth century Church of England is of a highly compromised church—with a predominance of Whig bishops—which was rationalistic and individualistic. Above all, it had limited organizational autonomy and was often used as the adjunct of the secular political power. Though the eighteenth-century church has tended to be seen as the 'darkness before the dawn', Carpenter's evaluation of its main features as a 'dessicated form of Anglicanism' [37] is not unfair.

Between this general discussion of the referents of legitimacy in the seventeenth- and eighteenth-century Church of England, and an assessment of Wesley's significance, there are two links which can be briefly mentioned. First, Wesley's father, who had a considerable influence on the religious development of both his sons, was a High Churchman of the Caroline school. As a result, in the opinion of Maldwyn Edwards, 'The brothers Wesley were rooted in orthodoxy from the Epworth Rectory days and their evangelical fervour was in one aspect only their earlier teaching becoming incandescent in their life and thought'. [38] Second, Wesley became very familiar with the writing of the Nonjurors, initially in his Oxford and Georgia period. 'It was, in the main, high church divinity which filled the books which Wesley took with him to Georgia.' [39] These themes suggest that we are justified in approaching early Methodism in terms of its continuity with existing religious organization rather than as a totally new innovation.

There is a wealth of evidence to show that Wesley referred back to the early church whenever he sought legitimacy for doctrinal and organizational principles. Indeed, this has been seen by some historians as the crucial distinction between the Wesleyans and the later Evangelical movement in the Church of England, which sought its legitimation in a rather different referent of tradition:

> There was one striking difference in general outlook [between Wesley and the Evangelicals] which has often been overlooked. Wesley had a great regard for the Primitive Church (many of his supposed innovations were derived from it); the Evan-

gelicals, especially as the movement developed and gained an ethos of its own, looked to the Church of the Reformation and to the Puritan tradition which had then arisen. [40]

Many similar interpretations and evidence from Wesley's own writing could be mustered to give the interpretation strong backing [41] and we will shortly deal with some of the precise details of the reinstatement of pristine organization which Wesley made, but it is necessary to add a note of caution to the discussion. Although the model of the early church was a very strong influence on Methodist organization, particularly in the early stages, to the extent that there is justification in tracing the origins of Wesley's movement to an already-existing tradition within the Church of England, there were other influences on it and these became more important as the movement grew in size: some of these will also be dealt with. But there is a tendency for some accounts to give great emphasis to the catholic element and to neglect any other. Partly this is due to the influence of the Oxford Movement on historical perspectives, but partly— notably more recently—it has been as a response to the ecumenical movement. [42] The opposite tendency is that which treats Methodism as an exclusively Puritan movement. [43] Both traditions can be traced in the Wesleyan movement, and if the present chapter seems to over-emphasize the latter's catholicity, this is only because we are mainly concerned with the early period of development when the traditional referent of the early church was undoubtedly of fundamental significance. Indeed, Wesley's appeal to antiquity is thrown into very clear relief when it is contrasted with the more typical ethos of the eighteenth-century church.

One other problem can be disposed of forthwith. The question arises whether Wesley's appeal to antiquity was the appeal to the early church which we have traced through the Laudian school or whether it was the more characteristically Puritan appeal to the Scriptural church. On this there is considerable agreement among historians that Wesley's model was the early church. In the thought and writings of the early Christian Fathers, Wesley found a firm basis for his 'innovations'. [44] This was not something which was discarded after the conversion of Wesley in 1738, for he made a spirited defence of a theological argument put forward by Waterland in 1749 which appealed to the tradition of the first three centuries of Christianity. [45] There is the interesting evidence of Balleine (who, it is worth noting, traces the pedigree of Evangelical churchmen only as far back as the Puritans, which means that Wesley's concern with the early church is not easily accommodated into his historical treatment): he quotes a memorandum of John Wesley during his Oxford period which shows the extent of Wesley's reliance on the model of the early church:

'I believe it is a duty to observe as far as I can (1) to baptise by immersion; (2) to use Water, Oblation of Elements, Invocation, Alms, a Prothesis, in the Eucharist; (3) to pray for the faithful departed; (4) to pray standing on Sunday in Pentecost; (5) to abstain from blood and things strangled.' It was only a passing phase, but it left its mark. To the end of his life Wesley was a Patristic student; he translated the Apostolic Fathers for the use of his preachers; and most of the things that were considered innovations in the societies that he organized later—the class-meetings, the love-feasts, the quarterly tickets, the day-break services, the watch-nights, the separate seats for men and women—were really revivals of customs of the Primitive Church. [46]

The *Christian Library* which Wesley had printed made use of works from the early Fathers and Roman Catholic writers and did not include any writings of Luther or Calvin, though their lives were included and there was a substantial quoting of Puritan divines. [47] Thus the early church was a most important referent of tradition in Wesley's legitimation, especially when apparent 'innovations' were concerned, and the fact that this appeal back to pristine origins was never abandoned is shown by Wesley's eventual separation from the Church of England (formally marked by his ordination of Coke in 1784), which was justified by reference to the church's pristine polity.

But two main factors resulted in the eventual divergence of Methodism from the Church of England. The first can be explained in terms of the routinization of a virtuoso religious style to form a mass religious organization. Thus, while early Methodism in the 'Holy Club' and Georgia phase corresponds very closely to the concept of religious virtuoso activity, there were subsequent selections from and modifications of the core tradition by those who subsequently became Methodists. [48] Briefly, by the end of the eighteenth century the Methodist local leadership was largely derived from small manufacturers and traders, who had a natural affinity with the aspects of Wesley's asceticism which were typically inner-worldly—the rejection of luxury, self-discipline, and family duty—and who found the ethical orientation a valuable source of disciplined labour: as Thompson puts it 'they [the Methodist leaders] fostered within the Methodist Church those elements most suited to make up the psychic component of the work-discipline of which the manufacturers stood most in need.' [49] But they found those aspects of Wesleyan asceticism which were basically other-worldly and derived from the tradition of the early church much less congenial. [50] Therefore, as a direct consequence of Methodism's success as a conversionist religious movement it underwent a process of development which led it away from its early status as an élitist, virtuoso group claiming an already-existing referent of tradition in the Church of England.

The other main factor in Methodism's divergence from the Church of England was the model of the early church which Wesley used as a basis for organizational changes as his movement became larger. Wesley's image of the early church was of an innovatory organization, typically in a state of flux. This is well demonstrated by his statement at the Fourth Annual Conference of 1747 that there was no thought of uniformity in the government of all the churches until the time of Constantine, and that there would not have been uniformity then if men had only consulted the word of God. [51] When in 1784 Wesley ordained Coke as the 'Superintendent of the Societies in America' he justified this 'innovation' by reference to Lord King's account of the primitive church, which had convinced him that, as a presbyter, he had the same right as a bishop to ordain. [52] Bishop Stillingfleet's *Irenicum* (1659), which treated forms of church government as inessential, gave added legitimacy to this interpretation of the early church. The model of the early church which Wesley employed and the later Tractarian version diverge basically on the issue of the innovatory nature of the early church, and later there will be a consideration of how the two distinct interpretations could be made while nevertheless being similarly located in the same referent of tradition. It is beyond doubt that Wesley and the Tractarians made comparable appeals back to the primitive church, which has led one writer to label it the 'ever-

recurring touchstone of agreement between the two movements.' [53]

Wesley's organizational reforms, as well as appealing back to
the early church polity, have on many points of organization been
compared to it. It has been said, for example, that

> ... the Methodists set up, alongside the Church, not by way of
> rivalry but of supplement, what was in effect a new organization.
> This organization was not the outcome of any premeditated
> design, but, as in the Primitive Church, the gradual response to
> the challenge of novel conditions and the disclosure of fresh
> needs. [54]

One of Wesley's most frequently-reiterated principles of organization (it was reinforced by the Conferences of 1765, 1782 and
1786) was the separation of men and women in his services, based
on the claim that this was an early church practice. Wesley was so
firmly convinced of this point that he seriously threatened never
again to set foot in a chapel where the sexes were mixed. It was
on exactly the same basis of legitimacy that lay preachers were
instituted after Wesley's return from Georgia. Similarly, the first
district visitors were favourably looked on as a revival of the
primitive church practice of appointing deaconesses: this, incidentally, is an interesting parallel with the later development of
sisterhoods in the Church of England. Wesley even found proof
of the antiquity of the practice which was eventually to become
almost synonymous with Nonconformity, hymn-singing:

> I was much surprised on reading an 'Essay on Music' wrote
> by one who is a thorough master of the subject, to find that the
> music of the ancients was as simple as that of the Methodists:
> that their music wholly consisted of melody, or the arrange-
> ment of single notes. [55]

Confession was another primitive practice which Wesley advocated, and an account of Wesley's period in Georgia which was
published by the principal land holders of the colony speaks of
his attempts to 're-establish confession, penance, mortifications ...
which he called Apostolic Constitutions'. [56] He insisted on the
necessity for confession to the extent of making it a condition for
Communicating. Further confirmation of the pristine legitimacy
of confession was provided by the Moravians, among whose

Bands group confession was practised, and it was introduced in this form into the Methodist 'Band' and later 'class' meetings.

Three of Wesley's most characteristic 'innovations' were the Love-Feast, a revival of the primitive *agape*, the Covenant Service and the Watchnight service. Wesley's own description of how the latter originated illustrates unambiguously his method of testing the legitimacy of apparently novel forms of worship and observance:

> About this time I was informed that several persons in Kingswood frequently met together at the school; and when they could spare the time, spent the greater part of the night in prayer, praise and thanksgiving. Some advised me to put an end to this; but, upon weighing the thing thoroughly *and comparing it with the practice of the ancient Christians*, I could see no cause to forbid it. Rather, I believed it might be made of more general use. [57]

Wesley did not always refer to the early church before he introduced some new practice (otherwise he could hardly have been 'surprised' by his discovery about hymn-singing) but he often did, and invariably if he could find pristine legitimacy for a practice which had been introduced on other grounds, so much the better. His ordination of Coke, which was the single most important innovation which separated him from the Church of England, shows that Wesley's allegiance to the established church was conditional on the extent to which the latter could be seen as conforming to the primary model of primitive Christianity. In this respect, Wesley and Newman had very much the same kind of conditional allegiance.

As is well known, Wesley always referred to himself as 'a clergyman of the High Church, son of a clergyman of the High Church, reared from his infancy in the most complete obedience.' [58] It is only in contrast to the low level of majority practice in the Church of England the Wesley's sacramentalism can properly be judged. During a period when the Communion service was a widely neglected part of Anglican worship, Wesley —even in the last eight years of his life (1783–90)—communicated on average seventy-two times a year. As far as this aspect of his Anglican practice was concerned, it was virtually constant from at least as early as 1735 when he preached a sermon on 'The Duty of Constant Communion'. [59] Thus, although the early church referent of tradition as shown in Wesley's reinstatement of primitive practice is most marked in the early period of his movement, and although his conception of the early church was much more free-floating than the High Church version, there are unmistakable continuities between the two, and there are good grounds for analysing the influence of the available Anglican tradition as an instance of what has been termed a 'revolution by tradition'. Wesley certainly saw the Methodist 'innovations' as reinstatements, and since during his lifetime he exercised a strong, at times autocratic, influence on Methodist development we cannot overlook his source of legitimacy.

Above all, the Methodist revival is best seen in contrast to the rest of eighteenth-century religion. The origins of Wesley's reforms have been contrasted with the predominantly Whig Church of England: it is also possible to draw a contrast between Wesleyan Methodism and the Evangelicals in the Church of England who succeeded them and with whom they share a superficial resemblance. The Anglican Evangelicals of the late eighteenth and early nineteenth centuries do not fit into precisely the same tradition as Wesley. Historians disagree quite considerably about their characteristics, but some conclusions can be drawn. The Evangelicals appear to have shared in the emotionalism characteristic of the wider Wesleyan revival, but they have commonly been seen as something of a theological backwater, a reaction against rationalism which allowed unfettered scope to the emotions and eventually developed an almost morbid preoccupation with death. As part of this reaction, intellectual pursuits were deprecated and reliance was placed substantially on Biblical literalism. [60] The contention that this was a comparatively sterile theological force is supported by Daniel-Rops' argument that the Evangelicals 'insisted more upon moral effort and charitable works than upon theological doctrine.' [61] To the extent that this was an attempt to contain evangelical zeal within the Church of England it can be described as having acquired some of the form but not the theological content of the Wesleyan revival. The Evangelicals made use of some of the evangelizing techniques of the Methodist preachers, though they rarely cut across the parish system of the Church of England by field-preaching, and they never attempted to form an autonomous religious organization: when they did establish organizations within the Church of England these were typically of the rational-bureaucratic type, for example the Church Missionary Society and the societies set up by the Clapham Sect. There was little attempt at traditional legitimation using the early church as a model among members of this movement.

Part of the reason why historians never give the Evangelicals the same importance as the Wesleyans was that, with the secession of the latter, a good deal of religious zeal had been lost to the Church of England. But the other reason fits well into the present analysis of traditional referents, for the Evangelicals had no strong notion of a pristine form of organization against which to compare the contemporary Church of England as a preliminary to their revivalist activity. As Carpenter concludes, 'A constitutional difference between the Evangelicals and Wesley was that, whereas Wesley formed his societies on what he believed to be the pattern of the primitive Church, the Evangelicals looked to the Reformation. They were in fact Puritans, though not in all respects.' [62] In terms of the present discussion, Carpenter's interpretation implies that the Evangelicals, by giving the Reformation pre-eminence in their traditional legitimations, were less able to make a radical critique of the contemporary Church of England than had the Wesleyans, whose choice of the early church as the model of pristine purity on which the Church of England's legitimacy was based had much greater potential for radical reinstatement.

Towards the end of the eighteenth and beginning of the nineteenth century there is evidence of a very similar tendency to that which preceded the Wesleyan revival, namely a decline in interest in the patristic period of church history. Wakeman sets the picture:

> Thus the whole tendency was to Protestant rather than Catholic theology. The Fathers and the Schoolmen and even the Caroline divines were put aside in favour of Luther, Calvin, Scott and Milner . . . It is true that there were a few clergy and laity scattered here and there through the country who, like John Keble's father, were the true spiritual descendants of Laud and Ken and Wilson and the High Churchmen of the seventeenth century. [63]

The inclusion of Milner (1744–97) on this list is not altogether justified, because, if anything, Milner provides the single most important intellectual link between the patristic interest of Wesley and the leaders of the Oxford Movement. Newman first came across the writings of the church Fathers through reading Milner. Elliott-Binns argues that Milner's *History of the Church of Christ*, which was brought out posthumously in stages between 1794 and 1809, revived an interest in the church Fathers which had almost completely died out in the eighteenth century, apart from Wesley. Balleine's judgement is even more straightforward: he thinks that Milner 'turned the attention of English readers to the almost forgotten writings of the early Fathers'. [64]

To continue a metaphor we have already used, the Tractarians can be seen as giving theological form to the Evangelical impulse, and there are several most important links between the two movements. For instance, there is the famous statement of Newman in his *Apologia* that: 'I almost owed my soul' to Thomas Scott. [65] A connection has already been established between Newman and Milner, and another link can be made between these two seemingly quite different movements by considering them as parallel attempts to establish a more vital form of Christianity. Both Evangelicals and Tractarians derived part of their orientation from a more general climate of the period which rejected reason as an arbiter of religious beliefs. It is not merely a question of the ideological parallels between the two movements, because there was a noticeable overlapping of personnel; even more significant for the present thesis is the observation that several of the founders of Anglo-Catholic religious communities came from Evangelical backgrounds. On this point, Allchin thinks that 'the longing for a life of holiness, for a living knowledge and love of God was integral to Evangelicalism as well as to the Oxford Movement. And the experienced quality of Evangelical theology, its stress on reality and life, is also in a different but related way a primary characteristic of any truly monastic theology.' [66] It was Father W. H. Frere, a Superior of the Community of the Resurrection, who gave the most precise assessment of the relationship between the Evangelical and Tractarian movements in relation to the revival of the religious life in the Church of England: 'In many ways it would be true to state that the Evangelical movement gave the spirit and the Catholic movement the form for this revival'. [67] Newman in particular embodies the relationship between the two movements, because he based his belief in God on direct apprehension, which was a strong Evangelical feature, but at the same time he regarded religion as dogma, a characteristically Catholic attitude: thus, 'experience and tradition stood side by side'. [68]

The referent of tradition adopted by the Tractarians was complex in the sense that different personnel gave differential emphasis to parts of it, and there was some change over time. But there was in the early phase of the movement an unmistakable stress on the tradition of the early church as a criterion for the rejection, retention or reinstatement of all aspects of the Church of England's doctrine and organization. The movement's leaders, particularly Pusey, explicitly interpreted their purpose as the revival of this traditional basis of Anglican organization, which they considered had been neglected or obscured. Pusey, who is perhaps the most consistent exponent of this tradition, put his trust in antiquity and advised his followers to look always to the first six centuries of Christianity, which meant that a disputed point must always be settled by an appeal to scholars. [69] This is an important point which goes a considerable way towards explaining the difference between Pusey and Newman, and the reason for the latter's defection, because Newman wanted a living, contemporary authority, and he eventually concluded that this was not available outside the Roman Catholic Church. While similarly basing his appeals on a reference back to the early church, Newman was much more unequivocally committed to what we have earlier characterized as the Catholic 'continuity' theory of church history. In the first year of the movement (1833) Newman had already stated his version of church tradition in Tract XI of the *Tracts for the Times*: 'Thus the visible Church is not a voluntary association of the day, but a continuation of one which existed in the age before us, and then again in the age before that; and so back till we come to the age of the Apostles.' [70]

The more characteristic emphasis at the start of the movement (and it can be put no stronger than that because there were disagreements among those Tractarians who remained Anglicans) was to refer to the fundamental authority of the early church and to reject as 'accretions' the supplementary traditions of the Roman Church, while at the same time equally avoiding the individualism and variety implicit in direct appeals to the Bible alone. On the first of these points, one of the clearest accounts is given by W. Palmer in his *Treatise on the Church* (third edition, 1872):

The difference between the Anglo-catholic and the popular Romish doctrine of tradition is this: The former only admits tradition as confirmatory of the true meaning of Scripture, the latter asserts that it is also *supplementary* to Scripture, conveying doctrines which Scripture has omitted . . . The authenticity of primitive tradition and its records, of Scripture and its doctrines, and of Christianity as a revelation, stand or fall together. [71]

On the second of these points, the rejection of direct interpretation of the Bible, Keble is one of the strongest reasoners, and he consistently maintained a crucial function for the church which was expressed in his dictum that 'the Church is to teach, the Bible to prove'. Keble drew a very clear distinction between an appeal back to the Bible and an appeal back to the early church as a means of understanding the Bible:

This use of apostolic tradition may well correct the presumptuous irreverence of disparaging the Fathers under a plea of magnifying Scripture. Here is a tradition so highly honoured by the Almighty Founder and Guide of the Church, as to be made the standard and rule of his own divine Scriptures. The very writings of the Apostles were first to be tried by it, before they could be incorporated into the canon. Thus the Scriptures themselves, as it were, do homage to the tradition of the Apostles; the despisers, therefore, of that tradition take part, inadvertently or profanely, with the despisers of the Scripture itself. [72]

But the importance of the early church referent of tradition for the process of organizational change with which we are now concerned, the 'revolution by tradition', lies in the use made of it in reforming the contemporary institution. In one sense, the goal of the Oxford Movement was preservative, for they were very much concerned to prevent the rejection of what they saw as central features of the Church of England's organization—principally the theological notion of an apostolic succession in the Anglican episcopate, which was then threatened by both the secular political authorities and by Low Church members of the Church of England. But in addition it was a significant reform movement, in which the Tractarians tried to reinstate aspects of ecclesiastical organization which were sanctioned by the example of the early church but neglected in contemporary organization. [73] The emphasis on frequent communion made by the Tractarians, together with preparation for communion which included fasting, were all introduced on the basis of a reference back to the practice of the early church. Likewise, the 'innovation' of daily services was legitimated on these grounds, as is clearly shown by the statement in one of Newman's sermons: 'I have now said enough to let you into the reasons why I have lately begun Daily Service in the Church. I felt that we were very unlike the early Christians if we went without it.' [74]

It is on the issue of daily services especially that we can find another parallel with the Wesleyan source of legitimacy, because both owed an obvious allegiance to certain aspects of the Reformation. In his summary of the various schools of churchmanship in the Church of England, Neill makes the following assessment of the nineteenth-century High Church attitude to the Reformation:

> Some think that the Reformation was on the whole a bad thing, but that it had certain redeeming features, such as the gift to the people of public worship in a tongue that they could under-stand. This is broadly the position of the Anglo-Catholic wing of the Anglican Churches. [75]

In fact, the marked emphasis on the Prayer Book shown by the leaders of the Oxford Movement is good evidence that they did not interpret their reforms as a complete rejection of the Reformation, though their attitude to it was markedly less positive than that of the Wesleyans. Rather, in reasserting the primacy of the pristine model of early church organization, their attitude to the Reformation became *conditional* on the extent to which it had preserved or reinstated this model. In this sense they certainly rejected legitimations which appealed back to the Reformation alone, as had Wesley, and Pusey demonstrates this orientation when he describes the attitude of the movement as '. . . reference to the ancient church, instead of the Reformers, as the ultimate expounder of the meaning of our Church'. [76] Even Hurrell Froude, whose dislike of the Reformers and preference for Rome had a strong influence on Newman, [77] was not prepared totally to reject the Reformation in arguing for a reinstatement of early church practice, particularly on the issue of daily services. [78] But emphasis on the Reformation was

weakened, and one result of this was to detract from an identification between Continental Protestants and the Church of
England. It was the persistence of this identification in the plans
for an Anglican-Lutheran bishopric in Jerusalem that contributed
to the eventual alienation of Newman from the Church of
England.

First and foremost, the leaders of the Oxford Movement were
concerned to re-emphasize the *spiritual* autonomy of the Church
of England in a period when this autonomy was seen as threatened,
both by the Liberal administration with its policy of church
reform and by the wider ideology of Liberalism which followed
the French Revolution. In this respect, the 'revolution by
tradition' which the Tractarians set out to accomplish by referring
back to a pristine and potentially highly valued period of church
history had as its purpose the demarcation of spheres of competence between the political and religious institutions. This
interpretation is very fully argued by Laski, who describes the
notion of autonomy advanced by the Tractarians. The Church of
England is a *'perfecta societas* set over against the State', [79] and as
part of this idea the early church becomes a firm point of reference
from which to set about the reform of the contemporary church:
'Out of the contemplation of the unalterable past is begotten the
motive force to the alteration of the present.' [80] To the extent
that both movements arose in periods when the Church of
England was subject to secular political pressure and thus can be
seen as attempts to restate the *spiritual* autonomy of the church,
Wesleyanism and Tractarianism share some common features
(though there are very important distinctions, some of which are
dealt with below).

So far attention has been directed towards traditional legitimacy
and the expansion of the Weberian concept in order to con-
ceptualize different *referents* of tradition within an organization
whose members have at their disposal different periods in its
history to which they may give differential emphasis. Using this
analytical concept, a common feature of the Wesleyan and
Tractarian reforms was found in the important role which both
movements attached to the tradition of the early church. This
referent was particularly valuable in claims to be reinstating
pristine beliefs and practices because it contained the notion of a
golden age in the church's history which could then be used to
compare unfavourably the contemporary Church of England. On

the other hand, there is little doubt that the model of the early church which Wesley used—at least after the Oxford and Georgia period—contained an important notion of flux, and it is to this distinguishing feature that another type of legitimate authority may be applied. For this part of the discussion, Weber's concept of charismatic authority is a valuable one. Up to this point the concept of traditional authority, with certain modifications, has been found a useful approach in explaining certain kinds of change within religious organizations. In the Church of England especially, the traditional component of positions in the organization is a most important factor, as Morgan discovered in his study of Anglican bishops:

> The examination of the continuities in the backgrounds of Anglican bishops and the relation of these to the nature of episcopal authority may be extended if we consider that this authority resides not merely in the institutionalized charisma of the office but also in the traditional values that it represents. Or, to put it another way, traditional values contribute to the essentially charismatic quality of the office. [81]

Morgan refers to the 'essentially charismatic quality' of the office of bishop. This may be worded slightly differently by saying that, since Christianity originated as a charismatic movement, the roles in any Christian organization at any time are either legitimated by, or are capable of being legitimated by reference to their charismatic basis. But since charisma is a potentially disruptive element, a church-type organization will typically employ a theory of office charisma rather than personal charisma, though the latter remains latent rather than completely disappearing. In the present context the point at issue is the very different effects on an organization such as the Church of England which personal and office charisma can have. The difference between the two types is very marked indeed. In the case of personal charisma, the personality and example of an exceptional individual are sufficient criteria for accepting the new obligations which the individual puts forward, without reference to, and frequently in defiance of, institutionalized authority—'It is written, but I say unto you'. In the case of office charisma the situation is almost the reverse: the charisma is objectified in, and dispensed through, institutionalized channels, so that the personal characteristics of the incumbent of a routinized charismatic office become to a considerable extent irrelevant. There is a clear example of this in Article XXVI of the Articles of Religion in the *Book of Common Prayer* of the Church of England (1562) which is here quoted in full:

Of the Unworthiness of the Ministers, which hinders not the effect of the Sacrament.

Although in the visible Church the evil be ever mingled with the good, and sometimes the evil have chief authority in the Ministration of the Word and Sacraments, yet forasmuch as they do not the same in their own name, but in Christ's, and do minister by his commission and authority, we may use their Ministry, both in hearing the Word of God, and in receiving of the Sacraments. Neither is the effect of Christ's ordinance taken away by their wickedness, nor the grace of God's gifts diminished from such as by faith and rightly do receive the Sacraments ministered unto them; which be effectual, because of Christ's institution and promise, although they be ministered by evil men. Nevertheless, it appertaineth to the discipline of the Church, that inquiry be made of evil Ministers, and that they be accused by those that have knowledge of their offences; and finally being found guilty, by just judgement be deposed.

It is in their reinterpretations of the charismatic component of the roles which they traced back to the model of the early church that the Methodists and Tractarians fundamentally diverged. Both movements were concerned to re-emphasize the charismatic content of roles within the Church of England in order to stress the latter's spiritual autonomy in the face of erosions of it by the secular political authorities, and this is their common point of departure. But the implications which the leaders of each movement took from the model of the early church were very different. The Wesleyans who, even in the 'Holy Club', had been impressed by the example of the African church of Tertullian, with its significant Montanist, *pneumatic* character, [82] placed considerable emphasis on the 'free-floating' nature of personal charisma. [83] Thus they tended to disregard legitimations which would have had the effect of crystallizing the roles within the Church of England into a formally autonomous hierarchy; instead, their improvisations tended to cut across the organizational boundaries of the Church of England and to emphasize personal charismatic qualities. This is nowhere more evident than in the characteristic

Methodist practice of field-preaching. The Tractarians were much more concerned to stress the routinized charismatic roles within the Church of England and in doing so they were attempting to strengthen and to crystallize the hierarchy of the church in order to protect the organization against what they saw as secular political and ideological attacks. This, Chadwick argues, was a necessary restatement in the church of the early nineteenth century [84] and it was explicit from the very beginning of the movement. In Tract I, Newman made the following appeal to the clergy:

> Therefore, my dear Brethren, act up to your professions. Let it not be said that you have neglected a gift; for if you have the Spirit of the Apostles on you, surely this *is* a great gift. 'Stir up the gift of God which is in you.' [85]

Thus both the Methodist and Tractarian movements began as in many respects similar 'revolutions by tradition' and both had as an ultimate goal the restatement of the spiritual autonomy of the Church of England: in short, they were attempts to differentiate the religious organization of the church from the institutions of the surrounding society. The Whig bishops of the eighteenth century have been described as the ecclesiastical wing of the Whig administration [86] and as clinging to the fleshpots of the establishment. [87] At the same time, the predominant ideology of the period was one of growing scepticism. Against this environment, Wesley stressed the spiritual uniqueness of the church which he initially found in the model of the early church. In a similar way, the Tractarians saw the Church of England as an institution threatened on the one hand by the attempts of a hostile Liberal administration to interfere in religious affairs, and on the other hand by the intellectual climate of Liberalism and the breakdown of traditional authority following the French Revolution. Sykes, like Chadwick, argues that the need for a high doctrine of the sovereignty and autonomy of the church is necessary in churches that wish to create their own 'perfect society' which is distinct from that of the State. This was something which was noted too by Laski, who makes an observation which might just as easily apply to the early Methodist movement. Laski notes:

> It is not a little curious that more attention should not have

been paid to the remarkable analogy between the Oxford
Movement and the Disruption of 1834 in the established
Church of Scotland. Each was essentially an anti-Erastian
movement. It was against an all-absorbtive state that each
group of men was contending . . . In each case, as was well
enough admitted by contemporaries, the attempt was made . . .
to work out a doctrine of the Church which, neglecting the
State, gave the Church the general organization of a perfect
society. [88]

The way in which different schools of churchmanship within the
Church of England legitimated the growth of sisterhoods,
deaconesses and brotherhoods, either by reference to some pristine
model of this 'perfect society' or by reference to more pragmatic
criteria, is the subject of the next chapter.

NOTES

1 A. MacIntyre, *Secularization and Moral Change* (London, Oxford University
Press, 1967).
2 For example, the articles by E. D. C. Brewer, 'Church and sect in
Methodism', *Social Forces*, vol. 30, 1952, pp. 400–8, and J. H. Chamber-
layne, 'From sect to church in British Methodism', *British Journal of
Sociology*, vol. 15 (2), 1964.
3 This portrayal of Tractarian attitudes to Methodism is found in
A. Skevington Wood, *The Inextinguishable Blaze. Spiritual Renewal and
Advance in the Eighteenth Century* (London, The Paternoster Press, 1960),
p. 16.
4 *Authorized Report of the Church Congress Held at Southampton, 1870*
(Southampton, Gutch and Cox, 1870), p. 84.
5 In fact, when the other denominations were mentioned there was sometimes a marked lack of diplomacy. Wackerbarth, one of the first to recom-
mend the formation of sisterhoods in the nineteenth century, was particularly acid about Dissenters in general: 'By the outward air of superior
sanctity adopted by the Dissenters, very many persons, who are seeking
a more perfect way than the ordinary practice and example of Churchmen
offer, are caught away from the Catholic faith to make shipwreck of their
Baptismal vow . . .' (Francis Diedrich Wackerbarth, *The Revival of Monastic
Institutions, and their Bearing on Society* [Colchester, W. Totham, 1839],
p. 13.)
6 This term comes from Gellner's concept of a neo-episodic theory of
social change, put forward in *Thought and Change* (London, Weidenfeld
and Nicolson, 1964).
7 Stephen Neill, *Anglicanism* (Harmondsworth, Middlesex, Penguin Books,
1965), pp. 31–4.
8 ibid., p. 35.

9 At his enthronement in 1945 Archbishop Fisher touched on this when he stated: 'The stresses within the Church, so far as they are due to tensions between divine truths imperfectly integrated by men, are signs of truthfulness and of health. . . . It is no accident that the Church in *this* country should be of *this* kind. . . . The stresses within the Church, and the unifying loyalty which controls them, have their counterpart in our secular history. . . . It is that tried and tested unity in our people which in these last years has brought us by God's providence through great perils and great sacrifices to the verge of a great deliverance. And the unifying forces have their roots and strength in that heritage of Christian Faith which the Church has implanted and preserved among us through the centuries.' (Charles Smyth, *The Church and the Nation* [London, Hodder and Stoughton, 1962], p. 14.)

10 The Anglo-Saxon church was, from the Reformation, sometimes used in conjunction with the 'Norman Yoke' theory: 'As the Reformation progressed, men like John Foxe, Archbishops Parker and Ussher looked back to Anglo-Saxon times for the pure primitive church, thus greatly stimulating Anglo-Saxon studies. For ecclesiastical corruption could be dated from the invasion of 1066, which the Pope had blessed.' (Christopher Hill, *Puritanism and Revolution* [London, Panther Books, 1968], p. 67.)

11 A. M. Allchin, *The Silent Rebellion* (London, S.C.M. Press, 1958), p. 38.

12 See, for example, Norman Sykes, *Church and State in England in the 18th Century* (London University Press, 1934).

13 S. C. Carpenter, *Eighteenth Century Church and People* (London, John Murray, 1959).

14 See Allchin, op. cit., 1958, pp. 39–40.

15 L. E. Elliott-Binns, *Religion in the Victorian Era* (London, Lutterworth Press, 1964), p. 104.

16 Allchin, op. cit., 1958, p. 38.

17 E. G. Rupp, *Studies in the Making of the English Protestant Tradition* (London, Cambridge University Press, 1947).

18 K. S. Latourette, *A History of Christianity* (London, Eyre and Spottiswoode, 1955), p. 837. Elsewhere, F. J. Taylor attributes the Reformation itself to the spread of popular knowledge about the Scriptures: 'The simple believer could not fail to be struck with the contrast between the picture of church life as it was presented to him in the pages of the New Testament and the prevailing ecclesiastical order with which he was familiar. It was an easy step to proceed to the conclusion that nothing more could be required as of necessity to be believed and practised on the part of the sixteenth-century Christian, than what was plainly to be read in the title-deeds of the faith.' (In Frederick William Dillistone (ed.), *Scripture and Tradition* [London, Lutterworth Press, 1955], p. 62.)

19 Norman Sykes, *From Sheldon to Secker* (London, Cambridge University Press, 1959), p. 168.

20 ibid., p. 168.

21 There is a parallel here with the more radical interpretations of the 'Norman Yoke' theory which were made by referring to Biblical traditions. See Christopher Hill, op. cit., Chapter 3, *passim*. The more 'ancient' the tradition the more radical the implications for the present.

22 F. L. Cross (ed.), *The Oxford Dictionary of the Christian Church* (London, Oxford University Press, 1963), p. 654.

23 Not only periods of church history have been used as bases for claims to legitimacy among schools of churchmanship in the Church of England, and the criterion of 'reason' has often been of critical importance. We will later find rational bureaucratic criteria used to justify the introduction of religious orders. However, at the moment we are concentrating on the specific importance of traditional authority, which we think forms a large part of the explanation of the different sub-groups in the Church of England.

24 There was some disagreement, even among Anglican High Churchmen, as to what constituted 'the early church'. On this point see Yngve Torgny Brilioth, *The Anglican Revival. Studies in the Oxford Movement* (London, Longmans, 1925), pp. 197–8: 'Nor could any agreement be arrived at as to where the limit of antiquity should be fixed. Newman himself mentions the different limits that were given. Ken holds with the undivided Church down to the schism between East and West. Bramhall says five centuries, Jewel six, and authoritative documents of the Reformation age vary between the time before Gregory I and the time up to Chalcedon. For his own part he does not go farther than to put the boundary of antiquity somewhere between 343 (Council of Sardica) and 787 (the seventh oecumenical council according to the Orthodox Church), but in any case with the chief emphasis on the first four centuries.' Apparently, the 'Higher' the Anglican, the longer the period attributed to 'the early church'.

25 W. K. Lowther Clarke, *Eighteenth Century Piety* (London, S.P.C.K., 1944), p. 32, my emphasis.

26 J. H. Newman, *Apologia Pro Vita Sua* (London, Longmans, Green, 1890), pp. 82–6.

27 Sykes, op. cit., 1934, pp. 17–18.

28 These were the members of the Church of England who, after 1688, scrupled to take the Oath of Allegiance to William and Mary on the grounds that by doing so they would break their previous oath to James II and his successors.

29 'Robert Nelson's [a Nonjuring layman] friends followed out their investigations of early Church history in no spirit of antiquarian inquiry, nor yet merely to find in them a treasure-house of weapons of argument wherewith to conduct their controversies, but mainly because their whole spirit was in sympathy with what they found there. Some were profoundly learned, others had no pretensions to extensive theological acquirements, but all his most congenial associates were imbued with the same feeling of deep respect for primitive antiquity.' C. J. Abbey and J. H. Overton, *The English Church in the Eighteenth Century* (London, Longmans, Green, 1878), p. 166. This might almost be a description of Wesley's 'Holy Club' at Oxford—compare, for example, the description on p. 118.

30 Abbey and Overton, op. cit., p. 167.

31 In this respect we could say that the Eastern Orthodox Church fulfilled the same function for High Churchmen as the American Indians did for Rousseau.

32 The significance of this will be made apparent later, when we argue that both Methodism and Tractarianism were attempts to secure the spiritual autonomy of the Church of England against political incursions. It is clearly much more effective to argue for autonomy on the basis of a model of antiquity than to use more contemporary models.

33 Gerald R. Cragg, *The Church and the Age of Reason* (London, Hodder and Stoughton, 1962), pp. 71–2.

34 Abbey and Overton, op. cit., p. 164. One aspect of this rejection of antiquity was the growth of Deism.

35 Abbey and Overton give several of these (ibid., pp. 163–5).

36 ibid., p. 163.

37 Carpenter, op. cit., 1959.

38 R. E. Davies and E. G. Rupp, *A History of the Methodist Church in Great Britain* (London, Epworth Press, 1965), vol. 1, p. 40.

39 ibid., the introductory essay by Rupp, p. xxix.

40 L. E. Elliott-Binns, *The Early Evangelicals* (London, Lutterworth Press, 1953), p. 215.

41 For example, Albert C. Outler, *John Wesley* (New York, Oxford University Press, 1964), p. 9: 'In the thought and piety of the early Church he discovered what he thereafter regarded as the normative pattern of catholic Christianity.'

42 An example of the Oxford Movement interpretation is William Simpson's *John Wesley and the Church of England* (London, S.P.C.K., 1934). Trevor Dearing's *Wesleyan and Tractarian Worship. An Ecumenical Study* (London, Epworth/S.P.C.K., 1966) is as it says, an ecumenical study.

43 For example, A. Skevington Wood, *The Inextinguishable Blaze* (London, Paternoster Press, 1960) and 'John Wesley's reversion to type', *Proceedings of the Wesley Historical Society*, vol. XXXV, December 1965, pp. 88–93.

44 For example, see Outler, op. cit., p. ix: 'To all these shaping forces he added the decisive influence of his own sustained immersion in the piety and wisdom of the early Christian fathers: Ignatius, Clement, Macarius, Ephraem Syrus, and others.'

45 Abbey and Overton, op. cit., p. 163. For the attack on Waterland which sparked this off, see Sykes, op. cit., 1959, p. 168.

46 G. R. Balleine, *A History of the Evangelical Party in the Church of England* (London, Church Book Room Press, 1951), p. 7.

47 Davies and Rupp, op. cit., pp. 50–1.

48 This is very well analysed by Bryan Turner in *Methodism in Leeds, 1914 to the Present Day*, Ph.D., Leeds, 1970.

49 E. P. Thompson, *The Making of the English Working Class* (Harmondsworth, Middx., Penguin Books, 1968), p. 390.

50 Turner finds valuable proof of this in the account by Lawson (in Davies and Rupp, op. cit., p. 207): 'Busy shop-keepers approved of that part of the Methodist discipline which in the name of God bade them "scorn delights and live laborious days". They had room for regular Sunday service and dutiful family prayers. However, the more ascetic and ecclesiastical discipline of "the morning preaching", the Friday fast, and of having one's heart "searched to the bottom" at the penitential Band was less congenial.' That this was something of which Wesley himself was

aware and disapproved is epitomized in his classic statement: 'For the Methodists in every place grew diligent and frugal; consequently they increase in goods. Hence they proportionately increase in pride, in anger, in the desire of the flesh, the desire of the eyes, and the pride of life. So, although the form of religion remains, the spirit is swiftly vanishing away.' (Southey, *Life of Wesley*, chap. XXXIX, Second American Edition, p. 308.)

51 It is significant that, in making this assertion, Wesley was approaching more the views of the Puritan Baxter who, at the Savoy Conference in 1661, had asked for the 'liberty of primitive times, when . . . no liturgical forms were imposed' or at least for the liberty afforded in the following ages when there were diversities of liturgies. See John T. Wilkinson, *1662 and After. Three Centuries of English Nonconformity* (London, Epworth Press, 1962), pp. 34–5.

52 King in fact defined a Presbyter as 'A person in Holy Orders having thereby an inherent Right to perform the whole office of a Bishop, but being possessed of no Place or Parish, nor actually discharging it, without the permission or consent of the Bishop of a Place or Parish'. (Davies and Rupp, op. cit., p. 69.)

53 Dearing, op. cit., p. 84.

54 Elliott-Binns, op. cit., 1953, p. 208.

55 Quoted by Dearing, op. cit., pp. 31–2.

56 Quoted ibid., p. 62.

57 Quoted ibid., p. 53 (letter of 1748, my emphasis). This is an interesting example of an *ex post facto* legitimation.

58 Quoted by Henri Daniel-Rops, *The Church in the Eighteenth Century*, transl. John Warrington (London, J. M. Dent and Sons, 1964), p. 177.

59 Material in Dearing, op. cit., p. 84.

60 Cragg, op. cit., chap. 10.

61 Daniel-Rops, op. cit., p. 178.

62 Carpenter, op. cit., p. 221. The importance of the Reformation tradition to the later Evangelicals was noted by Walter Farquhar Hook. See W. R. W. Stephens, *The Life and Letters of Walter Farquhar Hook* (London, Richard Bentley and Son, 1878), p. 283.

63 Henry Offley Wakeman, *An Introduction to the History of the Church of England* (London, Rivingtons, 1927), p. 451.

64 Balleine, op. cit., p. 6.

65 Newman, op. cit., 1890, p. 5.

66 A. M. Allchin, *George William Herbert. Some Aspects of his Teaching* (printed at the Convent of the Holy Name, Malvern Link, Worcestershire, n.d.), p. 11. The personnel cited by Allchin are: George William Herbert, founder of the Community of the Mission Sisters of the Holy Name of Jesus, Father R. M. Benson and Father Simeon Wilberforce O'Neill of the Society of St John the Evangelist, and Bishop George Wilkinson, founder of the Community of the Epiphany.

67 Quoted ibid., p. 15.

68 Elliott-Binns, op. cit., 1964, p. 93.

69 A. O. J. Cockshut, *Religious Controversies of the Nineteenth Century* (London, Methuen, 1966), general introduction.

70 ibid., p. 69.

71 Quoted by Owen Chadwick, *The Mind of the Oxford Movement* (London, Adam and Charles Black, 1960), pp. 131–3.

72 ibid., p. 127. J. W. C. Wand, *The Second Reform* (London, Faith Press, 1953), p. 51, says: '[The Tractarians'] . . . whole contention was that they were not introducing anything new but recalling the Church to its historic past. But reform is often most effective when it reminds us of the rock from which we are hewn. In any case a historical religion must always look back to its past. This was true even of the Evangelicals who sought to go back to the Bible and to the Christianity of the first generation. The Tractarians looked mainly to the Patristic period, but they were not afraid to call in also the witness of the Middle Ages.'

73 Again, Keble is a good example in this respect, as Chadwick points out (ibid., p. 39): 'Keble's theory is also, in a manner, preservative—keep the deposit. But it is not only preservative. He has begun to compare the teaching and practice, common or popular in the present Church of England, with the teaching or practice of antiquity, and to find the present Church wanting. Therefore the idea of primitive tradition is not only a preservative idea, but a quest for reform (Newman's "second reformation"), for the restoration of, or re-emphasis upon, those beliefs or practices approved or authorized by antiquity but wanting or fragmentary in the present age.'

74 Quoted in Dearing, op. cit., p. 34.

75 Neill, op. cit., p. 31.

76 E. B. Pusey, *What is Puseyism?* (Pusey House pamphlets).

77 For evidence of this see Geoffrey Faber, *Oxford Apostles* (Harmondsworth, Middlesex, Penguin Books, 1954), p. 245.

78 *Tracts*, I. i, No. 9, 'On Shortening The Church Services', by R. H. Froude, quoted in Dearing, op. cit., p. 34: 'The Services of the Church, as they now stand, are but a very small part of the ancient Christian worship. . . . The Services, as they were left by the Reformers, were, as they had been from the first ages—*Daily* Services; they are now *Weekly* Services. Are they not a fair way to become monthly?'

79 Harold J. Laski, *Studies in the Problem of Sovereignty* (New Haven, Yale University Press, 1917), p. 112.

80 Brilioth, op. cit., 1925, p. 205. Christopher H. Dawson, *The Spirit of the Oxford Movement* (London, Sheed and Ward, 1933), p. 134, makes a similar statement: 'The Oxford Movement . . . brought a new element into the religious life of the 19th century. It stood above all for the preservation of the spiritual identity of Christianity, and represents an attempt to restore the Catholic conception of an objective supernatural order and the Catholic idea of divine authority within the boundaries of the Established Church of Protestant England.'

81 D. H. J. Morgan, 'The social and educational background of Anglican bishops—continuities and changes', *British Journal of Sociology*, vol. XX, no. 3, September 1969, p. 302.

82 Balleine, op. cit., pp. 6–7, says of the 'Holy Club': 'As they read Tertullian, their hearts were enthralled by that ill-fated Church of North Africa with its stern enthusiasm, its austere discipline, its intensely prac-

tical religion, and the ambition seized them to revive those glorious days in England. They began to model their lives strictly on the lines of the African Church.'

83 The term is borrowed from S. M. Eisenstadt but it adequately describes the anti-institutional component of Methodism.

84 Chadwick, op. cit., p. 13: 'It was necessary, politically necessary, that the clergy of the Church of England should look to leaders who would declare that the authority of the Church does not rest upon the authority of the State; that the Church possesses a divine authority whatever the State may do, even if the State should be represented by an indifferent or a prosecuting government; that the authority of the bishop or the vicar rests not upon his national nor his social position, but upon his apostolic commission.'

85 Quoted by Cockshut, op. cit., p. 66. In the same tract the theory of apostolic succession is clearly summarized: 'It is plain then that he [the Bishop] but *transmits*; and that the Christian Ministry is a *succession*. And if we trace back the power of ordination from hand to hand, of course we shall come to the Apostles at last . . . all we, who have been ordained clergy, in the very form of our ordination acknowledged the doctrine of the Apostolical succession.' (ibid., p. 65.) Brilioth (op. cit., 1925) makes some interesting statements about the Tractarian doctrine of apostolic succession: 'One may therefore be fully justified in assuming that it was the pressure of the political situation . . . more than anything else—the necessity of finding a firm and unshakable foundation for a theory of the Church which could defy the assaults of the age, something objective in the deepest sense to put as a breakwater against what was regarded as the inundation of Liberal subjectivism, and also a short watchword as a signal and a standard in the hourly struggle—which made them catch at the principle of Apostolical Succession, sever it from the complex of ideas which gives it its correct import, and give it a formulation, the somewhat violent simplification of which was made possible by the absence of all disposition to a critical view of history.' (p. 183.) Wand (op. cit., p. 59) thinks that the practical result of the doctrine of apostolic succession 'was to hold up before the eyes of all men a vision of the Church as a self-contained unit quite independent of the State, subject in all essential matters to its own laws and jurisdiction'.

86 Cragg, op. cit.

87 Sykes, op. cit., 1934.

88 Quoted in Norman Sykes, *The English Religious Tradition* (London, S.C.M. Press, 1953), p. 87.

6

The Legitimation of Anglican Religious Orders in the Nineteenth Century

HAVING CONSTRUCTED a general model of the religious order, and having suggested a process of change based on the Weberian category of traditional authority which was found to be particularly useful in the analysis of religious organizations (since they often have a well-defined *normative* tradition or, as is the case in the Church of England, the possibility of several traditional models, each of which can be claimed to be legitimate) these constructs will now be applied to the nineteenth-century Church of England in order to test their validity and to interpret sociologically the growth of Anglican religious communities.

Firstly, it will be found useful to outline the main sources of legitimation for these institutions. There exists the basis for such a discussion in the analysis of different schools of 'churchmanship' in the Church of England, and this suggests an analysis of how the different groups interpreted the specific changes with which we are concerned. In the following two chapters the Anglican religious orders will be treated as a particular case within the ideal type, and by using this model it is possible to illuminate some of the special historical features of Anglican orders, as well as their continuities with Roman Catholic orders. Since the feature of religious orders which has had most stress laid upon it is their relationship with the wider church of which they form part, the following chapter will look closely at the problem of the authority nexus between the Anglican orders and the established officials of the church, especially the bishops. It will be argued in the last two chapters that the more explicitly 'theological' reaction to the Anglican religious orders was part of a wider set of social influences. Thus the distinct interpretation of each school of 'churchmanship' was closely aligned with social issues such as the status of women and the most effective way to solve certain social problems. By taking this line of approach it is possible to link the 'superstructure' of legitimations with the 'infrastructure' of nineteenth-century British society.

By way of introducing the various types of legitimation, the next few paragraphs will briefly outline the schools of 'churchmanship' in the Church of England. In the eighteenth century there was a more or less formal distinction between a High Church party, which saw itself as a continuation of the tradition of Laud and the Nonjurors and looked to the church Fathers as the basis of Anglican tradition, a Low Church party which was basically Erastian and looked to the Reformation as the reinstatement of the primitive, New Testament model of Christianity; and there was a Latitudinarian school, whose churchmanship was very much of the liberal, rational brand. By the end of the third decade of the nineteenth century, there had been a change in terminology, as Voll [1] describes. The term 'Low Church' had almost completely dropped out of use and the term 'Evangelical' became practically synonymous with this school. This was in itself an interesting development, because originally the Methodist precursors of the Evangelical movement had been marked by their attempt to revive in the Church of England the pristine purity of the early church. As Hook noted in a letter to T. P. Wood in 1836:

> It is perhaps now peculiarly erroneous, from the fact that those who stirred up the religious feelings in the country about fifty years ago, and their successors the Evangelical party have gone, not to the fountain head, not to the tradition as it was set a-flowing by the Apostles, and jealously watched and guarded by the primitive Church, but merely to the doctors of the Reformation, who, however praiseworthy in the resistance to Popery, were not of course armed at all points, and were better skilled most of them to pull down than to build up. [2]

As in the Low Church school of the eighteenth century, the nineteenth-century Evangelicals tended to regard the Reformation as a reinstatement of the primitive purity of the Gospel and rejected any notion of a church tradition other than this.

The High Church school, which at the beginning of the nineteenth century had been represented by such individuals as Thomas Sikes of Guisborough [3], and which had then been seen in terms of an antithesis between 'High' and 'Dry', had now come to be called the Tractarian party. It was only later that representatives of this school became popularly known as 'Ritualists' or 'Anglo-Catholics'. [4] As was shown in the last chapter, the early Tractarians—for example, Keble and Pusey, and especially Newman—in their emphasis on the church of the Fathers certainly saw themselves as part of a continuing High Church Anglican tradition: Newman 'often spoke of Archbishop Laud as seeing and hearing all that was going on and actually walking about Oxford'. [5]

The liberalism and rationalism of the Latitudinarians were best represented in the nineteenth century by the 'Broad Church' school of men like Coleridge and Arnold. Arnold provides an important insight into the type of legitimation which was most likely to be subscribed to by Broad Churchmen. In the first place, he very much distrusted any theory of the church which relied on the notion of tradition, and his formula of 'scripture plus contemporary expediency' is very clearly expressed in the following quotation, which amply demonstrates his method of applying the organizational claims of the contemporary church to the scriptural blueprint as a means of evaluating the latter:

> The Scripture, then, which is the sole and direct authority for all the truths of the Christian religion, is not, in the same way, an authority for the constitution and rules of the Christian church; that is, it does not furnish direct authority, but guides us only by analogy; or it gives us merely certain main principles, which we must apply to our own various circumstances. [6]

Kenneth Thompson's study of the development of bureaucratic administrative arrangements in the nineteenth and twentieth-century Church of England gives the Broad Church movement a key position in this process, and he notes:

> Liberal or Broad Churchmen were found to have had a primary orientation to the function of adaptation of the church system, and to have had as their major concern the articulation of that system with the larger community. [7]

Thus, to sum up, the three major schools of churchmanship in the nineteenth century may be expressed in a shorthand form as: Low Church—Scripture interpreted in terms of the Reformation church; High Church—Scripture interpreted in terms of the early church; Broad Church—Scripture interpreted in terms of instrumental dictates. Two of these interpretations fit perfectly into the 'mixed' Anglican tradition which has already been elaborated: the third, that of the Broad Church, while deriving its goals from the Scriptures, has elements which are close to Weber's category of rational-legal legitimation. It is therefore plausible to seek evidence of the way in which Anglican orders were 'presented' and accepted or rejected in terms of one of these three sources of authority. In this chapter I will show that sisterhoods were legitimated mainly by reference to the early church, deaconesses by reference to the Scriptural church, brotherhoods by reference to the medieval church, and all three by reference to the pragmatic principles of the Broad Church.

Two terms which will be extensively used in the discussion which follows require a brief definition. The term *deaconess* in the early church 'designated a woman officially charged with certain functions in the Church. The institution, though not the designation, apparently goes back to the Apostolic age'. [8] The office was associated originally with services provided by the church for women, for instance in looking after the female sick and poor, and in being present at interviews between bishops or priests and women, female baptisms and in the part of the church reserved for women. It appears that the 'welfare' and 'chaperone' functions of the deaconess were sometimes extended to include ministerial functions, and this, together with the decline in adult baptism, has been given as a reason for the decline in this office. [9] 'In the Church of England the order is described as "the one existing ordained ministry for women" to which they are "admitted by episcopal imposition of hands" conferring lifelong status.' [10]

The term *sisterhood* (the collective noun is significant, as will emerge in the later discussion) was neatly defined by the Rev. T. T. Carter (founder of the Community of St John the Baptist, Clewer) at the Oxford Church Congress of 1862: 'a sisterhood is a community of women, living a single life, in obedience to a fixed rule, with a common fund, seeking to advance the glory of God by the culture of their spiritual life, in closest union with Christ, and engaged in prayer or in works of mercy'. [11] The other characteristics he cites were at that time a rather more controversial matter of definition: for instance, he spoke of an 'abiding state of life' according to the 'call of God' to the soul (which almost amounts to the statement that sisterhoods require vows and vocation) and of a Superior who administers a rule, and a Spiritual Superior combining the functions of chaplain and warden. But the central features are clearly a stable community of single women living a common life.

THE TRADITIONAL LEGITIMATION OF THE SCRIPTURAL CHURCH: DEACONESSES

For that group of church members which tended to place the emphasis on a traditional conception of the Church of England which rested on the Reformation and the Gospel model, there could be little question about the type of traditional reinstatement in the field of women's role in the church: Low Church Anglicans were convinced that the only institution with the sanction of apostolic tradition was the deaconess.

The first Anglican sisterhood to be founded was the Park Village Sisterhood in 1845, although the real beginning of the Anglican revival of the religious life for women can be dated as Trinity Sunday, 1841, when Marian Rebecca Hughes privately took the three vows of Religion before Dr Pusey. The first group of deaconesses was formed in 1860 by William Pennefather, Vicar of St Jude's, Mildmay Park, and were known as the Mildmay Deaconesses, though as Carpenter points out: 'They were devoted women, but they were not Deaconesses in the historic sense of the term'.[12] The first deaconess in the Church of England was Miss Elizabeth Ferard, who was dedicated to her work by the Broad Church Bishop Tait of London in 1861.

A Convocation of Canterbury Report in 1858 had spoken of deaconesses as one type of women's work in the church, and in the following year a pamphlet was published with the title, *Church Deaconesses. The Revival of the Office of Deaconess Considered; with Practical Suggestions; etc.*, by the Rev. R. J. Hayne [P.H. 9634] in which it was argued that in the primitive church both married women and widows had been admitted to the office of deaconess, which was more flexible than the organization of sisterhoods:

It is true that here and there may be found already a few Sisterhoods established for carrying out many, if not all, of the kinds of work enumerated; and most valuable and devoted are their labours. But these Sisterhoods are generally quite local in their character, intended only to supply the wants of a particular institution or particular parish, and more conventual in their rule and arrangements than appears desirable or possible with the freer and more elastic system of work proposed for the deaconesses. [13]

The institution of Lutheran deaconesses at Kaiserwerth was fairly widely known in the Church of England before this; Florence Nightingale, for instance, had published a pamphlet describing the work of the deaconesses there in 1851. However, Kaiserwerth is best discussed in the context of those legitimations which were concerned with foreign 'competition' in the field of women's work. It is of interest here because in an undated pamphlet, *Some Account of the Deaconess-Work in the Christian Church*, the author, possibly Pastor Fliedner the founder of the Kaiserwerth Deaconesses, was extremely concerned to establish a *Biblical* pedigree for the office. This form of legitimation was precisely the one employed by Low Church protagonists in the Church of England.

Hence the debate between the supporters of sisterhoods on the one hand and deaconesses on the other begins around 1860. Although there are several arguments which appear again and again, some of which will be encountered in later chapters, the argument which appears with the most striking regularity is the one which appeals to the apostolic church as the sole source of authority.

For instance, the Lower House of the Convocation of Canterbury in 1861 debated the motion:

> That this house do agree to present to his Grace the Archbishop and the Upper House a respectful address, praying their Lordships to deliberate and agree on certain rules by which women, whose hearts God has moved to devote themselves exclusively to works of piety and charity, may be associated together on terms and conditions distinctly known as those which the Church of England has sanctioned and prescribed. [14]

This motion was proposed by the Rev. R. Seymour, and as Allchin notes, 'the notion does not refer by name to the sisterhoods, and although the report of the debate is headed "Religious Sisterhoods", the whole question of women's work in the Church is covered in the discussion'. [15] As will be argued later, there were good strategic grounds for appealing for the recognition of sisterhoods on wider grounds than those which were recognized in High Church circles, and Seymour's motion and introductory speech are excellent examples of this. [16]

The Rev. C. E. Kennaway, moving an amendment, said that while he wished the movement success, his impression was that there was not so much opposition as insensibility to the need for sisterhoods, the impression being that there was little call for such institutions. There must be many people present, he argued, who also thought them unnecessary. Admittedly, district visiting was a form of untrained work and nurses needed education but, he asked, was there any indication in Holy Scripture of how this want might be supplied? The answer, he found, was that Holy Scripture sanctioned deaconesses, and he cited various references from the New Testament. But his confusion about the nature of the existing sisterhoods became evident when he went on to advocate the formation of sisterhoods as being in some way synonymous with deaconesses. Although the debate lacked precision (Allchin thinks it had 'a certain unreality' about it [17]) the fact that Kennaway looked solely to Holy Scripture for his source of legitimacy and found mention of the deaconess signalled the start of an extensive controversy.

The issue was taken up again at the Church Congress in Oxford in July 1862, when the two kinds of women's work were more clearly presented. The debate on 'The Employment of Women in Works of Piety and Charity' was opened by the Rev. J. S. Howson, who spoke in favour of deaconesses. Howson became one of the main supporters of deaconesses in preference to sisterhoods, and he was probably expressing the view held by many Low Church and Broad Church clergy when, in his speeches at subsequent Church Congresses and in his published arguments, he regretted the formation of sisterhoods. He was followed at the 1862 Congress by Carter, whose definition of 'sisterhood' has already been quoted.

Howson published a pamphlet in 1862 called simply *Deaconesses* in which he put these arguments at greater length. [18] He made his preference quite clear:

It was a cause of peculiar mortification and disappointment, when the official employment of women in works of charity began to be really put into practice in the Church of England, to see this done in such a way as to deepen every prejudice, and to retard the establishment of a system of female ministration in harmony alike with Primitive times and the feelings and habits of the English people. [19]

In the same pamphlet, Howson admitted that he had not done justice to the sisterhoods who had, he agreed, been the real pioneers in women's church work, but this was because he was badly informed about them, having only visited Carter's sisterhood at Clewer. The rest of the argument is concerned with the relative *instrumental* merits of deaconesses and sisterhoods, but the debate about the traditional source of legitimation is taken up when Howson refers to the deaconess as a 'conspicuous figure' in the Apostolic Church, and he cites the authority of the 'Apostolic Constitutions' for the antiquity of the office. [20] Furthermore, the Acts of the Apostles often mention deaconesses and the Puritans in the Church of England had been the strongest supporters of them.

Also in 1862 there was an attempt to reclaim the term 'sisterhood' for a 'Protestant' usage. [21] Although the pamphlet was concerned not with deaconesses but with 'Bible and Domestic Missions' and had as its main theme the interesting concept of 'class native agency' (one of the variants of 'self help'). the explicitly Protestant critique of the current usage of the term 'sisterhood' and the attempt to redefine the family bond of humanity as the 'genuine institution of sisterhood' suggests that by this time sisterhoods had come to be clearly associated with the Tractarian party in the Church of England and the attempt to 'Protestantize' them further suggests that they had acquired a certain amount of prestige. At any rate, the pamphlet was concerned to indicate the 'conventual' nature of sisterhoods:

> The word Sisterhood has been used in England, hitherto, chiefly in connection with communities of charitable women, having more or less relation to a conventual system and establishment. Now WE WISH TO REDEEM IT to our evidently Protestant purpose, and make it sacred to a yet more intimate co-working in the school of life, than can even be attained during a term of education and training together towards a definite purpose. [22]

In 1866 the topic was again taken up on several occasions. George Cotton, Bishop of Calcutta, in a speech to the Bethune Society on the 5th April traced the systematic employment of

European women back to the Gospel. [23] Cotton traced the office through several centuries of church history, but not in order to demonstrate that the pedigree passed to a different form of developing women's organizations, namely the religious orders, which is the way that Tractarian apologists structured their arguments in favour of sisterhoods, but in order to show that the pristine office of deaconess was swamped by the other organizations:

> ... we find some traces of the office [of deaconess] down to the popedom of Gregory VII in the eleventh [century], when it was probably submerged under the general ascendancy of the monastic orders, both of men and women, bound by strict vows of celibacy; a system which finally triumphed under the unscrupulous administration of that imperious pontiff. We shall hear no more of parochial or congregational deaconesses till comparatively recent times. [24]

We will return to this speech by Cotton later, when we consider the nexus of theological legitimations and social attitudes, because Cotton is a particularly good example of an apologist whose conception of the status and role of women reinforced a fundamental theological position.

The 1866 Church Congress at York debated the subject of 'Female Ministrations', and the Earl of Devon spoke of the ordained female diaconate in the primitive church, the primitive *practical* character of which had degenerated until contemplation took the place of activity. Howson followed him, and explained that he would discuss deaconesses first because that subject was likely to rouse fewer sensibilities, and he expressed strong misgivings about the growth of sisterhoods:

> The first great fact that meets us is the establishment and growth of Sisterhoods in the Church of England. I do not deny that I look on much connected with these Sisterhoods with deep regret and with considerable apprehension. But for good or evil, or for both, Sisterhoods are now a great fact. [25]

He found it impossible to speak of these institutions without respect and admiration, and even if he had wanted to decry them he would have been restrained by 'the death of Dr Neale' (J. M. Neale, the founder of the Society of St Margaret, East Grinstead, in 1855). However, he still found himself able to describe some of his misgivings about sisterhoods in rather more detail. This is reminiscent of the polemical techniques of extreme Protestant controversialists like Hobart Seymour, who would admit that little was known about the interior life of convents and then proceed to engage in highly vivid speculations.

It was also in 1866 that the main participant in the Church Congress debates on the side of the sisterhoods, T. T. Carter, in an essay published in a volume devoted to 'Questions of the Day', dismissed the office of deaconess as a genuine example of the religious life using precisely the same period of church history as had its defenders:

> The earliest records relate to devoted women, and of these there were three classes—Widows, Virgins, and Deaconesses. The Deaconess was rather an office for Church-work than a state of life; and generally the selection was made from among the Widows or Virgins. We may therefore dismiss the idea of the Deaconess from our view. [26]

And in 1869 a pamphlet by J. M. Neale (also a sisterhood protagonist) which traced the development of both deaconesses and Sisters of Mercy in the early church was posthumously published. [27] Neale argued that to be a deaconess or a Sister of Mercy (the two offices he saw as indistinguishable) it was necessary (a) to be a widow; (b) to be at least 60 years of age; (c) to have been a mother; (d) to have been married only once; and (e) to have been always of exemplary character. These provisions he traces to St Paul's letter to Timothy about A.D. 55. Thirty-five years later, he argued, St Ignatius showed that vows of perpetual chastity were becoming more common, though St Paul's rule was so strictly followed that even as late as A.D. 200 Tertullian could state that it was monstrous that an unmarried woman should be ordained deaconess in her youth. It was developments in the organization of the church which were responsible for both the decline in the office of deaconess (for incumbents of that office began abrogating functions which were not originally theirs) and the growth of more contemplative forms of religious life for women, particularly in the fourth century when the church underwent a process of secularization after Constantine's conversion. Thus Neale uses the legitimation of the Gospel church to demonstrate the origin of sisterhoods as well as deaconesses, but it is to the more usual period of church history employed by

Tractarians that he looks for evidence of the decline of deaconesses and the growth of sisterhoods.

Whenever the subject of women's work in the church was discussed in Convocations, Church Congress or publications, much the same arguments were rehearsed. Thus at the Church Congress of 1875, after Carter had again read a paper on sisterhoods, the Rev. Arthur Gore argued that deaconesses were a more authentic 'primitive' revival. In the debate on sisterhoods and deaconesses in the Upper House of the Convocation of Canterbury in 1883, the Bishop of Winchester, while arguing that both types of institution were doing an immensely important job, thought that deaconesses were the most primitive forms of female activity in the church and suggested that the superior organization which was one of the reasons why the church had organized women collectively in sisterhoods might be obtained by having something in the nature of a deaconess home for training. At the 1885 Convocation he again spoke on the subject and made the interesting point that deaconesses were part of the primitive practice of the church but had fallen into abeyance, as had sisterhoods. But since the Reformation had been intended to revive primitive practice it was important to restore the office of deaconess. He quoted the Bishop of Durham's argument that the orders of the church were defective without deaconesses.

Similarly, at the York Convocation of 1884, in the debate on the 'Church Ministry of Women', Canon Trevor made clear the distinction between two possible sources of legitimation when he stated that what was required was a *Scriptural* precedent for the type of women's work, not the precedent of the primitive church. [28]

As late as 1914 very much the same legitimation was put forward by Cecilia Robinson, who acknowledged her debt to Dean Howson and supported deaconesses both on the grounds of their apostolic pedigree and on their survival over a long period of time:

> But grand as has been and is the work of the Sisterhoods, they could not fully meet the needs of the Church. Some other form of service was wanted, corresponding more closely with the parochial system. The Sister acted at the bidding of her Order; she was not under the direct control of the Bishop. Why should there not be other women, equally well disciplined and devoted,

but serving directly under the Clergy; handmaids of the Church, receiving a share in her ministry, ready for service wherever they were needed. Was there not such an order of women—ministers in the Church in Apostolic times, and had it not continued at work during more than half the Christian era? If so, why should not the Church in England return in this as in other matters to primitive usages, and restore an Institution which had proved so valuable in the first centuries? [29]

The reaction to organizational reforms in women's church work among groups which held the Low Church conception of a Reformed Church of England based largely on a Scriptural model was the substitution in place of the recently founded Anglican sisterhoods of the more Scriptural office of deaconess. The most that was accorded the existing sisterhoods was gratitude for the valuable practical work they had done. Apart from this there was regret, misapprehension and disapproval, coupled with the hope that deaconesses might become the principal agents of women's work in the Church of England.

THE TRADITIONAL LEGITIMATION OF THE EARLY CHURCH: SISTERHOODS

One of the most significant features to emerge from the historical material is the tendency of Tractarian apologists for the Anglican sisterhoods, in debates with members of other church parties who accepted a basically Scriptural source of legitimacy, to spend much of their argument in raking over the same ground but arriving at different conclusions. We have already noticed how J. M. Neale placed considerable emphasis on the Scriptural church. But like Neale, the Tractarian apologists broadened their terms of reference to take in the church of the Fathers, which is something the Low Church controversialists did not do. Clearly, maximum support can be gained for particular practices only by appealing to as broad a spectrum of legitimations as possible. [30]

As Brilioth notes [31], the exhaltation of virginity in the early Fathers made a strong impression on Pusey, especially when it was echoed in some of the seventeenth-century Anglican writers like Andrewes, Taylor and Law. Liddon's *Life* describes the importance for Pusey of the Catholic Fathers, especially St Augustine and St Jerome, who laid a very particular stress on the single life for men and women when consecrated to God. There is an interesting comment on the polemical use of church tradition in Liddon's account, for he says of the Fathers' writing on virginity:

> This side of their teaching had been lost sight of by that section of Anglican divines which regarded antiquity not as a guide in faith or morals, but merely as a storehouse of polemical weapons against the Church of Rome. [32]

Mention of Rome brings up the question of where to set limits on the tradition used as a source of legitimacy. The controversy over 'Romanizing' influences in the Anglican sisterhoods will be considered elsewhere, but there is a rather more basic point which can appropriately be considered now. The Church of England's Advisory Council on Religious Communities makes explicit in its *Directory* that a fairly broad basis of traditional legitimacy was sought by the Anglican orders:

> Whether the Community followed an active, contemplative or mixed life, it always envisaged the personal sanctification of its members by perpetual separation from the world under the obligation of the vows of Religion. In the formation and regulation of the various Communities the founders and first members looked to the long tradition and experience of the Western Church for guidance, but they did so in a spirit not of meticulous imitation, but of adaptation. [33]

The question of a Western church tradition was initially a vexed one, because it was bound up with the issue of Roman accretions. This seems to have been in the mind of Walter Farquhar Hook who, as vicar of Leeds, was engaged in a correspondence with Pusey in 1839–40 over the proposal to institute Sisters of Charity in the Church of England. Hook's solution to the problem of appealing to tradition without appearing too Roman was to suggest that Pusey should adopt 'Greek terms and forms rather than Latin ones; as less likely to give unnecessary offence'. And he added: 'Remember you are in advance of the age: deal tenderly with the babes'. [34]

It appears that the first religious sister in the Church of England, which technically speaking was Marian Hughes, also discovered a legitimation of sisterhoods in the Fathers of the church, whose writings she encountered through Newman. In 1840 Marian Hughes read Newman's *Church of the Fathers*:

In the notice of the life of St Demetrias, he [Newman] says, speaking of the requisites for the life and character of a Sister of Mercy: 'There is no reason why the English Church should not, from among its members, supply these requisites.' In her diary she writes, 'From this I resolved to dedicate my life, by God's Grace, and thus to prepare for the Day of Judgement'. [35]

Carter was one of the main legitimators of sisterhoods and, as was noted above, he took as his starting-point the New Testament church. He expressed this in much the sort of formula that has been documented in the present discussion:

> Monasticism, being as old as the New Testament itself, was also necessarily included in the Tractarian recall to the standards of the primitive Church. [36]

But the New Testament was only a point of departure, because when he came to document the evolution of institutions of the sort which were in the process of being revived as Anglican sisterhoods, he quoted extensively from later periods of church history. [37] He dealt with the question of vows in terms of three periods, and he put forward an explicit theory of development. The first period went to A.D. 458, when St Leo decreed that women should not receive the solemn benediction with the veil before the age of forty. The second period stretched from the Rule of St Benedict (A.D. 528) until, but excluding, the establishment of the religious orders of the Middle Ages; the third period was from the latter onward. Carter placed very great emphasis on the earliest period of monastic history, and he came to no definite conclusion about vows, but it is clear that he added church history to Scripture in his search for legitimation. As he stated:

> Before bringing these remarks to a close, it seems necessary to consider a question of practical moment to ourselves, which the conclusions gathered from *Holy Scripture, and the past history of the Church*, may enable us to solve. [38]

This was much the same source of legitimation as that which Carter put forward at the Church Congress of 1862 where he spoke of sisterhoods as traceable from the New Testament *through* the primitive church, and as Allchin notes of his speech on this occasion: 'He traces the origins of the institution to the New Testament and the Early Church.' [39]

A reviewer of the pamphlets by Cotton (which has already been mentioned) and Jameson (cited later) added the earliest ages of the church to the New Testament in his legitimation of contemporary sisterhoods:

> Surely then, this fact is an answer to the question, Can Sisterhoods exist in the Church of England in the present day? The Church of England is strictly Apostolic in constitution, and professes to be regulated on the model of the New Testament and of the earliest ages; and if Sisterhoods existed then, they can surely do so now, without there being the slightest necessity to alter the Church's framework and organization. [40]

One of the difficulties in interpreting such material is to know what the author understands by 'the early church': attention has already been given to the problem of different definitions of the early church by various Anglican divines. But one of the clearest claims to legitimacy resting on the church of the Fathers is that of Neale, who vividly describes the period when the growth of the first convents can be seen:

> I must take you back to the fourth century: when, though Martyrdom from the hands of the heathen was over, many and many a family must have had its father or grandfather among the martyrs: when men still lived, who bore about them the glorious scars of their profession, an eye torn out, an arm or leg lost; when together with the world entering, as it were, into the Church, laxity, and coldness, and negligence were beginning to enter too. There were great Saints in those days: there were men who had the every-day gift of miracles: there were Doctors whose words will be the comfort of the Church to the end of time. And let us see what the daughters of the Church were doing then. [41]

It is also interesting to note the source of legitimacy employed by those supporters of sisterhoods under attack who published sermons and pamphlets. For example, the Rev. John Martin preached a sermon in 1849 (published as a pamphlet the same year [P.H. 6245]) in which he defended Priscilla Sellon's sisterhood at Devonport, which was then under determined attack from supporters of a more 'Protestant' Church of England. A more recent account notes the basic contention of Martin's pamphlet:

He insisted that while we do not love the errors of medieval Christianity, as little do we love the corruptions of the last three centuries. But we do love the Catholic doctrines and pious practices of more primitive ages. [42]

This mention of medieval Christianity calls for a brief treatment of the Middle Ages as a period of church history on which legitimacy could be claimed. I think the evidence shows that, apart from the occasional eccentric or Romantic, the Middle Ages was much less important for the revival of religious communities in the Church of England than is sometimes supposed.

THE TRADITIONAL LEGITIMATION OF THE MEDIEVAL CHURCH: FRIARS AND ROMANTICS

Although there was a group within the Oxford Movement which saw 'the Middle Ages by moonlight', these tended to be minor figures and to be on the fringe of the movement. Certainly, as far as the public and 'official' utterances of those members of the Oxford Movement who were involved in the founding or legitimation of Anglican religious communities are concerned, the medieval church figures very little, and then only marginally.

Allchin reviews the influences on the Oxford Movement in terms of three periods of Catholic history:

There is first the example of monasticism in the patristic period, an influence of particular importance in the case of Pusey. There is secondly the example of medieval monasticism. The Tractarians, in their desire to assert the continuity of the post-Reformation Church of England with the medieval Church, possibly overestimated this debt. Certainly contemporary public opinion, shaped by Gothic and Romantic novels, always tended to think of Sisters in medieval terms. This was, from the point of view of accuracy and understanding, unfortunate; for the medieval Church had not used active orders of women, and the fascination which things medieval held for the early Victorians tended to disguise from the public the third and most direct source of the Sisterhoods' inspiration, the active orders founded in seventeenth-century France. [43]

Allchin goes on to link two more influences with the rise of the Oxford Movement. The first was the Romantic movement, particularly as represented in literature and architecture, which can be seen as a forerunner to the Oxford Movement. The poet Wordsworth had great influence on the Tractarians—especially on Keble, whose *Christian Year* has often been compared to the poet's work—and it was Wordsworth who wrote a sonnet to Miss Sellon when she was under attack from Protestant critics in 1849. Scott too gave the Middle Ages enormous popularity and his theology, if such it can be called, was commended as 'Catholic' by Keble himself. Another author made the comment:

> Sir Walter Scott was the first *historical* novelist that England produced. Whether he gave a reliable picture of social life in the Middle Ages may be doubted. [44]

In this connection it must be pointed out that in any 'revolution by tradition' the type of 'history' which is socially significant is the past which people create for themselves, rather than any objective chronicle of documented facts. The second major influence was the taste for Gothic architecture, and J. M. Neale (the founder of a sisterhood) was co-founder of the Cambridge Camden Society in 1839, with the goal of studying, cataloguing and restoring old buildings. Thus there was a convergence of popular attitudes around a medieval-Romantic-Gothic nexus, and this to some extent influenced the Anglican religious orders. It will be necessary later to consider the Romantic influence, but in the present context, where concern is specifically with the traditional sources of legitimation, it is important to note that the medieval church was very little used. Apart from the occasional eccentric like Father Ignatius of Llanthony there was little *explicit* concern with the medieval period.

One of the earliest and most direct references to medieval precedent is that of Sabine Baring-Gould in his essay 'On the Revival of Religious Confraternities' published in 1866. In a discussion which concentrates—as did all discussions on brotherhoods—on the state of large towns and the difficulties facing the Anglican clergy, especially when compared with the apparent success in such areas of the Dissenters, Baring-Gould made a strong plea for the recognition of precedent, and more specifically medieval precedent:

> We are wedded to precedent. Let us look to the precedent of the Middle Ages. Then, as now, the offices of the Church were not 'understood of the people'. Then, as now, there was

inefficiency among the parochial clergy. Then, as now, there were multitudes who would not come to church, so that the only chance for them was that the church should go to them. Then, as now, there was a dearth of educated clergy. And how did the church meet the difficulty? She founded Religious Orders. She gathered together under one roof men of all ranks and grades, and trained them in self-denial, in self-control, in the art of winning souls, in the art of preaching. Having educated them, she sent them forth through the length and breadth of the land, to occupy the pulpits of the parish churches, or to stand up on the wayside hedge, or on the steps of the market cross, and appeal to those who would not come to the House of GOD to hear. Was there a savour of heresy in the wind? North and south, east and west, flew these bare-footed, serge-frocked champions of orthodoxy, and in rude language, with argument telling home and forcible, they taught the people the right, and prepared them to combat the wrong. [45]

This appeal to the parallel of the medieval and nineteenth-century churches and to the precedent of the friars is a remarkably un-diluted one, and there are few comparable examples. It was much more common to subordinate the medieval referent to some other type of legitimation, for instance a rational-legal one, and in this way to deflect from a source of legitimacy that had very little support in the Church of England as a whole. Thus when the Report of both Houses of the Convocation of Canterbury on 'Organizations to reach classes now outside Religious Ministrations' was presented in 1889, and the arguments for and against brotherhoods were rehearsed, the medieval precedent was admitted to the discussion only insofar as it suggested a *useful* method of solving the problem. It was acknowledged that some might consider the plan to establish brotherhoods as being based on purely medieval precedents, but while it would be foolish to ignore the warnings of past experience, it would be equally foolish to refuse to use methods which, though they might be dangerous when they were abused, might also, if they were properly supervised, prove invaluable. Nor was this qualified attitude to the Middle Ages only found in Convocation debates, which might be expected to proceed on a more 'middle of the road' basis, for even a Tractarian biographer like Maria Trench found it necessary to draw on other than medieval comparisons when describing Ascot Priory:

There is a kind of medieval atmosphere about the whole thing (though combined with all modern comforts for the sick and weak)—a sort of aloofness from everything save love, and humility, and sweet indulgent tolerance for all, which I have never seen elsewhere in this world. [46]

It is this qualified medievalism—it might almost be epitomized as 'the Middle Ages with all mod. cons.'—which is most frequently encountered. There are more uncompromising representatives of this outlook, however, and none is more fascinating that Father Ignatius.

Father Ignatius reveals a curious mixture of characteristics: in part Evangelical Bible-wielder, in part faith-healer and in part the archetypal Gothic Romantic. It is quite apparent, however, that from a very early point in his career he was attracted by the example of the medieval church, and used it extensively as an organizational model. In an early pamphlet, published in 1863, the year the Benedictine brotherhood was founded, there was a reference to pre-Reformation monasticism when an appeal was made to the immense value of 'the mighty trumpet-voice of convent prayer rising from a thousand monks at Tintern on the smiling Wye, or echoing loud and deep from the mountain ravines in the stern Celtic wilds'. [47] It is worth noting that an appeal is also made in the same pamphlet to the Gospels and to the example of the primitive church. As a particularly good example of Ignatius's style, we might quote Attwater, who says of the eccentric monk:

He once wrote: 'We don't want any more namby-pamby, nineteenth-century-hearted men; we want only downright, brave, faithful, medieval-souled Welshmen and Englishmen, who can "leave all" and "give all" to "Jesus only".' [48]

It is notable from the examples picked that the medieval appeal was mainly concerned with brotherhoods. There are good reasons for this. Since woman's communities in the Middle Ages were for the most part enclosed, contemplative and 'conventual', and since these were precisely the accusations that Protestants and ultra-Protestants were levelling against the contemporary active sisterhoods (together with a great deal of innuendo and sensational reporting of numerous 'escapes') there was little to be gained in the case of women's communities by looking for a medieval precedent.

THE TRADITIONAL LEGITIMATION OF THE REFORMATION AND POST-REFORMATION CHURCH OF ENGLAND: THE REFORMERS; NICHOLAS FERRAR; SCHEMES AND PIOUS HOPES

It has been shown that there were a number of traditional referents which could be used to legitimate the introduction of deaconesses, sisterhoods and brotherhoods into the Church of England. The comparison between a distant, highly valued past and what can be seen as a decadent present is a potent source of leverage which has been typified as a 'revolution by tradition'. However, a most important basis of claims to traditional legitimacy lies in their ability to show *continuity* with a highly valued past, and such continuity will often be expressed in the form of a pedigree. For the majority tradition in the Church of England the Reformation represented a decisive break with previous tradition, and thus any claim to a Reformation and post-Reformation pedigree which the supporters of the newly formed religious orders were able to make—even if it was a fairly tenuous one—was highly significant. In this section I will show how the existence of a fairly weak but nevertheless identifiable pedigree provided the basis for nineteenth-century claims to continuity.

As we have seen, Low Church Anglicans who were most committed to the Reformation church were least likely to favour the new sisterhoods. In a similar way, Tractarians who were most in favour of the new sisterhoods and brotherhoods were also inclined to devalue the work of the Reformers: Froude grew to 'hate' them, and Littledale, in his paper on *Innovations* cast them in a very unfavourable light. [49] Biot has shown how the attitude of Luther and Calvin towards the dual standard and towards vows led to the elimination of the religious life in Continental Protestant churches during the sixteenth century, though significantly he excludes the Church of England from his terms of reference because it is not 'Protestant' in the strict sense of the word. [50] However, as was demonstrated in the 'mixed' tradition in the eighteenth-century Church of England, the Low Church party tended to view their church as a 'Protestant' body, sharing its identity and pedigree with Continental Lutheran and Calvinist bodies: this outlook will shortly be used to explain why the nineteenth-century Low Church Evangelicals were particularly keen to follow these Continental bodies by reviving the office of deaconess. But given that there was a party in the Church of England which placed such importance on the Reformation, this helps to explain why legitimators of sisterhoods sometimes tried to obtain maximum consensus for their appeals by including the Reformation church in them.

Of course, they were helped in this by the Book of Common Prayer, which often provided a common battleground in inter-Anglican disputes. While its provisions were accepted by the Evangelicals, they were also appealed to by Tractarians wishing to justify their more 'sacramental' view of the church. The most notable example of the latter is Newman's Tract 90, which tried to reconcile the doctrine contained in the 39 Articles of the Book of Common Prayer *not* with the doctrines of the primitive church but with those of the post-Tridentine Roman Catholic Church.[51] Thus it is not surprising to find reference being made back to the Prayer Book as a source of shared legitimation. Carter provides a useful example of this process, for in an essay on vows, he notes:

> Our Church Prayer Book recognizes this state as a distinct vocation and an abiding work of grace [speaking of celibacy], when in the exhortation at the commencement of the marriage service, it speaks of matrimony being ordained, 'that such persons as have not the gift of continency might marry, and keep themselves undefiled members of CHRIST'S BODY'. [52]

In his account of a visit to 'Brother Ignatius' (as he then styled himself) at Claydon, Charles Walker also made use of a Reformation precedent when he noted that Ridley had bemoaned the wholesale destruction of the monasteries, since these institutions were part of the primitive form of Christianity which he and the other Reformers were trying to reintroduce. Walker then went on to trace the line of Anglican theologians who had kept alive the ideal of the religious life in the post-Reformation Church of England. Very much the same argument was advanced four years later at the Church Congress of 1868, when Mr T. Gambier Parry, speaking on 'Authorized and Systematic Lay Agency, Male and Female' recalled that Latimer had protested against the dissolution of the monasteries and had wanted to retain at least two or three in each county as centres for learning, piety and charity. Like Walker, he traced the post-Reformation proponents of the Religious Life in the Church of England.

On the whole, the Reformation itself was not a very fruitful source of legitimation for the nineteenth-century communities. Some writers dismiss the Reformers altogether; for example, Harrison writes:

> The Reformers looked upon the Religious Life as at best, slavery; at worst, iniquity; and in either case, as subjection to popery. [53]

On the other hand, it is surprising how rarely a thorough-going 'Reformation Protestant' critique was made in official debates on sisterhoods and brotherhoods. It is true that the controversialists and pamphleteers of the nineteenth century had been citing the Reformation as the basis of their condemnation right from the start of the revival, with grotesque and sometimes thinly disguised sexual innuendo in the case of what T. Jay Williams calls 'the Protestant underworld' [54], but the Reformation argument never seemed to percolate through to Convocation debates in the nineteenth century. One frequently encounters an implied reference to the notion of 'conventual imprisonment', which the 'Reformation Protestant' press was so assiduously propagating, but it was not really until 1932 that a solid Reformation condemnation was made in Convocation, and then it emerged in the form of a very outspoken attack by the Bishop of Exeter. Although it comes strictly speaking outside the period of our study, it is worth looking at as indicating some of the 'unspoken' fears behind the nineteenth-century debates, without which the latter cannot properly be understood.

The occasion for the Bishop of Exeter's speech was the debate in the Upper House of the Canterbury Convocation on 1st June 1932, on the motion 'That this House receives the Draft Scheme for the Advisory Council on the Relations of Bishops and Communities, with the Regulations; and approves it; and invites the concurrence of the Lower House'. The Scheme was introduced by the Bishop of Truro, [55] and then the Bishop of Exeter opposed the establishment of an Advisory Council on the grounds that, for the first time since the Reformation, Convocation would be approving something which it had formerly condemned, and thus the policy of the Reformation would be formally reversed. The account of his speech continues:

> If they were going only to say that they approved of bodies of Christian men or Christian women living together under a

Rule, few indeed would be inclined to oppose or criticize; but they were doing far more than that. They were recognizing that which had proved, and would prove again, the source of very serious scandals, namely what were called 'permanent vows'. They were definitely recognizing that it was right for men and women to declare that they would continue to maintain throughout their whole life one or all of these three vows, namely, absolute obedience to the Superior of their monastery; that they would never marry; that they would never hold property, and surrender what they had—the vows of obedience, chastity and poverty. [56]

The bishop then went on to give an account of the evils of the religious life which was in every respect comparable to the type of ultra-Protestant pamphlets published by groups like the Protestant Alliance and the Protestant Truth Society. He gave a description of a girl of eighteen committing herself to the religious life and then later experiencing a terrible revulsion towards it: as a result she became a prisoner, he argued. And the history of monasteries was in his opinion even worse—a long record of sexual abnormalities developed by men who were almost maddened by segregation. Why was it, he asked, that in every country people loathed and hated the religious orders?

Thus, while the Reformation was of very limited use for the positive legitimation of religious communities, in the official debates on the subject it was not often drawn in on the side of the opponents of these communities: not explicitly, that is, although the sheer volume of pamphlets published from a 'Reformation Protestant' standpoint [57] must have underpinned the doubts and forebodings of those who saw the communities as an alien import.

The post-Reformation Church of England was a rather more fruitful area for the legitimation of the Anglican orders, because if it could be shown that they were in no way an innovation on the basis of Roman contemporary counterparts, but merely the continuing expression of a goal which had always existed in the Church of England, they were much more likely to gain widespread approval. There were, for example, a number of powerful individuals in the Church of England who still held to the more traditional 'High' conception of the church and found some of the Tractarian 'innovations' uncongenial, if not openly disloyal.

Among these conditional supporters of sisterhoods was Bishop Wilberforce of Oxford, and in a letter of 1854 he made it plain that the sort of legitimation he was prepared to accept must conform to the post-Reformation Anglican precedent which was laid down by divines who are normally associated with the 'High' School. He thinks there are three models on which a sisterhood like that at Clewer might be based: there is firstly the scheme which would be favoured by 'Romanizers', or those who wished to bring the arrangements of one Church of England as closely into line with those of the Roman Catholic Church as possible; secondly, there is the scheme of those who, while not being quite as attracted to Rome, would nevertheless like to see the Reformation revised; but:

> There is, III, the scheme of those who believe firmly and honestly that the system of the Reformed Church of England, as they find it in Bishop Andrewes, Rd. Hooker, and many more of like views with them, is the right system, is the Catholic system; who desire to bring out into life and reality and action its principles and powers, and to abide by it when so administered, and not to develop anything different from itself. Now, it is on this third scheme, honestly, heartily and completely adopted and maintained that I can, and on this alone that I can, have any share in organizing and promoting sisterhoods. [58]

Thus it was to make explicit the absence of any innovation in terms of the Church of England's organization that those who sought to legitimate the apparently 'new' communities looked to the post-Reformation church. They apparently had a good selection of schemes, attempts and pious hopes to choose from. Looking first at the three major historians of the movement, Cameron spends two or three pages on 'First Expressions in England Since the Reformation for the Need of Devoted Women', being mainly concerned with the seventeenth and early eighteenth centuries. [59] Allchin's first chapter 'From the Reformation to 1800' deals, in twenty-one pages of considerable detail, with the attitude of the Reformers and of subsequent Anglican theologians, as well as with particular proposals and schemes. [60] Anson's twenty-five-page introduction on 'The Call of the Cloister in the Seventeenth and Eighteenth Centuries' covers much the same ground but deals additionally with works of fiction which treated the subject. [61] What these histories show is the wide range of choice available to anyone looking for post-Reformation precedents in the Church of England. What is important here is the extent to which these precedents were used in the nineteenth century.

Newman certainly used the post-Reformation divines. As early as 1838, he quoted Bramhall, the seventeenth-century Archbishop of Armagh, who had spoken favourably of monasticism as being consistent with Reformed devotion. It is interesting that the quotation from Bramhall which Newman made use of in his public letter to the Margaret Professor of Divinity was very substantially hedged around with qualifications:

> The Irish Archbishop thought that: 'So as monasteries were restrained in their number and in their revenue, so as the monks were restrained from meddling between the Pastor and his flock ... so as the abler sort, when not taken up with higher studies and weightier employments, were inured to bestow their spare hours from their devotions in some profitable labour for the public good, that idleness might be stripped of the cloak of contemplative devotion, so as the vow of celibacy were reduced to the form of our English Universities, so long unmarried ... so as their blind obedience were more enlightened and secured by some certain rules and bounds ... and lastly so as all opinion of satisfaction and supererogation were removed, I do not see why Monasteries might not agree well enough with reformed devotion.' [62]

Despite his conditional acceptance of the principle of monasteries within the Church of England, Bramhall certainly believed that the dissolution was a mistake, and he wittily indicated this: ' ... We fear that covetousness had a great oar in the boat, and that sundry of the principal actors had a greater aim at the *goods* of the Church, than at the *good* of the Church ...' [63]

Pusey too found substantial support for the revival of the religious life in the post-Reformation divines, and Liddon, after mentioning the influence of the Catholic Fathers on Pusey, goes on to list the 'nobler minds in the English Church' who had never forgotten the importance of early Christian belief. Hooker, though married, had argued that a single life was 'more angelical and divine'; Bishop Andrewes was thankful for 'the Virgins, flowers of purity, celestial gems, brides of the Immaculate Lamb'; Bishop Montague distinguished between counsels and precepts; Laud had pointed out that in ecclesiastical promotions he preferred the single rather than the married man; Jeremy Taylor had called the voluntary celibate life 'the life of angels'; Thorndike thought the monastic life should be present in the Church of England and was a more perfect form of Christian life; Nicholas Ferrar (who will shortly be considered separately) and William Law were also good examples of the Anglican post-Reformation pedigree. [64]

Carter also found evidence for a continuing tradition, and he cited Andrewes and Ferrar as representative of it. He also found evidence in a work of 1698 by Sir George Wheeler called *The Protestant Monastery*. While recommending religious communities, especially of women, Wheeler thought that under existing circumstances there was little hope of this, and that private family piety was the only way to keep the monastic ideal alive. Carter quoted a passage which looked to a future time when it would be possible to reintroduce monastic communities:

> Yet, considering the great decay of Christian piety, and especially of devotion in this age, there seems to be but small hopes that anything of this nature [convents for single women] shall be brought to pass. Therefore, till it shall please God to send such unprejudiced times as may bring such commendable works to perfection, the pious conduct of private families shall be the monasteries that I shall most earnestly commend to all devout masters of them. [65]

J. M. Neale's novel *Ayton Priory or The Restored Monastery*, which was published in 1843, was a very early attempt to put before a popular audience the arguments in favour of a restoration of the religious life. He was distinctly pessimistic about the effectiveness of citing post-Reformation divines in claims to legitimacy, in view of the widespread prejudice against religious communities on the grounds that they were 'Roman':

> ... though we may bring forward passages, in which Divines of all classes, in our own church, have spoken of their [religious communities'] re-introduction as a desirable thing, from Bramhall and Thorndike down to Latimer and Burnet, the prejudice against them will be as obstinate, the outcry as clamourous as ever. [66]

Shortly after this, in 1845, a book by Samuel Fox, *Monks and Monasteries: Being an Account of English Monachism*, [67] presented several arguments in favour of reviving monastic institutions in the Church of England, one of which was attributed by Arch-bishop Leighton of Glasgow (1611–84). The form of the argu-ment will be dealt with at greater length in the next chapter, but it is important here to note that in Fox's book the argument is strengthened by attributing it to a post-Reformation church digni-tary. The argument simply says that it is essential to have monas-teries in the Church of England so that 'earnest men' will not be tempted to join another church, and Leighton regretted the fact that at the time of the Reformation the monasteries were abolished rather than being reformed. [68] One might rather crudely para-phrase this argument as, 'If we don't make provision, Rome will'.

Ferrar is a most important part of the revival of religious com-munities in the nineteenth-century Church of England, and his name continually reappears in several different contexts. One reason for his significance must undoubtedly lie in the fact that he founded a community of some thirty persons which continued in existence for twenty years (1626–46): most of the other names on the pre-Reformation pedigree had put forward schemes or pious hopes. [69] Also, he had come under attack from the Puritans in a pamphlet of 1646 called *The Arminian Nunnery* [70] and in the same year a Puritan raid brought the community to an end. This could not fail to strike the nineteenth-century revivers of the religious life as a similar situation to that of their own day, when the Evangelical and ultra-Protestant pamphleteers were very much on the offensive. The press and pamphlet attacks on the Devonport Sisterhood and the Lewes riot of 1857 involving J. M. Neale and the Society of St Margaret were motivated by much the same popular fear of popery as that which led to the destruction of Ferrar's community. Indeed, Carter makes use of a background of popular feeling against popery to suggest the extent to which Ferrar was a pioneer:

> ... the hatred and terror of Popery was still so great that few ventured openly to propose the foundation of a Religious Order, but their minds dwelt on the subject, and here or there, singly or in little groups, they strove after some fashion to live the life. [71]

The extent of the interest in Ferrar can be gauged by looking at the amount of literature published about him. In 1790 there was published a life of Ferrar by Peckard; another life was published in Bristol in 1829 and went through two editions; in 1837 another biography was published by Nisbet, the author's name being given as Macdonogh and the text being based on an unpublished life by Bishop Turner; in 1852 Masters published an abridgement of Peckard's earlier work; and in 1855 *Two Lives of Ferrar* was published by Mayor. In 1880, the publication of *John Inglesant* by J. H. Shorthouse, in which a few pages were devoted to a description of Ferrar's community at Little Gidding, brought the topic to a wider public. It was through reading Shorthouse's novel that Robert Hugh Benson, the son of E. W. Benson, Archbishop of Canterbury, onetime resident with the Community of the Resurrection (though never professed) and eventually a Roman Catholic convert and apologist, formed the idea of reviving the Little Gidding Community. In August 1897 he engaged in correspondence with the Rev. J. H. Molesworth about reviving Little Gidding, which Molesworth had just visited. The publication in 1892 of Carter's volume of essays on Ferrar by different writers is further evidence of the popularity of this example of seventeenth-century English piety at its high-water mark, which is how the Little Gidding Community has been widely interpreted.

The number of publications about, and references to, Nicholas Ferrar mark him out as a very strong focal point within the seventeenth-century Church of England for claims to Anglican precedent in the revival of religious orders. There is even one example of a descendant of Ferrar being personally involved in the founding of a new religious community in the nineteenth century—this is Henry Ernest Hardy, 'Father Andrew', one of the revivers of the Franciscan life and co-founder of the Society of the Divine Compassion in 1894. In her biography, Burne notes his distant 'High Church' ancestry and his immediate Evangelical parentage:

> Grace Maxwell Aiken, his ['Father Andrew's'] mother, was a descendant of Susannah, the sister of Nicholas Ferrar of Little Gidding. This descent from the Ferrars, who made the experiment of a revival of the religious life as a family group in the seventeenth century, may have played some part in the formation of the character of one who has been described as the greatest mystic in the Church of England of his time. The strong Evangelical piety of his parents must also have impressed itself upon his sensitive mind. [72]

To summarize the above section, the Tractarian legitimators of religious communities were not only able to appeal to primitive church tradition but to a tradition in the post-Reformation Church of England which had been a 'bearer' of the more pristine tradition: and not only had this High Church party maintained the ideal of religious orders *in abstracto*, but it had occasionally given rise to schemes, proposals, and in the case of Little Gidding to a stable community which had lasted for twenty years. Hence the importance of the latter for the nineteenth century.

RATIONAL-LEGAL LEGITIMATIONS AND 'MERE MECHANICAL ADMINISTRATION'

The quotation in this heading comes from an undated pamphlet *On Guilds, or Brotherhoods, as Supplying the Discipline of the Church* in which the author, William J. Irons, remarks: 'Wise spiritual rulers will certainly grow to feel among us, that the Church, as a community of souls, will not bear, what Christ never gave, a mere mechanical administration.' [73] This statement, as well as coinciding with the rather facile conclusion of Rudge that the New Testament does not sanction bureaucracy, [74] does provide a useful counterweight to the impression which is often conveyed by nineteenth-century Anglican writing, especially of the Broad Church school, that the church is best viewed as a business enterprise to be managed on criteria of efficiency and instrumentality. This pervasive image of the church is very evident in the legitimation of religious communities. Under the heading of rational-legal legitimations we will consider the extent to which administrative convenience could be used as a 'rationale' when the personnel belonging to the communities were themselves often indifferent to it.

There is an interesting contrast in the way religious communities originated in the early Western Church, that is, male contemplative groups, and the form the revival took in the nineteenth-century Church of England, where female active orders were the first products of the movement. At a very early stage in the growth of sisterhoods, however, a process of development was envisaged by the founders of sisterhoods—for instance Butler and Carter—which suggested that a growth in contemplative life would follow later. The argument was often put in the form of 'Martha's work before Mary's'. The place of the religious orders in the overall network of nineteenth-century charitable work is best treated separately, but we may readily distinguish legitimations based on instrumental interpretations of their role within the church and within society at large.

It is worth noting the wide measure of agreement which exists on the fact that the early sisterhoods were to a considerable extent responses to practical social needs. Allchin considers that 'after the call of God, which is the central factor in the revival of the communities, perhaps the most important impulse was given by the practical, social needs of the time. The communities must be seen as a part of the Church's attempt to adapt herself to a rapidly changing society'. [75] Cary also puts an interesting sociological interpretation on the revival:

> In most cases the realization of grave social and spiritual needs both created the demand and evoked the spiritual response. At the same time it should be recognized that the great secular events of the period were already beginning to set women free from the social restrictions that had debarred them from such activities in the past. [76]

Anson thinks that the realization of social problems together with the growing freedom of women were major factors in the growth of sisterhood [77], and he firmly suggests that the instrumental aspects of the sisterhoods was the only one to be recognized by the bishops of the Church of England: 'They [the bishops] regarded "Sisters" as being a class of unmarried women who lived together for the sake of devoting themselves to charitable work. The common life was a means towards carrying out a useful work; not an end in itself.' [78] It might therefore be expected that appeals to authority in the Church of England would be based on, or have a significant component of rational-legal legitimation.

And this is in fact the case. From the start, the movement was characterized by the instrumental orientation of its schemes. A pamphlet by the Rev. Alexander Dallas in 1826 which took the form of an open letter to the Bishop of London advocated the formation of 'Protestant Sisters of Charity' with the express purpose of improving medical care for the sick poor. Dallas described the Sisters of Charity in France and pointed out that since they went unmolested at the time of the French Revolution, they must have had a great deal of popular support. As well as providing a trained body of what amounted to district nurses, the sisterhood would also provide an occupation for women who might other-wise sink into poverty, for example the widows of clergy and tradesmen who were without independent support: indeed, no person should be allowed to enter the sisterhood whose income exceeded £100 a year. His biographer thinks the pamphlet 'contained very important suggestions at that time, and was widely circulated. It resulted in much interesting communication with Miss Fry, and in the plan being taken up by her, and ulti-mately carried out in the valuable nursing establishment in Devonshire Square, London...' [79] 'Miss Fry's establishment' was not opened until 1840, and there is the evidence of the further appeal by Robert Southey three years later to show that the Dallas pamphlet had little immediate effect.

Southey's appeal was made in his book *Sir Thomas More: or, Colloquies on the Progress and Prospects of Society*, and it was based on considerably more wide-ranging criteria than the single one of utility. In the first place, religious orders are seen as being a par-ticularly useful device for retaining *virtuosi* within a church, and this becomes an ingenious argument in favour of Anglican-Methodist unity:

> ... it is possible at this time, not indeed to bring the Methodists back to the Establishment from which they have erred and strayed, but to employ Methodism in aid of the Establishment, and embody as Church-Methodists those who would otherwise be drawn in to join one or other of the numerous squadrons of dissent...
>
> In this way ... they might be to the Church of England what its various fraternities are to the Church of Rome. [80]

Southey's appeal—'why then have you no Beguines, no Sisters of Charity?'—has been frequently quoted, and it illuminates an interesting aspect of the nineteenth-century awareness of foreign competition, but it is of note that Southey was concerned very explicitly with orders of women engaged in *practical* works of charity and piety. Otherwise, he shares the prejudice of every Protestant-minded Englishman of his day in thinking of *nunneries* as prisons:

> Nunneries are useful as Bedlams, which crazy women choose for themselves; but they are not Bedlams; they are Prisons; and it is not necessary that women should possess exhalted senti-ments, for them to be very miserable in confinement. [81]

Southey quoted the Dallas pamphlet and letters in *Blackwood's Magazine* and the *London Medical Gazette*, together with a letter from 'a country surgeon' which pessimistically suggested that the only people likely to be influenced by a proposal to introduce Sisters of Charity were the Church Methodists and the Society of Friends.

Although proposals were being exchanged in private correspondence, the only other pamphlet putting forward a public proposal for sisterhoods before the founding of the Park Village Sisterhood in 1845, with the exception of Neale's arguments in *Ayton Priory*, is the one by the Rev. Diedrich Wackerbarth: *The Revival of Monastic Institutions and their bearing upon Society considered with reference to the present condition of the Anglican Church.* [82] Wackerbarth pointed out that the parochial system was inadequate for the needs of church members, and went on to reiterate an argument first advanced by Leighton, that some institutional provision was necessary for the most 'ardent spirits' to prevent them becoming dissenters. One reason why the dissenters were so strong in large towns was that the Church of England's parochial system was weakest there, and colleges of unmarried priests would be of great assistance. Similarly, the system of religious education would be improved if priests with no parochial responsibilities could work in it. Such a body of unmarried clergy would more readily gain the affection of the working class and thus act as a greater moral influence on them than the overburdened parochial clergy. Wackerbarth concentrated especially on the religious claims for a revival of monastic institutions, but he was aware that the claim of work among the poor was a powerful one:

> [The author] is persuaded that the claims of Monachism might be powerfully urged on very various grounds, totally untouched by him, and perhaps on none more reasonably than on that of its high utility to the poorer classes of the community. [83]

If one looks at the list of reasons which Neale gives for the revival of monasteries in *Ayton Priory* (1843) they have a markedly instrumental tone to them. The reasons are: (1) monasteries would aid the missionary work of the Church in rural and industrial parishes; (2) they would be houses of learning; (3) they would provide the benefits of intercession; [84] (4) monastic houses could be used as asylums for orphaned clergy daughters, aged priests, and for retreats. [85] Neale provides an important example of instrumental legitimation because, since he was an accomplished ecclesiastical scholar, he could presumably have chosen to legitimate monastic institutions by reference to church history, which of course he did do to a certain extent. But the fact that the book as a whole was so clearly weighted in the direction of more practical problems (thus treating monasteries as means to ends which are defined pragmatically) shows the very strong pull of popular opinion towards a *practical* rather than a theologically defined role for the new religious communities. J. M. Neale's writing reveals the sort of compromise reached when it was necessary for a claim to legitimacy to be directed at a wide audience in an attempt to gain broad support.

There was a similar concern for the solution of practical problems among the founders of the first Anglican sisterhood at Park Village West in 1845. As Carpenter notes:

> A committee of influential laymen, including T. D. Acland, Lord Lyttelton, Lord Camden, Lord Clive, Lord John Manners, W. E. Gladstone and A. J. B. Hope, supported the project and in a sense were the initiators of it, but most of them were thinking more of the pastoral and nursing work which the Sisters would accomplish for the poor than of the devotional life which they would live. [86]

This emerges very clearly in the account of the initiation of the community given by Liddon, who shows how Pusey's conception of the enterprise was quite different from that of the laymen on the committee: 'To them it was less an effort once more to restore the consecrated single life than an attempt to relieve the misery and ignorance of the great towns, and as a tribute to the wisdom and forethought of Robert Southey.' [87] The sisterhood was originally planned as a practical memorial to Southey, who had died in 1843, and the Paper which was circulated by the lay members of the committee shortly after the foundation is almost exclusively devoted to practical concerns. [88] The signatories expressed concern for the state of the large cities and the fact that individual charity had so far had little impact. They pointed out the usefulness of female religious orders, both Catholic and Protestant, which were engaged in charitable work on the Continent, and suggested that the way to facilitate women's work in this country was to give them the protection of an institution, which was why the sisterhood was founded. The intended charitable work was detailed, and the Paper assured readers that the project was not in opposition to either the principles of the church or 'the opinions of its chief rulers' (Bishop Blomfield of London had in fact been consulted). This 'beginning of a series of experiments which resulted in many Sisterhoods' [89] was, as far as its lay founders were concerned, distinctly practical in its goals.

This kind of 'practical exigency' appears to have been the operating factor in most of the early sisterhoods, according to the public accounts which were given of them. But not all were so consciously planned as the Park Village Sisterhood. Among the sisterhoods which had originated for practical reasons and had only become institutionalized through a process of development rather than as the result of a conscious initial plan, the sisterhood founded by Carter at Clewer is fairly typical. The first stage of Clewer's growth was when, in response to the Appeal for a Church Penitentiary by John Armstrong [P.H. 6242], a Mrs Tennant in Clewer Village had offered her help, and had been assisted by two or three other ladies. It was when Mrs Tennant relinquished the work that the need was felt for *continuity and organization* if the enterprise was to be successful; this was the set of circumstances which called the sisterhood into being, as Carter states:

> As the work . . . went on, it soon became evident that it could not grow into a permanent institution, at least not on the same principles on which it had been commenced, if it were to remain dependent upon a succession of individuals, however capable. It was felt that it could be maintained and developed only by a Religious Community. [90]

This same argument—that the advantage of sisterhoods and brotherhoods lies in the *collective* and organized nature of their work—appears several times. Thus might an early nineteenth-century economist consider the advantages of the factory system over the domestic system of production.

There were protests against a too instrumental conception of the incipient religious communities (we shall shortly consider those that were put forward in Convocation and Church Congress debates) but they are less common than legitimations couched in utilitarian terms. The Broad Church Bishop Tait of London was, for example, not much in favour of the form of life chosen by the members of sisterhoods, but he was very willing to acknowledge the valuable practical work which they performed. Thus it is not surprising to find Tait under attack for not understanding what sisterhoods were:

> The Bishop of London, in his recent *Charge*, has expressed a strong sense of the usefulness of such institutions; but, looking only at their external effects, the Bishop regrets that their system assimilates so little to that of the foreign Deaconesses, and fondly looks forward to the day when increase of common sense shall induce the adoption of the Deaconess model. [91]

The fact that Tait should have wished the sisterhoods to conform more to the deaconess model is striking proof of his instrumental attitude to their work, and one cannot help speculating whether Tait did not have in mind the pamphlet on deaconesses by Howson, which had appeared only a few years before, and in which Howson had written:

> But then it might be said that the Deaconess-Institution is itself a sisterhood . . . Here I think it is important to mark a line of distinction which might easily be overlooked. Deaconess-*Institutions* are only means to an end. There might be deaconesses without them . . . So also with regard to the further point of associated residence, this is no necessary part of the plan. It is a question not of principle, but of detail, and to be settled by consideration of convenience for work, of fitness and propriety, and of spiritual benefit. [92]

The practical advantages of sisterhoods and brotherhoods were almost inevitably an area of major concern in the Convocation debates. The reason for this emphasis on secondary, instrumental concerns is not hard to find and is in a sense parallel to the argument put forward by MacIntyre in *Secularization and Moral Change*. Briefly, if one group in a specific social context wishes to appeal for support to another group, and if those two groups disagree over fundamental values and therefore tend not to share any substantial common ground over what is, or is not, a 'legitimate' claim, then a solution which avoids conflict is the appeal to secondary 'means' rather than primary values. All groups in the nineteenth-century Church of England were agreed in attaching a high degree of importance to practical schemes for ameliorating the spiritual and material conditions of the mass of the population, and concern with the instrumental aspect of sisterhood work was especially effective in concentrating the line of debates on an area less fraught with theological issues. It was, of course, possible to attack the sisterhoods on instrumental grounds—for instance, by arguing that their 'conventualism' detracted from their efficiency —and it was possible in the later debates to *question* the exclusive concern with 'inessentials' and to direct attention to the religious life of these institutions as being of primary importance, but for much of the nineteenth century the focus of Convocation debates was on practical results of religious communities, and this may account for the lack of any real polarization in the attitudes expressed.

By the time of the first debate on the subject of sisterhoods, in the 1862 Convocation of Canterbury (Lower House) the Crimean expedition—in which Florence Nightingale had included nurses from Anglican sisterhoods—had already provided evidence of the practical nature of the work which could be undertaken. Margaret Goodman, however, in a book published the following year, denied that sisterhoods were a particularly useful source of nursing talent. She describes the injunction in Sellon's sisterhood not to speak to people and not even to *look* at gentlemen in the streets. This was difficult to accomplish, she thought, and one of the sisters had continued this habit in the Crimea, which had considerably 'impaired her usefulness'. [93] Goodman, who had taken part in the Crimean venture, was in no doubt about the influence which sisterhoods had on 'active, useful nurses':

> . . . it seemed desirable to her [the authoress] also to describe some of the Romish Sisterhoods of a charitable kind, which have served as models for imitation by those who would fain pervert active, useful nurses into ascetic recluses; thus diverting the broad and beneficent stream of loving Christian charity into narrow and tortuous channels, directed by a proselytising party in the Church, but not of the Church. [94]

Archdeacon Ffoulkes, who spoke in favour of sisterhoods in the 1862 Convocation debate, had given two practical reasons for welcoming the growth of sisterhoods: they would be a great help in alleviating the burden of charitable work that fell on the wives of clergy; and the distinctive dress that they wore enabled them to penetrate the worst areas in slums so as to gain access to the afflicted. This last argument is the only one which Goodman was prepared to accept, as she said in her book of 1863:

The only valid plea for the segregation of charitable sisterhoods is, that their dress and religious character enable them to go into the worst haunts of poverty and crime, with immunity from harm or insult. [95]

At the 1866 Church Congress meeting the Earl of Devon spoke of the work done by the sisters in the London cholera epidemic of 1865. He valued the sisterhoods because of their good works, and was opposed to vows and the enforcement of 'peculiar religious observances'. His was a quite explicitly instrumental legitimation, for he thought that the *practical* nature of sisterhoods would convince those who were apprehensive about them:

> The real safeguard, however, against any dangers that may by some be apprehended, from the existence of Sisterhoods, is, the giving them a *practical* character, and treating as their primary regular and permanent duty, active work among the ignorant, the sick and the erring. [96]

In later debates there appeared a change of emphasis, as supporters of sisterhoods began to claim recognition for the life of these communities, the rational-legal legitimation having been largely accepted. 'That the Church of England has recognized and accepted Sisters' *work* is a gain to the Life of the Church', said Carter at the 1883 Church Congress; [97] what was now wanted was the recognition and acceptance of their *life*. This type of claim will be dealt with in the following chapter as an example of the process of reciprocal adjustment and convergence by means of which the religious orders and the Church of England arrived at a point of mutual acceptance.

Instrumental legitimation was even more evident in the debates on brotherhoods, where even highly emotive issues like vows were accepted on altogether instrumental criteria. In the Report in 1889 on 'Organizations to reach Classes now outside Religious Ministrations' an argument first began to be formulated in Convocation which was to carry a great deal of weight in subsequent debates, namely the idea of brotherhoods as a form of 'cheap labour'. It is interesting to note that it was precisely this argument that R. M. Benson had vigorously attacked at the 1888 Church Congress, and this supports Allchin's observation on the Church Congress, that because they were unofficial 'all shades of opinion in the Church of England were represented in their discussions'. [98] The Convocations, being official, necessarily picked their way with much more diplomacy through the various shades of opinion in the Church of England, which explains their greater readiness to accept secondary, instrumental legitimation.

Benson's speech at the 1888 Church Congress pointedly recognized this, for he began: 'I suppose I am not here to speak of the religious life as a vocation, but of some of its effects upon society, and the need of it in the present day.' [99] The bulk of his speech was concerned with vocation, however, and he made a strong argument in favour of concentrating on the spiritual rather than empirical aspects of the revival. The latter he attacked:

> I will not speak of religious communities as a means of getting work done very cheaply! Such an idea I can only regard as a sacrilege, an insult to God. [100]

He launched into a condemnation of the greed and materialism of the nineteenth century, which gave rise to the notion that God's work should be done without personal cost. Allchin thinks that Benson's speech is important because it made a crucial break from earlier preoccupations with the utilitarian aspects of communities. It is worth quoting Allchin at some length:

> . . . [Benson's] speech is the first occasion at a Church Congress, on which a member of a religious community had spoken of the inner justification of the religious life. Most speakers in earlier years, even men like Canon Carter, who, though the founder of a community, was not a member of one, had spoken of religious communities from outside, and had attempted to commend communities for the active works which they carried out. They had approached the question primarily in its utilitarian aspect. Fr. Benson cannot and will not do this. Even though he is speaking not of the life itself, but of 'its effects upon society', he talks not about the effects of what a community does, but the effects of what it is: i.e. the judgement which it brings on worldly society. In one matter events proved him absolutely right. Religious communities have to be based on what people believe to be a call from God, and not on utilitarian considerations. As Father Benson says, 'No tentative scheme of usefulness will have the necessary vitality'. The interest shown in religious communities for men, at this Church Congress, and in Convocation, and in the Church at

large, during the next three years, was a symptom of the need for such societies rather than the cause of them. As Fr. Herbert Kelly wrote, 'At this time there was a good deal of talk about brotherhoods out of which it will be remembered nothing came.' There clearly is a connexion between all that was said in this Congress and in Convocation on this subject, and the foundation between 1892 and 1894 of three communities for men, but it is not a simple relation of cause and effect. [101]

This point may be taken up by suggesting one possible reason why the Convocation calls for brotherhoods failed to elicit any immediate response; it was because the concept of a brotherhood with which most of the participants in the debates were working was so overwhelmingly instrumental that it contained little positive appeal to potential members of such brotherhoods. The 1889 Report, it was argued, contained the germ of a 'cheap labour' argument, and it also tended to concentrate on the practical goals and administrative arrangements of the proposed institutions. Subsequent debates were very much preoccupied with the relevance of brotherhoods as *means* of reinforcing the parish system in large towns, of gentling the masses, and of providing the necessary services without necessitating a substantial increase in finance, but the life of these brotherhoods was rarely seen as an *end* in itself. Practical issues were not the exclusive concern of the debates—'enthusiasm' and vows were discussed, for instance—but the overall impression is distinctly utilitarian. At the Convocation of 1890, Archdeacon Farrar said of vows:

Certainly we do not hold the view of St Thomas Aquinas, that vows give any special merit to the actions which they cover. We only value them because they add solemnity to obligation, stability to purpose, strength to will. [102]

In the following year's debate in the Upper House there was an element almost of *Realpolitik* in the Bishop of London, Dr Temple's recognition of vows, not as a matter of principle but of expediency. He argued in favour of accepting vows because otherwise they would lose potential recruits to the brotherhoods:

...I believe we must allow them to make these life-long engagements, or we shall certainly lose them. Moreover, I have very little doubt that in many cases they will form Brotherhoods of their own without reference to the Bishops or to the authority of the Bishops, and I do not believe such Brother-hoods will do the work nearly so well. [103]

Allchin's comment on this debate is a valuable postscript to a consideration of rational-legal legitimation: religious communities come into being, he states, 'rather because men feel themselves called by God to them, than because committees decide that they would be a convenient and cheap method of carrying out certain difficult pieces of work'. [104]

MIXED LEGITIMATIONS

The value of the Weberian concepts of legitimate authority lies in their analytical clarity, but they do not attempt to give a complete description of reality, only to indicate aspects of reality which are socially significant. Thus in the debates and arguments which were concerned with the incipient communities in the Church of England one never finds 'pure' legitimations. Indeed, it could be argued that proponents of religious communities might have a more widely based appeal by making use of the legitimations of other schools of churchmanship (bearing in mind that these are likewise analytical abstractions). Some examples of 'mixed legitimations' have already been given—J. M. Neale's *Deaconesses and Early Sisterhoods* made use of Gospel (Evangelical) and early church (Tractarian) precedent; T. T. Carter's speeches in debates made use of Gospel (Evangelical) and early church (Tractarian) precedent, together with rational-legal (Broad Church/secondary consensus) legitimation; Father Ignatius seems to have relied at one time or another on a whole range of legitimations.

One of the best examples of 'mixed legitimation' is in fact Seymour's speech at the 1861 Convocation, and we can discern in it several legitimations and subsidiary appeals: the legitimations have been traced above; and consideration will briefly be given to subsidiary appeals in the following section, since Seymour's speech suggests two of them. He first of all mentioned the fear often expressed that community life for women is foreign and un-English, a revival of the system abolished at the Reformation, but these are not the motives of the present founders (Reformation tradition reasserted; 'No Popery' fears discounted).

Seymour argued that the office of deaconess was absorbed by the monastic and conventual system of the Middle Ages, but the Reformation with its call for greater zeal demanded labourers such as the deaconesses of the 'early church' (Reformation tradition again reasserted; Middle Ages discounted; early church revived). He then cited the Kaiserwerth deaconesses to show that such institutions were not necessarily Roman (Protestant identification; suggestion of foreign competition) and he quoted from Southey (contemporary respected figure; instrumentalism and foreign competition in Southey) and Dr Arnold (Broad Church appeal), ending on the need for trained nurses (instrumental).

This sort of 'labelling' process could be applied to many of the most successful statements in favour of sisterhoods, and it illustrates the necessity for spreading appeals for legitimacy widely in the context of an institution—in this case the Church of England —where different groups had somewhat different definitions of a valid claim to legitimacy. Within High Church circles it was possible to present arguments in favour of sisterhoods on much more restricted criteria. When the 'audience' was not one which shared a similar definition of authority, a whole series of appeals were necessary, not all of them based on religious criteria. Two final sources of appeal can be listed.

OTHER IDEOLOGICAL SUBSIDIARIES
a. *Foreign competition*

The relevance of arguments based on what was being achieved by religious bodies in other western European countries was not only limited to proving that deaconesses or sisterhoods were 'Protestant'. There is an unmistakable theme of foreign competition in some statements of this sort, and it fits neatly into nineteenth-century awareness of a world economic market, especially as far as Germany was concerned; France too was the subject of a certain amount of 'ecclesiastical espionage'.

It is significant that the first proposal for women's institutions of this sort was couched in terms of the example of 'a neighbouring nation' and that the French 'Sisters of Charity' should be transposed into 'Protestant Sisters of Charity'. [105] One of the arguments put forward is that if the Roman Catholics can produce this amount of devotion, so can the Church of England. Southey's appeal three years later is much more explicit:

Why then have you [in Great Britain] no Beguines, no Sisters of Charity? Why in the most needful, the most merciful form that charity can take, have you not followed the example of the French and the Netherlanders? [106]

This formula—'why do we not have what France/Germany/the Netherlands have?'—was apparently a resilient one. At the time when Florence Nightingale was making up her mind to go to the Crimea, a letter appeared in *The Times* of 9th October 1854, asking the same question:

Why have we no Sisters of Charity? There are numbers of able-bodied and tender-hearted English women who would joyfully and with alacrity go out to devote themselves to nursing the sick and wounded, if they could be associated for that purpose, and placed under proper protection. [107]

The attitude which this kind of statement epitomized had apparently given rise to some French sarcasm, because in a book of 1855 which was cast in the same form as that of Dallas in 1826—describing the French Sisters of Charity and suggesting how they might be Anglicized—the author, apparently somewhat stung, comments:

The French say that they invent and the English imitate; some more politely say, they invent and the English perfect. [108]

Mention of Florence Nightingale inevitably leads to a consideration of Kaiserwerth deaconesses. Reference to a group of German Lutheran deaconesses as a justification for similar institutions in Britain had a strong appeal, partly because they were Protestant and also because Germany was the country most likely to be seen as a foreign competitor in the nineteenth century. Both Elizabeth Fry and Florence Nightingale visited Kaiserwerth; its founder, Pastor Fliedner, had visited England in his fund-raising tour; and the institution was greatly popularized by pamphlets and in speeches. [109]

In the first Convocation debate on the subject the Rev. C. E. Kennaway thought that since sisterhoods had been successful in Germany there was no reason why an English pastor should shrink from what had been successful there. But one of the most interesting appeals is that of Florence Nightingale, who speaks of Fliedner looking over his shoulder at the Roman Catholics at the same time as he appealed to the women of his own church; while Florence Nightingale herself looks over her shoulder at Fliedner, as she appeals to Englishwomen. The extract is from her obituary on Fliedner:

> In the midst of what others thought his success, his stirring voice was always heard crying, 'see, the Roman Church has its thousands of thousands of Sisters of Charity, of all orders. We have but a few hundreds. No more zealous proselytisers are found than these orders. And will you, the maidens of our Church, remain like idle cowards—you who might labour with equal zeal and greater light?'
>
> And what but this have we to say in England? There is such a chattering and noise here about 'fields' wanted for women's work. Yet every training institution with one voice tells the contrary tale; of applications innumerable for trained women to fill responsible posts, of few to fill them, of living materials wanted, situations and 'fields' being never wanting; of workers needed, not work. [110]

b. 'No Popery'

One of the most common accusations levelled against the religious orders in the Church of England was that they were 'foreign bodies' in the organism of the Church; more precisely, they were Romish. At the end of the following chapter there is a brief discussion of the extent to which the institutions could be seen as imitating or innovating. Here the emphasis is on a popular attitude and the attempt to dissociate the new institutions from it.

Southey had been one of the first to distinguish between 'nunneries', which were definitely Roman and detested, and Sisters of Charity:

> [England] is greviously in need of them! There is nothing Romish, nothing superstitious, nothing fanatical in such associations, nothing but what is rightous and holy . . . [111]

The importance of this kind of statement when popularizing sisterhoods can be judged by noting that in the first Convocation debate on the subject the Rev. C. E. Kennaway quoted precisely this passage from Southey. In connection with this debate, it is interesting to note that Seymour felt it necessary to make exactly the same distinction:

The English mind does not commend the vocation of the nun who is immured for life within the walls of a convent; often before she has had any experience of life, or any knowledge of herself; and where she is debarred from many of the offices of Christian love,—that, for example, of 'visiting the fatherless and widows in their affliction'; but it does admire and commend a life devoted in Christ's name to active charity. [112]

Bishop Wilberforce was one Anglican who had no hesitation in rejecting some of the practices of sisterhoods as 'Roman'. In a letter in 1850, he referred to terms like 'professed' and 'spouses of Christ' as 'un-Christian and savouring of the worst evils of Rome' [113], and in a letter of 1854 to T. T. Carter he stated:

If Sisterhoods cannot be maintained except upon a semi-Romanist scheme, with its *direction*, with its development of self-consciousness and morbid religious affection, with its exaltation of the contemplative life, its perpetual Confession, and its un-English tone, I am perfectly convinced that we had better have no Sisterhoods. [114]

While Wilberforce was prepared to sanction any sisterhood that was active, did not take women too young and, above all, avoided vows, he was sympathetic to fears of 'Popery'. At the 1868 Church Congress he said of sisterhoods: 'They labour under this most natural imputation that they are an attempt in our Reformed Church to imitate the system of nunneries in another Church.'[115]

On the other hand, at least one supporter of sisterhoods saw an evil motivation in the 'Popery' claim. Alexander Penrose Forbes, in his *Plea for Sisterhoods* of 1849, thought that God had been at work in reviving the religious life, but Satan had also been at work, putting on an angelic disguise and arguing that sisterhoods are 'Popish'. [116] One cannot help feeling that Forbes' image is partly justified in the case of many of the 'escaped and converted nuns' who were paraded by the Protestant press and publishers. Their claim to complete innocence (to the extent sometimes of claiming to have been drugged before being professed) in conjunction with their thinly-disguised Protestant postures and sexual innuendo give a strong impression of disingenuousness.

In this chapter attention has been directed at the process by which Anglican religious orders—an unfamiliar and often suspect type of organization—were legitimated. These legitimations derived from the basic models of ecclesiastical organization available in the different schools of churchmanship and provided a Scriptural justification of deaconesses which could be accommodated within a Low Church perspective; an early church model of sisterhoods, from which the High Church party justified their apparent 'innovations'; and a medieval model for brotherhoods which, suitably modernized, held some significance in the organic view of industrial society at the end of the nineteenth century. Instrumental appeals were highly characteristic of the period and also avoided theological conflict. There were, finally, the fears of foreign competition and Popery which legitimators had to take into account.

NOTES

1 Dieter Voll, *Catholic Evangelicalism* (London, Faith Press, 1963).
2 W. R. W. Stephens, *The Life and Letters of Walter Farquhar Hook*, 2 vols (London, Richard Bentley and Son, 1878), p. 283.
3 Sikes of Guisborough is frequently credited with having predicted the rise and course of the Oxford Movement. The relevant passage is in Henry Parry Liddon, *Life of Edward Bouverie Pusey* (London, Longmans, 1893–7), vol. I, pp. 257–8.
4 Voll, op. cit., 1963.
5 Anne Mozley, *Reminiscences*, vol. 1, p. 180, quoted in Robert Dudley Middleton, *Keble, Froude and Newman* (Canterbury, Gibbs and Sons, 1933).
6 Thomas Arnold, *Christian Life. Its Course, Its Hindrances, And Its Helps* (London, B. Followes, 1841), p. xliv.
7 Kenneth A. Thompson, *Bureaucracy and Church Reform* (London, Oxford University Press, 1970), p. 239.
8 *Oxford Dictionary of the Christian Church* (London, Oxford University Press, 1958), p. 377.
9 ibid., p. 377.
10 ibid., p. 377.
11 *Report of the Proceedings of the Church Congress of 1862, Oxford* (Oxford and London, J. H. and J. Parker, 1862), p. 128.
12 Spencer Cecil Carpenter, *Church and People, 1789–1889* (London, S.P.C.K., 1933), p. 412.
13 Pusey House Pamphlet No. 9634, p. 10. The prefix 'P.H.' in the text refers to Pusey House Pamphlets.
14 [Convocation of Canterbury], *Chronicle of Convocation* (London, 1859, 1861 Convocation), p. 881.
15 Arthur Macdonald Allchin, *The Silent Rebellion* (London, S.C.M., 1958), p. 157.

16 See the section on 'mixed legitimations' later in this chapter.

17 Allchin, op. cit., 1958, p. 160.

18 The pamphlet was based on an article which had originally been published in the *Quarterly Review* of 1860.

19 John Saul Howson, *Deaconesses* (London, Longman, Green, Longman and Roberts, 1862), p. vii.

20 On the Apostolic Constitutions *The Oxford Dictionary of the Christian Church* says (p. 73): 'A collection of ecclesiastical law dating from the latter half of the 4th cent. and almost certainly of Syrian provenance. The full title is "Ordinances of the Holy Apostles through Clement"... There are good grounds for identifying the compiler with the 4th cent. interpolater of St. Ignatius' Epp., and there are also some indications that he was an Arian. The work is a valuable witness to the religious practices and beliefs of its period.'

21 *The True Institution of Sisterhood: Or, A Message and its Messengers.* By L. N. R.

22 ibid., p. 25.

23 George Edward Lynch Cotton, Bishop of Calcutta, *The Employment of Women in Religious and Charitable Works: A Lecture Delivered before the Bethune Society, the 5th April, 1866* ... Published by desire of the Society, 1866.

24 ibid., p. 8.

25 *Proceedings of the Church Congress Held at York, 1866* (York, John Sampson, 1867), p. 190.

26 Thomas Thellusson Carter, 'Vows, and their relation to Religious Communities', in Orby Shipley (ed.), *The Church and the World: Essays on Questions of the Day*, first series (London, Longmans, Green, Reader and Dyer, 1866), p. 371.

27 John Mason Neale, *Deaconesses and Early Sisterhoods* (London, 1869). (Two Sermons preached in the Oratory of St. Margarets, East Grinstead, Advent, 1857.)

28 *York Journal of Convocation*, London, York, 1861–1884 Report.

29 Cecilia Robinson, *The Ministry of Deaconesses* (London, Methuen, 1914), pp. 105–6.

30 Such attempts to override, or at least to circumvent competing ideologies is characteristic of political legitimation in England.

31 Yngve Torgny Brilioth, *The Anglican Revival. Studies in the Oxford Movement* (London, Longmans, 1925) the section on Tractarian Piety.

32 Henry Parry Liddon, op. cit., vol. III, p. 7.

33 Advisory Council on Religious Communities, *A Directory of the Religious Life* (London, S.P.C.K., 1943), pp. 1–2.

34 Liddon, op. cit., vol. III, p. 7.

35 Robert Townsend Warner, *Marian Rebecca Hughes* (Oxford, printed at the University Press by John Johnson, 1933), pp. 8–9.

36 [Thomas Thellusson Carter], *The Founders of Clewer* (London, A. R. Mowbray, 1952), p. 17.

37 Carter in Shipley (ed.), op. cit., 1866, pp. 370–9.

38 ibid., p. 391 (my italics).

39 Allchin, op. cit., 1958, p. 140.

40 [Anna Bronwell Jameson], 'Sisters of Charity . . .' (Review of Jameson and Cotton, n.d.).

41 Neale, op. cit., 1869, p. 12.

42 W. J. S. Simpson, *The History of the Anglo-Catholic Revival from 1845* (London, Allen and Unwin, 1932) p. 233.

43 Allchin, op. cit., 1958, pp. 37–8. The question of a medieval tradition as part of the background to the revival of Anglican communities in the nineteenth century brings into clear relief the difference between a 'public' *legitimation* and the conscious or unconscious *model* which lies behind the activity for which legitimation is claimed. The externals of the revival certainly suggest a strong medieval component, and there is some justification in regarding medievalism as an 'unofficial' image and the early church as an 'official' source of legitimation. The medieval church was poor as a source of legitimation—it was not old enough or original enough to provide a sufficiently firm basis for reform—and it never found widespread acceptance in the public presentation of the Tractarian movement, but it may well have been a significant latent factor. There is an interesting discussion of the issues involved in this in Claude Levi-Strauss, *Structural Anthropology* (New York and London, Basic Books, 1963), p. 281: 'A structural model may be conscious or unconscious without this difference affecting its nature. It can only be said that when the structure of a certain type of phenomenon does not lie at a great depth, it is more likely that some kind of model, standing as a screen to hide it, will exist in the collective consciousness. For conscious models, which are usually known as "norms", are by definition very poor ones, since they are not intended to explain the phenomena but to perpetuate them. Therefore, structural analysis is confronted with a strange paradox well known to the linguist, that is: the more obvious structural organization is, the more difficult it becomes to reach it because of the inaccurate conscious models lying across the path which leads to it.' This seems especially pertinent to our present analysis, because in the 'public' Convocation debates, as will shortly be seen, the most frequently used conscious model was that of a pragmatic, instrumental organization. This was a 'screen' for the more radical divergence of legitimations based on rather different church traditions, and at an even deeper level in the case of some of the Tractarian apologists we might suggest that the medieval church played an important role in providing an 'unofficial' model.

44 Charles Lock Eastlake, *A History of the Gothic Revival* (London, Longmans, Green, 1872), p. 113.

45 Sabine Baring-Gould in Shipley (ed.), op. cit., 1866, pp. 103–104.

46 Pusey House Pamphlet No. 72207.

47 Pusey House Pamphlet No. 1103. (Hereafter Pusey House pamphlets which are listed in the Bibliography are simply prefixed 'P.H.'.)

48 Donald Attwater, *Father Ignatius of Llanthony* (London, Cassell, 1931), p. 80.

49 Richard Frederick Littledale, *Innovations* (Oxford, A. R. Mowbray, 1868). (A lecture delivered in the Assembly Rooms, Liverpool, 23rd April, 1868.)

50 François Biot, O.P., *The Rise of Protestant Monasticism*, transl. W. J. Kerrigan (Dublin, Helicon, 1963).

51 As Clarke pointedly remarks: 'A person who conscientiously subscribes a document [*sic*] according to his judgement of the grammatical sense is free from any obligation to rule himself by the supposed opinions either of compilers or imposers.' (Charles Philip Stewart Clarke, *The Oxford Movement and After* [London and Oxford, A. R. Mowbray, 1932], p. 101.)

52 Thomas Thellusson Carter, *Vows and the Religious State*. I. *Vows and their relation to Religious Communities*. II. *The Religious State and Age of Profession* (London, J. Masters, 1881), p. 61.

53 T. D. Harrison, *Every Man's Story of the Oxford Movement* (London, A. R. Mowbray, 1932) p. 120. See also Charles Walker, *Three Months in an English Monastery* (London, Murray, 1864).

54 Thomas Jay Williams, *Priscilla Lydia Sellon* (London, S.P.C.K., 1950), p. 56.

55 W. H. Frere, one-time Superior of the Community of the Resurrection and, with Charles Gore (Bishop of Oxford from 1911 to 1919) at that time one of the few Anglican bishops to have been a member of a community.

56 *Canterbury Chronicle of Convocation*, Upper House, 1st June, 1932, pp. 202–3.

57 For a selection of controversial pamphlets see Pusey House Pamphlets nos. 6249, 6250, 6252, 6253, 6257, 6262, 6265, 6273, 10183, 11522, 12000, 12299, 12905, 13985, 71164, 71591.

58 Reginald G. Wilberforce, *Bishop Wilberforce* (Oxford and London, A. R. Mowbray, 1905), p. 325.

59 Allan T. Cameron, *The Religious Communities of the Church of England* (London, Faith Press, 1918), pp. 8–10.

60 Allchin, op. cit., 1958 (first chapter).

61 Anson, op. cit., pp. 1–25. Other pedigrees of this type can be found in Sidney Leslie Ollard, *A Short History of the Oxford Movement* (London, Faith Press Reprints, 1963); Talbot Dilworth Harrison, *Every Man's Story of the Oxford Movement* op. cit. p. 121; and in Anson's earlier work, *The Benedictines of Caldey* (London, Burns, Oates, 1940).

62 Quoted in William John Sparrow Simpson, op. cit. 230.

63 Quoted in Anson, op. cit., 1964, p. 4.

64 Henry Parry Liddon, op. cit., vol. 3, pp. 2–4.

65 Thomas Thellusson Carter (ed.), *Nicholas Ferrar. His Household and His Friends* (London, Longmans, Green, 1892), p. 103.

66 John Mason Neale, *Ayton Priory or the Restored Monastery* (Cambridge, Deightons, 1843), p. iv.

67 The dedication on the title-page is to Lord John Manners, one of the leading figures in the 'Young England' movement and a member of the committee which founded the Park Village Sisterhood.

68 See Samuel Fox, *Monks and Monasteries: Being an Account of English Monachism* (London, James Burns, 1845 [B. M. catalogue gives 1840]). For details of Leighton's argument, which was in turn derived from Bishop Burnet, see Erasmus Middleton, *The Genuine Works of R.*

Leighton, D.D., Archbishop of Glasgow . . . to which is now Prefixed the Life of the Author (London, W. Baynes, 1819), vol. 1, pp. xxiii–iv.

69 The exceptions were Sancroft, who was the spiritual director of a group of twelve ladies who wished to form a 'Protestant Nunnery' (which in the event did not materialize) and, possibly, Stephens, who implied in a pamphlet that such a community which had actually been proposed by him was already in existence. See Anson, op. cit., 1964, p. 15 and p. 17.

70 See the extract from a Puritan pamphlet, 'The Arminian Nunnery' in Paul Elmer More and Frank Leslie Cross (eds.), Anglicanism: The Thought and Practise of the Church of England. Illustrated from the Religious Literature of the Seventeenth Century (London, S.P.C.K., 1951), p. 737.

71 Thomas Thellusson Carter, Nicholas Ferrar. His Household and his Friends (London, Longmans, Green, 1892), p. 102.

72 Kathleen E. Burne, The Life and Letters of Father Andrew, S.D.C. (London and Oxford, A. R. Mowbray, 1948), pp. 10–11.

73 P.H. 7627, p. 21.

74 Peter F. Rudge, Ministry and Management (London, Tavistock Publications, 1968), pp. 39–40.

75 Allchin, op. cit., 1958, p. 40.

76 Henry Lucius Moultrie Cary, in Norman Powell Williams and Charles Harris, Northern Catholicism. Centenary Studies in the Oxford and Parallel Movements (London, 1933), p. 339.

77 P. F. Anson, The Benedictines of Caldey (London, Burns, Oates, 1940), p. xvii.

78 ibid., p. xx.

79 Anne B. Dallas, Incidents in the Life and Ministry of the Rev. A. R. C. Dallas (London, James Nisbet, 1871), p. 224.

80 Robert Southey, Sir Thomas More: Or, Colloquies on the progress and prospects of Society (London, 1829), vol. 2, p. 82.

81 ibid., vol. 1, p. 403.

82 P.H. 6241. Wackerbarth went over to Rome in 1842.

83 ibid., p. x.

84 This argument validating religious orders, which Troeltsch makes considerable use of, became in the nineteenth-century Church of England almost a principle of 'spiritual utility'. A pamphlet of 1862, for instance, makes the following comment:
  'This is what is termed a practical age, and things are judged according to the results they are seen to produce. But who knows the blessings we may be reaping, even now, from the constant intercessions which arose day and night to GOD from our old Religious Houses.' [P.H. 6269, p. 11.]

85 See Arthur Geoffrey Lough, The Influence of John Mason Neale (London, S.P.C.K., 1962), pp. 45–7.

86 Spencer Cecil Carpenter, Church and People, 1789–1889 (London, S.P.C.K., 1933), p. 180.

87 Henry Parry Liddon, Life of Edward Bouverie Pusey (London, Longmans, 1893–7), vol. III, p. 18.

88 ibid., vol. III, pp. 18–21.

89 ibid., vol. III, p. 21.

90 Thomas Thellusson Carter, *Harriet Monsell. A Memoir* (London, J. Masters, 1884), p. 34.

91 Orby Shipley (ed.), *The Church and the World: Essays on Questions of the Day*, second series (London, Longmans, Green, Reader and Dyer, 1867), p. 166.

92 Howson, op. cit., pp. xii–xiii.

93 Margaret Goodman, *Sisterhoods in the Church of England: With Notices of Some Charitable Sisterhoods in the Romish Church* (London, Smith, Elder, 1863).

94 ibid., p. xiii.

95 ibid., p. xii.

96 *Proceedings of the Church Congress Held at York . . . 1865* (York, John Sampson, 1867), p. 185.

97 *The Official Report of the Church Congress Held at Reading . . . 1883* (London, Bemrose, 1883) and quoted in Allchin (op. cit., 1958), p. 149.

98 Allchin, op. cit., 1958, p. 139.

99 *The Official Report of the Church Congress Held at Manchester, 1888* (London, Bemrose, 1888), p. 724.

100 ibid., p. 728.

101 Allchin, op. cit., 1958, p. 152.

102 *Chronicle of the Convocation of Canterbury*, 1890, p. 26.

103 Quoted in Allchin, op. cit., 1958, p. 174.

104 ibid., p. 174.

105 P.H. 12554.

106 Southey, op. cit., II, p. 318.

107 Sir Edward Cook, *The Life of Florence Nightingale* (London, Macmillan, 1913), vol. I, p. 148.

108 *Sisters of Charity and some Visits with them* (London, Joseph Masters, 1855), p. 77.

109 For instance, in the pamphlet which was probably written by Fliedner himself, *Some Account of Deaconess-work in the Christian Church*.

110 Florence Nightingale, 'Death of Pastor Fliedner' (reprinted from *Evangelical Christendom*, 1864).

111 Southey, op. cit., II, pp. 330–1.

112 P.H. 6268.

113 A. R. Ashwell, *Life of Bishop Wilberforce* (London, John Murray, 1883), vol. 3, p. 330.

114 ibid., vol. 3, p. 328.

115 Quoted in Allchin, op. cit., 1958, p. 144.

116 Alexander Penrose Forbes, *A Plea for Sisterhoods* (London, Joseph Masters, 1849).

7

Religious Orders in the Nineteenth-Century Church of England and the Ideal Type: The Problem of Authority

THE GENERALIZED ideal type which was put forward in chapter 2 as a means of indicating the most significant sociological aspects of religious orders can now be applied to the specific historical case with which we are concerned. Some divergence from the type must be expected, but such divergence should be a source of valuable insight into the historical context of nineteenth-century Anglican orders. This is in fact the case in two of the major features of religious orders—their relationship with the parent church and their insistence on total commitment. These take on a highly distinct character, and other features, for instance the conception of the order as a collection of *virtuosi*, undergo a process of adaptation, so that the *virtuosi* concept emerges as an argument in favour of providing special facilities for such members of the church to prevent them joining other churches and denominations, rather than as the organizational recognition of two distinct levels of moral attainment, as is the case in official Roman Catholic conceptions.

In this and the next chapter the ideal type will be used to throw into clear relief the specific features of nineteenth-century orders. The feature which emerges with great clarity is the problem of establishing formal lines of authority between the orders and the parent church, a large sector of which was more or less hostile to the principle on which they were based or was indifferent to their aims. 'Authority' in the case of a complex and diffuse institution like the Church of England is not easy to identify. However, we may expect to find indications of it in Convocation resolutions (if resolutions is the right word for issues that were often never resolved), in links between brotherhoods and the parochial structure, in the autonomy or lack of it which individual communities showed in decision-making, in relations with individual bishops, and in the internal development of patterns of authority, often from obscure, even secretive beginnings. In all of these areas the Anglican orders show a characteristic divergence from the ideal type.

This chapter is therefore concerned exclusively with the first characteristic of the ideal type:

1. The religious order only exists as part of a church.

Membership of a wider church, it was argued earlier, is a key characteristic of religious orders, since one of the most significant influences on them is that the ultimate source of authority is located externally in a more universalistic religious organization. And this feature, more than any other, was the one which gave the Anglican orders much of their distinctiveness, as well as presenting them with a great many problems. The cause of the problem relates directly to the way in which the early sisterhoods and brotherhoods were legitimated, for, as was shown in the previous chapter, these organizations were the creation of, and received complete support from only a section of the Church of England. This section, the Tractarian party, worked with a model of church structure which could certainly be claimed as a valid part of Anglican tradition, but which was not universally accepted by members of the Church of England: the two other major parties in the nineteenth century, the Evangelicals and the Broad Churchmen, had very different traditional or instrumental conceptions. Since the Anglican bishops were, on the whole, drawn from Broad Church and Evangelical backgrounds, the religious orders were faced from the outset with a parent church whose principal representatives of authority were either openly hostile, or misunderstood the goals of the orders, or at best greeted these new groups with conditional acceptance, as in the case of Bishop Wilberforce. Reinforcing certain of these attitudes was of course the generally hostile attitude to the Roman Catholic Church. The Anglican orders were not unlike Roman orders, and this chapter will consider the extent to which the former were seen as imitations of the latter.

The Advisory Council's Directory applies the three fundamental principles of the religious life in the Western Church to the Anglican orders:

These fundamental principles are: (1) an entire self-consecration to God under vows of a greater or less degree both of permanence and of dispensability; (2) a common life under rule administered by duly constituted authority; (3) a loyal recognition of the authority of the Church. [1]

But it was not in fact until 1897 that the Church of England first officially recognized these bodies, as the *Directory* points out:

It was not until the close of those first fifty years of growth and stabilization that any general recognition of Religious and Community life was accorded by ecclesiastical authority. At the Lambeth Conference of 1897 the subject of Religious Communities was raised and considered by a committee of the Conference in a spirit of sympathetic appreciation, with express thanksgiving to God for 'The manifold tokens of His blessing upon the revival of Religious Communities in our branch of the Catholic Church.' [2]

Thus it was inevitable that the early attempts to revive the religious life should have been '. . . for the most part private and self-contained; they were unsupported by ecclesiastical authority, and often gravely suspect, and embarrassed by discouragement or opposition.' [3]

The earliest proposal for the establishment of sisterhoods, the open letter by Dallas, envisaged them as parochial organizations, being under the control of the parish clergy. Wackerbarth's proposal was concerned more with general principles than with a detailed scheme, and consequently he did not specifically deal with the authority relationship between the orders and the Church of England. But in 1843, Neale's *Ayton Priory* took up the issue and proposed that the monastic houses he envisaged should be placed under the authority of the bishop. There is a considerable difference between the parochial and episcopal source of authority, as Pusey himself noted. It is bound up with the question of continuity in the fulfilling of long-term goals, the element of community, the relative merits of sisterhoods and deaconesses, but above all with the degree of autonomy available with each system: this discussion will be resumed under the second feature of the ideal type. What is important here is to note that early schemes did find it necessary to specify the authority link between the orders and the Church of England.

But there were some interesting perceptions of where the authority of the Church of England lay—not surprisingly, since there was a whole range of possible sources of legitimation which different groups employed. Pusey, for example, made an explicit distinction between the authority of the Church of England and the authority of its bishops, as Benson shows:

> When one who was alongside of him tottered from the faith, and said, 'we trusted the Bishops, and they have failed', Dr. Pusey said, 'I never trusted the Bishops; I trusted the Church of England'. [4]

Pusey's attitude to episcopal authority was apparent from the first foundation of the Park Village Sisterhood. It was necessary to devise a daily routine of devotions for the sisters, and this was done by adapting the seven Hours of the Breviary in such a way that the bishop would not be offended, as Pusey pointed out in a letter of 1848 to one of the lay members of the committee, Mr A. J. B. Hope:

> We know of no resource but to go to the same source from which our English Prayer-book is taken, and to give them such devotions *as we felt sure we could ourselves use in the Bishop's presence . . . There is, of course, nothing discountenanced or only half-countenanced by the Church of England . . . there is no passage read from a Father which I could not myself preach in a sermon before the Bishop, nor any prayer which the Bishop himself might not use.* [5]

But later in the same letter, Pusey put forward an argument which showed that to him the authority of the bishop was secondary to his own interpretation of the authority of the Church of England. He told Hope that he regretted the Bishop of London's disapproval of his 'adaptation' of Roman books. He would have altered anything the bishop disapproved of as being contrary to the English Church, and he continued:

> *But in these adaptations I admitted whatever I believed to be true,* believing it *not* to be *contrary to the teaching of the Church of England*: in the Devotions of the Sisters there is *nothing but what is countenanced and* sanctioned in principle by the Church of England. [6]

Pusey's attitude shows very clearly what was the result in terms of relationships with the episcopacy of seeing the Church of

England primarily as a normative organization rather than an instrumental one: if the norms on which the organization was based were paramount then it was without question legitimate to appeal directly to them rather than necessarily making use of hierarchical channels of authority.

The concept of a normative model which was distinct from the existing structure of the church seems to have been particularly evident in the early attempts at reviving the Benedictine life in the Church of England. Father Ignatius, for example, often referred to his monastery as being exempt from episcopal juris-diction simply because it *was* a monastery and he cited in support of his claim the many 'exempt monasteries' in the Middle Ages and in contemporary times. Attwater turns this argument con-vincingly against Ignatius by showing that the exemption was a privilege at first granted by the bishops themselves and then made part of the Roman Catholic Church's Canon Law (which of course Ignatius repudiated). Furthermore, the Fourth Canon of the Council of Chalcedon (which took place in A.D. 451 and could therefore be incorporated in the 'primitive practice' to which Ignatius also appealed) laid down that nobody could found a monastery without the approval of the local bishop; and, adds Attwater, 'there can be no doubt what was the will of the nine-teenth-century bishops of Norwich or St David's'. [7]

After the Lambeth Conference of 1897, when general principles for the regulation of the religious life had been laid down, there could be less dispute about the Church of England's official position *vis-à-vis* new communities and thus less 'bargaining' about the normative basis of the church's authority. Perhaps it was in part as a result of this more clearly defined relationship that the Caldey Benedictines were able to engage in such a conscious process of decision-making over the period 1912–13 which finally led them corporately to enter the Roman Church. [8] It is much more difficult to take a physical step of separation when the extent to which a connection had ever existed was a matter of evaluation rather than of official demarcation.

This was never more clearly demonstrated than in some of the early disputes between sisterhoods and bishops over vows. As Anson notes:

Some of the Sisterhoods, when it was a matter of giving up vows for the sake of having episcopal approval and Visitorship, decided that the former were more important than the latter, and chose their independence rather than conform to the rulings of the authorities of the Church to which they belonged. [9]

The ease with which some of the early sisterhoods could sever ties with their diocesan bishop—and also the ease with which some bishops washed their hands of troublesome sisterhoods—suggests that the place of the latter within the church's authority structure was extremely tenuous. In the sort of situation we are concerned with here, it can be seen that the sisterhoods, by appealing to a source of legitimacy which was normative rather than formal, and the respective bishops, by appealing to a formal and institutional source of legitimacy, were faced with the problem of bargaining over the contract on which legitimacy might be based. Thus the sisterhoods could claim that they were not subverting authority by declaring their independence since no mutual agreement over the nature of the contract existed. In fact, what is found increasingly throughout the nineteenth century, and much more obviously in the twentieth century, is the framing of just such a mutual source of legitimacy on which a less ambiguous perception of authority could be based. The sisterhoods and brotherhoods recognized the advantages which could be gained on their side from a less precarious status within the formal structure of the Church of England. The bishops likewise recognized on their part the immensely valuable role which such highly committed bodies of men and women could play within the wider church. The result was a convergence of interests and a fairly flexible core of legitimation around which there could still be bargaining but which nevertheless provided a sufficiently reciprocal basis on which to elaborate authority relationships.

There were those among the early founders of sisterhoods who were extremely careful to specify a policy of complete submission to the order of the Church of England, by which was meant the contemporary arrangement of the Church rather than some normatively defined model of church order. Among these was Carter, who stated:

> I strongly feel that Sisterhoods should be kept in harmony with Church order. They will occasionally have their own special days of observances, and these ought, I think, to have the bishop's sanction; and further, they ought not to interfere with

Church services, at least so far as Sundays and Holy Days, for which a special service is provided, are concerned. [10]

Carter went on to note that the chapels of religious communities were private to the extent that they could not be interfered with from outside, but even this did not put them outside the provisions of church order, and priests who officiated in such chapels ought to protect church order. Carter was an interesting example of a founder of a sisterhood who put forward quite 'advanced' views on such things as vows (though in public debate he tended to leave the issue open), but whose relationship with his diocesan bishop, Samuel Wilberforce, seems to have been remarkably deferential and to have caused a split between himself and Pusey, who was spiritual director of the Clewer community. At all events, Carter's attitude to Pusey seems to have been somewhat ambivalent. Allchin suggests that around 1851, when the sisterhood was founded, Carter sought Pusey's advice, since the latter had a great deal of experience and was also the spiritual director of Mrs Monsell, who became Superior of the Community of St John the Baptist, as the sisterhood was called. However, Bishop Wilberforce, who was invited to become Visitor of the Society, was at that time very worried about Pusey's influence and it was not long before Pusey was removed from his role of spiritual director. In Allchin's account is the explanation that: 'There also seems to have been some difference of opinion between Carter and Pusey on this question [of spiritual director], if not on matters of principle, at least on methods and approach.' [11] If the account by Reginald Wilberforce in the biography of his father is correct, there was more than a dispute between Carter and Pusey, since in 1850–51 Carter had written a series of letters to the bishop complaining that Pusey's teaching was 'unhealthy, if not actually perverting', [12] especially in relation to Confession. Partly as a result of these complaints, Pusey was requested not to preach in the diocese of Oxford, and because Carter had asked Wilberforce not to name him as the complainant all the blame consequently fell on the bishop. It is hardly surprising that in these and similar circumstances, it was sometimes difficult to articulate the authority relationships both inside the community and between the community and the wider church.

Some of the opposition shown to the early sisterhoods from

parochial clergy was immensely fierce. Donovan, for instance, describes the reaction to J. M. Neale's community:

> The first steps [in founding the Society of St Margaret at East Grinstead] were taken in 1854 and by 1856 the Sisterhood had gained a footing. Authority was, as usual, far from sympathetic. The vicar of the parish expressed the benevolent wish that infectious disease might break out so that he could ask the Sisterhoods to undertake the first case of it, with the pious wish that it would get rid of them! [13]

Authority at a higher level, however, while it might not be at all favourable towards (or even in some cases conversant with) the principles on which the incipient communities were founded, was prepared at a fairly early stage in their development to discuss the ways in which the authority relationship might be regularized. Nor was this discussion concerned purely with means of controlling the communities; interest was also expressed in their protection.

ANGLICAN RELIGIOUS ORDERS AND THE CONVOCATIONS

In his speech to the Canterbury Convocations of 1861 and 1862, Seymour explained that he had brought forward a motion asking for the establishment of rules by which women's institutions might be officially attached to the Church of England because he thought that such institutions should be done justice if they were to do the church's work; he was also convinced that the 'scandalous proceedings' at one or two sisterhoods could be attributed to the fact that the church had no rules for ordering such institutions. The last reason had been the main one in bringing the motion forward, for as he explained:

> I was led to give notice of this resolution . . . by a feeling of indignation, entertained in common with many, at the recurrence of these scandals; and by an impression that if the Church looks on at these things and does nothing, the blame of such scandals lies with her rather than with her individual members. [14]

Fortunately, there are one or two first-hand accounts of what the life was like in some of these Anglican sisterhoods, and evidence will later be given of the sort of difficulties which arose when the authority structure was so loose. But it should be noted in connection with Seymour's speech that although one or two notable scandals had been behind his introducing the motion, he did feel that because of the lack of any clearly laid down position, the sisterhoods were in a state of perpetual uncertainty.

Other speakers in the debate agreed with the necessity for a clear relationship between the church and those institutions, and the Rev. A. Oxenden thought that 'any extravagancies into which they have fallen are owing to the fact that they have been left to themselves'. [15] But an amendment to the precisely-worded motion of Seymour asking for 'certain rules' was proposed by the Rev. C. E. Kennaway, asking simply for sanction and guidance. This was seconded by Sir George Prevost, who thought the matter was not yet ripe for a code of rules, and Seymour accepted the amendment. Such a characteristically Anglican aversion to codification was immediately taken up by the Rev. M. W. Mayow, who said he was sorry that Seymour had accepted the amendment because it would be difficult to regulate sisterhoods without formal rules and this might be a cause of delay in setting them up. Archdeacon Denison also thought that the amendment was a less practical course of action because its terms were vague and general: this, he thought (with genuine insight into the ecclesiastical administration of his day) was not calculated to elicit the most practical reply from the bishops in the Upper House of Convocation. In the event, the amendment was carried, and at least one person was gratified by the freedom which this decision left to the sisterhoods: at the Church Congress of 1862, Pusey stated that he was glad Convocation had decided not to legislate on this matter because such legislation would have been too narrowing: rules, he thought, came after experience. This conception of natural growth being the most valuable form of progress in the revival of the religious life is often encountered in the nineteenth-century literature, but for Pusey there was a shrewd notion of strategy, as his advice in 1865 to the group of individuals which included R. M. Benson and resulted in the formation of the Society of St John the Evangelist indisputably shows:

. . . Pusey was present and, conscious that a Victorian bishop would generally say 'Don't!' if he were asked, but might look the other way if confronted with a *fait accompli*, advised Benson to act first and seek ecclesiastical sanction afterwards. [16]

Sisterhoods and deaconesses were next discussed in Convocation in 1875, when a Committee of the Lower House was given the task of preparing a Report on Sisterhoods, Brotherhoods and Deaconesses: this Report was presented and debated at the Convocation of 1878. By 1878, it may be noted, some forty-three sisterhoods and ten brotherhoods had already been founded, [17] so they must have appeared considerably less ephemeral than at the time of the first Convocation discussion in 1861 (when there existed twenty sisterhoods or Deaconess Institutions and only three brotherhoods). The Report was therefore able to cite a great deal of factual data on these institutions and their relationship with ecclesiastical authority. Fear was expressed that those communities which failed to seek and obtain the recognition of the authorities of the church might lapse into practices that were alien to the Church of England. Queries had been sent to the existing institutions and replies had been received from the four larger communities of All Saints (founded 1851), Clewer, Wantage and East Grinstead, and from ten smaller sisterhoods. The Report then went on to describe the various arrangements by which the communities were related to the wider church. At Wantage, the duties of warden were performed by one who acted as a commissary of the bishop, and this was agreed to be satisfactory by both sides. The Bishop of Oxford visited the community annually, and both at Wantage and at Clewer, the final profession of sisters was made in the presence of the bishop. No alteration in the Rule of any of the four largest sisterhoods was made without the permission of the episcopal visitor, and every sister had a right of appeal to him. The chaplain and sub-chaplain were generally elected by the sisters themselves but had to be sanctioned by the bishop. In the smaller communities the bishop was often a visitor and he usually agreed to appoint the chaplain.

That these institutions were no longer small and marginal growths in the framework of the Church of England can best be judged by quoting the valuable statistics contained in the Report on the number of members these communities contained. The number of sisters, novices and postulants connected with the four largest sisterhoods was not less than 460 and in the smaller communities in the Province of Canterbury from which replies had been received there were not less than 200. To this total should be added the numbers in the Province of York, the nonrespondents and the associate sisters (much like the Third Orders of the Roman Catholic orders), so the sisterhoods were an influential section of the Church of England if numbers are important. Their influence was increased by the interest which individuals of considerable prominence in one field or another took in their progress: Gladstone and Lord John Manners have already been cited as members of the committee of laymen which was responsible for founding the Park Village Sisterhood; Charles Lindley, Viscount Halifax, was instrumental in the original plans for founding the Society of St John the Evangelist; and the popular authoress, Charlotte Mary Yonge, was an associate of the Wantage Community—a role that was especially suited to the public relations work which was a large part of the early search for public support for such ventures.

The 1878 Report also mentioned brotherhoods, pointing out that although one had existed for a number of years (the Society of St John the Evangelist) they had considerably fewer members. There were in addition a limited number of deaconesses, who had the advantage of archiepiscopal recognition and regulation. Deaconesses were completely subject to the existing authorities. In a concluding section, the Report found no evidence that bishops who were hostile to sisterhoods had used their visatorial powers to oppress them, and it also suggested that smaller sisterhoods would be better off if they were affiliated to larger ones.

In the course of the debate on the Report, Archdeacon Ffoulkes wondered why brotherhoods and deaconesses had not matched the growth of sisterhoods, and suggested that in the case of women's organizations it might be because sisterhoods offered a higher ideal. He pointed out that so far only four or five bishops had offered their protection to the communities, and he thought that more should do so. Archdeacon Emery was much more in favour of deaconesses because while sisterhoods tended to work autonomously, deaconesses worked more distinctly under a bishop. His contribution to the problem of why there were more sisters than deaconesses was that the former had their life directed for them, which was what women needed: this explanation, as a later chapter will show, reverses the most frequently encountered view of deaconesses, which held that *they* were most subject to direction and control. Prevost followed this by proposing a vote of thanks to those prelates who had been friendly towards the communities and had maintained a just authority without unnecessary interference. He was seconded by Canon Butler (founder of the Wantage Community in 1848) who said he had not intended the matter of sisterhoods to be brought before the House so soon, since the church usually allowed institutions within to grow before it considered them. Later in the debate, which was centred on the two issues of whether or not perpetual vows should be permitted and how detailed should be the rules which the church laid down for these institutions, Prebendary Ainslie put forward the argument that to bring private and voluntary institutions like the sisterhoods under the authority of synods of the church was an infringement of their personal liberty. The existing situation showed, he argued, that progress could be made in the face of non-recognition and even opposition, so why should the sisterhoods be singled out for control by the synod and not the other voluntary associations [18] which formed part of the church? Episcopal authority was needed, he thought, but it should go no further than that. Canon Rawlinson agreed, and contended that the bishops individually, and not in synod, were *executives*, but Archdeacon Lord A. Compton thought it was illogical to argue that sisterhoods were private institutions with which the church should not interfere and then to ask the church to interfere by arguing in favour of episcopal authority. Butler stated that the sisters themselves really did desire to have some authority from the church. The eventual outcome of this debate was the appointment of a joint committee of both Houses to lay down the general principles on which the recognition and regulation of these institutions could be achieved.

This committee never met, and the next discussion of sisterhoods and deaconesses was in 1883 when the Upper House had the issue raised once again, this time by the Bishop of Winchester. He found it difficult to know what sort of authority these institutions needed to be under: some sisters, he thought, considered themselves answerable only to the bishop who originally gave them his licence. The Bishop of Lincoln thought that the question of these societies of women ought to be taken up by the bishops in synod if they were to be offered episcopal protection. The Bishop of Truro suggested a committee to look into the position of sisterhoods, because it was not the latters' fault that they had grown up outside the church, and he thought it would be difficult to bring some of them under episcopal control at this late stage. There was agreement on this last point from the Bishop of

London, who saw one of the barriers in the way of episcopal control as being the way that branch houses were frequently set up in other dioceses, and the Bishop of Exeter thought it should be in the power of the bishop as visitor with authority over the mother house that branch houses were not founded in other dioceses without the permission of the respective bishops. At the end of this debate the joint committee which had never met was discharged and a committee of the Upper House was appointed to look into the relationship of sisterhoods and deaconesses to the church.

In 1885, Reports were presented at both the Convocation of Canterbury and the Convocation of York, and the Bishop of Winchester, who presented the Report to the Canterbury Convocation, observed that the members of the committee had not seen the York Report on the same topic. The Canterbury Report's sympathetic treatment of the sisterhoods is attributed by Allchin to the presence on the Committee of G. H. Wilkinson, Bishop of Truro, who had founded a sisterhood, the Community of the Epiphany in 1883: 'For the first time there was a member of the episcopate who had an intimate knowledge of the inner life of a sisterhood.' [19] This Report was a significant step in what we have referred to above as the process of 'bargaining' to establish an agreed basis for mutual agreement on authority, by the church in its formal decision-making role on the one hand, and by sisterhoods on the other. It recognized that the charitable work done by the sisterhoods was only one aspect of their activities, and that for the sisters themselves the life of the community was just as important:

> Nor is charity the only, or perhaps the chief motive which inspires the desire to enter such Communities. Experience shows that, in point of fact, some women are conscious of a call which binds them, as they believe, to dedicate themselves wholly and irrevocably to a life of special devotion to God. [20]

The committee would not accept vows, however, and they suggested a framework within which sisterhoods could operate. The bishop should agree the Rule of a particular community and should have visiting powers and admit sisters. In the case of a branch house, the bishop of the diocese in which it was situated should have authority over it, and relationships with the parochial clergy must depend on the bishops, though the clergy ought always to be consulted when external work was being undertaken in their parish. The Upper House asked the committee to continue meeting and to prepare Resolutions based on the Report and submit them to the House, but due to death and illness among the committee's members this was never done. There was an interesting sequel to the Report, however, and it shows once more how a concession on the part of the church authorities made it possible for the relationship between the sisterhoods and the wider Church of England to be regularized on a formal basis. The issue was taken up again in 1890 when a new committee was appointed which presented Resolutions based on the 1885 Report. The eventual outcome was approval of the Resolutions almost without alteration, but the important development as far as official authority relationships were concerned is described by Allchin:

> The delay of the last five years proved fortunate for the Sisterhoods. The fine distinction between promises and vows, which had been made in 1885, was lost sight of in 1890, and, apparently without anyone noticing it, what had originally been described as a promise *to* the Bishop became a promise *in the presence* of the Bishop. Although this did not expressly sanction life-long vows, it clearly permitted it, for a promise in the presence of the Bishop could be, and was, taken to mean a vow to God. Thus the practice of most of the Sisterhoods was recognized, and the Upper House was saved from passing a resolution which would have prevented nearly all the communities from seeking episcopal recognition. [21]

The 1883 Report of the Convocation of York on 'The Church Ministry of Women' contained similar ideas to those of the 1883 Canterbury Report in that the bishop was given the primary role, both in the official dedication of the sister to her work and in dispensing her, should this be needed, from sisterhood life. In the course of a debate concerned, as it seems, more with the terminology surrounding religious communities than the principles on which they were based (for instance, the Dean of Chester thought that the use of the word 'chastity' in sisterhoods implied that marriage was a source of defilement, and Canon Knowles objected to the expression '*called* by the Holy Ghost', since '*moved . . .*' was more in keeping with Prayer Book language), Canon Body plainly based his argument on a situation which had often been envisaged by the early founders, for example Pusey, but which now very obviously applied. Sisterhoods, he pointed out, were a *fait accompli*:

> Another point upon which he [Canon Body] desired to lay emphasis was that, as a matter of fact, sisterhoods existed. It was not a question whether they should be called into being; they existed already, and the question of most practical importance was how to bring them into such a state of ecclesiastical recognition and dependency as might save them from such lamentable developments as might grow up if they left them independent of the control of the Church. [22]

In the same debate a point of view was expressed by the Archdeacon of the East Riding which, it is arguable, if taken into account from the very beginning of Convocation's concern with women's institutions in 1861, might have made the case for sisterhoods somewhat harder to advocate: he simply thought that they should not be dealing with two such vast subjects as deaconesses and sisterhoods together. Strategically—though this is not to say as the result of a conscious plan—it was to the advantage of the advocates of sisterhoods to have deaconesses and sisterhoods debated at the same time. We have noted Allchin's observation that the first debate was characterized by 'unreality' because at that time many of the participants were not sure what the main differences between the two types of institution were. The differences were, of course, quite radical (in terms of our distinction between sources of traditional legitimacy in the Church of England, each institution was located in a different period of church history) but the distinction was less obvious if the common characteristic of deaconesses and sisterhoods, the fact that they were two types of charitable work for churchwomen, was the one around which the debate took shape. In terms of MacIntyre's concept, a consensus about the secondary issues relating to the two types of institution detracted from a primary, and possibly disruptive concern with their theological basis: in the event, the latter emerged as a very detailed concentration on points of terminology. This amounts to saying that, if an advocate of deaconesses wanted to criticize sisterhoods in a debate concerned with both, he would tend to express a preference for the former and then go on to catalogue their particular advantages rather than concentrating on a negative attack on the latter. Thus eventually the official concession over vows was accepted almost without anyone being aware of its significance. And it is interesting to note that the outstanding 'Protestant' onslaught at the 1932 Convocation came not during a debate on sisterhoods and deaconesses but on religious communities. The issue was consequently a much more 'open' one, and the opportunity to make a specific attack was taken.

BROTHERHOODS AND AUTHORITY WITHIN THE CHURCH OF ENGLAND

The question of brotherhoods and their relationship to ecclesiastical authority was never such a vexed one as that of sisterhoods. In the first place, they were male institutions, and this meant that ascribed sexual characteristics gave a greater degree of role freedom than was accorded to women. An argument which will be explored later is that the early sisterhoods demonstrated something akin to an incipient feminism, and this was without doubt one of the reasons for their unpopularity in certain quarters. Secondly, at least part of the proposals for brotherhoods envisaged them as being composed of celibate clergy, who by virtue of their ordination already had an official authority position within the church. Thirdly, brotherhoods were somewhat analogous to the colleges of Oxford and Cambridge in that they were celibate communities. Fourthly, such institutions were almost invariably described as supplementary to, and supportive of, the parochial system in large towns, which placed them in a co-operative relationship with the church from the beginning. But finally, and perhaps most important, they were called into being by the Convocations themselves, or at least could be claimed to have been. In this sense they were creatures of the wider church in the same way that the Dominicans originated quite specifically as an organization founded to defend the church.

In 1889 a committee of both Houses of the Convocation of Canterbury produced a Report on 'Organizations to reach classes now outside Religious Ministrations'. This committee, incidentally, had been set up as the result of a debate in 1888 which had been particularly concerned with the apparent success of the Salvation Army and the Methodists in reaching the lowest

strata in the population. Four possible solutions to the inefficiency of the urban parochial system were suggested: (1) a large-
scale subdivision of parishes; (2) a large increase in clerical staff;
(3) a substantial increase in Lay Leaders in Missions; and (4):

> Establishing under Episcopal sanction and control in our large
> towns Brotherhoods of clergy living together bound during
> such residence to celibacy, receiving nothing beyond their
> board and lodging, and pledged to render their services at the
> bidding of their Warden, whenever asked for by Incum-
> bents. [23]

In order to gain some impression of people's reaction to these
proposals, questionnaires had been sent to eighty 'able and
experienced clergymen and laymen', and of those who replied
(both to the whole questionnaire and to particular items in it) the
numbers in favour of each scheme were:

Scheme	Pro.	Con.
1	12	22
2	35	0
3	2	19
4	48	5*

* A similar straw poll conducted by the Convocation of York at the same time
found, out of 117 returned questionnaires, 64 in favour and 28 against brotherhoods.

While there was clearly the largest number in favour of brotherhoods, some of the voting on other alternatives is interesting.
For instance, the subdivision of parishes was not very much
favoured, partly perhaps because of the possible drop in income:
at all events, the Report pointed out that the Ecclesiastical Com-
missioners were unable to find the funds to endow new districts.
The second proposal met with unanimous support but was also
impracticable because of lack of funds (and one gets the impression when reading the Report that this was the point at which the
'cheap labour' argument began to emerge). The interesting
rejection of the proposal to increase the number of lay readers
shows that the clergy were concerned to preserve their professional status and it suggests too that the conception of brotherhoods in the majority of people's minds was of organizations of
ordained clergy, as indeed they predominantly were.

As was outlined in the section on instrumental legitimations, most of the argument about brotherhoods revolved around their role as supplementary adjuncts to the parochial system; since they were to be ancillary organizations they were clearly subject to the authority of the bishop and of the local incumbent. There were still a few misgivings about the extent to which brotherhoods could be subjected to ecclesiastical authority, however, and in the 1890 debate on the Report Archdeacon Farrar spoke in favour of putting brotherhoods in strict subordination to the authority of the bishop of each diocese in which they were established, and believed they should only operate by invitation from, and under the sanction of, the parochial clergy. He did not want to see the establishment of an *imperium in imperio* and a clash between the secular and regular clergy. In a vivid analogy, he said he was confident that the church would be strong enough to control its creation, unlike Frankenstein and his monster. It might almost have been in echo of Farrar that the Rev. E. K. Talbot, speaking in the debate on Religious Communities at the York Convocation of 1934, said:

> The religious communities desired in no kind of way to be regarded as abnormal freaks of the Church. They desired to be considered as constituting a normal feature of the life of the Church wherever that life was in full vigour. Moreover, for the healthy development of the communities it was of great importance that there should be some regulation and control. [24]

As well as those proponents of religious orders in the nineteenth-century Church of England who put forward the classical claim to be providing a necessary service for the church by means of their vicarious oblation, which was pointed out in one case as being close to a notion of 'spiritual utility', there were those with experience of the Anglican communities who tried to articulate their relationship with the church in organizational terms. Paul Bull, of the Community of the Resurrection, looked at the revival of the religious life in retrospect and in the early years of the twentieth century, and interpreted it in terms of growth within an adaptive and organicist church. This is an example of the systemic theory used by Rudge, [25] and it is an interesting statement, in organizational terms, of a process which was interpreted by other writers in theological terms, when the religious orders would be seen as examples of 'living' Christianity or 'Catholicity':

> Differentiation of function is essential in the life of every highly developed body . . . In her work of healing the disease of the human race, the Church is well served by her ordinary practitioners, the parish priests. But their work of edification surely needs supplementing by differentiation of function, by missioners who are specialists in the work of conversion, by students in every branch of knowledge, who in a life of prayer and worship and communion draw from the heart of God the secret of wisdom for the healing of the nation. Many of our best thinkers are quite unfitted for the routine work of parish priests, but can consecrate their great gifts to the service of God in the cloister. [26]

This passage, which was written outside the period being studied, but was partly an interpretation of the nineteenth-century revival, presents an interesting version of the secularization debate. There are two main editions of the secularization argument which may for convenience be labelled 'ancient' and 'modern'. [27] The 'ancient' argument points out that in the fourth century, when the church ceased to be a persecuted and other-worldly minority group and became the official religion of the Roman Empire, it experienced a process of compromise and institutionalization which is closely related to, if not actually synonymous with, the process often defined as secularization. Against this interpretation prominence has already been given to the argument of many writers concerned with the religious life, that it was at precisely this period in the church's history that virtuoso communities, linked with the church but acting as a counterweight to its worldly compromise, grew up. The 'modern' edition of the secularization argument states, briefly, that as institutions become more and more differentiated, in the sense of occupying a more and more specific area of competence, then the church, which originally had diffuse functions, occupies a less and less significant social role. [28] The passage from Bull suggests an alternative interpretation: that the process of differentiation involves the church just as it involves other institutions, and that the revival of the religious life which began in the nineteenth-century Church of England was one aspect of the adaptation of the church's organization to enable it to fulfil more effectively its specialized religious functions.

THE INDEPENDENCE OF ANGLICAN RELIGIOUS ORDERS

Despite the immense progress that was made at the meetings of Convocation, it is nevertheless true that even at the end of the century the relationships between some communities and the church of which they claimed to be part were fairly unstable. The communal secession of the Caldey Island Benedictines which occurred in 1913 was the result of the development of increasing autonomy within the community coupled with a certain amount of lack of compromise on the part of the church authorities. [29] It is of course inevitable in cases where formal authority structures are not completely delineated, that individual personalities will figure much more prominently in disputes over authority roles. This is why individual Anglican bishops were so significant in the history of the developing relationship between the Church of England and its religious orders, as Bishop Gore was in the particular case of the Caldey Benedictines. But it was recognized that a formal definition of authority relationships was more satisfactory than an inherently unstable network of personal ties, just as in the early church the friendly relationships which existed between certain bishops and the first monks were gradually superceded, at least within Western Christendom, by more formal regulations. The need for such a development in the Church of England was gradually recognized by Convocation, and at the 1878 meeting of Canterbury Convocation, Archdeacon Iles put forward a particularly valid plea for uniformity in the regulation of sisterhoods, since if the matter was left to the discretion of individual bishops the founders of sisterhoods would tend to shop around the different dioceses to find which one suited them best because of a sympathetic bishop. On the side of the communities themselves there was a similar recognition of the need for a well-defined source of authority, and it was given a theological validation by R. M. Benson in a letter of 1882, which shows Benson's important role as a mediator in the process of agreeing on a settled relationship between the church and its orders. On the one hand he demanded that the authorities of the church should recognize the spiritual as well as the instrumental goals of the communities—it was 'sacrilege' to consider orders solely as means—but elsewhere he could be equally firm on the necessity by obedience:

> If *Religious* are to criticize, what is *the world* to do? If the Religious has not learnt to be silent, how will he attain the salvation promised to the lowly? The bishop ought to feel that he can act towards us with a hearty confidence in our simple co-operation. [30]

Nevertheless, it was still possible at the end of the nineteenth century for a sisterhood to renounce ecclesiastical authority almost at the stroke of a pen, which suggests that authority relationships were still tenuous and not yet institutionalized. The most obvious example of this is the case of the Sisters of the Church and Archbishop Benson. The sisterhood had been founded in 1870 by Miss Emily Ayckbowm (or Ayckbown) [31] in connection with a large charity organization which she had also founded known as the Church Extension Association (1863). Around the year 1895 the sisterhood and the association came under attack from two sources, the Protestant Alliance and the Charity Organization Society: the former made the charge, which was almost universal in ultra-Protestant pamphlets of the nineteenth century, that the sisters were cruel to the orphans in their care, using 'mechanical restraints' to control them and 'cruelly tearing portions of their body' with sharp spikes; the latter made the equally common and (for them) heinous charge that the CEA had distributed indiscriminate charity. Added to this was the secession from the sisterhood of a group of fourteen sisters (eleven professed and three novices) who expressed dissatisfaction with the administration of the community and the CEA. They were unhappy about the rapid growth of the sisterhood (it totalled 160 sisters at the time), about the way the religious life of the community was sacrificed to the immense pressure of work, about the lack of consultation with the Council of Sisters; and they further complained that the sisterhood had no visitor.

There were links with the ecclesiastical authorities. Dr Jackson, the Bishop of London (who succeeded Tait in 1869) 'took a fatherly interest in the new Sisterhood', [32] gave it his blessing and approval and licensed the Rev. R. C. Kirkpatrick as its chaplain. But it was not until 1903 that the Bishop of London filled the office of visitor, and in 1895 the community's lack of official support was a source of real weakness. In 1892 the

Archbishop of Canterbury had accepted the position of Patron of the CEA, *not* Visitor of the Community. In 1894 the archbishop, E. W. Benson, inquired about the terms on which illegitimate children were taken in by the orphanage, and he was not altogether satisfied by the reply he received. [33] As can be judged from his biography, Benson's attitude to sisterhoods was an uncompromising blend of gratitude for the work they did and rejection of the principles on which they were based. In one conversation he is reported as having said:

> No one can admire more than I do the magnificent work that they do, but I consider it to be individual work for Christ, and not conducted on Church lines; I have several times remonstrated about this, and my views are perfectly well known . . . [34]

But on a visit to the sisterhood in 1889 he had apparently adopted a more conciliatory attitude for he described the atmosphere as 'dignity, gravity, silence, beauty' and communicated to the mother superior that he thought they were 'a very *formidable* body' [35] (though perhaps there is a somewhat patronizing tone in this epithet). A diary entry of 22nd May 1890, certainly gives evidence of Benson's disapproval of the system of authority which sisterhoods were prepared to work under, and it shows his insight into one of the most important distinctions between Anglican and Roman religious orders, namely the presence or absence of a Pope to whom authority could be owed directly. He writes:

> I have had a letter from A   expressing gratitude on behalf of Sisterhoods for the kindliness of the Bishops towards them. But saying that they do not consider themselves as Diocesan but as 'Church-wide'. The Bishop of the Diocese has no relation to them, only that Bishop whom they elect Visitor and he only as Visitor. The Bishop of the Diocese may license their Clergy, but I think the old man really implies that if he does not, it does not matter.
>
> The old monastic bodies would have lasted till now if they had not been exempt from Diocesan jurisdiction so that they had no friends when the covetousness arose. But as regards themselves they were at least under discipline to the Pope; these are under no one but their chaplain, so that a pres-

byterian system has started up in the heart of episcopacy, and if the Bishops pressed them hard there would be not much hesitation in adhering to the Church of Rome. I believe this secret practice to savour much of Rome. [36]

In January 1895 Benson proposed that he should inquire into the affairs of the community and should become its official visitor on condition that the sisters agreed prior to this to abide by his decisions. This the sisters refused to do, the mother superior on her part being reluctant to put the community under the authority of someone who had little practical experience of sisterhoods. They then announced their intention of removing his name and that of all other male patrons from their literature, and of having only patronesses in future. Consequently Lord Nelson, who was then President of the CEA, was later also asked to resign. Benson's diary gives his reaction to these events:

The Mother Superior is the most comically audacious Mother in the Universe. After I began my enquiry into the rumours against them as Patron, she calmly dropped her list of Patrons. Now that Lord Nelson has joined me in telling her that her Sisterhood ought to have a fixed constitution and a Visitor, she has told him she must not expose him to so much obloquy and therefore dismisses him from his Chairmanship. Such daring simplicity will no doubt have its reward. I wrote again to her saying that her method of receiving illegitimate children, sum down, no questions asked, entirely taken charge of for life, is facilitating vice. [37]

Allchin identifies the main cause of the trouble as lack of confidence between the sisters and the archbishop, and Nelson himself wrote that 'A feeling unfortunately sprang up among the sisters that the archbishop was prejudiced against them'. [38] In assessing the significance of this incident, Allchin argues that it shows the problems which still existed for these communities at the end of the nineteenth century, 'both as regards relations with with the episcopate, and with public opinion. So long as the work of a community remained small, it might avoid criticism, but once it became powerful and important its activities had to come before the public eye'. [39] It could also be pointed out that a community which existed without a formal episcopal visitor and which could sever what unofficial links it did have with such apparent ease was liable to come under attack for precisely this element of independence.

Many of those who were concerned with the relationship between the new communities and the Church of England were as concerned with the repercussions which the lack of definition had on the internal structure of the communities. In part, the problem could be identified as one of an absence of traditional regulation of the church/order relationship. Simpson points out the lack of any 'recent Anglican tradition, no modern precedents, no experience' and he adds to this the 'pathetic instances of instability, of unsuitable persons' together with 'defections and secessions'. [40] Pusey too was aware of the dangers which were concomitant with the absence of a tradition: 'Enthusiasm without discipline was not enough to keep the new movement out of the pitfalls of fanaticism and ascetic indiscretion.' [41] One of the results of this lack of an Anglican tradition of religious orders was a phenomenon which writers have found typical of many nineteenth-century Roman Catholic communities of women, which may be summarized in the word 'stiffness'.[42] One historical account describes how the first woman in the Church of England to take vows since the Reformation found the contrast between long-established Roman Catholic communities on the Continent and the first Anglican sisterhood:

> The Park Village Sisters were 'loving and devout, but learning their life, not sure as to minute usages, which gave them a coldness and stiffness of manner'. While Miss Hughes was 'grateful for the love around her', the atmosphere of constraint 'made her less at home than she had been with the Ursulines in Bayeux'. [43]

Whether the absence of any previous decision by the authorities of the Church of England to sanction the sorts of communities that grew up actually *impaired* their growth, as some were prepared to argue, seems open to doubt. Others, like Pusey, thought that the freedom to evolve new forms of community life that resulted from the absence of official definition was a positive benefit; and it does appear significant that over the thirty-year period during which the Canterbury Convocation was discussing the issue of regulation, the type of regulation proposed changed radically. A direct consequence of the lack of episcopal guidance and direction was the tendency to proliferation shown by the communities. In the absence of continuity and predictability in relationships with authority communities tended to spring up as and when the local incumbent and bishop were sympathetic: thus 'there was a tendency for small new communities to spring up where the purposes aimed at could have been better achieved through the medium of one of those already in existence'. [44] It might be added that while the Roman Catholic Church had a strong, centralized authority with no (serious) alternative, the Church of England had both a fragmented basis of authority *and* a fairly influential alternative in the shape of the Church of Rome.

This is one more aspect of the importance of personal ties of authority in the absence of institutionalized ones, which could have disruptive effects on the internal organization of communities. Although such a process had its most severe repercussions in the early history of the revival of Anglican orders with the resulting defections and schisms, it is still a subject of discussion at the present time. In his Address, 'Authority in the Religious Life' which was delivered at the Conference of Wardens and Superiors of Religious Communities in 1960, William O'Brien spoke of the need for an external source of constitutional authority in the case of Anglican communities which was now available:

> It is a matter for thankfulness that the Church in England *now* gives to our communities *her authority* to administer a life of worship and service to almighty God in the religious state . . . The Rule and Constitution of each community provide the law of living and discipline which is to be administered within it. This must have the approval of the Church and be subject to her general supervision through the episcopal Visitor and the Warden of the Community. [45]

O'Brien then went on to speak of the problem of personal authority, and there are possibly valid grounds for projecting the problem back into the nineteenth century on the simple argument that if the problem was apparent when external authority *was* available it must have been even more endemic when it was not. The situation O'Brien indicated was where the mother superior tended to call forth loyalty from the sisters on the basis of her personal attractiveness: this, he argued, was not the same thing as a *spiritual* source of authority and it caused disruption when the mother superior gave way to her successor. In the first sisterhoods the effect on continuity and predictability of such a substitution of personal in the place of institutional authority must have generated a great amount of anomie and instability. One of the critics of sisterhoods, Margaret Cusack, who had herself belonged to the Park Village Sisterhood, described the atmosphere of the early sisterhoods (with an obvious nod in the direction of her Protestant readers):

> I could not for a moment deceive myself into the belief that Sisterhoods were in any way recognized by the Protestant Church. I knew we were simply a private institution, a sort of fancy experiment, whose existence depended on individuals who might or might not continue their support. Our numbers were few, and we rarely received a new member; so that it seemed not only possible but probable that we might die out. It was not a very cheering prospect; and yet I clung to it, loved it, and would not for any consideration have returned to my family. [46]

A much more detailed and objective account, which is sympathetic but at the same time critical, is the one given by Alice Bennett in *Through an Anglican Sisterhood to Rome*. She gives a very full account of the impact on internal organization which the tenuous authority position with regard to the Church of England caused. In the first place, there were pressures in the novitiate that induced the new applicant to remain a member:

> In the case of a novice with a good disposition, an adaptable temperament, and nothing as to vocation or non-vocation very marked, it is not so easy to say she would not be influenced to stay. *Consciously* influenced she would not be, but the whole atmosphere would be in favour of her 'persevering'. The ideal of the novitiate was to 'forget those things that were behind and to press on' to the day when the final step would be taken and the novice would become a professed sister. It was inevitable that there should be the strong if unexpressed feeling that to 'leave the novitiate was to fail', and on a sensitive ambitious temperament it would have a great effect. This was enhanced by the very unsympathetic attitude of the Bishops; and knowing many of the clergy also disapproved of Sister-

hoods, the novices felt that to discuss a difficulty as to vocation with anyone but the mistress was hardly loyal . . . [47]

Another reason why there were informal sanctions against leaving was the fact that even at that time sisterhoods were regarded as an experimental area of the Church of England and if anyone did leave this was taken by the unsympathetic observers in the wider church as well as in society at large *not* as proof of the mistaken vocation of one woman but as demonstrating the overall inappropriateness of sisterhoods. Bennett describes how at ceremonies like clothing and profession, when clergy from outside would be present, she and her fellow novices would scan the congregation in an attempt to 'size up' which clergy were in favour of sisterhoods and which disapproved. This in itself must have contributed to a very unsettling atmosphere. In 1907 Bennett went to join the Anglican Benedictine Sisterhood at West Malling in Kent, where she found grave difficulties over the problem of authority. One of the most serious difficulties occurred when she decided to leave and told the chaplain, 'Father F' of her decision:

> Unfortunately Father F did not wish me to discuss my difficulties with the Bishop, knowing his lordship was not much in favour of Sisterhoods, and would in any case advise me to leave. [48]

COMMUNITIES AND INDIVIDUAL BISHOPS

As a general rule it can be said that the Anglican bishops, who were very much concerned with social and moral problems, approved to a considerable extent the work that the sisterhoods were doing, but were not prepared to sanction the kind of community and ritual life that these groups of women were really aiming at. Some bishops were more friendly towards them than others—Bishop Wilberforce of Oxford was particularly helpful in a strong-minded manner at a very early stage in the growth of these institutions. Some bishops who were markedly hostile to the communities were simply bypassed, a process which must have done much to reinforce their suspicion that these communities were disruptive influences. In the debate of the Upper House of Convocation in 1883, for instance, the Bishop of Chichester complained that there was a large institution in his diocese (presumably the East Grinstead sisterhood) to which he had been unable to obtain entry, and he thought there would be more understanding if the sisters allowed bishops more information.

It is ironic to note that some bishops who indirectly called the sisterhoods into being by their public appeals for more charitable work to be undertaken, especially in large urban areas, later found themselves in uneasy confrontation with their unruly 'offspring'. On 1st January 1848, Dr Phillpotts, Bishop of Exeter, made an appeal for help in Devonport, where a population of 26,000 was without a parish church. Lydia Sellon read this appeal in a newspaper, offered her services to the bishop and in April of the same year began work in the slums of Devonport. On the 27th October the bishop officially sanctioned the formation of 'The Church of England Sisterhood of Mercy in Devonport and Plymouth' and gave Sellon and her companion, Miss Catherine Chambers, his blessing and benediction. There were attacks on the community from the very beginning, some of them centring on Pusey's connection with it, and in February 1849 Phillpotts, as visitor, held a public inquiry which ended in the acquittal of the sisters from all blame and the bishop's publicly expressed approval of the community. But in 1852 the attacks were renewed, this time by the Rev. James Spurrell, who had obtained information from a sister who had recently seceded [P.H. 6250] and a pamphlet debate took place [P.H. 6251, 6252, 6253, 6256, 6257, 6258]. The bishop, who was alarmed by these attacks and considered he did not sufficiently control the institution to be known as its Visitor, relinquished that office. At the same time he hoped they would carry on and wished them well [P.H. 6255], an action which attracted some criticism, as T. J. Williams notes:

> The Christian Observer, which had no love for either the Bishop of Exeter or Lady Superior of Devonport, made caustic comment: 'From the first, the Bishop gave Miss Sellon the broadest and most distinguishing support. He flattered her in public and stimulated her in private . . . And now, in a moment, with much of that soft eloquence . . . of which he is so emphatically a master, having invested her in the silken robe of his praise, proceeds to throw her overboard.' [49]

This kind of ambivalence, which was prepared to accept the valuable contribution made by sisterhoods and brotherhoods to the work of the church, without protecting them at the same time from extreme Protestant attacks, was understandably a source of bitterness among those who were reviving religious communities. As one writer comments on episcopal ambivalence: 'Nor are the Anglican bishops any whit less ready than their Roman brethren to benefit by the services of inexpensive curates [from the brotherhoods] in the dioceses.' [50]

Of course, the trouble between certain communities and certain bishops was partly due to the traditional Anglican notion of the role of bishop, which was perhaps not invested with the same amount of formal authority as was that of his Roman Catholic counterpart. Charles Gore, of the Community of the Resurrection and subsequently Bishop of Worcester and Oxford, was singularly disrespectful about his own office:

> While a Bishop, and having an enormous influence on the Church, [Gore] wrote: 'Bishops are useless creatures', and 'It is barely possible to combine the activities of being a good Christian and a good Bishop.' [51]

But one of the most typical reactions of the bishops was probably due to a strong feeling of conservatism, and Williams's description of Bishop Blomfield when faced with the development of the Park Village Sisterhood best epitomizes this:

> Dr. Blomfield (true to the ancient proverb, *'Episcopus Anglicus semper pavidus'*) was more or less afraid . . . [52]

Nor was the fear altogether unprovoked, because the early sisterhoods tended to grow up very quietly—with one or two exceptions—and to shun publicity, partly because they saw this as part of their vocation. It is worth noting that Walter Walsh's ultra-Protestant exposure is called 'The *Secret* History of the Oxford Movement'. This accusation became particularly directed at the incipient religious communities because, in attempting to revive an institution which had been missing from the Church of England for 300 years, and therefore had no tradition on which to be based, many of the founders of communities believed that the only way to engage in such ventures was to begin quietly and unobserved, and to allow the communities to go through a process of spontaneous growth. This was not altogether unconnected with the tactic of the *fait accompli*, as with Pusey, but it did have another justification.

QUIET BEGINNINGS AND PRIOR CONSULTATION

There was a great amount of concern with this problem around 1840, when preliminary discussions were going on among Pusey, Newman, Keble and Hook about the best way to institute sisterhoods. Newman was much concerned about spontaneous growth and in a letter of 21st February 1840, he wrote:

> . . . Pusey is at present very eager about setting up Sisters of Mercy. I feel sure that such institutions are the only means of saving some of our best members from turning Roman Catholics; and yet I despair of such societies being *made* externally. They must be the expression of an inward principle. All one can do is to offer the opportunity. I am sceptical, too, whether they can be set up without a quasi-vow. [53]

Hook, it seems, was in favour of 'staggering' the process by which they were made public, and of 'exhibiting works before principle. Let the good be done before we tell people why and how it is done'. [54] Pusey had written to Hook in December 1839 proposing the formation of sisterhoods, and Hook replied in 1840, proposing among other things that they should use Greek rather than Latin terms. He suggested that Pusey should train an elderly lady, 'full of zeal and discretion, and thoroughly imbued with right principles' and should send her to Leeds where she could take lodgings with two or three other women. He continued:

> Let their object be known to none but myself, and I would speak of them merely as well-disposed persons willing to assist my curates and myself, as other persons do, in visiting the sick. [55]

No rules should be drawn up to begin with and there should be no distinctive dress, but after at least twelve months there could be a meeting of any friends interested in helping the establishment, and at that meeting the rules and dress could be decided on the basis of experience. Hook remained consistently in favour of 'secret' beginnings and natural growth, as can be seen very clearly from a letter he wrote to W. E. Gladstone on 22nd January 1844, in which he protested the impossibility of 'founding' a sisterhood:

As to an Order of Mercy, the fact that people talk of establishing such a thing is proof that it will not succeed—at least, to my mind. In the kingdom of grace, as in the kingdom of nature, great things are the result of small beginnings. If you had told me that you had lately discovered a society of persons, calling themselves an Order of Mercy, who though only five or six in number had been for the last ten years doing immense good, and it was intended to add to their efficiency, then I should hope for success; they would have framed rules as practical men, and they would have had their existence, and gained certain supporters, before the world could attack them . . . The fact is, that no institution of a religious character will answer, which has not for its immediate object the promotion of God's glory by the increase of piety in the individuals forming it. As they become pious, they, for the glory of God, will do good works, and will undertake the visiting of the poor; but if the direct object be the relief of the poor, the institution will only supply a better class of overseers. [56]

Hook indeed showed a very profound consciousness of the spiritual growth required by genuine religious communities, but his argument, while recognizing the importance of spiritual dynamism, seemed to favour complete organizational inertia.

Samuel Wilberforce himself, as a Dean in 1844, gave much the same sort of advice to a lady who wished to form a sisterhood. He advised her to be very cautious indeed and suggested she should begin with 'small and unobserved steps'. [57] Butler of Wantage, who had a close relationship with Wilberforce when the latter was Bishop of Oxford, put forward much the same ideas. Mention has already been made of his comment at the 1878 meeting of Convocation, that the church should have let the sisterhoods grow before debating them, and in an Address of 1873 he remarked that:

. . . hard work and little show has ever been the mark of this Community . . . Is not the Hidden Life the ideal of the true Sister, and where can she find it sooner than in extreme simplicity, a quiet exterior, and in deep humility. [58]

Butler was very far from being the Machiavellian conspirator that founders of communities were often made out to be, and he justified his demand for a quiet, hidden existence in theological

terms; but it is not difficult to equate an aversion for publicity
with some kind of mysterious proceedings, and this was readily
seized on by some opponents of sisterhoods, Howson among
them:

> It is only when there is some impenetrable mystery in a Sister-
> hood that we are inclined to become indignant. Wherever there
> is mystery there is suspicion, and to excite even causeless
> suspicion, in controversial times, is inexcusable. [59]

In many cases there was consultation with the local bishop,
whose authority and sanction were sought, before founding a
new community. There was prior consultation with Bishop
Blomfield over the Park Village Sisterhood, though when it
actually came to showing him the Rule which had been drawn up,
there was a certain coyness, as Pusey explained in his letter to
A. J. B. Hope in 1848:

> When it was done [the grafting together of the various Rules],
> Dodsworth and myself looked over it, with a view to what the
> Bishop of London would think; and several little points were
> altered (language chiefly) on his saying, 'The Bishop would not
> like that'. This was kept to be shown to the Bishop, whenever
> trial enough had been made of the institution, for him to be
> ready to take it up. *We could not bring it before him sooner, without
> asking him to do the very thing* which he naturally did not wish to
> do yet. For if he saw the rules and sanctioned them, the Sister-
> hood would have been at once under his sanction. This we
> wished, but could not ask for. [60]

According to Cusack, in his adaptation of existing Rules, Pusey
rejected entirely the part of the Constitutions of the Nuns of the
Visitation which authorized an appeal to the bishop in the event
of a dispute between the Superior and the Spiritual Father. And
although the bishop's reaction had been kept firmly in mind when
the Rule was originally framed, it appears that in 1849, when
Blomfield applied to see the Rule, he very much objected to the
sisters being described as 'spouses of our Lord, completely
separated from the world'. [61] Perhaps the letter from John
Manners to G. W. E. Russell, which the latter quotes in his
biography, *Dr. Pusey*, best conveys the sort of consultation that
went on with Blomfield before the sisterhood was formed.
Manners quoted from a note he made at the time:

Had an interview with the Bishop of London about the Sisters of Mercy, at which he said it was dangerous in such times as ours to propose such a scheme. . . . But, after discussing the chief points and agreeing on most of them, he said he would consult with the Archbishop, and so the matter rested for a couple of months; and he has now written me a letter which I think will authorize us to proceed. [62]

On the other hand, since this was the first organized attempt to start a sisterhood, and since Blomfield was so clearly *pavidus*, it is hardly surprising that this was as solid a basis of authority that the committee of ecclesiastical *entrepreneurs* could obtain.

Given a more friendly bishop who was involved and consulted from the start, together with a founder who wished to provide active work for women first and foremost and then by a process of 'spiritual gradualism' allow the life of such a community to develop, the situation could be very different—as is shown by the Wantage sisterhood. In an Address in 1849, the year after the sisterhood was begun, Butler stated:

Moreover in this present time surely Martha's work must be the fittest preparation for Mary's. Surely it is hard to leave this world after many years spent therein, suddenly to renounce that increasing activity of mind and body, so common in this generation; the heart languishes for want of that to which it has been used, the sudden revulsion is too great, there is danger of formalism; it is unnatural to take up a life of entire prayer and contemplation without some preparation, some gradual step-by-step beginning. Martha's part seems well fitted for this. [63]

Simplicity and loyalty to the Church of England were made the two principles around which the Wantage Sisterhood was organized. When asked to state the aim of the community, Butler once gave it as

. . . simple, honest loyalty to the Church to which it belongs, that is the Church of England, the Church of our native land. . . . We wish to follow in the steps of those great men who heralded the great Catholic Revival in the Church of England, and who never 'left their first love', as Dr. Pusey, Mr. Keble, Charles Marriott, Hugh James Rose, and others of their kind . . . [64]

In 1850 when Archdeacon Manning, who had recommended the
first superior, and the superior herself, Miss Elizabeth Lockhart,
both went over to Rome, it was to his diocesan bishop, Wilberforce of Oxford, that Butler turned. Wilberforce gave his strong
support, and in a later comment on these events Butler saw the
relationship between the sisterhood and the Church of England
as being very much due to the influence of this bishop. The outcome was the continuation of the sisterhood and in 1854 the
official appointment of Harriet Monsell as superior of the sisterhood, a most significant event, as Butler noted in the *Parish
Journal*:

> The Bishop went in the morning to the Home and there
> instituted Sister Harriet. This seems a most important step, and
> probably she is the first ecclesiastically appointed Superior in an
> English house of this kind since the Reformation! [65]

INNOVATION OR IMITATION?

An important aspect of the relationship between the religious
orders and the Church of England is the extent to which the new
communities can be seen as innovations, having little continuity
with the traditions of the church, or as imitations of specifically
Roman Catholic institutions. In one sense these two characteristics
can be viewed as polar opposites, since a logical concomitant of
claiming that a particular institution is not a copy of another is to
claim that it is new. A particularly good example of this is provided by Mosley's account of the way in which the original Rule
of the Community of the Resurrection was drawn up:

> The Rule of the Order was to be new, not based directly on
> Benedictine or Dominican patterns. The aim was to reproduce
> the life of the first Christians, of whom it is recorded in the Acts
> of the Apostles that 'they continued steadfastly in the Apostles'
> teaching and fellowship, in the breaking of bread and the
> prayers'. [66]

The problem which revivers of the religious life faced in the
nineteenth century was that they wished to institute active
women's orders (indeed, the authorities of the Church of England
were unlikely to sanction any other form of life) but most of the
available models of this kind of institution were to be found in

the post-Reformation Roman Catholic Church. The Rule of the Sisters of Charity of St Vincent de Paul which Pusey consulted when framing the Rule for the Park Village Sisterhood was written in 1655, and the Rule of the active women's branch of the Congregation inspired by de Sales, which Carter adapted for use at Clewer and Neale for East Grinstead, was probably written around 1610. [67] As Prestige points out, Pusey's practice of adapting Roman Rules and manuals of devotion, which resulted in popular attacks on him, was due to the lack of anything else. In the absence of native creations, selective transplants were necessary. On the other hand, Liddon doubts whether Pusey gained much from his visit to a Roman Catholic sisterhood:

> . . . Pusey had intended to visit Ireland in 1840 in order to make inquiries respecting the working of the Roman Catholic Sisterhoods in that country. He carried out this project in 1841, but although he visited some convents, and witnessed the reception of a Sister, there is no evidence of his having gathered from this quarter much experience or information which could be turned to account in his projects for Anglican Sisterhoods. [68]

This argument over the extent of imitation is very closely related to a chicken-and-egg argument which emerged in the nineteenth century with regard to evidence of catholicity. As Simpson puts it, wherever catholicism prevails, monasticism appears. R. M. Benson expressed it slightly differently:

> Any sectarian body, if it falls into a state of degradation, loses all capacity of self-recovery; it has no Divine life. The sect may show forth great powers for a time, but it will be only for a time; very soon the phraseology and the habits which seem to constitute its very goodness may become miserable forms of deceit and corruption, and there is no possibility of restoring that which was before. But in the Church of God there is a personal sanctity of the Holy Ghost, and all the holiness of the Church comes from His personal operation dwelling within the Church. [70]

According to this interpretation, the impetus towards the revival of the religious life had a supernatural source and any apparent imitation was purely incidental: since the origin of the revival was beyond human control, it would have happened anyway.

But the argument could be stood on its head, and in a pamphlet of 1863 'Brother Ignatius' seemed to do precisely that. [71] He argued that the national Church of England had no hand in the dissolution of the monasteries, which was solely Henry VIII's doing, and as a result of this the Church of England was deprived of one of the chief and ancient features of catholic religion. The lack of monasteries was an argument against the catholicity of the Church of England so they should be restored. In this interpretation, or so it seems, the causal direction is reversed and takes the form: if we do not revive monasteries, we will not be called catholic. Perhaps Ignatius, in his clumsy but guileless way, had stumbled on an unspoken and even unconscious idea in the minds of monastic restorers, but it implies that imitation may have been a more important factor in the revival than the more 'spiritual' argument suggests. [72]

There are fragments of evidence, however, which lead to the conclusion that among some of the more central figures in the revival there was little conscious imitation. Miss Sellon's outraged disclaimer that she was running a nunnery is one such fragment and is worth quoting as a suitable note on which to end this chapter. The disclaimer came at the public inquiry by the Bishop of Exeter in 1849, when Miss Sellon was questioned by the bishop:

Q. You are called the 'Lady Superior'. Did you adopt that title in order to mark the similarity of this institution to conventual ones?

A. I do not know what is understood by conventual.

Q. Was it your intention to imitate the Convents in Roman Catholic countries?

A. No! no! my lord.

Q. Did you intend to make it a Nunnery?

A. OH, DEAR, NO! [73]

NOTES

1 Advisory Council on Religious Communities, *A Directory of the Religious Life* (London, S.P.C.K., 1943), pp. 6–7.
2 ibid., p. 3.
3 ibid., p. 1.
4 Richard Meux Benson, *The Revival of the Religious Life* (London, 1900), p. 169.

5 Henry Parry Liddon, *Life of Edward Bouverie Pusey* (London, Longmans, 1892–7), vol. III, p. 25 (original emphasis).

6 ibid., p. 26, original emphasis.

7 Donald Attwater, *Father Ignatius of Llanthony* (London, Cassell, 1931), p. 72.

8 Peter Frederick Anson, *The Benedictines of Caldey* (London, Burns, Oates, 1940), chap. 10.

9 ibid., p. xx.

10 [Thomas Thellusson Carter], *The Founders of Clewer* (London, A. R. Mowbray, 1952), p. 27. There is an interesting parallel here with Wesley, who was similarly concerned not to compete with established church services.

11 Arthur Macdonald Allchin, *The Silent Rebellion* (London, S.C.M., 1958), p. 73.

12 Reginald G. Wilberforce, *Bishop Wilberforce* (Oxford and London, A. R. Mowbray, 1905), p. 53.

13 Marcus Fitzgerald Grain Donovan, *After the Tractarians* (London, Phillip Allan), p. 43.

14 Quoted by Allchin, op. cit., 1958, p. 158.

15 Quoted by ibid., p. 159.

16 John Gilbert Lockhart, *Charles Lindley, Viscount Halifax* (London, Geoffrey Bles, 1935–36, vol. 1, p. 118.

17 Anson, op. cit., 1964, pp. 594–6.

18 He particularly had in mind Missionary Societies.

19 Allchin, op. cit., 1958, p. 166.

20 Quoted in ibid., p. 166.

21 ibid., p. 167.

22 *Journal of the York Convocation*, 1883, p. 97.

23 *Chronicle of the Convocation of Canterbury*, 1889, p. 2.

24 *Journal of the York Convocation*, 1934, p. 86.

25 Rudge, op. cit., pp. 29–31.

26 Paul Bertie Bull, *The Revival of the Religious Life* (London, Edward Arnold, 1914), pp. 230–1.

27 See M. Hill, *A Sociology of Religion* (London, Heinemann, 1973), pp. 232–4.

28 Bryan Wilson incorporates this into his definition of secularization: 'By secularization, as already explained, is meant the process whereby religious thinking, practice and institutions lose social significance' (*Religion in Secular Society* [London, Watts, 1966], p. xiv). He also links differentiation with professionalization: 'In a society which is highly professionalized, and which now no longer expects to discover (amateur) saints any more than it believes in amateur clinicians, the role of the clergy becomes more distinctive within religious institutions, and becomes more specifically, and more circumscribedly, religious' (ibid., p. xviii).

29 On this issue see Peter Frederick Anson, *The Benedictines of Caldey* (London, Burns, Oates, 1940), pp. 162–3 and George Leonard Prestige, *The Life of Charles Gore* (London, Heinemann, 1935).

30 George Congreve and W. H. Longridge, *Letters of R. M. Benson* (London, Oxford, A. R. Mowbray, 1916), p. 52.

31 See Allchin, op. cit., 1958, p. 205 ff.

32 ibid., p. 440.
33 The issue of illegitimate children may appear to be a trivial one, but there was a great deal of unease about some of the types of charitable work which 'respectable' women were expected to engage in, and penitentiaries, orphanages and lying-in hospitals were all subject to the extreme innuendo of ultra-Protestant pamphleteers (see, for a perfect example, the book by William Hogan *Auricular Confession and Popish Nunneries* [London, G. B. Dyer and Co., 1846]. That the founders of religious communities were aware of the possible misinterpretation that might be put on their activities is illustrated by Bishop Grafton's advice to very clearly distinguish who were the members of the *community* and who were the *inmates*.
34 Arthur Christopher Benson, *The Life of Edward White Benson* (London, Macmillan, 1899), vol. I, p. 594.
35 ibid., vol. II, p. 273.
36 ibid., vol. II, p. 307.
37 ibid., vol. II, p. 640.
38 Quoted in Allchin, op. cit., 1958, p. 215.
39 ibid., p. 216.
40 William John Sparrow Simpson, *The History of the Anglo-Catholic Revival from 1805* (London, Allen and Unwin, 1932), p. 243.
41 George Leonard Prestige, *Pusey* (London, Philip Allan, 1933) p. 115.
42 See Chapter 2, footnote 55.
43 Thomas Jay Williams and Allan Walter Campbell, *The Park Village Sisterhood* (London, S.P.C.K., 1965), p. 30.
44 Frank Leslie Cross, *Darwell Stone* (Westminster, Dacre Press, 1943), p. 212.
45 William Braithwaite O'Brien, *A Cowley Father's Letters* (London, Todd, 1962), p. 151.
46 Margaret A. Cusack, *Five Years in a Protestant Sisterhood and Ten Years in a Catholic Convent* (London, Longmans, Green, 1869), pp. 69–70.
47 Alice Horlock Bennett, *Through an Anglican Sisterhood to Rome* (London, Longmans, 1914), p. 26.
48 ibid., p. 126.
49 Thomas Jay Williams, *Priscilla Lydia Sellon* (London, S.P.C.K., 1950), p. 116.
50 Anselm Hughes, *The Rivers of the Flood. A Personal Account of the Catholic Revival in England in the Twentieth Century* (London, Faith Press, 1961), pp. 114–15.
51 Nicholas Mosley, *The Life of Raymond Raynes* (London, Faith Press, 1961), p. 35.
52 Williams, op. cit., 1950, p. 28.
53 Liddon, op. cit., vol. III, p. 6.
54 ibid, vol. III, p. 7.
55 ibid., vol. III, p. 7.
56 W. R. W. Stephens, *The Life and Letters of Walter Farquhar Hook* (London, Richard Bentley and Son, 1878), vol. I, pp. 226–7.
57 Ashwell, op. cit., vol. 3, p. 292.
58 Arthur John Butler, *Life and Letters of William John Butler* (London, Macmillan, 1897), p. 131.
59 Howson, op. cit., pp. 138–9.

60 Liddon, op. cit., vol. III, p. 22.
61 Cusack, op. cit., quoted by Anson, op. cit., 1964, p. 230.
62 George William Erskine Russell, *Dr. Pusey* (Oxford, London, A. R. Mowbray, 1907), p. 63.
63 Arthur John Butler, op. cit., p. 153.
64 ibid., p. 154.
65 ibid., p. 142.
66 Mosley, op. cit., p. 35.
67 Eleanor A. Towle (*John Mason Neale* [London, Longmans, 1906], p. 234) says of the Rules which Neale consulted: 'The Rule of St. Margaret's, East Grinstead, was founded upon that of the Visitation of S. Francis de Sales before he converted his community into a cloistered order; but it had its origins in the principles governing and animating the Society of S. Vincent de Paul.'
68 Liddon, op. cit., vol. III, p. 11.
69 Simpson, op. cit., 1932.
70 Richard Meux Benson, *The Revival of the Religious Life* (London, 1900), p. 154.
71 P.H. 1103.
72 There was a very similar argument, based on utilitarian criteria, about the problem of 'surplus women' and this will be taken up in the final chapter.
73 P.H. 6244, pp. 65–6. See also P.H. 6251, where Sellon again denies knowing anything about Roman orders.

8

The Ideal Type and the Nineteenth-Century
Anglican Orders: Further Considerations

THE FIRST PROPOSITION of the ideal type—which was that orders exist only as part of a wider church—seemed to indicate a significant feature of the Church of England revival, namely the process of articulating an agreed authority relationship so that the orders themselves could receive official sanction, and thus stabilize their internal authority structure, while the church was able to utilize the spiritual and instrumental provisions of these virtuoso communities on a regularized basis. The other features of the ideal type provide equally valuable insights into 'problem areas' in this study, and the present chapter will complete the discussion of the model set out in chapter 2.

2. Though part of a church, the religious order always maintains a certain degree of moral and organizational autonomy.
   One of the main formative influences on the Oxford Movement, it was argued, was the growing tendency towards State interference in the Church of England of the early nineteenth century. Laski gave great prominence to this precipitating factor, and in chapter 6 it was cited as a parallel component in the origin of the Wesleyan revival. It is therefore interesting to note that a contemporary writer saw religious orders (he was talking specifically about 'Religious Confraternities') as one kind of 'solution' to the problem of the intense agitation generated among High Church Anglicans as a result of pressure by the State. [1]
   Writing in 1866, Baring-Gould argued:

There is a danger looming in the Church horizon likely to precipitate the formation of Religious Confraternities. We mean the threatened attempt to interfere with the liberties of the English Church on the part of Government, to compromise its orthodoxy by Privy Council decisions, and to curtail its ritual, thereby striking a blow at its doctrine. [2]

He thought it was uncertain what line the bishops would take on this issue, but their support was not worth counting on in view of their recent oppression of 'the Catholic party'. The bishops were not a particularly courageous lot, he went on, and he suggested that when the bill to alter priests' vestments was introduced into Parliament, the episcopal mitre should go too and be replaced by a white feather. How could their support be gained when they owed their position and their income to the State? Baring-Gould spoke of two possible courses of action if the State should attempt to interfere with doctrine and ritual: the first was secession to Rome; the second was the establishment of a Free Church; both alternatives were 'too violent to be contemplated with composure'. [3]

He thought the weaknesses of the Roman Church had been thoroughly probed by Anglicans, so that the 'leakage' Rome-ward had almost stopped. Furthermore, the precedent of the Non-jurors' schism was a warning against separating into a Free Church.

> But the revival of monastic orders would present no such difficulties; and the liberty enjoyed by Religious Confraternities, and their freedom from episcopal supervision, would render such asylums peculiarly tasteful to the aggrieved. It would be a split in the Church of England, but not a secession from it. [4]

Such a move would almost certainly cause bitterness and contention between 'regulars' and 'seculars', but as long as 'violent measures' were not employed against such a movement, no real split need occur.

This is an interesting and highly sophisticated justification of religious orders, and it is not far removed from the 'counterweight' idea put forward to explain the development of monasticism in the church of the fourth century. It says, in effect, that if the wider church cannot preserve its autonomy (from the State or from the secular society) then certain groups will attempt, without abandoning altogether the more universalistic religious institution, to preserve a system of selective autonomy.

Almost certainly, the Oxford Movement's reassertion of the 'spiritual' and autonomous basis of authority in the Church of England had a very important predisposing influence on the revival of religious communities, and it is part of the search for proofs of 'catholicity'.

Almost inevitably, in view of the attitudes and theological direction of the bishops, the early communities were autonomous growths—'private and self-contained . . . unsupported by ecclesiastical authority, and often gravely suspect', as the Advisory Council's *Directory* puts it. [5] The dialogue which developed between the new institutions and the authorities of the Church of England was first of all concerned with the issue of whether a certain degree of autonomy was necessarily evidence of disloyalty; and later, as the orders became a more familiar aspect of the Church of England and as relationships between the church and the communities became institutionalized, the question was more one of the definition of acceptable limits to the autonomy which had now been more or less agreed in principle.

The need for organizational autonomy was perceived by Pusey from the very beginning of the sisterhood movement, and he also noticed a feature of the historical development of religious orders—the tendency for decentralization to result in the imposition of a high degree of control at all levels by the authorities of the wider church, and for a high degree of autonomy to be possible only on the basis of considerable internal centralization in the orders. [6] Thus he always rejected the idea of forming 'parish sisterhoods'. Liddon points out that the Park Village experiment led to several attempts at imitating it. 'More than one clergyman thought that he might "start a Sisterhood" just as he would institute a coal-club, with a view to better carrying out his own duties to his parishioners; and Pusey was asked for counsel and assistance.' [7] Pusey's experience of founding sisterhoods had, however, convinced him of the complexities involved and he was doubtful whether many parish priests had the necessary knowledge and skill. 'He was inclined to discourage entirely the tendency to multiply small local Sisterhoods; and of late years the wisdom of this advice has been generally recognized.' [8] Liddon quotes from a letter by Pusey to the Rev. D. S. Govett in 1855:

. . . I think that the plan of clergy 'forming Sisterhoods' is an amiable mistake. Of course the clergy can help . . . Many can carry on a work: few can begin it. Sisters can only be trained in a Sisterhood: and, if God gives the increase, future Superiors would come best from the training in existing Sisterhoods... [9]

Perhaps the clearest indication of Pusey's preference for centralized orders rather than parish sisterhoods is given by the 1864–5 negotiations with Arthur Stanton over St Saviour's Church in Leeds, summarized by Clarke:

When in 1864 Dr. Pusey invited Arthur Stanton of S. Alban's, Holborn, to become Vicar of S. Saviour's, Leeds, the offer would have been accepted if Pusey had not objected to Stanton's intention of founding a sisterhood to work immediately under himself, while Dr. Pusey proposed to introduce sisters from the Devonport Community. Stanton was only twenty-five at the time. [10]

Clarke then referred back to the letter of 1855 which is quoted above, setting the whole discussion in the context of a remarkable proliferation of small sisterhoods, with all this implied for a stable and continuous source of authority:

Enthusiastic would-be-founders embarked on the task with a light-heartedness, or perhaps one should say with a faith and courage that almost takes one's breath away. It seemed the most natural thing in the world for a zealous parish priest, surrounded by needs with which only women could cope, to found a Sisterhood. [11]

The Pusey–Stanton episode is worth citing in some detail because it throws light on the question of centralized sisterhoods as a means of achieving autonomy and continuity, as well as other major questions such as the degree of direction required by women—something which will emerge in the following chapter when the subject of the status of women is taken up. Stanton was curate of St Alban's, Holborn (a centre of the 'Ritualist' development of the Oxford Movement under Alexander Mackonochie), and in September 1864 he wrote to Pusey saying that he understood Pusey was looking for someone to work at St Saviour's in Leeds, that he was interested in this possibility, and that he knew of someone else who would fit in with the work of St Saviour's and would form the nucleus of a brotherhood: this was Arthur Tooth. Pusey at first replied that he had someone else in mind, but when this eventually fell through the negotiations with Stanton and Tooth were taken up again. Stanton and Tooth travelled to Oxford together, where they had an interview with Pusey, as a result of which they apparently considered the matter settled. However, on 10th January 1865, Pusey wrote to Stanton: (a) asking him to give an account of the extent of his ritual practices, and (b) querying a letter which had arrived that day from Tooth mentioning the foundation of a sisterhood 'under your [i.e. Stanton and/or Tooth's] supervision under all its details'. [12] Tooth had furthermore stated that no other society should work in the parish. At this point Pusey spoke of his own plan for a sisterhood which had been formulated by Sellon: 'The Plan, which the Lady Superior at Devonport had undertaken at my request, was not at all Parochial.' [13] He stressed that in his opinion sisterhood work should be *independent* and that young clergy should not be involved with a society of women Religious. One reason was that mother superiors would often be old enough to be the younger clergy's mothers. He continued:

> My own conviction is that Clergy who become, in fact, the supervisors of houses of religious women have taken (it may be from the necessity of the case, and the inexperience or want of decision of those whom they invited to be the nominal Superior) an office which cannot last. For it cannot be supposed that the Parochial Clergy in any given Parish should always be eminently qualified to undertake the direction of government of a religious society of women. [14]

Pusey thought it would take enough of Stanton and Tooth's energy to found their proposed brotherhood without taking on any other projects. In a further letter of 14th January, Pusey argued that another reason for allowing sisterhoods autonomy was the need to let women direct their own work. He argued:

> I think that it is a wrong ambition of men to wish to have the direction of the work of women. I should fear that it would be for the injury of both. Women ought to understand their own work, the education and care of young women; or they would not be fit for it at all. [15]

The opinion expressed in this passage has obvious implications for the status of women in general.

A long correspondence ensued, in which a secondary theme

emerged—the respect for Miss Sellon and the Devonport Sister-hood founded by her under Pusey's guidance—which suggested a personal motive in Pusey's judgement as well as a statement of general principles. In one letter Pusey remarks:

> I saw the cramping effect of Mr. Dodsworth's plan of making the Sisterhood at Park Village, a sort of district visiting society. The sisters got disheartened in their work. The society started with new life, when it joined the Devonport Society and carried out the expansive plans of the Lady Superior in full co-operation with the clergy, but directed by herself. [16]

The amalgamation of the two sisterhoods described by Pusey in his letter had occurred in 1856, partly as a result of Dodsworth's defection to Rome in 1851, and, significantly, partly in response to the Crimean nursing expedition led by Florence Nightingale in 1854, when it became obvious that solidarity on a more universalistic basis than that provided by a parochial unit was an effective means of support in a highly demanding situation. But Pusey's defence of Sellon against 'unkindliness' throughout the correspondence and his presentation of her as a model of the kind of centralized sisterhood he wished to see formed had disadvantages in that it deflected attention from an important issue of principle to a 'latent' personal reason. As Tooth commented: 'Dr. Pusey was urgent in Miss Sellon's favour.' [17]

Nevertheless, Pusey's concern was distinctly with the necessity for providing an autonomous basis for the sisterhoods' organization which would remove the uncertainties and discontinuities of a parochial foundation. One of his more amusing statements rejecting the parochial notion is the following:

> In this way, [under the direction of the parish priest] sisters of mercy should live like the Scythians in their wagons, and, like gypsies, be ready to remove, on the warning of the Parish Priest, as the gypsies do at that of the parish constable. [18]

Another observer who noted the disadvantage of sisterhoods being founded on an individualistic basis was Florence Night-ingale. She was most concerned to develop a system of nursing on formal rather than personal criteria, so that changes could be made in the system as and when they were needed. She criticized sisterhoods because she believed that they relied too much on the zeal of their founders: 'Her chief criticism of sisterhoods was that when the founders were gone, change would often set in, and high professions become mere words. "Lillies that fester smell far worse than weeds". ' [19] This was very much the tendency which Pusey feared in the proliferation of parish sisterhoods, and some measure of the instability of the smaller sisterhoods can be estimated from Anson's chronological list of nineteenth-century foundations. [20] Of sixty-one sisterhoods founded in the Church of England [21] between 1845 and 1900, twenty-six had become extinct by 1964 (most of them after a relatively short period of time).

As was argued in the previous chapter, much of the developing relationship between the religious orders and the Church of England in its 'official' capacity—as represented by the bishops and the Convocation decisions—can be seen as a convergence of 'interests' whereby the church came to accept that a certain degree of autonomy was a necessary feature of the communities, while the communities gradually recognized the advantage of episcopal recognition and protection. By the 1880s the Convocation debates on brotherhoods and sisterhoods had lost a great deal of their argument in favour of rigorous and detailed control of the whole range of the communities' organization and show a greater willingness to accept autonomy and self-regulation by the communities, especially on points of detail. A good example of the liberal attitude is provided in the 1885 debate of the Convocation of York, when the Archdeacon of Durham said he wanted the sisterhoods to have a large amount of liberty, and he also wished that the bishops would show a large amount of paternal affection and interest towards them. Above all, he implored the members of Convocation not to be pedantic over points of detail in the regulations they drew up for the sisterhoods, as the Report shows:

> But he did implore them, if they were going to do the thing at all, to do it thoroughly, to set it on a right footing and not to try and hamper them with the contemptible little regulations about not allowing vows, and not allowing the bishops to demand from them the belief that they were inspired by the spirit of God. [22]

Mandell Creighton, when Bishop of London at the end of the nineteenth century (1897–1901), had more friendly relations with the sisterhoods which existed in his diocese than his predecessor

Bishop (whose encounter with Emily Ayckbowm was described in the last chapter) but shared Benson's views on the office of visitor (it will be remembered that the Sisters of the Church did not have an official visitor until 1903) and thus he believed that the autonomy of any sisterhood must be conditional on the acceptance of a visitor. His views were very clearly expressed in the criticisms he made of the constitution of a new sisterhood, and it is notable that in the same passage he emphasized *autonomy* as a desirable goal:

> Generally I think you have given too great power to the warden, whose office ought not to contain anything that affects initiative of new work or interference with the executive, which I would advise you to reserve to the superior.
>
> The community should be self-governing. You invite a warden to help you on the lines which you have laid down: there is no need that he should have any power to alter or direct them. He is your spiritual officer, let him have influence, not power, within your constitution.
>
> But I feel strongly that the office of visitor ought to be in accordance with ancient precedent. I see some of the suggestions indicate a jealousy of the visitor. This is the bad point about sisterhoods. They want to be absolutely independent, obedient only to their own will. Such a claim is entirely unworthy. We must all work in obedience and cannot afford to do without it. But observe, the obedience is only to your constitution. The office of visitor is merely that of guardian and interpreter of the Statutes. He has no power of interference. He has merely to pronounce if you are keeping your own laws. The proposal to depose him if you do not like him is subversive of all rule. He is your judge chosen by yourselves: he must be for life, and must be independent of your will. He must have a veto on change of the constitution in important matters: for by undertaking the post he gives a guarantee to the general public of your object and your methods. You must not use him and then throw him away when you are started. A bishop is already visitor of many institutions, he is not likely to interfere unless there is strong cause. The fear is of too little rather than too much. [23]

That Creighton saw the office of visitor as being just as much a way of protecting the autonomy of the Anglican orders as a way of containing that autonomy within limits which would guarantee the orders an official standing within the Church of England emerges from this extended quotation, and elsewhere he re-iterated the visatorial function of protecting autonomy when he stated: 'What communities suffer from is unauthorized inter-vention from outside. This can only be met by immediate reference to the visitor. Communities now find this a real ad-vantage.' [24]

It is interesting to note that Father Cary, of the Society of St John the Evangelist, one of the strongest defenders of the autonomy of the religious life, especially in the 1930s, against what he saw as being formalistic encroachments on the part of the newly formed Advisory Council on Religious Communities, noted the importance of referring back to an early period of church history to justify autonomy within Anglican com-munities. Cary thought that

> . . . the Religious Life of the English Church is the true child of the Catholic Revival, inasmuch as its appeal lies to the history and spirit of the earlier ages before Papal authority, through the action of Innocent III (A.D. 1215), took to itself the ultimate control over all Religious Life. [25]

He argued that ideally each religious community was a family based on the voluntary association of its members on its own terms, and thus it lay outside 'the inquisitorial control of Ecclesi-astical authority'. This organizational autonomy he extended also to the moral autonomy of each community, and in another account he spoke of the need for each community to 'set its own spiritual purity and vitality before all other considerations'. [26] This 'advanced' moral theory of the religious life is one which is not frequently encountered in nineteenth-century debate: for the most part the earlier institutions were in public debate more occupied in demonstrating their legitimate position within the Church of England.

But they were often called upon to justify ritual 'innovations', and this they did by reference to the post-Reformation High Church practice of eminent figures, some of whom have already been discussed, and also to the more pragmatic demands of the work or events of a chance nature. It is interesting that the Communion service should have played a major part in the early controversies at the Devonport Sisterhood. One of the accusations made at the Bishop of Exeter's inquiry was that Dr Pusey had illegally celebrated Holy Communion in the House of the sisterhood whilst visiting the community at Christmas 1848. This was justified on the grounds that the service used was the office for the Communion of the Sick, the patient having been Philip Pusey. (Reservation of the Blessed Sacrament, an important Ritualistic observance, was later justified under the same Rubric.) The bishop also used pragmatic grounds to soften opposition to the Sisters' wearing of crosses, which he regretted, but added: 'Ladies are ladies'. [27] And the ritual observance of the sisterhood, which marked a divergence from the normal Anglican practice of the period, was later justified by the biographer of the local (sympathetic) incumbent, George Prynne, on similar apparently pragmatic grounds. Prynne explained:

> . . . I gave her [one of the Sisters] Holy Communion, which she longed for, and in the morning she was dead. It was during the raging of the cholera that the Sisters asked to be allowed to receive Holy Communion daily to strengthen them for their daily work.

and his biographer adds:

> It is believed that this was the first restoration of the Daily Eucharist in the Church of England since the Reformation . . . [28]

The biographer in this case—Albert Kelway, one of the 'darkness before the dawn' portrayers of the eighteenth-century Church of England [29]—was not as diligent as he might have been in looking for a precedent, though with John Wesley among the short list of possible selections it is perhaps understandable. The general point, however is still valid. Many of the 'autonomous' beliefs and practices ('autonomous' in the sense that they represented deviations from predominant norms of observance in the nineteenth-century Church of England) were justified on criteria other than primarily theological ones, and thus fit the characteristic pattern of pragmatic avoidance of theological conflict. Daily Holy Communion was linked with the need for support during a period of stress—in this case a cholera epidemic—just as some of the later support for vows was seen as a way of attracting recruits who might otherwise be alienated.

3. In the main tradition of Christianity the religious order can never be dualistic in the sense of rejecting the world as totally evil (though its theology may occasionally approximate very nearly to a form of dualism) although it both totally rejects any compromise of its conception of the Gospel ethic and isolates or insulates itself against normal social intercourse.

There is an important link between the Evangelical movement of the early nineteenth century, with its profoundly imbued sense of evil and the fundamental depravity of man, and the leaders of the Tractarian revival and there is a very important link indeed between the Evangelicals and the founders of communities. [30] One of the most thorough appraisals of the wider affinity is that by Voll, and on the special place of the communities he says:

> ... the origin of these Communities goes hand in hand with the appearance of Evangelical undercurrents in the Oxford Movement. The same historical forces lie behind Missions and behind the revived Religious Life. Without attempting an exhaustive definition, we see the renaissance of the monastic ideal as a symptom of Catholic Evangelicalism in the Anglican Church of the Victorian Age. [31]

An outstanding representative of this Evangelicalism was Father R. M. Benson of the Society of St John the Evangelist. Many of his utterances were indistinguishable from those of Evangelical writers: 'People must live in their Bibles, and they will find the nourishing power which is therein. It is of no use to believe the Bible at second hand. We must use it devotionally, so as to learn its truth by experience and constant colloquy with God.' [32] It is therefore not altogether surprising to find that a writer on 'The Spirit of Father Benson' [33] notes that Benson stands apart from modern schools of theology which have come into being in the twentieth century, particularly with regard to his concept of evil as an extremely powerful force, though the writer adds that Benson's conception of evil was not the same as that of a Manichean dualist. However, some measure of his 'dualism' emerges from the sort of statement which Benson made about the active life as against the contemplative. Prayer comes first: 'All else is accidental. It is the contemplative life gazing up to God and doing battle with Satan, which is the essential characteristic of all Christian life.' [34]

It was earlier argued that one of the ways in which the dualistic equivalent within religious orders could be accommodated within the wider church was by interpreting the orders as 'forward troops' in a widespread battle. Benson undoubtedly made this a very strong feature of the religious life in his presentation of it:

. . . [Christ's 'society of the regenerate'] mingled itself with the world in a way very different from that which was the divine Will. It had been the divine intention that this society, keeping itself separate from all contact with the world, should absorb the world into itself. But on the contrary this society chose rather to yield itself up to various forms of contact and alliance with the world, and so it became absorbed in the world.

Nevertheless, from age to age increasingly, there was within the Church the cry of the spiritual life. The life of Adam was forfeited by his sin, but however the degradation of Christendom might increase, the life of the Church could never be forfeited. This living power within the Church made itself manifest from age to age, speaking in various forms; and thus individuals were called away from the world, whose aim should be to realize that which God had intended for His Church. They were to rise up to a life of separation from the world, and yet were still to realize the social law of being under which man was formed. [35]

Benson is thus a very good example of a combination of the dualistic tendency of religious orders, given a highly characteristic content by the Evangelical background of the nineteenth-century Church of England, and the classical monastic notion of a religious order providing 'vicarious oblation' for the rest of the church with the concomitant notion of preventing the church's complete compromise with a basically evil society. This theme is especially characteristic of the S.S.J.E., for we find Benson's contemporary George Congreve putting forward a highly dualistic concept of fallen nature:

Then, next, let us go on to think of nature as not only powerless because dead without God; not neutral merely, but hostile. 'The flesh listeth against the Spirit.' Because Satan is the prince of this world, our fallen nature is fallen under his dominion, and it can only act as the instrument of God, so far as it is given up by man purely to God, and delivered by divine grace from the tyranny of Satan. [36]

The Society of St John the Evangelist was, of course, a well-established and officially sanctioned order within the Church of England, and hence its self-image of a reformist group, criticizing and reminding the church of its fundamentally other-worldly nature was not likely to be seen as subversive, especially when the language used by its main protagonists was so much like that of the Evangelicals, who were very often the main antagonists of religious orders. Father Ignatius used similar Evangelical language and he expressed similar intentions towards the Church of England when, in *The Epistle of Ignatius, the Monk, to his disciples in the Lord Jesus*, he gave his object as: 'to form a glowing centre of love for Jesus within the pale of the English Church, to enkindle the coals, the burning coals of fire, with which to heap the heads of our fellow churchmen, and our fellow citizens of those sects which are alien to the Church.' [37] But Ignatius's method of heaping coals was rather different from those of the S.S.J.E., involving for instance a public denunciation at the 1893 Birmingham Church Congress of Charles Gore's *Lux Mundi* which took the form of an occupation of the platform when Gore was called on to speak, together with Ignatian nuns in the street proclaiming anathema on Gore from placards.

Another feature of the religious order's specific interpretation of the dualistic confrontation with the forces of evil—the particular significance of prayer in the middle of the night—is a persistent theme in Anglican accounts of religious orders. One example of this has already been given above (page 34) and there are many others. For instance, an ex-monk of Llanthony in his account of prayers at 2 a.m. casually remarks: 'When you come to think of what all the other people in the World are doing at 2 a.m., there is very little worship of God going on . . . more likely the Devil.' [38] Just to show how continuous this theme is, we might cite a pamphlet of 1935 by an Anglican religious, in which the events of 2 a.m. are made more explicit:

No doubt many Christians, as they wake in the night in London and listen to the traffic which never stops, think of the traffic in souls in London Streets and the bitter sufferings of the destitute. They may be glad then to remember that the Contemplative monks and nuns are up and praying. Who can tell how many Souls are saved by their costly prayers in the cold, dark winter nights? [39]

This concern with a direct effect of the wider process which Troeltsch calls 'vicarious oblation' is an interesting recurrent notion going far back in Christian history and may be best understood in the nineteenth century as an example of what has earlier been termed 'spiritual utility': whenever it appears, however, it is tinged with the Evangelical concern with sin.

As far as the insulation of special dress is concerned, this was given a highly instrumental interpretation by the nineteenth-century sisterhoods. In addition, while a distinctive dress for 'respectable' women was viewed as a protective form of insulation, preventing insults and embarrassing advances in slum districts, it was ultimately as a means towards gaining social *access* to poverty-stricken families that this initial insulation was of value. There is little disagreement about its value, and again it is interesting to note that the characteristic response to a charge that sisterhoods were copies of Roman convents was by recourse to an instrumental legitimation. Even Margaret Goodman, as was seen in the last chapter, agreed that the dress was a valuable means of gaining access to poor areas in cities. Nor was it only sisterhoods who made use of this practice, for in the 1863 Annual Report of the North London Deaconesses' Institution we read: 'Deaconesses, protected by their dress and office, have been able to penetrate localities which, under ordinary circumstances, could scarcely have been assigned to district visitors.' [40]

The earliest evidence does not unequivocally bear out this argument, however, for in the first, understandably secretive days of the Park Village Sisterhood even the simple black costume aroused the suspicion that they were 'disguised Roman Catholics'. Mr Dodsworth, the local incumbent, advised them to wear 'a more ordinary dress' in the street, and he especially favoured the idea of 'black and white, with coloured shawls' because it would show they were not nuns, but the only concession made was 'a little white about the neck'. [41] However, popular attitudes had apparently changed by 1849, for in *The Guardian* of 17th January that year it was stated that:

> There are many places, also, where no woman could visit the sick and the poor and be safe from insult, *whose very dress and appearance did not shield her* as one unmistakeably consecrated to religion. [42]

From then onwards there was widespread acceptance of the

principle of a special dress—which might have been thought one of the most likely practices to be condemned as a 'Romish imitation'—and we find few overt attacks in Convocation debates and Church Congresses.

Very occasionally, the question of the symbolism of the dress arose, as was in the case in 1881–2 when Bishop G. H. Wilkinson was engaged in founding the Community of the Epiphany. In a letter to Miss Julian Warrender, the eventual mother foundress, in March 1882, Wilkinson writes:

> You will consider about the dress. I feel that we ought not to put any woman in an uncomfortable position by giving her a dress which will expose her to remark, and you will know better than I do how to avoid this danger.
>
> Personally, I like every colour better than black, and I dislike long trains which are always being trodden upon; and, on principle, I object to any head-dress which is an imitation of the trappings of death, for we are not only dead but risen in Him. [43]

As in the case of other features of the ideal type, the nineteenth-century Anglican orders shows a specific historical deviation from the model on the question of insulation and special dress.

4. The religious order demands total commitment.

Under the heading of total commitment appears the issue which dominated all the debates of Convocations and Church Congresses in the nineteenth century. A very distinctive complex of historical factors resulted in a development from a situation in which no form of vow could receive official sanction to one in which, with certain conditions, the Church of England was prepared to give its sanction to the three religious vows of poverty, chastity and obedience, in most cases for life. As was suggested earlier, the bishops' concession on this point was a most important step in the process of drawing the existing orders into an official position of authority within the Church of England.

To understand the position of different groups within the Church of England on the issue of vows it is necessary to look at some of the statements of the Reformers—in this case the Continental Reformers, Luther and Calvin—because these theologians were prominent in the pedigree of that school of Anglican churchmanship which went 'not to the fountain head', as Hook put it, but to 'the doctors of the Reformation'. [44] The Evangelicals of the post-1836 period tended to interpret the Scriptural blueprint in terms of the Reformation church, and the latter had laid down a fairly precise position on vows, as Biot shows. [45]

Luther's attitude to the religious life was, at first, close to the traditional Catholic conception—he himself had been a member of the austere Hermits of St Augustine—and after his excommunication he began to envisage a reformation of the religious life which would still retain the value of perpetual commitment. It was Luther's colleague Melanchthon who found no justification for monastic vows in Scripture and argued that monastic vows were not special but should be the aim of all Christians. Luther eventually came to reject monastic vows since they were 'contrary to the word of God because they established a *particular* and *superior* way, one different from the Gospel way, which is to say different, finally, from the way of the one and only Mediator'. [46]

Calvin is rather more difficult to pin down on the subject of vows partly because, unlike Luther, he had no personal experience of them, but he rejected the distinction between counsels and precepts and he thought the lawfulness of vows must be judged on three criteria: (a) The question of the person to whom the vow was made—vows were promises to God and were valueless unless pleasing to God, but since He had revealed what was pleasing to Him, no additional human contrivance could have any value. (b) The question of the person making the vow—a vow must be in the power of the person who makes it otherwise it was meaningless, and it should not curtail the liberty which God had given man; thus a vow of celibacy was inadmissible because it consisted in promising something which did not depend on man himself without a call from God to such a form of life except temporarily, and it showed contempt for the God-given freedom to marry. (c) The question of why the vow was made—there were only four lawful purposes; as regards the past, to render thanks or to do penance; as regards the future, to protect oneself against dangers or to incite oneself to the performance of duties. On all these criteria the vow of baptism was wholly legitimate, more so because it was God-willed. But monastic vows were rejected.

Calvin noted that the monks often cited the primitive church as their justification but Calvin thought the contrast between the primitive (Augustinian) monks and contemporary monks showed the extent of corruption of the latter. But what was even more reprehensible was that the monks claimed their life to be a state of perfection, and in this way—a most interesting claim in the light of the interpretation of religious orders as a means of institution-alizing schism—the monks had formed schismatic sects:

> By their state of perfection, and by the profession by which they entered this state and which they considered as a second bap-tism, the monks separated themselves from the Church; having a rule of behaviour of their own, they wished to receive the sacraments separately from others, they cut themselves off from the fellowship of the faithful, and thus formed schismatic conventicles, or sects, each attached to some particular learned teacher, and hostile to one another. [47]

The *Augsburg Confession*, which, being more a profession of faith than a doctrinal treatise, can be seen as having a more binding effect, was even more blunt on the subject of vows: 'Monastic vows are null and void; they bind no one.' [48]

Insofar as statements of Continental Protestant opinion had an influence on the Church of England in the nineteenth century—and it is here argued that they influenced at least one major school of churchmanship, the Evangelicals—then the practice of taking vows of religion was a difficult one to incorporate within the overall framework of the church. The problem becomes an even more acute one when it is noted that vows were the most usual form of expressing total commitment, and such commitment was without doubt the goal of most of those who entered Anglican orders. From the evidence of the early Tractarian period it is quite clear that some of the leaders of the Oxford Movement found it difficult to incorporate the idea of vows within the Anglican system of beliefs. Newman in particular maintained this attitude over a long time. In 1830 he remarked in a letter to Froude:

> I have thought vows [for example, of celibacy] are evidences of *want of faith* [in the sense of *fidei*, trust]. Why should we look to the morrow? It will be given us to do what is our duty as the day comes; to bind duty by forestalment is to pay up manna for seven days; it will corrupt us. [49]

Again, in his letter to Bowden of 1840, he speaks of being sceptical about setting up Sisters of Mercy 'without a quasi-vow', of which he disapproves.

Although there had been considerable publicity of the utilitarian functions which communities might serve (in the works of Dallas, Southey and Wackerbarth), thus making it tactically a more viable means of reintroducing the religious life into the Church of England, it seems clear that since the motive behind this kind of life was primarily one of self-consecration, we might expect to find the question of vows emerging at an early stage. Indeed, the *origin* of the newly revived Religious Life was in the form of a vow. On Trinity Sunday (6th June) 1841, Pusey wrote to Newman explaining that 'A young lady, who is very grateful for your teaching, is purposing today to take a vow of holy celibacy'. [50] He explained that she had 'difficulties and anxieties' in her position, that she had attended St Mary's Church (where Newman was vicar) since first coming to Oxford, and that she would be taking Communion there that day. He continued in a manner that shows just how secretly the procedure had to be carried out: 'It was wished that you should know it and remember her. You will know her by her being dressed in white with an ivory cross . . .' [51] The fact that vows of this sort were not part of the officially-recognized practice of the Church of England also emerges from the form in which the vows were taken, which was by using a translation of the Roman Pontifical. [52] The 'young lady' involved was Marian Rebecca Hughes, the twenty-four-year-old daughter of the Rector of Shenington in Gloucestershire, and although she travelled to the Continent to see how the religious life was lived in Roman Catholic communities, it was not until 1851 that she felt sufficiently free from domestic ties to found what eventually became the Society of the Holy and Undivided Trinity.

Two years later J. M. Neale, in *Ayton Priory*, took up the subject of vows. He concluded that in the existing state of the church they were not possible, but he thought they were essential to a monastic establishment, and the reason he gave was more one of the establishment of a stable community than a recognition of total self-commitment (again, one should note the audience for whom his book was intended) for he wrote: 'A monastery without vows would be little better than a religious hotel.' [53] His suggested solution was to fix two limits to vows, three months and five years, with the possibility of renewal after five years. Thus Neale, like Pusey, believed in the necessity for vows from the very beginning of the revival: others, like Carter and Butler, gradually came to accept them as necessary. As Allchin notes, 'whereas Pusey approached the problems of sisterhood life with a mind already formed, Carter only very gradually developed his views on the subject'. [54] Both Carter and Butler were prepared to let the matter rest and to await the process of natural development by which sisterhoods would become a more accepted part of the church and could begin to press claims for the recognition of aspects of their life other than the 'external' instrumental features which won recognition very early in the public debates.

Both Butler and Carter had a close relationship with their diocesan, Bishop Wilberforce of Oxford, whose relationships with sisterhoods were remarkably cordial and 'enlightened' in comparison with those of other nineteenth-century bishops. But on the question of vows he was completely firm and never altered his opinion that vows were incompatible with the teaching of the Church of England. A diary entry of 1860 notes: 'November 30— Clewer . . . admission of three Sisters—two rejected—would not consent to altering rule about *no vows*.' [55] His definitive statement on the issue came at the Church Congress of 1862. It is interesting to note that he was preceded in the discussion by Pusey, who made an attempt to deflect concern from the question of vows to the general issue of vocation. Pusey contended that 'every objection against the religious life as a *permanent state* which the individual cannot leave without sin, denies, in fact, that she can have been called by God. It is not a question of vows'. [56] But it was very much a question of vows as far as Wilberforce was concerned, for he stated:

> But if it was to be imagined from the silence of any, that those who were silent went on to approve in the first place of *vows of celibacy* being made for life, or secondly, of vows of celibacy being made for a fixed time by those who give themselves to that life, I believe it would be an entire mistake of the meeting. I am bound to say this, in order that there may be no mistake, as one holding the office God has given me, that I should not have felt at liberty to take any part in the arrangements of any sisterhood of which such vows formed a part . . . [57]

This speech became a crucial point of reference in subsequent Convocation debates for any opponent of the principle of taking vows. Wilberforce's reasons for rejecting vows were (a) that they were unscriptural; (b) that the Church of England did not sanction them; (c) that they interfered with religious liberty. Behind these arguments was the belief that vows were Roman, as Wilberforce suggested in a letter of 1867: 'I see nothing in the sister's life which is at all Roman, if vows of perpetual obligation are not taken.' [58]

Although vows were not officially recognized by Convocation until 1891, [59] they in fact existed in several communities: indeed, the first action Pusey took when reviving the religious life for women was to sanction the vows of Marian Hughes; and one of the arguments advanced (in favour of sanctioning vows) in the Convocation debate of 1891 was that unless this was done it would be impossible to bring some communities under the authority of the Church of England. Even in the communities which had an official relationship with a bishop who did not sanction vows, as was the case at Clewer and Wantage under Wilberforce, there was an unwritten assumption that the life was perpetual, and this later developed into the belief that a formal recognition of this in the shape of a vow was necessary. Carter explained the origin of this process in a letter of 1863:

The rule which says no vow or engagement is to be understood by the service which confirms a Sister, but only an obligation of obedience while in the Sisterhood, is read out to the Sisters once a week, and the service itself is also clear on the same point. If, then, as is alleged against us, we impress on the Sisters the idea of 'a vow, or insert dedication', we should be ourselves liars, and make all the Sisters liars, and place ourselves and them in this enviable position weekly. There is, indeed, *bona fide* no such thing done, or attempted to be done. But I will tell you what may not unnaturally have given rise to such an imputation.

It has always been the feeling of the Sisters that their purpose and conviction is a lifelong dedication of themselves. I never knew any one during the last ten or twelve years apply to be admitted who did not view what she believed to be her calling of God in this light. We have no need to teach it, if we desired to do so. They assume it as a preliminary; that if thought worthy to be a Sister at all, it must be for life. They have taught it me, not I them. The idea of going back and returning to the world, marrying, etc., is thought an impossibility by every one of them. [60]

He went on to describe the idea of being a sister for a time and then leaving as though having never been a sister, as 'foreign to the animus of the whole body'. But he was also careful to add that if domestic circumstances demanded it the sister would leave the sisterhood and go home to fulfil her duty.

Thus in the matter of vows, as in the matter of an active or a contemplative life, there are signs of a gradual change. It was possible to introduce the religious life in a fairly complete form, usually by the wholesale adoption or adaptation of Roman models. But in any case, whether by a similar process of imitation or, as those who were closely connected with Anglican communities certainly believed, by a natural growth which reinforced the idea that Anglican orders were genuinely an organic part of the church, the formal recognition of vows and the tendency towards contemplative forms of life (the 'Martha to Mary' trend) seemed to occur in orders which had begun with very little overt intention of instituting these practices. Whatever the reason, it is not difficult to explain the factors operating in the original attempts to form active communities without vows, since these were least likely to arouse hostility and could clearly legitimate themselves. One can also explain the later development of vows, since the formal recognition of total commitment was an important means of stabilizing and institutionalizing the communities.

5. The religious order demands considerably more obedience from its members than the wider church demands from either its lay members or its clergy.

The problem of obedience within Anglican orders may be divided into two aspects. There is firstly the problem of the *personnel* in these orders, and secondly the problem of the *legitimacy* of internal channels of authority. As a general rule it can be said that the presence of a body of recruits who had not been pre-socialized according to institutionalized personality types [61] into the norms of the religious life, and who were furthermore 'deviants' in the sense that they had rejected the predominant authority structure of Victorian family life, together with the lack of any unequivocal external legitimacy from the Church of

England, combined to create a situation in which obedience as
it was understood in Roman Catholic orders was often difficult
to achieve.

Before the first sisterhood was even founded, Newman had
noted the difficulty of maintaining the stability of such a community without obedience, and in a letter of 1840 he did not put
forward a very optimistic forecast: 'Women (no, nor men still
less) would not live together without quarrelling, as things are
among us. A very strong religious principle and a tight discipline
would be necessary.' [62] The result, as was suggested in Marian
Hughes's impression of the Park Village Sisterhood, could
occasionally be 'stiffness' instead of the more traditionally
moderated observance of communities whose foundation was
less recent. This must have been all the more evident when the
Rule was an imported, albeit adapted, set of injunctions, as was
the case with the Park Village Sisterhood. Hook's letter to Pusey
in which he suggested that principles were needed for a sisterhood
from the beginning, but rules had to be formed on the basis of
experience, [63] together with the later example of Wantage,
where the Rule went through a process of development (always
based on Roman precedents but interpreted very much in terms
of the practical experience of the community), [64] give an indication of the insight which some founders showed by institutionalizing the necessary degree of obedience and formal
control while keeping them compatible with the particular social
norms of the community's personnel. Although it might be
claimed that in adopting an already existing Roman Rule 'the
experience of the Western Church' was the most reliable guide,
it must be remembered that the Church of England had been
without many of the 'modal personalities' which the Roman
church was able to put forward as models for the socialization of
the young members of the church, and which Mecklin finds so
characteristically attached to the concept of sainthood. In short,
there was a very vague definition of the role of sister. Neither
were there any autonomous roles for women in general, so that
the problem existed on two fronts.

This is strikingly demonstrated in the case of Sellon and the
Devonport Sisterhood, within which—even in the opinion of a
sympathetic observer [65]—the life involved considerable rigour
and often arbitrary discipline. Sellon herself seems to have had a
highly authoritarian image of her role as superior: Anson calls

her 'the would-be Abess-General of all the Sisterhoods in the Church of England' [66] and her biographer thinks that 'she was imbued with the love of regimentation and discipline and, above all, with that rigid insistence on obedience which marked the organization and direction of her life work'. [67] But at least part of the explanation of her conception of obedience and of the role of superior is that she was unsure what the traditional definition was. The author of *Five Years in a Protestant Sisterhood* thinks that Sellon 'realized in her own person the Protestant idea of a Lady Abbess' and she added in a somewhat double-edged plea:

> Once more do not blame her. How could she have done otherwise? She believed, or if she did not express it in words, she certainly expressed it in acts, that the Lady Abbess was a person to be exalted on a mighty pinnacle of honour, to be reverenced with almost idolatrous worship, to be obeyed without the slightest consideration as to whether her commands were right or wrong; to rule without being in any way under rule; to subject others to the most severe exactions, and not be subject herself to any law whatsoever. [68]

The reason, as Anson sees it, was that, since Sellon's position was recognized by neither the civil nor the ecclesiastical law a hundred years ago, 'there was then no law to which she could have been subjected herself'. [69] And he cites Cusack's opinion that

> [Sellon] had entered on a certain state of life without the slightest knowledge of its duties or requirements. The only excuse for her having undertaken duties of which she knew nothing, and for attempting to teach others a kind of life of which she was herself perfectly ignorant was simply that, as long as she remained externally a member of the Protestant Church, she could not do otherwise . . . It was a case of the blind leading the blind. [70]

It is usually the question of obedience that is given greatest prominence by those who attack Sellon's sisterhood. The Rev. James Spurrell, in his 'exposure' of the society in 1852 thought that the rule enjoining complete obedience turned the members into automatons. [71] He spoke of three Rules within the Devonport Sisterhood, one of them of a contemplative type, and Sellon gave her version of this in her reply:

This society is composed of three Orders or Rules. One rule is for those who live in community, working amongst the poor, engaged in active laborious life; a second is for those who from sickness or other causes are unable to undertake this laborious work, but who wish to live a quiet life engaged in reading and prayer and such occupations as best suit their health, such as needlework, writing &c., all of which is a great assistance to those who are actively employed and who have less time. The third rule or order is for those, married or unmarried, who live in the world, not in our community, but who wish to belong to us, and to assist our work in different ways. [72]

Goodman, another of the critics of the Devonport Sisterhood, clearly indicated the relationship between internal obedience and external authority when she argued that obedience to a superior together with freedom from outside scrutiny was a dangerous and alarming development. If the inmates of lunatic asylums could be protected by law, she thought the inmates of convents should have the same protection—this was an argument which became the major proposal of the later Conventual Inquiry Society. Every entrant to the Devonport Sisterhood, according to Goodman, promised absolute obedience to Miss Sellon, and the vow of obedience was one of the main sources of trouble. Just how difficult it must have been to introduce the traditional observances of religious communities emerges from the sisters' reaction to the Chapter of Faults, for 'they said it was by no means conducive to love and charity in the house, for a Sister to tell every unkind and censorious thought about another which had crossed her mind, or every little depreciating remark they may have made'. [73]

In the later part of the nineteenth century, when the religious life for women was sufficiently well established in the Church of England for traditions and conventions to have grown up, and when the important process of official acceptance by the church had given the internal authority structure of the orders greater legitimacy, obedience was much less a problem area, and it is possible to find theological vindications of the Rules, as for instance in the work translated by R. M. Benson for the use of Sisters of Mercy:

Bear always in mind that there is no detail of your Rule which may not and will not help to sanctify you; and that if you despise little things, you imperil your salvation. [74]

6. The religious order is locally community-based and to some degree always forms a quasi-familial Gemeinschaft *and a permanent, participating ritual group.*

At first the collectivity of a sisterhood tended to be seen by the church at large, and even by some of those who were closely connected with these institutions, as a *means* to an end; as a way of achieving stability, continuity, concerted action and psychological support for members. Howson, the supporter of deaconesses, thought the fact that sisterhoods were group-based was an advantage which deaconesses did not have. Penitentiary work in particular was thought to be an area in which group activity by women was a source of support for them and—most important—a substitute family group for those in their care. This was a widely perceived function and it was alluded to by a Scottish Commissioner in Lunacy in a pamphlet of 1866 appealing for sisterhoods in asylums:

> It is natural to expect, and it is opportune, that, at a time when the efficacy of the home and family life in the cure or amelioration of certain forms of alienation is recognised, the aid of women, acting under religious or compassionate and, above all, motherly motives, should be invoked. That such an artificial maternity may have contributed to the success of the thousand communities that have sprung up, succoured and humanised their fellow-beings in the Western Church, is highly probable. But it was scarcely fictitious under such circumstances, as professed nuns were wedded to the Church, spouses of Christ, and bore the endearing names of mother and sister. The magic of such titles was felt and made use of in the hospitals of the Crimea. [75]

It was not really until the issue of brotherhoods arose that the idea of a religious community for its own sake became common in public debate. Of course, evidence of this kind of development within the sisterhoods appears at a fairly early stage, when the contemplative, more internally oriented kind of life grew out of the external works of charity. But it was R. M. Benson and George Congreve who really gave the community goal its first expression and its public presentation. As early as 1865, Benson spoke of 'the difference between a Brotherhood within the Church and a sect outside of it. A sect throbs with the passion of earth: a Brotherhood glows with the light of heaven, concentrated indeed within itself, losing nothing of its diffusive integrity by that concentration . . .' [76] In the Church Congress debate of 1888 he spoke of religious communities 'supporting the soul' and giving a greater depth to individuals. Benson and Congreve had a very similar conception of the community base of the religious life and they often put forward the idea of community as a more pristine and perfectionist form of Christian life. Two quotations, the first from Benson and the second from Congreve, reveal how far the concept of religious community as an end in itself had developed in the case of brotherhoods from the more instrumental, even associational, way in which sisterhoods were perceived: [77]

> Nor is our Society a society drawn out of the Church, but drawn together within the Church. And it is not drawn together as supplying something wanting in the communion of Saints, but as the means to arrive at the recognition of that communion. The object of all Religious Societies is to gather up, and, as it were, focus the love which ought to animate the whole body of the Church Catholic. The existence of smaller communities than the whole Church certainly implies something wanting, some imperfection, in the state of Christendom, but the infirmities of human nature necessarily obscure the divine glory which belongs to the Church. So it was that in early times such communities rose up, in which that love might be more perfectly obtained. [78]

> Fellowship, brotherhood, is of the essence of the Religious life, whether of Cenobite or of Solitary. The Religious orders did not create brotherhood as if it were a fantastic device of medieval devotion, which had its day, and is now to be regarded only among the half-forgotten curiosities of a past age.

> Religious brotherhood is not an imperfection tolerated for the present on account of the incurable weakness of human nature; it is a sacrament of Divine Love, a means towards perfection, a type of all Christian life . . . [79]

Thus the *gemeinschaftlich* characteristics of the Anglican religious orders gradually evolved out of a combination of theological and instrumental conceptions and were by the end of the nineteenth century interpreted in predominantly normative terms. This movement is closely related to the gradual emergence of the contemplative kind of life in communities that had been originally active.

7. *The religious order is originally a lay movement with considerable lay participation, and this remains as an ideal though it may be eroded by the church as a means of maintaining control.*

It is no accident that the revival of the religious life in the nineteenth-century Church of England should have been initiated by women's communities. Victorian women, faced with a choice between a highly valued role of wife and mother and an indeterminate role as spinster, sought to make provision for a greater range of laywomen's roles within a church which had previously allocated almost no roles at all to women: in fact, the only available role was the one which fitted the predominant conception of family life, namely the role of clergyman's wife. If evidence is needed that the wives of clergy were valued as a source of devoted female labour in the Church of England one has only to scan the debates and pamphlets on sisterhoods and deaconesses. Those which disapprove of sisterhoods always point to the wives of clergy as embodying the genuine form of female work in the Church of England, and proponents of sisterhoods often made approving statements about the valiant work done by these unpaid ancillaries, while suggesting how the system might be aided by sisterhoods.

One reason for the preference for deaconesses over sisterhoods among some sections of opinion may have been that the former were in a real sense office-holders in the church rather than bodies of more or less independent laywomen. In the debate of the Upper House of the Convocation of Canterbury in 1890 it was pointed out that deaconesses were admitted to their office by the laying-on of hands by the bishop and thus it was impossible to cease being a deaconess without the bishop's release or deposition. Thus, it was argued, this was not a *lay* movement like the sisterhoods. The office of deaconess may have appeared more directly a part of the official hierarchy of the Church of England and thus less subversive of authority, although in a previous Convocation debate the office had been shown to be different to, and carrying less functions than that of deacon.

Church Congress debates tended to see lay participation as an important feature of the revival of such institutions. The Church Congress debate of 1868 on this topic was headed 'Authorized and Systematic Lay Agency, Male and Female', and it was opened by Dean Howson of Chester, who said that at the present time the laity were required to do much of the work which had previously been done by the clergy, and in some cases the former could do the work better. He went on to make some interesting comparisons with other Christian groups. The Presbyterians and the Methodists, he argued, gave the laity a much more important role than did the Church of England, which, because it was a State church with good endowments, had allowed its clergy and laity to become complacent. In its attitude to the laity it was almost stiffer than the Roman Church. The next speaker, T. Gambier Parry, thought that since the dissolution of the monasteries, lay work in the Church of England had been weak and spasmodic. *Organization* was needed because lay work was unsatisfactory when it was not submitted to discipline and a rule. He made the very important observation (which will be considered at length under the next heading) that by reviving lay orders, the church would be giving authority and occupation to those of its members who were at present becoming schismatic. It was often pointed out that unless special provision was made for the more zealous lay element in the Church of England, they would find their vocation in another religious body.

In the last decade of the nineteenth century there was an explicit attempt to organize the laity into a kind of 'Third Order' on Roman lines. This was known as the Parochial or Third Order (Anglican), and it had been influenced by Canon Body, who explained that the term 'Third Order' not because of its connection with any other *particular* order but because it was modelled on the plan of the Third Order of St Francis. It was to be under the authority of the parochial system, as Rule 7 of the Order explained:

> To be duly subordinate to the ordained Clergy, as taking part in the Parochial system in which they [members of the Order] are placed. [80]

A similar type of organization, though based more on the idea of 'cells' of activists, was founded in 1943 under the name of 'The Servants of Christ the King'.

Part of the reason for the important stress placed on the *lay* element in Anglican religious communities can be explained by using an institutional analogy of David Hume's 'oscillation' theory of religion. [81] The Tractarian revival, by emphasizing the important routinized charismatic role of the clergy in the doctrine of Apostolic Succession, had presented an image of a church in which priestly vocation was especially prestigious. In order to 'mediate' between the ordinary mass of the laity and the now re-emphasized status of the clergy, it was necessary to have organizations of laity fulfilling a specialized vocation. The concept of hierarchy was clearly present in the Parochial Order, one description of which noted:

> The Diaconate is the next step to which we of the Third Order look forward, if we wish to proceed further in the Church's ranks; and as there are both men and women deacons, it does not seem unreasonable to ask for a Third or Outer Order to be added, to embrace the innumerable good people at work in our Church, and fill up a certain gap between the Diaconate and the ordinary Church member, who may unfortunately be often very unfit at first to become even a member of the Third Order. [82]

In this 'professionalization of everyone', which the doctrine of *successio* together with the more general process of differentiation had initiated within the Church of England, the orders of laymen and laywomen were accorded the particular function of 'go-betweens', as Paul Bull suggested in 1914:

> Now the widespread revival of the Religious Life would help to bridge over the gap between the priesthood and the laity by affording to men who are not called to or fitted for the priesthood an opportunity for special consecration to the service of God. [83]

8. The religious order is a collection of religious virtuosi *with an uncompromising interpretation of the Gospel ethic which is sanctioned by the church but is not put forward as necessary for all.*

Martin's contention that Protestantism rejects the dual standard and sees that 'all men are called to be tertiaries', [84] together with the evidence presented by Biot, suggests that it might be possible to find a characteristic modification of this feature of the ideal type in the case of nineteenth-century Anglican orders. What does emerge is a general refusal on the part of the church authorities at the beginning of the revival to accept anything resembling a theology of counsels and precepts, but to perceive with great clarity the need to make provision for particularly zealous or 'enthusiastic' laymen in order to prevent their defection to Rome or to the Dissenters (with the consequent loss of especially useful talent from the Church of England). At the same time, the concept of the dual standard was an accepted part of the 'private' image of religious orders. Benson is a particuarly important figure in the discussion because he put forward the notion of reciprocity, whereby the orders provided special services for the church and thereby guaranteed its spiritual autonomy. The images which were used to portray this relationship in public statements saw orders in terms of 'reservoirs of religion' or 'power stations'.

On the Reformation rejection of the dual standard we have already quoted Biot, [85] and a statement by Bishop Wilberforce at the Oxford Church Congress of 1862 shows how most Anglicans saw the issue:

> One single word on the use of the term 'religious'. I confess, after all that has been said, that I have the very deepest objection in any way whatever to applying the word 'religious' to such a life. I think it was adopted at a time when the standard of lay piety was very low . . . [86]

The Protestant line of criticism is well demonstrated in the book *Maude; or The Anglican Sister of Mercy*, which was sufficiently popular to go through two editions (1869 and 1895). The account is of an Anglican sister who later saw the error of her ways and became converted to Protestantism—the common theme of almost all Protestant 'exposures':

> Maude at this time had no notion of Christ being made unto us by God sanctification (1 Cor. i. 30); and neither in the books given her to read, nor in the instructions of the Mother Superior, was it ever hinted to her that the true Christian is in Christ, and that the True Christian is 'accepted in the beloved' (Eph. i. 6). [87]

Similarly, a Protestant Alliance Tract argued that

> The gospel was given for mankind at large, but man's boasted wisdom devises a rule of greater perfection than any given in that holy book; and thus enters asceticism, which destroys Christian charity and fosters self-sufficiency and spiritual pride, while it engenders self-absorption, selfishness and want of feeling. [88]

But the importance of the notion of making 'special provision' for *virtuosi* within the Church of England as a means of preventing their secession to other bodies cannot be overstated. It emerged in the very first proposals for sisterhoods and it permeated the whole public debate in Convocation, Church Congresses and pamphlets. Dallas's original pamphlet countered the argument that Protestantism was not capable of arousing sufficient devotion to sustain Sisters of Charity by maintaining that 'the Protestant reformed religion, when faithfully received into the heart, *is* capable of producing the degree of excitement required for the performance of such duties as will be proposed for English Sisters of Charity'. [89] Southey not only saw Anglican orders as a means of preventing schism among present *virtuoso* members of the church but as a way of repairing the breach between the Church of England and the Wesleyan Methodists. Wackerbarth's proposal in 1839 made very much the same point, for he thought that Dissenters were 'frequently persons really devoted to the cause of holiness, and who, disgusted at the laxity and imperfect acquiescence of professed Churchmen, in the dogmas and practice enjoined by the Catholic Faith, seek for a more perfect way than what conformity with the common *practice* of churchmen offers'. [90] Since perfectionism in the present state of the church led to sectarianism, it was *expedient* that these *virtuosi* should be provided with an outlet within the Church of England. Wacker- barth's argument is worth quoting at this point because it draws together many of the themes which have been dealt with in other contexts:

By the outward air of superior sanctity adopted by the Dis- senters, very many persons, who are seeking a more perfect way than the ordinary practice and example of Churchmen offer, are caught away from the Catholic faith to make ship- wreck of their Baptismal vow, and they who should have been among the foremost ranks of the Church of CHRIST, are carried away to swell, by their character and influence, the motley legions of heresy and schism. And is it not in a certain degree, the duty, or perhaps I shall gain more attention in the present age if I ask, is it not *expedient*, that we should provide some means whereby these ardent spirits may be satisfied in their out-puttings for holiness and more intimate union with CHRIST, without leaving the communion of the Church? [91]

Wackerbarth himself solved this dilemma by joining the Roman communion three years later. Newman, who followed him in 1845, had remarked of the proposed sisterhoods in 1840: 'I feel sure that such institutions are the only means of saving some of our best members from turning Roman Catholics . . .' [92]

Seymour's first speech to Convocation on the subject took up this argument, and he asked: 'Can the Church of England, can any Church, afford to lose the benefit of that zeal and love and devotion which rises above the ordinary level of religious life?' [93] In the debate on Seymour's motion at the 1862 Convocation he was followed by Archdeacon Ffoulkes, who used the example of the loss of Wesley to support the *virtuoso* argument:

> Had greater wisdom been shown 100 years ago, Wesley and Whitfield had never been driven out of the Church; and now that the Spirit of God moves the hearts of noble women to offer themselves for God's service, are we to refuse to cast around them the shield of our protection, and suffer them to be reproached for their labours for Christ's sake? [94]

The Wesleyan analogy was especially important in Church Congress debates, where there was apparently less hesitation about the value of 'enthusiasm'. At the 1862 Congress Pusey made a detailed argument on this basis:

> The Church of England should be large enough to contain every soul who would, with devoted heart, labour for her. We mourn now that Wesley was not led to form an order within the Church, rather than rend those thousands and thousands from her. We mourn here the loss of deep devoted fealty, of strong intellectual energy, of clear-sighted faith, of ardent piety, lost to us; we, the older of us, see them yet in their places, which they fill no more, as they used to go up and down labouring among us. Let us take heed how it is repeated. The longing for the religious life is deeply and widely spread amid our Christian ladies. Women are guided not by controversial arguments, but by intuitive feeling. Controversy they leave to us. But every religious woman whom God draws to more devoted service will obey that call, and if a veto is put upon their longing to lead the religious life, as it was in the primitive Church, here, she will seek it elsewhere. Alas for our Church, if she be again deprived of her flower and her promise. [95]

An even more emotive reference to Wesley—parallelling New-man's idea that Laud was 'present' in the Oxford of the early Tractarians—was made at the Church Congress of 1870, when the Rev. George Body, speaking in a debate on 'Agencies for the Kindling and Revival of Spiritual Life' (i.e. parochial missions), said:

> I think if John Wesley could rise up in our midst today, that his great and noble heart—and a greater and nobler never beat in England—would beat with exultation and joy as he saw the prelates, the priests, and the laity of the English Church gathered together in solemn conference to consider this question—how the masses of the people may be awakened to the knowledge of the Fatherhood of their God, to the love of their Redeemer, and to the power of the Eternal Spirit. And if this be true, let us remember that John Wesley did in his day, to a great degree, what we want to do today. [96]

This suggests that the supporters of religious orders in the Church of England—from Southey to Pusey and Body—cast Wesley very much in the role of an outcast *virtuoso*, used this as an argument against stifling the zeal of the contemporary examples of this spirit, and in some cases, for instance Southey, saw in the Wesleyan Methodists potential personnel for the proposed new orders.

After the 1851 Religious Census had showed that in the thirty-four largest towns more than half the population professed no religion whatsoever, a proposal was made to found an Order of Repentance, with the main goal of preaching to the masses but with the subsidiary goal of 'providing, in the Church of England, a lawful channel for the zeal of her laymen, so that they may not be tempted, either to quench the spirit within them, or to become schismatical'. [97] Also during the 1860s the Benedictine Brotherhood of Claydon ('Brother Ignatius') put forward an appeal which combined the notion of 'special provision' for *virtuosi* with the explicit idea of a dual standard:

> [The Church of England] also gives occasion to many zealous and earnest souls, to leave her pale, as many have done, because she does not supply them with the means for following the 'evangelical counsels of perfection' in a regular and monastic life. [98]

There had always been justifications of the new religious communities as being composed of people with a very special desire to follow God but the theological concept of two types of morality, one for the mass of Christians and the other for a rather special group, was not especially prominent in public debate, partly because it was unlikely to command very wide support. A pamphlet of 1862, however, on *The Two Ways of Christian Life*, [99] explicitly put forward this argument. It stated that those aspects of ecclesiastical provision which had been permitted on account of human weakness had now become the rule, while attempts at reform had been swept away. In establishing a pedigree within the Church of England for a dual standard the author made the characteristic reference back to a High Church source, in this case the Nonjuror, William Law, who had described the existence from the very earliest days of Christianity of two types of life, one for the average Christian, the other a less worldly and a superior way of life. In this pamphlet an appeal was made for the public to understand not only the activity of sisterhoods, but the religious basis of their internal life as well. Another example of the dual morality argument is provided by a sermon of 1866, in which an extremely élitist viewpoint was put forward:

> Religious communities have a distinct and separate calling, and they only ask to be let alone in the enjoyment of those higher privileges to which the Holy Ghost has called them. [100]

R. M. Benson, perhaps more than any other individual involved in the revival of religious communities in the nineteenth-century Church of England, succeeded in articulating a *virtuoso* concept of the community without pushing this to an extreme form of élitism. He did this by arguing that the religious community was not following a different set of norms from those of the wider church, but was simply *concentrating* those characteristics that served to distinguish the church from other institutions. This has already been discussed, especially in the context of his statement that 'The object of all Religious societies is to gather up and, as it were, focus the love which ought to animate the whole body of the Church Catholic'. [101] Such intensification of the life of the church in its communities does put the latter in a special position, however, as Benson noted for his own order: 'Our Society ought to be one of the great principles and powers of spiritual instruction to the Church at large.' [102]

The way in which religious orders may be interpreted as providing special *virtuoso* functions for the wider church comes very close at times to the kind of instrumental legitimations which, it was suggested earlier, were so important in the introduction of these institutions. Paul Bull, for example, who has a clear notion of the relevance of precepts and counsels for the theoretical justification of religious communities, uses a somewhat more instrumental notion towards the end of his discussion:

> The chief need of the Church is the restoration of monasteries as 'power stations' for the generation and development of spiritual power. [103]

And another writer, who seems to share Gibbon's disgust for the way ascetics cast off their civic and domestic duties at the fall of the Roman Empire, uses a similar analogy:

> Now, if society is to be permeated by religion, there must be reservoirs of religion; like those great storage places up among the hills which feed the pipes by which water is carried to every home in the city. [104]

This argument continued by asking whether monasticism was the best shape for this purely religious life in modern times, but the pursuit of religion for its own sake was a necessity: the rest was a matter only of form. It is not surprising that this predominantly instrumental conception was challenged in a book published two years later:

> The Religious Life is an end in itself. Just as a well-ordered family coming to settle in a place cannot help influencing for good those among whom its members live, so a Religious Community which keeps its silence, prays and meditates, will be a centre of spiritual life and light. [105]

9. The individual member of a religious order is basically seeking personal perfection, whether such perfection is defined in terms of individual or social goals or of an active or contemplative life.

It seems that Pusey, even before any sisterhood had been formed, had realized that the only motivational basis for the foundation of a community was personal perfectionism. When in 1840 he sent to Hook's sister, who was contemplating joining some sisterhood, a paper describing a Quaker scheme for supplying Guy's Hospital with nurses, he complained that he could not find in the plan 'as proposed, those moral features which alone command success in such enterprises. It only contemplated so much self-denial as was essential for a nurse's work'. [106] He wrote:

> Its error seems to be the prevailing error of the day, that money will produce everything. Persons of Christian temper, self-devotion, self-denial, are to start up at the touch of this golden wand, instead of being raised up as God's blessing and gift to his Church. [107]

In an undated sermon, Pusey defined the basis of religious perfection as very distinctly a form of self-denial: 'In the religious life, you can be as nothing, outwardly as well as in your own eyes. Sink deep then in your own nothingness.' [108]

Even in the case of an institution like Carter's sisterhood at Clewer, where the moral basis was not consciously derived at the outset from a study of classical Roman orders, the counsels of perfection were made the first principle in the Constitutions of the community:

> The Community of St John the Baptist is instituted for the promotion of the honour and worship due to Almighty God for the cultivation of the counsels and graces which He has taught as the way of perfection, and for active service, both in spiritual and corporal works of mercy. [109]

But once again, it appears to be in the less 'public' statements of the goals of religious orders in the early period of the revival that the orientation towards personal perfection is most clearly expressed. In the pamphlet which was quoted using William Law as a precedent, the following antiinstrumental view is put forward:

> The salvation, and assistance of others, has always been one leading idea in Religious Houses, whose inmates have ever performed numberless deeds of mercy. But this was not all; for they laboured earnestly to advance in the path of self-conquest, and in 'the acquirement of those interior virtues, without which exterior works are of little avail in the eyes of GOD'. Their chief thought has ever been the consecration of themselves to God. [110]

It is quite evident that as a contemplative type of life developed out of the earlier active life of the first sisterhoods, the goal of personal perfection was more and more recognized as having primacy and was given theological expression. But this goal still tended to remain 'private'—to be given expression, for example, in sermons to the members of communities, in devotional works and in personal correspondence—while the more 'public' statement of goals was more heavily weighted in favour of utilitarian motives.

As far as the social definition of perfection was concerned, Benson again is a prominent figure, along with Congreve. Benson argued that the purpose for which a religious community existed —the sanctification of the individual—would be found to be in accordance with the social goals of the Society. But the object of a religious community is invariably 'to strive after perfection. Whatever subordinate objects may be connected with the Life, this is its primary object. It is our duty to strive after perfection, and without this strife the Religious Life is a mockery'. [111]

To some critics of religious orders the life was, indeed, a mockery. One of the most trenchant of these critics, Margaret Goodman, made the goal of perfection a principal target:

> I suppose, fallen beings as we are, the wisest disposition of time on earth would be such a one as would best fit us for the presence of God, holy angels, and saints in the mansions beyond the grave. But, setting aside the question whether such a life causes us to neglect social duties, it is doubtful if a life directed by these rules really trains the soul to any high degree of holiness, or is elevating to the character. It appeared to some who watched it, to have the effect of narrowing the sympathies, of engendering ignorance, self-conceit, and spiritual pride, and of altogether destroying simplicity and self-forgetfulness. [112]

10. Membership of a religious order may only be gained and maintained by proof of special merit.

When Pusey wrote to Miss Hughes in 1843 he saw a very useful test of entry lying entirely outside the religious orders themselves:

> The difficulties which people have to go through before they enter upon it [the religious life] are a means of disciplining them to enter upon it aright; and they, meantime, may be disciplining themselves by learning to give up more readily

their own wills, bearing contradiction cheerfully, as well as growing continually in the grace and love and fear of God. [113]

Pusey was in favour of applying to women the same tests of vocation as those applied to men, for in his speech at the 1862 Church Congress he said, of female vocations:

> Of course, the fact that any individual is so called [by God] must be tested somehow, as in our own case. But as we, the clergy, are expected to come to a conviction that 'we are inwardly moved by the Holy Ghost to take up this office', that 'we are duly called according to the will of our Lord Jesus Christ', so it must be possible for women to come to the same conviction, if there be any such call to them. [114]

But the Pusey principle of parental prohibition was not a foolproof test of entry by any means, and there is evidence that the entrants to the very first sisterhood at Park Village, although 'ardent and sincere in their desire to dedicate themselves to God and the Service of His poor in the Religious Life' were not at all adequately socialized. Most of them were, it seems, over thirty, and their 'habits of thought and action had been moulded by domestic and social traditions alien to the Catholic ideal of religious vocation'. [115] Furthermore, there is evidence that parental opposition was as much likely to keep a novice whose vocation was shaky *inside* a sisterhood—since the comments that would meet such a person when she returned to her parental home were likely to be unpleasant and unsympathetic—as it would be to thoroughly test the postulant *before* entry. [116]

It seems that lack of experience in some cases led to mistakes in the matter of preserving a high degree of exclusiveness in the treatment of full members. Goodman accuses Sellon of letting women whose previous lives were 'not unsullied' mix with pure women. [117] This was a point which was taken up by Grafton, who advised mother superiors not to allow their orders to be used as reformatories. If a scandal arose, he argued, nobody was going to be too careful about distinguishing between the fully professed sisters and those who had been put there to reform. [118] However, if properly regulated, a sisterhood could ensure a proper standard of entry, and Grafton was careful to stress this in his more public statements. Echoing the point first made by Cardinal Wiseman, [119] that convents were locked from inside, Grafton maintained that:

It is not such an easy thing to become a sister as the world imagines. The doors of a well-regulated sisterhood swing open with comparative ease to those within seeking egress, but are opened slowly, and only after long and patient waiting, to those without. [120]

In this statement, Grafton was clearly attempting to define sisterhoods as selective groups of *virtuosi* against the prevailing Protestant image of them as 'Papal garrisons'.

NOTES

1 Sabine Baring-Gould, 'On the revival of religious confraternities', in Orby Shipley (ed.), *The Church and the World: Essays on Questions of the Day*, first series (London, Longmans, Green, Reader and Dyer, 1866).
2 ibid., p. 107.
3 ibid., p. 107.
4 ibid., p. 108.
5 Advisory Council on Religious Communities, *A Directory of the Religious Life* (London, S.P.C.K., 1943), p. 1.
6 This process has already been traced in the case of the Benedictine Order.
7 Liddon, op. cit., III, p. 32.
8 ibid., III, p. 32.
9 ibid., III, p. 32.
10 Charles Philip Stewart Clarke, *The Oxford Movement and After* (London, Oxford, A. R. Mowbray, 1932), p. 256.
11 ibid., p. 255.
12 George William Erskine Russell, *Arthur Stanton: A Memoir* (London, Longmans, 1917), p. 54.
13 ibid., p. 55.
14 ibid., pp. 55–6. This is the same kind of development as that which was characteristic of the very earliest forms of monasticism among the Egyptian hermits, where the gradual replacement of *personal* ties of loyalty and authority by formal ties was an important aspect of institutionalization. It ought to be added that even when a sisterhood is not parish-based it may well happen that a branch house within a particular parish ceases to operate because of a change in parish clergy—but of course there is a great difference between the loss of a *branch* house and the loss of the only community that exists.
15 ibid., pp. 57–8.
16 ibid., p. 64.
17 ibid., p. 69.
18 ibid., p. 67.
19 Rosalind Nash, *A Sketch of the Life of Florence Nightingale* (London, S.P.C.K., 1937), p. 23.

20 Anson, op. cit., 1964, pp. 593–600.

21 This includes the Church of Ireland and of Scotland.

22 *York Journal of Convocation*, 1885 Report, p. 104.

23 Louise Creighton, *Life and Letters of Mandell Creighton* (London, Longmans, Green, 1904), vol. II, pp. 270–1.

24 ibid., II, p. 271.

25 H. L. M. Cary in Norman Powell Williams and Charles Harris, *Northern Catholicism. Centenary Studies in the Oxford and Parallel Movements* (London, 1933), pp. 347–8.

26 Henry Lucius Moultrie Cary, *Called of God* (London, Oxford, A. R. Mowbray, 1937), p. 16.

27 Quoted in Allchin, op. cit., 1958, p. 14.

28 Albert Clifton Kelway, *George Rundle Prynne: A Chapter in the Early History of the Catholic Revival*, 1905, p. 54.

29 For example, see Albert Clifton Kelway, *The Story of the Catholic Revival* (London, Philip Allan, 1933).

30 See above, p. 124.

31 Dieter Voll, *Catholic Evangelicalism* (London, Faith Press, 1963), p. 132.

32 [Richard Meux Benson], *Thoughts of Father Benson* (London, Oxford, A. R. Mowbray, 1933), p. 10.

33 H. L. M. Cary in *The Religious Vocation* (London, A. R. Mowbray, 1939).

34 Richard Meux Benson, *The Followers of the Lamb* (London, Longmans, 1900), p. 6.

35 Richard Meux Benson, *Instructions on the Religious Life* (Oxford, S.S.J.E., 1927–51, 1951), p. 21.

36 George Congreve, *The Incarnation and the Religious Life* (Oxford, S.S.J.E., 1929), p. 24.

37 P.H. 13575, p. 8.

38 Bertram George Aubrey Cannell, *From Monk to Busman* (London, Skeffington and Son, 1935), p. 36.

39 *Monks and Nuns in Modern Days, by a Religious* (London, Church Literature Assoc., 1935), p. 8.

40 *The Second Annual Report and Balance Sheet of the North London Deaconesses' Institution*, 1863, p. 5.

41 Maria Trench, *The Story of Dr. Pusey's Life* (London, Longmans, 1900), p. 274. Quoted by Anson, op. cit., 1964, p. 274. Trench also reports that as early as 1840 a Mr Perceval Ward had written to Pusey with details of the Sisters of Charity of St Vincent de Paul—a branch of which was to be founded at Hastings—and he added: 'I do not know whether they have any distinctive dress, but this would appear indispensable in the low haunts of our cities' (p. 164).

42 *Memos Relating to the Society of the Holy Trinity* (London, Terry, 1907), pp. 5–6. See also P.H. 12899.

43 Arthur James Mason, *Memoir of George Howard Wilkinson* (London, Longmans, 1909), vol. II, p. 149. Apparently Wilkinson did not share the taste of Pusey's daughter, Lucy, who in 1842, when on a visit to an Irish convent of the Sisters of Charity with her father, was asked by the superior which of the postulants' dresses she liked best, and chose the black one. 'The nun was evidently much impressed by such a choice in

a child just twelve years old.' (Trench, quoted by Allchin, op. cit., 1958, p. 225.)

44 See above, Chap. 6, note 2.

45 François Biot, *The Rise of Protestant Monasticism*, transl. W. J. Kerrigan (Dublin, Helicon, 1963).

46 ibid., p. 16.

47 ibid., p. 34.

48 ibid., p. 55.

49 Anne Mozley, *Letters and Correspondence of J. H. Newman* (London, Longmans, Green, 1891), vol. II, p. 220.

50 Liddon, op. cit., III, p. 10.

51 ibid., p. 10.

52 Pontificals are the liturgical books of the Roman Catholic Church and contain the prayers and ceremonies celebrated by bishops. Uniformity was first achieved by the authoritative edition issued by Clement VIII in 1596.

53 John Mason Neale, *Ayton Priory: Or, The Restored Monastery* (Cambridge, Deightons, 1843), p. 187. On the whole question of Neale's attitude to vows, see Lough, op. cit., pp. 61–3.

54 Allchin, op. cit., 1958, pp. 73–4.

55 Ashwell, op. cit., III, p. 332. This was later to be used as an argument against alienating recruits to the brotherhoods formed at the end of the nineteenth century.

56 *Report of the Proceedings of the Church Congress of 1862, Held in . . . Oxford* (Oxford and London, J. H. and J. Parker, 1862), p. 141.

57 *ibid.*, p. 149.

58 Ashwell, *op. cit.*, III, p. 332.

59 See Allchin, op. cit., 1958, p. 167. T. T. Carter seems to have envisaged an earlier, 'unofficial' approval of vows, for in *Harriet Monsell* (op. cit., pp. xii–xiii) he says: 'Much has been said of late, and much that I cannot but deem needlessly alarming and unreasonable, on the vexed question of vows. At the late Reading Congress [1883], at the end of the morning's debate in the large Congress Hall, on the comparative merits of the Sisterhood and the Deaconess principles, it was generally felt that they agreed in representing the self-devotion intended in either state as life-long. And a vow is but the outward expression of a lifelong devotion. It simply implies a vocation of GOD, in which one so called should abide with Him to the end. Every safeguard indeed should be taken against possible error, but this may be ensured both on the side of the Community, and that of its members, if there be, according to long established principle, wisely regulated authority, and a recognised system of dispensation.'

60 William Henry Hutchings, *Life and Letters of Thomas Thelluson Carter* (London, Longmans, 1904), pp. 104–5.

61 Principally, the ideal of Roman Catholic sainthood.

62 Liddon, op. cit., III, p. 10.

63 ibid., III, p. 7.

64 On the influences in the Wantage Rule, see Anson, op. cit., 1964, pp. 250–1.

65 G. W. E. Russell, op. cit., 1907.

66 Anson, op. cit., 1964, p. 265.

67 T. J. Williams, op. cit., 1950, p. 106.

68 Quoted in Anson, op. cit., 1964, p. 103.

69 ibid., p. 266.

70 Quoted ibid., p. 266.

71 P.H. 6250.

72 P.H. 6251, p. 7.

73 Margaret Goodman, op. cit., 1863.

74 Richard Meux Benson, *The Religious Life Portrayed for the Use of Sisters of Mercy* (London, 1898), p. 46.

75 P.H. 71403, p. 20.

76 P.H. 72865, p. 9.

77 Although the internal conceptions of sisterhoods were much more in terms of a community *per se* than was their external image.

78 R. M. Benson, *The Religious Vocation*, op. cit., pp. 80–1.

79 George Congreve, *Christian Progress: with Other Papers and Addresses* (London, Longmans, 1910), p. 198.

80 [Parochial Order], *The Dawn Breaking* (London, Skeffington, 1896), p. 17.

81 See M. Hill, *A Sociology of Religion*, op. cit., pp. 23–4.

82 [Parochial Order], *The Parochial, or Third Order (Anglican)* (Oxford, London, A. R. Mowbray, 1901), p. 5.

83 Paul Bertie Bull, *The Revival of the Religious Life* (London, Edward Arnold, 1914), p. 227.

84 D. A. Martin, *Pacifism* (London, Routledge and Kegan Paul, 1965), p. 163.

85 See this chapter, pages 243–244, for relevant passages in Biot.

86 *Church Congress of 1862*, op. cit., p. 149.

87 *The Anglican Sister of Mercy* (London, Eliot, Stock, 1895), p. 45.

88 P.H. 12299, p. 4.

89 P.H. 12554, p. 22.

90 P.H. 6241, p. 12.

91 ibid., pp. 13–14.

92 Liddon, op. cit., III, p. 6.

93 P.H. 6268, p. 20.

94 *Chronicle of the Convocation of Canterbury*, 1862, p. 881.

95 P.H. 6276, col. c.

96 *Authorized Report of the Church Congress held at Southampton . . . 1870* (Southampton, Gutch and Cox, 1870), p. 84.

97 P.H. 71474, pp. 4–5.

98 P.H. 1103, p. 5.

99 P.H. 6269.

100 P.H. 7852, p. 8.

101 R. M. Benson, *Religious Vocation*, op. cit., pp. 80–1.

102 ibid., p. 258.

103 P.B. Bull, op. cit., p. 231.

104 Charles Bigg, *Wayside Sketches in Ecclesiastical History* (London, Longmans, Green, 1906), p. 135.

105 Albert Clifton Kelway, *A Franciscan Revival. The Story of the Society of the Divine Compassion* (Plaistow, privately printed), p. 9.

106 Liddon, op. cit., III, p. 9.

107 ibid., III, p. 9.

108 P.H. 74137, p. 2.

109 Hutchings, op. cit., p. 101. See ibid., p. 121, for a meditation by Carter on 'If thou wilt be perfect . . .'

110 P.H. 6269, p. 7.

111 R. M. Benson, op. cit., 1927–51; 1927, p. 7.

112 Margaret Goodman, *Experiences of an English Sister of Mercy* (London, Smith, Elder, 1862), pp. 7–8.

113 Liddon, op. cit., III, p. 12.

114 P.H. 6276, col. a.

115 T. J. Williams, op. cit., 1950, p. 24. See also Orby Shipley (ed.), op. cit., second series, pp. 175–87.

116 On this see A. H. Bennett, op. cit., p. 27.

117 M. Goodman, op. cit., 1863, chap. 12.

118 This advice is given by Charles Chapman Grafton in *A Journey Godward of a Servant of Jesus Christ* (Milwaukee, Young Churchman Co., 1910).

119 See P.H. 13637.

120 P.H. 72013, p. 8.

9

The Role of Women in Victorian Society: Sisterhoods, Deaconesses and the Growth of Nursing

IN THIS and the final chapter the study of the legitimation and internal structure of Anglican religious orders will be anchored in an analysis of some of the main features of the secular environment in which they developed. Of particular interest is the way in which the specifically religious legitimation of these new institutions was very often coupled with, or even derived from, a secular role-definition. Thus the supporters of sisterhoods worked with an incipiently feminist conception of the role of women and insisted on the right of women to organize their own activities. Those who favoured deaconesses, on the other hand, were far more likely to accept the prevailing role-definition of women and to regard them as in need of men's control and direction. In the context of secular roles for working women, nursing was an occupation which enabled a compromise to be made between the traditional woman's role of service and drudgery and the newer, more autonomous role of professional employee. Sisterhoods provided an important link between the old and the new kinds of women's work and they are intimately connected with the growth of secular nursing.

THE STATUS OF WOMEN AND INCIPIENT FEMINISM

The nuclear family of the Victorian middle class served a most important social function by translating the breadwinner's income into symbols of status. 'Respectability' was the fundamental norm, and for the Victorian middle class leisure for women became synonymous with respectability: thus the crucial distinction between lady and woman was laid down in terms of work and non-work. From the literature available it appears that the cult of uselessness, which for middle class women was a basic part of the demand for conspicuous consumption, became a well-defined characteristic of the wife's role. Since a wife had to spend money so as to produce the greatest possible impression of wealth as a mark of status, a great deal of time and energy was spent on refining manners and cultivating 'ornamental' tastes. Temperament and function were rigidly divided for men and women, and a more sharply differentiated set of functions was given to the woman's role based on impersonally defined—and sometimes genetically attributed—features, such as: 'All women have a good sense of colour'. The man's superiority was established and marriage was virtually the *only* occupation open to women of the middle class, partly because a very inadequate education left them extremely dependent on their husbands. One writer has summed up the personality type which tended to emerge from this environment: '. . . from all accounts, middle class women seem to have been narrow-minded, emotional, self-centred, snobbish and morbid'. [1]

Several of these points can be illustrated from historical material which is specifically concerned with the formation and growth of sisterhoods. Southey, for example, noted that on the Continent women were very active in a number of fields, but that as soon as an Englishwoman tried to earn her own living she lost caste. [2] And it was Charlotte Mary Yonge, the novelist, who described to William Butler of Wantage the inadequacy of her up-bringing for any practical undertaking in a letter of 1868:

> My dear Mr. Butler—Thanks. I wish I felt more worthy of being an Exterior Sister, but I am thankful to be joined to what is good, though I do not think you would care to have me if you knew how I 'shrink when hard service must be done,' and what a spoilt child I have been ever since I grew up, very nearly useless in anything practical. [3]

It is highly significant that Butler's earliest and most cherished goal—shown by the fact that he was somewhat disappointed when the Wantage sisterhood turned to penitentiary work—was the education of women. It was precisely this goal that was urged by early feminists like Mrs Jameson, who in 1855 commented:

> , . . the education given to our women is merely calculated to render them ornamental and well-informed; but it does not

train them, even those who are so inclined and fitted by nature, to be effective instruments of social improvement. Whether men, without the assistance and sympathetic approval of well-educated women, are likely to improve and elevate the moral tone of society, or work out good in any especial sphere or profession, is, I think, hardly a question. [4]

It is in a discussion of the inadequacy of women's education that Carpenter suggests that even inside the church there was little scope for women in the nineteenth century:

Apart from 'parish work,' done by trained Sisters, or Deaconesses, by other untrained wholetime workers, or by the occasional efforts of benevolent amateurs, there was not much scope for the activity of Christian women. Even the work of education was still a lightly tilled field, and often one to which untrained women gave themselves when they had to do something and did not know what else to do. [5]

Nevertheless, changes can be detected in the expectations of women quite early in the nineteenth century, and the evidence goes some way towards explaining why it was that pioneer women emerged in the first place and how they could attract personnel to their different enterprises. Dunbar, for instance, argues that:

[1837–57] . . . was a time when the rising prosperity of the middle classes should have made for increased comfort and security, and therefore for women's contentment with their lot. It was, in fact, a period when the frustrations and discontents of women came to a head below the surface of life, and presently broke through. [6]

It almost certainly required a considerable amount of determination for aspiring members of the early sisterhoods and middle class female occupations to break free from their family ties, as A. H. Bennett acknowledged when she wrote that: 'Nearly every novice had had to undergo much opposition, if not petty persecution, before she had succeeded in entering the Sisterhood . . .' [7] It is interesting too that at least one advocate of the religious life for women turned the argument that the nun's vocation involved loss of liberty convincingly against his ultra-Protestant antagonists by suggesting that the life vows of marriage were a more likely source of despotism. [8]

One of the most frequently cited examples of a woman who had broken through male prejudice and had thus shown the way for other women to do likewise was, of course, Florence Nightingale. Especially after the Crimean expedition when, according to Jameson, she had broken through 'what Goethe calls a "Chinese wall of prejudices" . . . and established a precedent which will indeed "multiply the good to all time" ', [9] Miss Nightingale became the most important symbol of the early feminist movement. However, her role in the wider attempt to improve the status of women is rather more complex. Although there is some truth in her biographer's claim that: 'Because she was a woman, her early life was one long struggle for liberation from circumstance and social prepossessions', [10] it is also significant that she was reared in a family with strong progressive, Benthamite and rationalistic inclinations. Thus there was less family opposition than in the case, for instance, of some of the women who joined sisterhoods against the will of their parents and later became rather pathetic objects in pamphlet disputes. One of the few occasions when Florence Nightingale's career seemed likely to be disrupted by family commitments was in 1853, when she had to return from training in Paris to help nurse her grandmother. This incident serves to illustrate the type of role which many women who did not marry and did not seek an independent occupation came to adopt, namely the role of unemployed spinster, of which Dunbar says:

She became the aunt, the nurse, the useful member of the family who had no responsibilities of her own, the person whom the others could call upon for help in any emergency. [11]

The general attitude to the spinster was well defined. While the middle class married woman had a status and a recognized position in society, the unmarried woman of thirty was already an object of pity and took her place in the family as an unsuccessful human being. It was largely as a result of the work done by individuals like Florence Nightingale and by the Anglican sisterhoods that female celibacy became defined as a role which might be consciously chosen, and thus it lost some of its negative valuation. Nightingale herself positively valued spinsterhood and explicitly *chose* it (as will be seen in the next chapter, for many spinsters the unmarried state was a *necessity*). She was even prepared to give credit to the primitive church on this point, though in a somewhat two-edged way:

> I think some [women] have every reason for not marrying and that for these it is much better to educate the children who are already in the world and can't be got out of it, than to bring more into it. The Primitive Church clearly thought so too, and provided accordingly; and though no doubt the Primitive Church was in many matters an old woman, yet I think the experience of ages has proved her right in this. [12]

Perhaps a more important factor in the redefinition of women's roles was the occupation through which the redefinition was achieved. The role of nurse was one which could very easily be defined in terms of masculine conceptions of women's 'natural' attributes. Thus a pamphlet of 1866 appealing for sisterhoods to undertake nursing in lunatic asylums noted that there was a universal cry for women's emancipation and rights, and pointed out that it was woman's *hereditary right* to care for the afflicted. [13] As with other attributes—such as the appreciation of colour—a male expectation of the female role was transposed into a 'natural' characteristic. Furthermore, it has long been noted that most masculine tasks fall into the category of 'exploit' while female tasks are best class as 'drudgery': the Victorian conception of woman as being more 'willing' to glory in drudgery was the male validation of this distinction. The fact that many of the duties of nurses resembled simple domestic tasks—and it is worth noting that until quite recently the nurses' uniform in some hospitals was basically the same as that of a nineteenth-century domestic servant—meant that the occupation of nurse could be accommodated within traditional male expectations about the role of women. Florence Nightingale certainly adopted this as *part* of her conception of nursing, for she referred to the occupation as 'this coarse, repulsive, servile, noble work'. [14] On the other hand, she was very concerned to stress that she was training professional nurses and not just specialized domestics; or, as Edwards-Rees explains:

> There was at first no domestic training. Florence Nightingale was emphatic that 'students should not scour, it is a waste of time'. For the care of the sick, she said, 'is, after all, the real purpose of their being there, not to act as lifts, water-carriers,

beasts of burden or steam engines—articles whose labour can be had at vastly less cost than that of educated human beings'. This point was only slowly grasped. [15]

One reason why the point was only slowly grasped can be attributed to the Victorian male idea of 'sublime drudgery'. Another important definition of women was that they were 'less independent, less capable of initiative and less creative than are men, and, for that reason, stand in need of masculine guidance'. [16] This dependent role was particularly evident in the case of nursing, which was an ancillary professional group under the direction of the medical profession. The latter, with very few exceptions in the nineteenth century, was a predominantly male profession, and so in this respect the prevailing definition of the role of women remained substantially unchallenged by the growth of nursing. To the extent that nursing could be perceived in terms of existing male conceptions of the female role, it was relatively easier for middle class women to enter this profession than most others. Elizabeth Garrett Anderson's struggle to gain entry to the medical profession, was, by contrast, a very difficult and bitter one.

Just as the popular image of nursing conformed with male role-expectations, so the office of deaconess had not only a theological justification but broadly conformed to Victorian male conceptions of the status of women. It is evidence of the predominantly *virtuoso* and feminist motivation behind the development of sisterhoods that the less radical alternative available in the office of deaconess was of comparatively little importance.

The 'dependent' role of deaconess is well illustrated by Howson in 1862 in one of the most influential pamphlets on the subject. Having disclaimed both the feminist argument and the argument that woman's place was exclusively in a family as being too extreme, Howson put forward the office of deaconess as a 'happy medium'. Above all, woman's position in society was *to help*, and the Greek equivalent of 'deaconess' signified helpful service. Much the same attitude was expressed by the Bishop of Winchester at the 1885 meeting of Canterbury Convocation. He described the mode of admission to the office of deaconess and the need for a deaconess institution for training and occasional retirement. This was necessary because 'women need more support than men'. [17] Cotton, another supporter of deaconesses, had a clear idea of 'natural' distinctions between women and men and thought that women's education should be moral education, of the *heart* and not of the head, because that was where the particular attributes of women lay. He also gave prominence to the work of the wives and daughters of the Protestant clergy:

> The Protestants had lost the aid of female devotion by the abolition of nunneries, but they had gained the services of the wives and daughters of a reformed priesthood. The Roman Catholics, still retaining the celibacy of the clergy, could not have the latter, but tried to make up for it by an enormous increase of the former. [18]

The idea that family duties were paramount is very characteristic of nineteenth-century discussions of women's work. The statement made by Bishop Tait in his Diocesan Charge of 1866 is an excellent example:

> The rules which I have myself laid down as most necessary in my dealing with such communities [the sisterhoods] have been the following:—To point out that the first of all duties are those which we owe to our family. Family ties are imposed direct by God. If family duties are overlooked, God's blessing can never be expected on any efforts which we make for His Church. Every community, therefore, of Sisters or Deaconesses ought to consist of persons who have fully satisfied all family obligations. [19]

Against this widely held view of the status of women the early sisterhoods can be seen as representing limited but implicitly feminist goals. Butler's interest in women's education and Pusey's contention in the Stanton/Tooth debate that women should govern themselves have already been cited, and there are many other examples. In 1840 Pusey wrote to Mr W. Greenhill, who was studying medicine in Paris and had obtained for Pusey the rules of the Sisters of the Order of St Augustine and those of St Vincent de Paul. In the context of a discussion about vows for women, Pusey commented, 'We, who are admitted to the priesthood, are under vows; we devote ourselves for a whole life; why should not women also for their offices?' [20] J. M. Neale, in a sermon of 1857, made an implicit comparison between the status of women in pre-Christian society and in Victorian society:

... woman was at best the plaything, at the worst the slave of man. All heathen ideas of woman's happiness lay in marriage; without that, hers was a wasted existence. [21]

At the 1862 Church Congress Pusey again argued in favour of treating male and female vocations equally. He said he believed that the Holy Ghost had been moving men's minds in recent times, and just as the clergy must attest that they had been called by God, why should not God call women too? This speech was made during the debate in which the question of vows was raised and in which the Bishop of Oxford made his definitive statement on the issue.

But the prevailing male conception asserted itself in many different ways. In pamphlet debates, for instance, the fact that sisterhoods were opposed to one of the central norms of female behaviour could be used in arguments that they were 'unnatural' or un-English. Diana Campbell contended in her attack on Miss Sellon's sisterhood that the arrangement of the convent was 'masculine' and unsuited to delicate English women. [22] One pamphlet writer even censured Sellon for replying to attacks like these: women, he thought, should be seen and not heard. [23] More extreme pamphleteers, of whom Hobart Seymour is an excellent example, described the 'conventual imprisonment' of English women and appealed to the sense of outrage of all Englishmen to have these institutions suppressed.

More fundamental than these pamphlet attacks, however, was the influence exerted on female communities by the kind of recruit they attracted. The women who entered sisterhoods had been socialized in a society which gave them a subordinate and ornamental role, thus: 'Their habits of thought and action had been moulded by domestic and social traditions alien to the Catholic ideal of religious vocation.' [24] In these circumstances the women who entered an Anglican sisterhood were 'deviant' in that they had rejected some of the central values of Victorian society. It is hardly surprising that these women should have alienated even some of their strongest defenders. Charles Lindley, for instance, wrote to his father:

> Miss Sellon is quite extraordinary. She was a woman against whom I have always had a sort of prejudice, but I am learning to see how unjust I have been. She may have her faults—who has not?—but her energy and her power of organization are

marvellous—and the work she is doing at her hospital is thoroughly good and satisfactory, and would delight you from its method and arrangement. [25]

The type of recruit who joined a sisterhood because she found it impossible to live with her parents—and this type must have been fairly common when there were so few alternatives open to her—was likely to be a disruptive influence within the sisterhood. The problem was clearly perceived at the time, for in an essay published in 1867 the writer noted:

No Postulants turn out more unsatisfactory than those who offer themselves for community life because they cannot have their own way at home, or cannot live in unity with their own kindred. When the novelty of their position has worn off, their self-will and discontent rise up as strongly as ever; and, after causing much discomfort and trouble to all around them, they generally fly off to some fresh and untried scene of action, or return to the former situation, which had previously been so intolerable. These are they who cause most annoyance in a Sisterhood, and most scandal in the World. Their hyperbolical and foolish praise of the Institution on first joining it, is as pernicious and disagreeable as their sweeping condemnation of it when its novelty has worn off. And though charity, hoping all things, sometimes admits unfit persons such as these into a religious Community, they too often prove a most sore thorn in its side. [26]

The writer went on to quote St Francis de Sales' warning to avoid mutinous and opinionated women—a reminder that the problems of Anglican sisterhoods were not exclusively attributable to their Victorian environment.

Another problem was the enormous amount of publicity and attention that was given to these groups of women, which were originally small in number. A consequence of this was noted by Keble in 1845 when he referred to the Park Village Sisterhood:

It strikes me that there is a particular danger incident to persons situated as those Sisters are among us, viz. that being so very few, and among persons so deeply interested for them and their undertaking, they may very easily think too much of themselves and be made too much of, and I could fancy that it might be necessary to do some violence to ourselves in order not to flatter them unconsciously. On this, as on other accounts, I wish I could hear of their number increasing. [27]

This problem became less acute as the number of women in the sisterhoods increased: in 1878 there were at least 660 professed sisters in the Province of Canterbury alone, and in 1912 there were at least 1,300 professed sisters in the whole of the Church of England. [28] In addition, the growth of other occupations for middle class woman deflected some of the attention from the sisterhoods.

One of the common features which appeared both in the growth of nursing and in Anglican sisterhoods was the emergence of an internal form of stratification, with middle class and especially upper middle class women forming an élite. It was partly because this group in the wider society provided many of the early recruits to nursing and the sisterhoods, but also because the pioneering work of demonstrating how effective women could be in relatively independent roles required the example of upper class women if the ecclesiastical and medical authorities were to be sufficiently influenced. The growth of nursing is very interesting in this respect because the emergence of internal stratification was an unintended—and for the most part strongly resisted—development. Florence Nightingale in particular saw it as antithetical to her conception of the professional nurse, but she was eventually forced to accept the situation.

Nursing was originally a form of domestic service, and it is quite clear that Florence Nightingale originally set out to recruit her trainees from exactly this class of woman. After her experience in the Crimea and in hospitals in several countries, she very much disliked the idea of 'ladies' being involved in nursing: she thought they were too prone to have 'spiritual flirtations' with the patients. As Rosalind Nash, who knew Florence Nightingale from middle-age onwards, makes very clear, Nightingale saw the best material for good nurses in the class of women who worked for a living, which she elsewhere specified as the upper levels of the domestic servant class:

She dreaded the false sentiment and 'puffery' which had attached itself to nursing and had turned the heads of some of her first following. She dreaded the invasion of superficial enthusiasts into 'this coarse, repulsive, servile, noble work'. The object, she soberly conceived, was to improve hospitals by training and improving in character 'that section of the large class of women supporting themselves by labour who take to hospital nursing as a livelihood.' Some of these might be induced 'in the long run' to value 'usefulness and the service of God in the relief of man' as well as maintenance. A proportion of gentlewomen might be added, but she was not at first too hopeful of gentlewomen. [29]

Abel-Smith thinks that it was almost by accident that Florence Nightingale popularized nursing as an occupation for ladies. Certainly, the Annual Report of the Nightingale Fund in 1862 was fairly condescending on the subject of 'lady' nurses:

Persons of superior manners and education, ladies in fact, are not as a rule the best qualified, but rather women of somewhat more than ordinary intelligence emanating from those classes in which women are habitually employed in earning their own livelihood. Ladies, however, are not excluded; on the contrary, where sufficient evidence is shown that they intend to pursue the calling as a business, and have these qualifications which will fit them to become superintendents, their admission would be considered an advantage. [30]

It was, however, an almost inevitable process. In the first place these 'lady' ('special') nurses were able to pay for their own training, and this was something which the early training schools could not ignore because it meant that they could thus subsidize the training of the group of 'probationer' nurses and add to their number. Secondly, Florence Nightingale was pioneering something which received considerable opposition from the medical profession and thus she needed a body of strong, educated and articulate lieutenants who could be sent out to found training schools in other hospitals, and these qualities were more readily available in the higher strata. As R. K. Merton shows, Nightingale recognized that it was education rather than status that was responsible for their upward mobility in the profession. He quotes her on this point:

Unquestionably, she observed, 'the educated will be more likely to rise to the post of Superintendent, but *not* because they are ladies [and she meant ladies in the Victorian sense] but because they are educated'. [31]

This factor must have been a crucial consideration, for by looking at the progress of some of the early Nightingale matrons it is possible to appreciate the enormous pressures there were against their work. Nightingale expected almost superhuman strength of character in her matrons and when one of them, Lucy Osburn, appeared to give in under sustained opposition after being appointed to the Sydney Infirmary, New South Wales, she never entirely trusted her again.

And, indeed, the entry of 'ladies' into nursing created problems as well as solving them. The social origins of some hospital doctors were fairly low, and the acute status anxiety which was caused when these 'lady' nurses, whose *occupational* status was lower than that of the doctors but whose *social* status was often considerably higher, came into the hospitals, created much tension and occasionally erupted as conflict. Given all these influences, the following description of the Nightingale reform seems to be misleading:

> When her work was over, the hierarchy of the servants' hall characteristic of eighteenth- and early nineteenth-century hospital nursing had given place to a hierarchy based on breeding, education and training. [32]

The 'servants' hall' was not replaced, because 'probationer' nurses still provided the equivalent of a domestic servant class; rather, the group of nurses as a whole internalized its own authority in the form of the elite of 'lady' nurses. Nutting and Dock explain this:

> The weak point . . . in the composition of the early English schools was their inheritance and continuation in modified form of the servant-nurse, though it would have been hard not to accept and continue to some extent a class distinction which was ingrained in the social order and had so long characterised the hospital service under both lay and religious governing bodies: Kaiserwerth had ignored all class distinctions, and so had Mrs. Fry's institute, but caste had reappeared in the later German organisations, and in the nursing orders of the Anglican Church. [33]

Social differences asserted themselves in the Anglican sister-hoods for two main reasons. Firstly, the work which was done by those sisterhoods engaged in charitable work among the poor or deprived could only be done, it was thought, by 'ladies'. This view was especially strong in the case of penitentiary work, as an Appeal by Butler of Wantage shows:

> And first, it seems necessary that [Houses of Refuge] should be carried on by Ladies, united as a Sisterhood, since these poor persons [the penitents] require constant watchfulness . . . The discipline, so necessary to aid the work of the Chaplain in their repentance, must be carried out by those who can unite firmness with gentleness: who will be faithful to their charge in requiring obedience, while they enforce it in the spirit of love. Need I stop to prove, that such powers, added to devotion of heart, are hardly to be found, except in those of gentle birth and education. [34]

The paternalistic conception of charitable work which was characteristic of Victorian society, and which was particularly apparent in the Settlement Movement, saw the possibility of moral influence being exerted as a result of the involvement of 'respectable' men and women in social problems. A pamphlet of 1866 demonstrates this basic idea very well, again in the case of a House of Mercy:

> I do not believe there is a penitent in the House who does not feel the real force of that 'faith working by love' which is brought before them in the lives of the Sisters. They see these ladies of gentle birth and nurture, whom they know to be in every possible way so superior to themselves, living among them apart from their friends, apart from all the ordinary pleasures and enjoyments of life, for the sole purpose of guiding them into the way of peace. [35]

There was a very explicit equation between Christian virtue and social superiority in some minds. At the Church Congress of 1866, for instance, Archdeacon Harris made a reference to his ideal of the Christian 'lady':

> If we can bring poor, fallen, abandoned creatures under the rule of Christianity in its very highest form—and surely there is no higher form than that of a highly educated, devout English woman— . . . we may, solely as a matter of reason, imagine we shall yet have results greater in quantity and higher in quality than is possible when the penitents come into contact

with those who naturally, without any fault of their own, have not the same advantages. [36]

It was not only thought that the working class might benefit from the example set by the Anglican sisters, however. In his account of the Sisters of the Poor at St Michael's, Shoreditch, Nihill explained that there were three good reasons why the sisters did all their own domestic work: (a) it was economical, and thus more money could be spent on the poor; (b) their doctor thought it was good for them; and (c) it set a good example to girls of a higher social class, who apparently scorned domestic work. Enlarging on the third of these reasons, Nihill wondered what happened to these 'ornamental' women when they got married. [37] Presumably their 'ornamental' features were an important part of their marriage prospects, since they had to be *part* of their husband's conspicuous consumption. [38]

The second reason why it was so important to state publicly that the sisterhoods were composed of ladies (in both the social and the moral conception of the term) was the simple one of attracting recruits. Thus Commander Sellon, defending his daughter against pamphlet attacks, was very concerned to show that there were no vermin in the sisters' quarters, but 'should a stray visitor occasionally be imported in the dresses of the Sisters, he is soon expelled'. [39] He further pointed out that the laundress's bill was a heavy item of expenditure. Carter was another who faced this issue when the question of setting up a penitentiary was raised:

> . . . when these ideas were at first ventilated, they were considered more than quixotic. The idea, it was thought, would be enough to deter young ladies from offering themselves for Sisters, and families from allowing them to enter Sisterhoods, where such a work was carried on. It aroused a complex objection, first to Sisterhood life in itself, and then to the work for which Sisterhoods were being formed. [40]

In view of this, it is not surprising to find in the pamphlets which Carter wrote for public circulation that there is a firm denial of some of the accusations made against penitentiary work. In one pamphlet he argued that there was in his experience no danger of 'contamination' of the ladies by the girls in their care—and the purer the ladies, the less likely was such contamination. 'Dignity' and 'distance' were key words in this pamphlet. [41] Despite such obvious concern with the more educated and refined members of sisterhoods, Carter elsewhere stated that there were both higher and lower class women in his sisterhood, [42] though its ethos was distinctly hierarchical in a social and moral sense:

> The Sisters will be careful to show towards the Penitents in their manner, speech, etc. such tenderness and pity as would become a forgiving parent dealing with a prodigal child, returning home, yet nevertheless they will preserve such distance and propriety of demeanour as become ladies dealing with persons of inferior rank, and fallen even from that rank by their sins. [43]

On the other hand, there is the evidence of Frere, who was familiar with the structure and workings of Anglican religious orders, that by the beginning of the twentieth century there was a wider social mixture in the sisterhoods: 'In most of them there is a considerable blending of classes, the well-to-do and the poorer each contributing some Sisters to the community.' [44]

THE IMPORTANCE OF SISTERHOODS FOR THE GROWTH OF NURSING AND OTHER FEMALE OCCUPATIONS

One of the most frequently encountered interpretations in the sociology of religion is of religion as a *transitional* phenomenon, providing symbols, organization or personnel in a situation of rapid social change. Worsley, for example, in his study of Cargo Cults, argues that these forms of millennial movements provide symbolic meaning for members of a traditional society which has been disrupted by colonization and he further postulates that the religious symbols are only transitional and will eventually be replaced by revolutionary political ideologies. [45] The study by Kevin Clements of the ideological response to social disruption caused by the Depression in New Zealand shows how, in a situation of complete breakdown in the political interpretation of events, certain religious groups provided symbols which served to articulate a new basis for social and economic organization. These symbols were eventually adopted by reformist political groups and passed out of the sphere of religion, but only after the Christian denominations had served a crucial transitional function. [46] In a very similar way the Anglican sisterhoods, and to a certain extent also the Roman Catholic orders of women, provided important transitional functions in the growth of secular nursing and female occupations generally.

It often seems to be implied, and it is sometimes explicitly stated, that Florence Nightingale 'invented' modern nursing. This is not absolutely correct. She undoubtedly did a great deal to popularize her own system of training, administration and organization of hospital nursing, but she had several antecedents from whom she learned a great deal. Nutting and Dock speak of 'the dark period of nursing' from the latter part of the seventeenth century to the middle of the nineteenth:

> Solely among the religious orders did nursing remain an interest and some remnants of technique survive. The result was that in this period the general level of nursing fell far below that of earlier period.
>
> In England, where the religious orders had been suppressed, and no substitute organisation given, it might almost be said that no nursing class at all remained during this period. [47]

However, although these do not relate to *hospital* nursing, there are two manuals of instructions for nurses in private houses dated 1825 (*The Good Nurse*) and 1836 (*The Nurse's Manual*), which seem to contain as much practical instruction on nursing procedure as does Florence Nightingale's later book, *Notes on Nursing*: the 1825 book actually runs to forty-seven chapters. In more ways than one, religious sisterhoods can be argued to have provided a transition between the older, inefficient type of hospital nursing and the later professional nursing for which Florence Nightingale was largely responsible. A lot of the reform in nursing which the sisterhoods began and which Nightingale continued can best be described as 'public relations' work. R. K. Merton actually uses this term in relation to Florence Nightingale:

> . . . she was interested in the evolving role of the nurse in society, and so she proceeded methodically to transform the public image of the nurse. In part, she did this by becoming a one-woman bureau of public relations, . . . but only in part. Beyond this, she undertook to change the public conception of the nurse by remaking the realities of what a nurse actually was. [48]

With this *caveat* against analysing the reforms in nursing in terms of the charisma of one woman, however exceptional, most of the available material suggests strongly that in pre-Nightingale hospitals the level of nursing was poor, partly, as Abel-Smith suggests, because in the early nineteenth century neither rich nor poor *chose* to be treated in hospital: the only difference being that the former could back their choice with money to pay private medical attendants. The most common type of nurse in this period was apparently the sort which Dickens took as his model for Sairey Gamp: frequently drunk on gin—doubtless as a reaction to intolerable strains—and not infrequently dishonest in their handling of the belongings of patients in their care. These descriptions are not just impressions, judging from the frequent references in reports of hospitals to the poor quality of nursing.

Edward-Rees, in her history of the nursing profession, shows precisely how the Anglican sisterhoods assisted in the transitional stage between the older, brutalized form of nursing and the professional system introduced by Florence Nightingale. The discussion is concerned with Miss Sellon's sisterhood in Devonport and with the Sisters of St John's House, founded like the Devonport sisterhood in 1848:

> These small ventures are important, for soon people were to be shocked into demanding new standards of nursing. They wished to avoid appointing nurses of the old type but it took time to attract the good to a profession with so bad a name, and still more time to train them. Meanwhile the sick had to be nursed and the hospitals used for training staffed by people who could set reasonably good standards. These little Sisterhoods provided a few women to break the vicious circle. And without them the call to Scutari could hardly have been answered. [49]

In this context it is interesting to find that Florence Nightingale had in her earlier career thought of founding a sisterhood for hospital nursing, as she described in a letter of 1845:

> —Well, I do not much like talking about it, but I thought something like a Protestant Sisterhood, without vows, for women of educated feelings, might be established. But there have been difficulties about my very first step, which terrified Mama. I do not mean the physically revolting parts of a hospital, but things about the surgeons and nurses which you may guess. [50]

Perhaps the most significant aspect of her mother's disapproval was that it was not directed against the *religious* ambition but against the realities of early nineteenth-century nursing.

Later in her career, Nightingale became less happy about sisterhood nursing—her remark about lilies and weeds has already been quoted—but it was almost inevitable that she became intimately involved with them. When she was seeking practical experience of hospital nursing it was to the religious communities (mainly Roman Catholic, though this was 'on account, not of their dogmas, but of their deeds', [51]) and to Fliedner's deaconess institution at Kaiserwerth that she turned. Again, when personnel were needed for the Crimean expedition, these were mainly provided by the Anglican sisterhoods and Roman Catholic orders. Even so, her attitude to them seems to have remained somewhat ambivalent:

'I think,' wrote Monckton Milnes to his wife, 'that Florence always much distrusted the Sisterhood matter,' and such was the case. Her inner thought was that no vows were needed other than the nurse's own fitness for the calling and devotion to it. But she was engaged in the crusade of a pioneer, and had to consider what was practically expedient and immediately feasible, as well as what was theoretically reasonable . . . She did not like the religious orders in themselves; they only 'become beautiful,' she said, 'as an expedient, a temporary condition, an antidote to present evils.' [52]

Others among the early Nightingale nurses seem to have been alienated by the sisterhoods. Agnes Elizabeth Jones, who was one of the first matrons, was also an Evangelical. This made her choice of a training school for her primary goal of nursing rather difficult, as she herself indicated:

If I wish to be trained for practical usefulness, nothing else will do, says Miss Nightingale, than a year's training in a London hospital. There are but two open, King's College and St. Thomas's. Well, if ever I contemplated the first, which I did not with its High Church head, it was at an end when I found I must become a sister to do so. And at St. Thomas's, I must be prepared to enter as a common nurse; my companions there, moral and respectable, but not, as a body, Christian women. Miss N. dwelt on all this, and yet I do not feel it would really lower me to do so. [53]

Using R. K. Merton's concept of the 'public relations' work done by Florence Nightingale for nursing as a whole, it is possible to trace the intricate relationships between sisterhoods, deaconesses and secular nursing. Initially, secular nursing was a low status and repellent occupation which no 'respectable' women would enter. However, individuals like Florence Nightingale and Elizabeth Fry saw the need for improved standards of nursing and concluded that the only way this could be achieved was by attracting a more educated and therefore socially superior class of women into the occupation. Sisterhoods were too closely identified with one party in the Church of England and also inculcated certain norms of vocation and self sacrifice that were inimical to the growth of a professional ethos—the latter being Miss Nightingale's primary goal. On the other hand, the sisterhoods and deaconesses were already in existence and contained not only trained nursing personnel but furthermore women of a high social status. Thus, by making use of these groups of women in the Crimean expedition she was able to project an image of the new kind of nurse and to bring nursing into prominence as a potential occupation for the educated spinsters who were needed to reform the hospitals. At the same time, the success of the Crimean episode and the immense personal popularity of Miss Nightingale began to be reflected back on the sisterhoods and, as is shown by the Convocation debates, they became accepted on the grounds of their utility.

Much documentation could be given to this process, but some of the most important evidence will suffice. Forbes in his early article put the process of redefining the status of all female occupations into a wider context by arguing that,

> The village schoolmistress, matrons of institutions, nurses, would be of a wholly different order, if they had the pattern of a 'Sister of Mercy' performing the same offices. Each rank feels ennobled when persons are chosen out of it to a noble office. Those who are not drawn towards it, are yet drawn upwards, by the example of such as, from among themselves, are led to higher aims. [54]

There were attacks on sisterhood nurses for being 'narrow and sectarian' and for proselytizing among patients, as for example in the Rev. William Niven's letter to the Governors of St George's Hospital in 1866, [55] but in reply to this kind of attack the merits

of sisterhood nursing—as acknowledged by Florence Nightingale
herself—could always be cited:

> Wherever sisterhoods (under proper, as Miss Nightingale
> writes in her 'Notes on Hospitals', secular control), have
> undertaken nursing in hospitals, whether at home or abroad,
> whether Protestant or Roman Catholic, their great merits are
> acknowledged, and scarcely one of the evils enumerated above
> finds a place. [56]

There were observers who very clearly saw how women from
the higher social classes had first of all been attracted into nursing
by the example of women from a similar class background in the
sisterhoods:

> It is due to the memory of those who took the lead in founding
> St. John's House . . . to place here upon record that they were
> among the first in the present century to recognise the fact,
> and to act upon the principle, that the work of nursing the sick
> is a high and holy one, *to which Christian women of gentle and noble
> families may be glad to* dedicate themselves; and that, in order
> that the class of professional nurses, whether in hospitals, or in
> private families, should be impressed with a just sense of the
> dignity of their office, they ought to have before their eyes the
> examples of women in the *higher ranks of society, consecrating* freely
> and joyfully their health and strength to *the glory and service of
> God,* for the love of Christ, in the work of tending the sick in
> the wards of hospitals, and at the bedsides of the rich and
> poor. [57] (original italics)

Nor was this relationship typical only of the sisterhoods. Deaconesses too were thought to be a valuable influence on the occupational role-definition of nursing, for exactly the same social
reasons as those which were attributed to sisterhoods: 'The
presence in the wards of women of education and refinement,
gives a tone to a Hospital which nothing else can supply.' [58]

The opposite direction of influence, whereby sisterhoods
received public approval as a result of the nursing work which
was sometimes, but not always, exclusively performed by them,
is very well illustrated in Convocation debates. As Archdeacon
Ffoulkes stated at the 1878 meeting of the Lower House of
Canterbury Convocation:

The value of Sisterhoods has been brought before the eyes of the nation by the Crimean War, and the names of Miss Nightingale and Miss Sellon, and of the East Grinstead Sisters will long be remembered as having taught the people of this country the true character of women's work. [59]

Later in the same debate Canon Jeffreys commented, 'It has been said that these institutions cannot exist without public opinion. Why, they have created themselves against public opinion. ("Hear, hear")'. [60] This was largely true, and it is perhaps in the way the early sisterhoods provided a transitional stage between the older, debased form of nursing and Florence Nightingale's professional organization of nursing that these institutions can be seen exerting an independent influence on the growth of the nursing profession.

The ambivalent attitude towards sisterhoods sometimes emerged in the extent to which observers were prepared to admit that these organizations were important as pre-Nightingale pioneers in nursing. A reviewer of Jameson's and Cotton's pamphlets thought that the sisterhoods had gained more from secular nursing than *vice versa*:

It is true that some of the Sisterhoods in England had already arisen before Miss Nightingale appeared on the field; but it was her name which first turned the current of popular feeling in their favour, and brought all parties to that general state of accord in which they are at present, that Sisterhoods ought to be organized, and were capable, under proper control and management, of unmixed benefit to all classes of the community. [61]

However, in the same pamphlet the writer advocated sisters (in the religious sense) to act as superiors over the ordinary nurses. The extract at the same time provides yet another insight into Victorian ideas of moral and social equivalents, since it is impossible to discern whether by 'higher order' the writer is referring to the social hierarchy, the moral hierarchy, or both combined:

We much wish that the staff of Hospital Nurses could be organized under the same kind of agency, having a lady who would work for pure love's sake at its head, and who would infuse into the staff that would be under her management and control, some of her own spirit and principle. Our hospital nurses at present are too much of the hireling order, and although in many cases they do their own work well, we hear frequent complaints of their conduct in the matter of habits of intemperance and other evil courses, which the constant presence among them of an element of higher order would go far to check and remove. [62]

The sisterhoods, then, originated as organizations with practical charitable goals and in some ways pioneered the field for secular reformers, as well as enjoying some of the reflected public acclaim of the secular reformers. Mention has already been made of the tendency for sisterhoods to develop a more contemplative devotional life and to abandon in some respects their active vocation. The interpretation which is often put on this 'Martha to Mary' process is that the revival of the religious life for women in the Church of England had always been a primarily *religious* movement and the fact that early sisterhoods had an active character was partly a response to the climate of opinion in Victorian society, which imposed criteria of efficiency on every form of enterprise, and partly a 'strategic' choice, since the conventual aspect of women's communities was the least congenial to the majority of church dignitaries. Another plausible explanation is that, since the social problems which the sisterhoods set out to ameliorate proved more and more intractable, pragmatic solutions were gradually replaced by non-empirical ones. such an argument would probably be couched in terms of disappointment and a communitarian turning inwards, and the study of millennial movements has shown that when an activist, revolutionary phase of development meets with defeat, the reaction is very often a growth of quietism and introspection.

There is, however, a third explanation which fits well into the 'transitional' view of religious institutions. As the State and other secular agencies took over many of the fields of charitable work which had originally been within the scope of the sisterhoods, the latter tended more and more to concentrate on the specifically religious aspects of the life they had adopted:

The heroic efforts of the first sisterhoods in the cholera epidemics of the mid-nineteenth century resulted in a very notable change in public estimation. In the present age, the justification of these active works is no longer needed to the same extent, and . . . several of the women's communities have revised their original Rules and Constitutions during the last few decades with a greater emphasis upon contemplation or enclosure or both. [63]

The key concept is again that of 'differentiation', and there are parallels in other areas of society. Just as it has been argued that other institutions have taken over 'non-essential' functions of the family and have left it to provide 'core' functions, so it can be argued that religious institutions have more and more tended to fulfil specifically 'religious' functions. Whether or not this can be termed 'desecularization' is an interesting problem.

NOTES

1 See L. Davidoff, *The employment of married women in England 1850–1950* (unpub. M.A. thesis, L.S.E., 1956).

2 Southey, op. cit., vol. 2, p. 300.

3 Christabel Rose Coleridge, *Charlotte Mary Yonge. Her Life and Letters.* London, New York, Macmillan & Co., 1903, pp. 237–8.

4 Anna Bronwell Jameson, *Sisters of Charity Catholic and Protestant at Home and Abroad* (London, Longmans, Brown, Green and Longmans, 1855), pp. 60–1.

5 S. C. Carpenter, op. cit., 1933, p. 413.

6 Janet Dunbar, *The Early Victorian Woman: Some Aspects of her Life* (London, Harraps, 1953), p. 6.

7 A. H. Bennett, op. cit., p. 27.

8 P.H. 6248.

9 Jameson, op. cit., p. 105.

10 Sir Edward Cook, *The Life of Florence Nightingale* (London, Macmillan, 1913), vol. 1, p. 5.

11 Dunbar, op. cit., p. 22.

12 Cook, op. cit., vol. 1, p. 5.

13 P.H. 71403.

14 Rosalind Nash, *A Sketch of the Life of Florence Nightingale* (London, S.P.C.K., 1937), p. 20.

15 Desiree Edwards-Rees, *The Story of Nursing* (London, Constable, 1965), p. 60. See also the article by George Devereux and Florence R. Weiner, 'The occupational status of nurses', *American Sociological Review*, vol. 15 (1950), p. 628.

16 Devereux and Weiner, op. cit., p. 630.

17 *Convocation of Canterbury Report*, 1885, p. 276.

18 George Edward Lynch Cotton, *The Employment of Women in Religious and Charitable Works: A Lecture delivered before the Bethune Society, 5th April, 1866*, pp. 14–15. Cary in Williams and Harris (op. cit.) also refers to the ideal of exemplary family life in the parsonage.

19 R. T. Davidson and W. Benham, *Life of A. C. Tait* (London, Macmillan, 1891) vol. 1, p. 468.
20 Liddon, op. cit., vol. 3, p. 8.
21 J. M. Neale, op. cit., 1869, p. 4.
22 P.H. 6253.
23 P.H. 6257.
24 T. J. Williams, op. cit., 1950, p. 24.
25 Lockhart, op. cit., vol. 1, p. 135.
26 Orby Shipley, op. cit., 1867, p. 177.
27 Maria Trench, *The Story of Dr. Pusey's Life* (London, Longmans, 1900), p. 276.
28 The source of this is Sidney Leslie Ollard, *The Anglo-Catholic Revival* (London, Oxford, A. R. Mowbray, 1925).
29 Nash, op. cit., p. 20.
30 Quoted in F. N. L. Poynter, *The Evolution of Hospitals in Britain* (London, Pitmans Medical, 1964), p. 247.
31 American Nurses' Association, *Issues in the Growth of a Profession*, presented at the 41st convention of the American Nurses' Association, Atlantic City, New Jersey, 19th June, 1958, p. 8.
32 In Poynter, op. cit., p. 245.
33 M. Adelaide Nutting and Lavinia L. Dock, *A History of Nursing* (New York and London, Pitman, 1907), vol. 2, pp. 184–5.
34 P.H. 323, pp. 3–4.
35 P.H. 1086, p. 3.
36 *Church Congress of 1866*, op. cit., p. 194.
37 Henry Daniel Nihill, *The Sisters of the Poor at St. Michael's, Shoreditch, and their Work* (London, private circulation, 1870); and *Sisters of the Poor and their Work* (London, Kegan Paul, 1887).
38 See Alan Deacon and Michael Hill, 'The problem of "surplus women" in the nineteenth century', in M. Hill (ed.), *A Sociological Yearbook of Religion in Britain—5* (London, S.C.M. Press, 1972).
39 P.H. 6256.
40 Hutchings, op. cit., p. 85.
41 P.H. 6259.
42 P.H. 70887.
43 P.H. 6259, p. 3.
44 Walter Howard Frere, *English Church Ways* (London, John Murray, 1914), p. 87.
45 Peter Worsley, op. cit., especially concluding chapter.
46 See the article by Kevin Clements in the *Sociological Yearbook of Religion in Britain—4*, ed. M. Hill (London, S.C.M. Press, 1971).
47 Nutting and Dock, op. cit., vol. 1, p. 500.
48 Quoted in Poynter, op. cit., p. 245.
49 Edward-Rees, op. cit., p. 41.
50 Cook, op. cit., vol. 1, p. 44.
51 ibid., p. 54.
52 ibid., p. 62.
53 *Memorials of Agnes Elizabeth Jones by her sister, with introduction by Florence Nightingale* (London, Strahan, 1871), p. 251.

54 Forbes, op. cit., pp. 15–16.
55 P.H. 6273.
56 P.H. 6274, p. 15.
57 P.H. 5060, p. 11.
58 North London Deaconess Institution, op. cit., p. 6.
59 *Report of Convocation*, 1878, op. cit., p. 239.
60 ibid., p. 255.
61 *Review of Jameson and Cotton* (British Museum), p. 7.
62 ibid., p. 9.
63 A. Hughes, op. cit., p. 117.

10

Anglican Religious Orders in Their Secular Context: Social and Demographic Influences on Sisterhoods and Brotherhoods

THERE ARE various levels on which social influences can be seen working on the Anglican orders of the nineteenth century. In the previous chapter it was shown that the legitimation of these institutions sometimes relied for its impact on social factors and role definitions which derived from a secular source. In this final chapter we will consider three ways in which the secular environment strongly and directly influenced the growth of religious orders. There is no intention of providing an overriding epiphenomenalist explanation of these movements, but simply of suggesting those areas in which social influences were more clearly defined. The first of these centres on the effect which sisterhoods, and especially their founders, were thought to have on family life, and the friction this caused between communities and their local environment. Secondly, the influence on female communities of the demographic imbalance which resulted in many women not marrying will be traced. Thirdly, and finally, the brotherhoods will be seen as a very direct response to the problems of big cities and as a means of reconciling economic differences, a role in which they were occasionally envisaged as a counter-revolutionary task force.

SISTERHOODS AS A SUBVERSIVE INFLUENCE ON FAMILIES

One of the commonest themes of Protestant attacks on Catholicism in general (in which category Tractarianism was invariably included) and on the religious life in particular was the subversive influence of priests and convents on the authority of the family. In a society in which the family was considered a most important social institution, the effectiveness of this point of attack may well be appreciated. The revived practice of Confession was regarded with especially deep suspicion as a form of spy system whereby the priest could gain information about and secretly influence the domestic arrangements of unwary Englishmen. [1] The idea that convents exerted a subversive influence on families had a considerable impact on the sisterhoods and the fact that this attitude was recognized and taken into account by founders and supporters of sisterhoods can be judged by their public statements denying any depreciation of marriage. Liddon commented in a sermon:

> It is not a question of depreciating marriage, but of insisting upon the spiritual advantages of a single life freely undertaken for the glory of God . . . [2]

In the debate of Canterbury Convocation in 1862, when sisterhoods were discussed for the first time, Seymour assured his audience that he had no wish to devalue marriage. Similarly, Forbes argued in his pamphlet that voluntary celibacy would *ennoble* the unmarried state, which was so often not chosen willingly. [3] At the Church Congress of 1862 Carter of Clewer mentioned two possible objections to sisterhoods: firstly, there was the fear that sisterhoods would interfere with family ties and duties; and secondly, it was thought that they represented a disparagement of domestic life. Both these fears were, in his opinion, groundless. He returned to the second of these objections at the Church Congress of 1878, when he stated that sisterhoods were 'not to be regarded as casting any reflection on other forms of life or service, least of all on family life'. [4] However, in the same debate the Rev. G. W. Weldon plainly argued that home life was being devalued by the sisterhoods and he quoted the phrase, 'The trivial round, the common task . . .' to draw a contrast between active benevolence and contemplative devotion.

It is interesting to note that Florence Nightingale was confronted by exactly the same accusation of disrupting family life in her early career. Thus, when she was making preparations for the Crimean expedition and was trying to gather together a group of nurses to accompany her, a sketch of her background and personal qualities was put in *The Examiner* and later in *The Times*. The article was phrased in a very reassuring way:

> Her friends and acquaintances are of all classes and persuasions, but her happiest place is at home, in the centre of a very large

band of accomplished relatives, and in simplest obedience to her admiring parents. [5]

Comments Tooley, 'The last clause would satisfy apprehensive people that a young lady of such unusual attainments was not a "revolting daughter".' [6] Despite these disclaimers, it seems probable that at least some of the new recruits had strong family reasons for wanting to join a sisterhood. It must also have been the case, as A. H. Bennett suggests, that there were some women in sisterhoods who were not completely committed to the life but who could not sever themselves from the community because they had initially been obliged to reject family ties in order to gain entrance. Whatever the actual situation, it is highly significant that supporters of sisterhoods found it necessary to reiterate their support for conventional family loyalties. Miss Sellon's brother, writing in defence of sisterhoods in 1849, went very far indeed in this direction:

> And although but few of the daughters of England's Church can enter into these companies of energetic women; although but few, under present circumstances, have any right, even if they have the desire, thus wholly to separate themselves from the common cares of daily life, and devote themselves to the service of CHRIST; yet there is no reason why the sister's life may not be virtually practised, and in a way as pleasing to GOD in the quiet English home. [7]

The way in which Protestant appeals to the integrity of the family were employed against the sisterhoods is well illustrated by the book: *Maude; or the Anglican Sister of Mercy*. In the 1869 edition the basic objection was clearly stated:

> [God] has given us our home ties and duties; and to set these aside for work planned and devised by ourselves is *not* in reality following Him, but following *ourselves*. [8]

The second edition of the book in 1895 made even more explicit the Protestant critique of sisterhoods, and it described the reaction that was required from the heads of families. Having given details of the revival of 'priestcraft' and the Confessional the author says:

> Neither will [priestcraft] regain its sway in Christian families

where the heads of them are determined that the integrity of the family shall be upheld. [9]

Very often the founders and spiritual advisers of sisterhoods were identified as disrupters of domestic harmony. In this respect the cases of W. J. E. Bennett and Dr Pusey are typical and very similar. In 1850—against the background of intense popular disapproval which followed the Pope's re-establishment of a hierarchy in Great Britain—the Bishop of London wrote to the Rev. W. J. E. Bennett, vicar of St Barnabas', Pimlico, accusing him of Romanist ritual tendencies and of receiving sisters (to what the bishop called a 'society of females [with] . . . almost every peculiarity of a nunnery but the name' [10]) without the approval of their parents. The particular accusation concerned a young woman who in the event wrote to the bishop assuring him that she had her parents' consent and that Mr Bennett had remained an intimate friend of her father throughout. The accusation against Pusey was made in *The Times* of 20th December 1866, and concerned a young woman who, it was said, had been persuaded by him to take a vow of celibacy for two years without the knowledge or consent of her parents. In this case the father was still alive and wrote to the newspaper completely denying the story. [11]

By far the most notable case of parental disapproval was the dispute, which was precipitated by a riot, between J. M. Neale and the Rev. John Scobell of Lewes, Sussex, in 1857. Scobell's daughter had entered Neale's sisterhood at East Grinstead against her father's wishes. Shortly afterwards she contracted scarlet fever and died, but not before she had been permitted to write a will in which she bequeathed £400 to the sisterhood. This seems to have greatly annoyed Scobell, who proceeded to circulate a number of rumours—including the insinuation that the scarlet fever had been engineered by the sisters and that his daughter had subsequently been persuaded to make a will in favour of the sisterhood. On the evening of the funeral at Lewes, J. N. Neale and the sisters were attacked by a mob and only with difficulty succeeded in reaching the railway station under police escort. There followed a bitter pamphlet battle in which Scobell accused the Puseyites of 'capturing' his daughter and warned that no home was safe with such machinations going on. In his reply Neale alleged that Scobell had used his position as *paterfamilias* in a despotic manner, opening his twenty-seven-year-old daughter's mail, reading her diary to the rest of the family and generally behaving in a cruel and overbearing way. Whatever the truth of the accusations and counter-accusations a good deal of harm was done to the sisterhood. The Bishop of Chichester, another *pavidus* bishop, withdrew the little support he had given the sisterhood and it took some time to restore confidence in it among the public at large.

THE FEMALE SURPLUS

When at the Canterbury Convocation of 1862 Seymour made the first speech on the subject of sisterhoods, he noted that there was no lack of women to join them because there were many women with no home duties to fulfil. Here he was referring to one of the most widely perceived social problems of the nineteenth century, that of 'surplus' or 'redundant' women—a consequence of the male/female imbalance in the population of Great Britain. In 1855 Mrs Jameson made a speech in which she said:

> The subject becomes one of awful importance when we consider, that in the last census of 1851, there appears an excess of the female over the male population of Great Britain of more than half a million, the proportion being 104 women to 100 men. How shall we employ this superfluity of the 'feminine element' in society, how turn it to good and useful purposes, instead of allowing it to run to waste? Take of these 500,000 superfluous women only the one-hundredth part, say 5,000 women, who are willing to work for good, to join the communion of labour, under a directing power, if only they knew how—if only they could *learn* how—best to do their work, and if employment were open to them—what a phalanx it would be if properly organised! [12]

Dunbar attributes the surplus at least in part to the high rate of emigration of men:

> There was a still more urgent need for women's education; the whole question was bound up with the problem of their freedom to work for a living. The high rate of emigration among young men at that period of commercial expansion meant that there was a surplus of unmarried middle-class women left at home. Many of these, on the death of father or brother, had no means of support . . . [13]

This explanation is open to question because, while the problem of the 'redundant' woman was (or was certainly presented as) a middle class problem, the vast majority of emigrants who left Brtain for America and the colonies in the first half of the nineteenth century were working class. [14]

The demographic imbalance had advantages and disadvantages for the growth of sisterhoods, just as it did for the growth of other female occupations such as nursing. In brief, while it created a pool of potential recruits it was also arguable that these were not necessarily the most highly motivated women to recruit from. Using an analogy which has been applied to patterns of urbanization, when 'pull' factors operate—as was the case with pioneers like Florence Nightingale, who positively rejected offers of marriage in order to pursue a career which had been previously chosen—there is likely to be higher morale and more commitment to the occupational role than when predominantly 'push' factors operate. In the latter case there is likely to be what has been called in another context a 'reluctant labour force'. [15] In general, writers tended to welcome the demographic opportunity and wished to channel the female surplus into sisterhoods, deaconesses and other women's occupations, though other commentators added a substantial note of dissent.

Southey's *Colloquies* took up the issue, and this was one of the earliest references to the problem in the nineteenth century. It is argued:

> Considering the condition of single women in the middle classes, it is not speaking too strongly to assert, that the establishment of protestant nunneries, upon a wise plan and liberal scale, would be the greatest benefit that could possibly be conferred upon these kingdoms. [16]

Forbes, who anticipated that voluntary celibacy would raise the status of spinsters generally, similarly thought that, when marriage was not possible it was a noble course of action to join a sisterhood:

> To marry, to guide the house, to bear children, to educate them in the fear and love of GOD, is the customary lot and duty of women. But in any artificial state of society (such as our own is in a high degree) many cannot meet with such marriage as would be real happiness to them. [17]

For these women, thought Forbes, it was a valuable alternative to join a sisterhood. Two years later Florence Nightingale pointed out that it was misguided to be complacent about the single life for women in a society in which very few roles for single women were provided:

> It has become of late the fashion, both of novel and of sermon writers, to cry up 'old maids', to inveigh against regarding marriage as the vocation of all women, to declare that a single life is as happy as a married one, if people would but think so. So is the air as good an element for fish as the water, if they did but know how to live in it. Show us how to be single, and we will agree. But hitherto we have not found that young English women have been convinced. And we must confess that, *in the present state of things*, their horror of being 'old maids' seems perfectly justified; it is not merely a foolish desire for the pomp and circumstance of marriage—a 'life without love, and an activity without an aim' is horrible in idea, and wearisome in reality. [18]

The fate of well-to-do spinsters who had no particular occupation was often described as a pitiable one, and in a pamphlet of 1855 it was suggested that they might provide ready recruits to sisterhoods. The writer thought that the plight of the wealthy spinsters was more pitiable than that of the poor one, and a description was given of a boarding house in Paris which was full of spinsters from Great Britain and in which the landlord was the only man. 'Was this a sisterhood? No; but each lady there belonged to an order very common in, and much dispersed over the continent—the order of British Idlers.' [19] In welcoming the demographic opportunity which the female surplus provided for the expansion of sisterhoods, some of their protagonists were even prepared to detect the hand of Divine Providence at work in the Registrar General's statistics. Speaking at the Church Congress of 1866, Archdeacon Harris noted:

> The two last census [*sic*] have revealed a singular state of Christian society within our own country—namely, the immense preponderance of the female sex. The last census, I believe, showed a preponderance of something like half a million. This will lead to more female employment, some will say; but I view it as a remarkably providential feature of the present day,

that when there is this anomalous state of society, God has created amongst us a high vocation, a high calling, a vocation in the highest sense of the word of God calling his servants to do a particular work for Him. [20]

One of the best examples of a commentator who seriously doubted the relevance of census figures for the revival of female activity in the nineteenth-century church was Howson, who was mainly concerned with deaconesses. He had published an article on the subject in the *Quarterly Review* of September 1860, and in his pamphlet of 1862 he noted with amusement that one of the least important arguments of his 1860 article (that the preponderance of males in the British population made it necessary to find employment for women) had been greatly amplified by reviewers. It was true, he agreed, that the census statistics had only recently been closely scrutinized and that they opened some serious questions, but ' . . . it would be a great delusion to suppose that the establishment of a system of Deaconesses would redress the evils which, however keenly felt before, have now been clearly defined by help of the Census'. [21] When there was a female surplus, he continued, it did suggest that there were some specific ministries providentially assigned to the female sex, but a surplus on the existing scale—which had doubtless in part been caused by male emigration—could only be put right by planned female emigration. Similar arguments were applied to sisterhoods. Margaret Goodman, for example, who was a strong albeit extremely perceptive critic of sisterhoods, commented:

> It would appear from the writings of some persons, who urge the multiplication of sisterhoods, that they think them desirable because calculated to prove a blessing to women who have nothing to do: a mode of existence for ladies who, after every effort on their part, from the supply not equalling the demand, are unable to find husbands; or a refuge for the woe-worn, weary and disappointed. For neither of these three classes will a sisterhood prove a home. The work is far too real to be performed by lagging hands. [22]

On the ultra-Protestant fringe even direr fears were voiced, and a pamphlet of 1872 warned that the sex imbalance was attracting Jesuits to England with the intention of expanding the 'papal garrisons' (monasteries and convents) so that the whole of the country might be placed in subjection to the Pope. Female emigration to the colonies was urged.

THE BROTHERHOODS AND URBAN ISSUES

The debate over the apparent failure of the urban parochial system covered many different aspects, but Anglican brotherhoods were one of the most frequently advocated solutions. Froude was one of the first Tractarians to advocate brotherhoods principally for the needs of a fast-expanding population. In 1833 he wrote that the present situation seemed to offer possibilities 'for reviving the monastic system. Certainly colleges of unmarried priests would be the cheapest way of providing effectively for the spiritual wants of a large population'. [23] Around 1838 Pusey was also thinking about the possibility of colleges of celibate clergy in large towns. Others had also given thoughts to the problem, and in his pamphlet of 1839 Wackerbarth started from the premise that the parochial system was inadequate:

> It is, I presume, admitted on all hands, or at least very generally felt, that in the present state of the Church's fortunes and funds, the Parochial system alone is altogether inadequate to the necessities of the Faithful. [24]

Having described the apparent success of the Dissenters, who were evangelizing in large towns as well as making good use of their members' enthusiasm, he returned to the failure of the parish system and argued,

> . . . it appears to me, that a College of unmarried Priests, such as the rulers of a Monastic Institution ought in all cases to be, with a body of religious brethren under them, would be of incalculable efficacy in counteracting the evil above-stated. [25]

However, early attempts to found brotherhoods were not particularly noticeable for their involvement in urban evangelism. Newman's community at Littlemore was primarily contemplative, as was the curious experiment at Leeds which Hook described to Pusey in a letter of 1843:

> I am uneasy about Mr. Aitkin . . . He has fitted up the schoolroom adjoining his church with cells, each containing a bed and a cross; he has some young men with him who have forsaken all; his rule is very strict; he has daily Communion; they fast

till four every Wednesday, when he allows himself, and themselves, meat; on Friday they fast till four and then have fish. In
the meantime he, having a family residing five miles away,
sleeps in his cell four times a week . . . ; his wife complains of
his neglecting his six or more children. [26]

Another reference was made to the problem of the large towns in
1845, when Samuel Fox prefaced his highly informative book on
monks and monasteries in England with a call for brotherhoods
to engage in the work of converting the masses in large towns. In
1861 a concrete proposal was made to Bishop Tait of London by
a layman who had tested the opinion of clergy of different schools
of churchmanship and had found general approval for a 'better
organization of voluntary lay assistance in aid of the efforts of the
parochial clergy' (as Tait termed the scheme [27]). The proposal
was couched in fairly general terms, and so was the bishop's reply
expressing approval for the scheme but pointing out that the word
'order' might create difficulties.

In his essay of 1866, Baring-Gould argued that the parish
system itself was not necessarily a failure but was simply being
expected to do work which it had never been intended to do. [28]
The success of the Dissenters was not only due to their freedom
from the parish system but also to the more popular idiom of their
forms of worship. Such techniques were not to be rejected out of
hand by the Church of England since they might be extremely
valuable. The solution was, he thought, to introduce missionary
brotherhoods into the Church of England as a supplement to the
existing parish system and as a specialized means of coping with
the problem of the 'unchurched masses' in the large towns. This
was precisely what the Society of St John the Evangelist, which
was founded in 1866, set out to do. The SSJE proved to be one
of the most successful Anglican brotherhoods.

The Society of the Holy Cross, an association of ritualist clergy
and hence a major target of ultra-Protestant spokesmen like John
Kensit and Walter Walsh, published around 1866–7 a Memorial to
the Archbishop of Canterbury in which Brother Ignatius was
stoutly defended and the Archbishop's sanction for his work requested. The pamphlet also asked the Archbishop to consider the
establishment of 'Religious Orders of Men, living and working
under Episcopal direction, in the Church of England'. [29] Archbishop Longley replied that he found little support among the

bishops for the opinions expressed by the subscribers to the Memorial and declined the responsibility of taking any steps for the re-establishment of 'Religious Orders of Men, with a name and habit distinctive of their calling and order'. [30] The Society of the Holy Cross regarded work among the poorer areas of cities as a major field of its activities, for in a vindication of their organization in 1877 they demanded:

> If there is this Protestant zeal for religion, why did it not pre-occupy those slums, in our large towns, into which Mr. Lowder and Mr. Mackonochie have found their way? [31]

One of the most explicitly political reasons for introducing brotherhoods into cities was made in the debate of the 1889 Canterbury Convocation on the Report on Brotherhoods. It shows, perhaps better than any other source, how a theological position and a particular view of society could combine to give double justification to an ostensibly religious reform. The speaker was the Dean of Lincoln (W. J. Butler, founder of the Wantage Sisterhood) and his subject was the lack of religious observance in industrial cities. He reminded the other members

> ... that unless they could bring that love of Christ into the heart of their congregations, there was no possible means of reconciling differences of rank and *status* ... Unless they could reconcile these distances at any moment there might be a fierce outbreak of the lower classes, which would sweep away the dignity and the prosperity of this country. ... Unless they could in some way or other teach the people that there was something which would compensate for all the miseries of the present life, they were living on the edge of a volcano. [32]

He also saw the advantage of having devoted clergy, committed to the ideal of poverty, who would thus set an example to the working poor among whom they lived:

> Some had very bitter words to say about clergymen, whom they looked upon as men rolling in money. What was wanted was to bring before these people a body of men, thorough gentlemen, highly educated it might be, but living on something like the same terms as themselves. [33]

The sisterhoods and brotherhoods in the nineteenth-century Church of England took the form they did as a result of influences from two main directions. Firstly, there was the theological conception of the reinstatement of primitive tradition which involved the revival of specific organizational features which had been characteristic of the early church. Different parties within the Church of England had quite different ideas of what constituted the legitimate form of ancillary organization to meet the demands of a rapidly changing society, and the High Church party's reintroduction of the religious life was one of these. Secondly, there were the influences exerted by the structure and ethos of Victorian society. These had a profound influence on the shape taken by these reinstated forms of organization, and on the way the latter were legitimated within the church and in society at large. Some of the most interesting features appear at the point where the theological and social influences converge. Thus, for example, the two competing types of women's work in the church—deaconesses and sisterhoods—could be referred back to different periods of church history which were accepted in claims to legitimacy by different church parties. Deaconesses were more acceptable to the Low Church party which referred back to the Gospel church, and sisterhoods were an offshoot of the High Church party which had a strong conception of the early church tradition. Sisterhoods and deaconesses also represented more or less conflicting definitions of the role of women in Victorian society. Likewise, the brotherhoods could be viewed primarily in theological or pragmatic terms, but even to observers who were most sympathetic to the non-instrumental claims of the religious life, the latent political functions of such institutions were of great importance.

It is especially in situations like these, when religious and social influences are intricately related, that an ideal type of religious organization is most helpful: it provides a relatively stable and to a certain degree 'external' point of reference by means of which the empirical complexities may be unravelled. In the study of religious organizations and beliefs this enables us to anchor the legitimations derived from a theological source in their secular environment without at the same time having to adopt an epiphenomenalist perspective. This, in the last analysis, is the only way in which a sociological interpretation of religion can develop.

NOTES

1 For evidence of this, see the pamphlets by such writers as Cayla and Hogan, where Confession and conventualism are treated in the same context.

2 P.H. 12781, p. 19.

3 A. P. Forbes, op. cit.

4 *Church Congress of 1878*, op. cit., p. 56.

5 Sarah A. Tooley, *The Life of Florence Nightingale* (London, S. H. Bousfield, 1904), p. 112.

6 ibid., p. 112.

7 P.H. 6243, p. 11.

8 *Maude; or the Anglican Sister of Mercy*, edited by Miss Whately (London, Harrison, 1869), pp. 18–19.

9 *The Anglican Sister of Mercy* (London, Eliot Stock, 1895), p. 57.

10 W. J. E. Bennett, op. cit., p. 92.

11 Liddon, op. cit., vol. 3, pp. 190–1.

12 Jameson, op. cit., p. 56. By my crude calculations, which agree with the figure of half a million, the ratio of females to males was more like 105 to 100 and it hovered between 105 and 107 to 100 from 1801 to 1901. Incidentally, in 1929 Wanda Neff began her book, *Victorian Working Women* with a discussion of this problem which misquoted Jameson, then quibbled with her figures, and made the classic mistake of failing to distinguish England and Britain. She says: 'Mrs. Jameson in 1851 proclaimed from the lecture-platform that there was an excess of half a million women in England. [*sic*] The census figures allow 365,159. [*sic*] The Napoleonic Wars could be held directly responsible for only a small part of this disproportion which the census had recorded since 1801.'

Neff's book is often quoted as a source of information about Victorian women, but it should be treated with care. She thinks that the Empire with its demand for men in the Civil Service was one disruptive factor, but another was more interesting. The census figures for 1851 show that 24·86 per cent of women at 30 years of age were unmarried, 17·89 per cent aged 35 and 11·88 per cent aged 50. But out of every 100 men in 1851 in England and Wales 25·89 per cent were not married at the age of 30, 18 at the age of 35 and 10·74 per cent aged 50. Says Neff, 'Women were "redundant" then, not because there were too many of them, but because the men did not marry'. (p. 12).

13 Dunbar, op. cit., p. 133.

14 Five million people—of whom about three-quarters were men—are estimated to have emigrated between 1800 and 1850. I am indebted for this and other points in this section to Mr Alan Deacon, whose undergraduate dissertation, 'The Social Position of the Unmarried Woman in the Mid-Victorian Period and its Relationship to the Development of Philanthropy', (L.S.E., 1969) contains excellent documentation and interpretation of this topic.

15 See the article by E. James, 'Women at work in twentieth-century Britain', *Manchester School*, September 1962. The push/pull analogy refers

to the analysis of urbanization in Western and contemporary developing societies which Hoselitz gives in *City, Factory and Economic Growth*.

16 Southey, op. cit., vol. 2, p. 36.

17 Forbes, op. cit., pp. 11–12.

18 Florence Nightingale, *The Institution of Kaiserwerth on the Rhine* (London, 1851), pp. 6–7.

19 *Sisters of Charity and some visits with them* (London, Joseph Masters, 1855), p. 70.

20 *Church Congress of 1866*, op. cit., p. 194.

21 Howson, op. cit., p. xix.

22 Margaret Goodman, *Sisterhoods in the Church of England* (London, Smith, Elder, 1863), p. 268.

23 Quoted in Brilioth, op. cit., 1925, p. 246.

24 P.H. 6241, pp. 5–6.

25 ibid., pp. 20–1.

26 Quoted in C. P. S. Clarke, op. cit., p. 251.

27 Davidson and Benham, op. cit., pp. 501–2.

28 Orby Shipley (ed.), op. cit., 1866, p. 93.

29 Quoted in James Embry, *The Catholic Movement and the Society of the Holy Cross* (London, Faith Press, 1931), p. 28.

30 ibid., p. 29.

31 P.H. 1732, p. vi.

32 *Report of Convocation*, 1889, p. 242.

33 ibid., p. 243.

A Select Bibliography of Works on nineteenth-century Anglican orders

Adderley, Hon. James Granville, *In Slums and Society* (London, T. Fisher Unwin, 1916).

Advisory Council on Religious Communities, *A Directory of the Religious Life* (London, S.P.C.K., 1943).

Advisory Council on Religious Communities, *Guide to the Religious Communities of the Anglican Communion* (London, A. R. Mowbray, 1962).

(*All for All*), Religious Vocation by a Religious of S. Peter's Community, Woking (London, Faith Press, second edition, 1946).

Allchin, Arthur Macdonald, *The Silent Rebellion* (London, S.C.M., 1958).

Allchin, Arthur Macdonald, *George William Herbert: Some Aspects of his Teaching* (privately printed at the Convent of the Holy Name, Malvern Link, Worcestershire, n.d.).

Anglican Sister of Mercy, *The Anglican Sister of Mercey* (London, Eliot Stock, 1895).

Annie Louisa, Mother General of the Community of St Mary the Virgin, Wantage, *A Memoir of Mother Annie Louisa* (Wantage, Convent of St Mary the Virgin, 1953).

Anson, Peter Frederick, *The Benedictines of Caldey* (London, Burns, Oates, 1940).

Anson, Peter Frederick, *A Roving Recluse* (Cork, Merger Press, 1946).

Anson, Peter Frederick, *Abbot Extraordinary. A Memoir of Aelred Carlyle, Monk & Missionary, 187?–1955* (London, Faith Press, 1958).

Anson, Peter Frederick, *Bishop at Large* (London, Faber and Faber, 1964).

Anson, Peter Frederick and Campbell, A. W., *The Call of the Cloister* (London, S.P.C.K., 1964).

Arnold, Thomas, *Christian Life, its Course, its Hindrances, and its Helps* (London, B. Fellowes, 1841).

Ashwell, Arthur Rawson, *Life of the Right Reverend Samuel Wilberforce* (London, John Murray, 1880–2, vol. 3).

Attwater, Donald, *Father Ignatius of Llanthony* (London, Cassell, 1931).

Ayckbowm, Mother Emily, *A Valiant Victorian. The Life and Times of Mother E. A. 1836–1900 of the Community of the Sisters of the Church* (London, A. R. Mowbray, 1964).

Baker, Joseph Ellis, *The Novel and the Oxford Movement* (Princeton, Princeton Studies in English No. 8, 1932).

Baring-Gould, Sabine, 'On the revival of religious confraternities', in *The Church and the World: Essays on Questions of the Day*, ed. Orby Shipley, first series (London, Longmans, Green, Reader and Dyer, 1866).

Bennett, Alice Horlock, *Through an Anglican Sisterhood to Rome* (London, Longmans, 1914).

Bennett, Rev. Frederick, *The Story of W. J. E. Bennett . . . and of his Part in the Oxford Church Movement of the Nineteenth Century* (London, Longmans, 1909).

Bennett, Rosemary Howard, *I Choose the Cloister* (London, Hodder and Stoughton, 1956).

Benson, Arthur Christopher, *The Life of Edward White Benson, Sometime Archbishop of Canterbury* (London, Macmillan, 1899).

Benson, Richard Meux, *The Principles of Brotherhood. An Address* (Oxford, 1865).

Benson, Richard Meux, *The Religious Life Portrayed for the Use of Sisters of Mercy*, transl. from the French (London, 1898).

Benson, Richard Meux, *The Revival of the Religious Life* (1900).

Benson, Richard Meux, *The Followers of the Lamb* (London, Longmans, 1900).

Benson, Richard Meux, *Instructions on the Religious Life* (Oxford, S.S.J.E., 1927–51).

[Benson, Richard Meux], *Thoughts of Father Benson* (London, Oxford, A. R. Mowbray, 1933) [The Churchman's Penny Library, New Series].

Benson, Richard Meux, *The Religious Vocation* (London, A. R. Mowbray, 1939).

Bertouch, Beatrice De Baroness, *The Life of Father Ignatius O.S.B., The Monk of Llanthony* (London, Methuen, 1904).

Bigg, Charles, *Wayside Sketches in Ecclesiastical History* (London, Longmans, Green, 1906).

Biggs, Charles Richard Davey, *Berkyngechurche by the Tower. The Story and Work of Allhallows, Barking* (London, Waterlow and Sons, 1899).

Binns, L. E. Elliott, *Religion in the Victorian Era* (London, Lutterworth Press, 1964).

Biot, François, O.P., *The Rise of Protestant Monasticism*, transl. W. J. Kerrigan (Dublin, Helicon, 1963).

Brandreth, Henry Reynard Turner, *Dr. Lee of Lambeth. A Chapter in Parenthesis in the History of the Oxford Movement* (London, S.P.C.K., 1951).

Brandreth, Henry Reynard Turner, *Episcopi Vagantes and the Anglican Church* (London, S.P.C.K., 1947).

Brandreth, Henry Reynard Turner, *The Oratory of the Good Shepherd. An Historical Sketch* (Cambridge, Oratory of the Good Shepherd, 1958).

Bridges, Robert Seymour, *Three Friends* (Digby Mackworth Dolben, Richard Watson Dixon, Henry Bradley) (London, Oxford University Press, 1932).

Brilioth, Yngve Torgny, *The Anglican Revival. Studies in the Oxford Movement* (London, Longmans, 1925).

Brilioth, Yngve Torgny, *Three Lectures on Evangelicalism and the Oxford Movement* (London, Oxford University Press, 1934).

Briscoe, John Fetherstonhaugh, *V. S. S. Coles, Letters, Papers, Addresses, Hymns and Verses* (London, A. R. Mowbray, 1930).

Browne, Edward George Kirwan, *History of the Tractarian Movement* (Dublin, James Duffy, 1856).

Browne, Edward George Kirwan, *Annals of the Tractarian Movement. From 1842 to 1860* . . . (London, The Author, third edition, 1861).

Bull, Paul Bertie, C.R., *The Revival of the Religious Life* (London, Edward Arnold, 1914).

Burne, Kathleen E., *The Life and Letters of Father Andrew, S.D.C.* (London, Oxford, A. R. Mowbray, 1948).

Burne, Kathleen E., *Love's Fulfilment* (Father Andrew) (London, A. R. Mowbray, 1957).

Butler, Arthur John, *Life and Letters of William John Butler* (Dean of Lincoln) (London, Macmillan, 1897).

Butler, William John (Dean of Lincoln), *Butler of Wantage. His Inheritance and his Legacy* (Westminster, Dacre Press, 1948).

Cameron, Allan T., *The Religious Communities of the Church of England* (London, Faith Press, 1918).

Cannell, Bertram George Aubrey, *From Monk to Busman* (London, Skeffington and Son, 1935).

Carpenter, Spencer Cecil, *Church & People, 1789–1889* (London, S.P.C.K., 1933).

Carter, Thomas Thellusson, *Objections to Sisterhoods Considered, In a Letter to a Parent* (London, F. and J. Rivington, 1853).

Carter, Thomas Thellusson, *Vows and the Religious State. I. Vows, and their relation to Religious Communities. II. The Religious State and Age of Profession* (London, J. Masters, 1881).

Carter, Thomas Thellusson, *Harriet Monsell. A Memoir* (London, J. Masters, 1884).

Carter, Thomas Thellusson (ed.), *Nicholas Ferrar. His Household and his Friends* (London, Longmans, Green, 1892).

Carter, Thomas Thellusson, *Manual of Devotion for Sisters of Mercy* (London, Longmans, Green, fifth edition, vol. 1, 1897).

[Carter, Thomas Thellusson], *The Founders of Clewer* (London, A. R. Mowbray, 1952).

Carter, Thomas Thellusson, 'Vows, and their relation to Religious Communities', in *The Church and the World: Essays on Questions of the Day*, ed. Orby Shipley, first series (London, Longmans, Green, Reader and Dyer, 1866).

Cary, Henry Lucius Moultrie, *Called of God* (London and Oxford, A. R. Mowbray, 1937).

Cary, Henry Lucius Moultrie, *Hortus Inclusus*—An Essay on the Contemplative Life (Westminster, Pax House, 1944).

[Cecile, Mother], *Mother Cecile in South Africa, 1883–1906. Foundress of the Community of the Resurrection of our Lord. Compiled by a Sister of the Community* (London, S.P.C.K., 1930).

Chadwick, Owen, *The Mind of the Oxford Movement* (London, Adam and Charles Black, 1960).

Church, Richard William, *The Oxford Movement. Twelve Years. 1833–1845* (London, Macmillan, (1891) 1900).

Church Congress of 1862, Report of the Proceedings of the, held in the Sheldonian Theatre and Town Hall, Oxford . . . (Oxford and London, J. H. and J. Parker, 1862).

Church Congress held at York, . . . 1866, . . . Proceedings of the (York, John Sampson, 1867).

Church Congress, held at Dublin . . . 1868, Authorized Report of the (Dublin, Hodges, Smith and Foster, 1868).

Church Congress held at Southampton . . . 1870, Authorized Report of the (Southampton, Gutch and Cox, 1870).

Church Congress held at Stoke-on-Trent . . . 1875, Authorized Report of the (London, William Wells Gardner, 1875).

Church Congress held at Sheffield . . . 1878, The Official Report of the (Sheffield, Pawson and Brailsford, 1879).

Church Congress held at Reading . . . 1883, The Official Report of the (London, Bemrose and Sons, 1883).

Church Congress held at Manchester, 1888, The Official Report of the (London, Bemrose and Sons, 1888).

Church Congress held at Birmingham, 1893, The Official Report of the (London, Bemrose and Sons, 1893).

Clarke, Charles Philip Stewart, *The Oxford Movement and After* (London and Oxford, A. R. Mowbray, 1932).

Cockshut, A. O. J., *Religious Controversies of the Nineteenth Century: Selected Documents* (London, Methuen, 1966).

Coleridge, Christabel Rose, *Charlotte Mary Yonge. Her Life and Letters* (London and New York, Macmillan, 1903).

[Community of St Mary The Virgin, Wantage], *A Hundred Years of Blessing* (London, S.P.C.K., 1946).

[Community of the Holy Family], *A Service of Praise for All Hallows Tide* (London, 1930).

[Community of the Resurrection], *Mirfield Essays in Christian Belief* (London, Faith Press, 1962).

[Community of the Resurrection], *The Call to the Religious Life* (Huddersfield, Mirfield Publications, 1963).

Congreve, George, *Christian Progress; with Other Papers and Addresses* (London, Longmans, 1910).

Congreve, George and Longridge, W. H., *Letters of R. M. Benson* (London and Oxford, A. R. Mowbray, 1916).

Congreve, George, *The Incarnation and the Religious Life* (Oxford, S.S.J.E., 1929).

[Convocation of Canterbury], *Chronicle of Convocation* (London, 1859–)

[Convocation of York], *Journal of Convocation* (London, York, 1861–)

Cook, Sir Edward, *The Life of Florence Nightingale* (London, Macmillan, 1913).

Cope, Zachary, *Six Disciples of Florence Nightingale* (London, Pitman Medical, 1961).

Cornish, Francis Ware, *The English Church in the Nineteenth Century*, in W. R. W. Stephens and W. Hunt, *A History of the English Church*, vol. 8 (London, Macmillan, 1910).

Cotton, George Edward Lynch, Bishop of Calcutta, *The Employment of Women in Religious and Charitable Works: A Lecture Delivered before the Bethune Society, the 5th April, 1866* . . . (Published by desire of the Society, 1866).

Creighton, Mandell, *The National Church in the Middle Ages* (London, Simpkin, Marshall, Hamilton, Kent; Church Defence Depot, 1895).

Creighton, Mandell, *The Idea of a National Church. An Address* (London, S.P.C.K., 1898).

Creighton, Louise, *Life and Letters of Mandell Creighton* (London, Longmans, Green, 1904).

Creighton, Mandell, *The Claims of the Common Life* (London, Longmans, Green, 1905).

Cross, Frank Leslie, *The Oxford Movement and the Seventeenth Century*, Oxford Movement Centenary Series (London, S.P.C.K., 1933).

Cross, Frank Leslie, *Darwell Stone* (Westminster, Dacre Press, 1943).

Curtis, Geoffrey William Seymour, *William of Glasshampton. Friar: Monk: Solitary* (London, S.P.C.K., 1947).

[Cusack, Margaret A.], *Five Years in a Protestant Sisterhood and Ten Years in a Catholic Convent* (London, Longmans, Green, 1869).

[Dallas, Alexander Robert Charles], *Protestant Sisters of Charity; A letter addressed to the Lord Bishop of London . . . 1826.*

Dallas, Anne B., *Incidents in the Life and Ministry of the Rev. A. R. C. Dallas* (London, James Nisbet, 1871).

Davidson, Randall Thomas and Benham, William, *Life of Archibald Campbell Tait* (London and New York, Macmillan, 1891).

Dawson, Christopher H., *The Spirit of the Oxford Movement* (London, Sheed and Ward, 1933).

Dearing, Trevor, *Wesleyan and Tractarian Worship* (London, Epworth Press/S.P.C.K., 1966).

Dillistone, Frederick William, *Scripture and Tradition* (London, Lutterworth Press, 1955).

Dix, Morgan, *Instructions on the Religious Life* (London, Oxford, A. R. Mowbray, 1910).

Donovan, Marcus Fitzgerald Grain, *After the Tractarians* (London, Philip Allan, 1933).

Dunbar, Janet, *The Early Victorian Woman; Some Aspects of her Life* (London, Harrap, 1953).

Eastlake, Charles Lock, *A History of the Gothic Revival* (London, Longmans, Green, 1872).

Edwards-Rees, Desiree, *The Story of Nursing* (London, Constable, 1965).

Embry, James, *The Catholic Movement and the Society of the Holy Cross* (London, Faith Press, 1931).

Faber, Geoffrey, *Oxford Apostles* (Harmondsworth, Middlesex, Penguin Books, 1954).

Fairweather, Eugene R. (ed.), *The Oxford Movement* (New York, Oxford University Press, 1964).

[Fliedner, Theodor], *Life of Pastor Fliedner . . .* transl. C. Winkworth (London, 1867).

Forbes, Alexander Penrose, *A Plea for Sisterhoods* (London, Joseph Masters, 1849).

Fox, Samuel, *Monks and Monasteries: being an account of English Monachism* (London, James Burns, 1845, catalogue gives 1840).

Frere, Walter Howard, *English Church Ways* (London, John Murray, 1914).

Froude, Richard Hurrell, *Remains of the Late Rev. R. H. F.* (London, Derby, Rivington, 1838, 39).

Gannon, David, *Father Paul of Graymoor* (New York, Macmillan, 1959).

[Good Nurse, The], *The Good Nurse: or, Hints on the Management of the Sick and Lying-In Chamber, and the Nursery*, dedicated, by permission, to Mrs Priscilla Wakefield (London, 1825).

Goodman, Margaret, *Experiences of an English Sister of Mercy* (London, Smith, Elder, 1862).

Goodman, Margaret, *Sisterhoods in the Church of England: with Notices of some Charitable Sisterhoods in the Romish Church* (London, Smith, Elder, 1863).

Grafton, Charles Chapman, Bp. of Fond du Lac., *The Works of the Rt. Rev. C. C. Grafton* (New York, Longmans) (vol. IV *A Journey Godward . . .*; vol. V *Vocation or the Call of the Divine Master to a Sister's Life: And other writings on the Religious Life*; vol. VII *Letters and Addresses*).

Harrison, Talbot Dilworth, *Every Man's Story of the Oxford Movement* (London and Oxford, A. R. Mowbray, 1932).

Heanley, Robert Marshall, *A Memoir of Edward Steere* (London, George Bell, 1888).

Howson, John Saul, *Deaconesses* (London, Longman, Green, Longman and Roberts, 1862).

Hughes, Anselm, *The Rivers of the Flood. A Personal Account of the Catholic Revival in England in the Twentieth Century* (London, Faith Press, 1961).

Hutchings, William Henry, *Life and Letters of Thomas Thellusson Carter* (London, Longmans, 1903).

Jameson, Anna Bronwell, *Sisters of Charity Catholic and Protestant, at Home and Abroad* (London, Longman, Brown, Green and Longmans, 1855).

[Jameson, Anna Bronwell], *Sisters of Charity* . . . Review of Jameson and Cotton (q.v.) (n.d.).

Johnston, John Octavius, *Life and Letters of Henry Parry Liddon* (London, Longmans, 1904).

Jones, Agnes Elizabeth, *Memorials of Agnes Elizabeth Jones by her Sister, with introduction by Florence Nightingale* (London, Strahan, 1871).

[Kaiserwerth], *Some Account of the Deaconess-Work in the Christian Church* (Fliedner?) (Kaiserwerth, n.d.).

Keble, John, *The Christian Year* (Oxford and London, James Parker, 1873).

Kelly, Herbert Hamilton, *An Idea in the Working: an Account of the S.S.M.* (London, 1908).

Kelly, Herbert Hamilton, *Vocation and Recruiting of Candidates for Holy orders,* (London, S.P.C.K., 1908).

[Kelly, Herbert, S.S.M.], *No Pious Person. Autobiographical Recollections, Edited by George Every, S.S.M.* (London, The Faith Press, 1960).

Kelway, Albert Clifton, *George Rundle Prynne. A Chapter in the Early History of the Catholic Revival,* 1905.

Kelway, Albert Clifton, *A Franciscan Revival. The Story of the Society of the Divine Compassion* (printed, for private circulation only, by the Society, at the Whitwell Press, Plaistow).

Kelway, Albert Clifton, *The Story of the Catholic Revival* (London, Philip Allan, 1933).

Liddon, Henry Parry, *Life of Edward Bouverie Pusey* (London, Longmans, 1893–7).

Littledale, Richard Frederick, *Innovations* (Oxford, A. R. Mowbray, 1868) (a lecture delivered in the Assembly Rooms, Liverpool, 23rd April 1868).

Lloyd, Roger Bradshaigh, *The Church of England in the Twentieth Century* (London, Longmans, Green, 1946, 50).

Lloyd, Roger, *An Adventure in Discipleship. The Servants of Christ the King* (London, Longmans, Green, 1953).

Lock, Walter, *John Keble. A Biography* (London, Methuen, 1891).

Lockhart, John Gilbert, *Charles Lindley, Viscount Halifax* (London, Geoffrey Bles, 1935, 36).

Longridge, George, *A History of the Oxford Mission to Calcutta* (London and Oxford, A. R. Mowbray, 1910).

Lough, Arthur Geoffrey, *The Influence of John Mason Neale* (London, S.P.C.K., 1962).

Lowder, Charles Fuge, *Ten Years in St. George's Mission* (London, G. J. Plamer, 1867).

Lowder, Charles Fuge, *Twenty-one Years in St. George's Mission* (London, Rivingtons, 1877).

[Lowder, Charles Fuge], *Charles Lowder, a Biography* (Maria Trench) (London, Kegan Paul, Trench, ninth edition, 1883).

Lyne, Joseph Leycester (Father Ignatius), *May a Monk serve God in the Church of England, or not? A Letter to the Lord Bishop of London by Ignatius, Deacon of the Church of England, and Monk of the Order of S. Benedict* (Oxford, A. R. Mowbray, 1870).

Macaulay, Rose, *Letters to a Friend* (London, Collins, 1961).

Macaulay, Rose, *Last Letters to a Friend* (London, Collins, 1962).

Mackay, Henry Falconar Barclay, *Saints and Leaders* (London, Society of SS. Peter and Paul, P. Allan, 1928).

Macleod, George, *We shall re-build. The work of the Iona Community on mainland and on island* (Glasgow, The Iona Community, n.d.).

Mare, Margaret Laura and Percival, Alicia Constance, *Victorian Best-Seller. The World of Charlotte M. Yonge* (London, Harrap, 1947).

Marshall, Arthur Calder, *The Enthusiast* (London, Faber and Faber, 1962).

Martindale, Cyril Charles, S.J., *The Life of Monsignor Robert Hugh Benson* (London, Longmans, 1916).

Mason, Arthur James, *Memoir of George Howard Wilkinson* (London, Longmans, 1909).

Maude; or the Anglican Sister of Mercy, edited by Miss Whately, Authoress of 'Life of Archbishop Whately' (London, Harrison, 1869).

Maughan, Herbert Hamilton, *Wagner of Brighton* (Loughlinstown, Coelian Press, 1949).

May, James Lewis, *The Oxford Movement. Its History and its Future* (London, John Lane, 1933).

Middleton, Robert Dudley, *Keble, Froude and Newman* (Canterbury, Gibbs and Sons, 1933).

Middleton, Robert Dudley, *Newman at Oxford* (London, Oxford University Press, 1950).

[Monk, A.], *Brother Placidus and why he became a Monk. A tale for the times, by a Monk of New Llanthony Abbey, Abergavenny, Monmouthshire. (Llanthony Tales—No. 1)* (Brighton, J. Bray, 1870).

Mosley, Nicholas, *The Life of Raymond Raynes* (London, Faith Press, 1961).

Mozley, Anne, *Letters and Correspondence of J. H. Newman* (London, Longmans, Green, 1891).

[N., H., *of St Mary's Home, Stone, Dartford*], *Twenty-Three Years in a House of Mercy* (London, Rivingtons, 1886).

Nash, Rosalind, *A Sketch of the Life of Florence Nightingale* (London, S.P.C.K., 1937).

Neale, John Mason, *Ayton Priory; or, The Restored Monastery* (Cambridge, Deightons, 1843).

Neale, John Mason, *Deaconesses, and Early Sisterhoods*—two Sermons preached in the Oratory of S. Margarets, East Grinstead, Advent, 1857 (London, 1869).

Neale, John Mason, *Selections from the Writings of J. M. N.* (London, Rivingtons, 1884).

Neale, John Mason, *Letters of John Mason Neale . . . Selected and Edited by his daughter* (London, Longmans, 1910).

Neale, John Mason, *The Bible and the Bible Only, the Religion of Protestants . . .* (London and Oxford, A. R. Mowbray, 1915).

Neff, Wanda Fraiken, *Victorian Working Women: An Historical and Literary Study of Women in British Industries and Professions 1832–1850* (New York, Columbia University Press, 1929).

Neil, Stephen, *Anglicanism* (Harmondsworth, Middlesex, Penguin Books, 1965).

Newman, John Henry, *The Church of the Fathers* (London, Rivingtons, 1840).

Newman, John Henry, *Apologia Pro Vita Sua* (London, Longmans, Green, 1890).

Nias, John Charles Somerset, *Flame from an Oxford Cloister* (London, Faith Press, 1961).

Nightingale, Florence, *The Institution of Kaiserwerth on the Rhine* (London, printed by the inmates of the London Ragged Colonial Training School, 1851).

Nightingale, Florence, *Notes on Nursing* (first published 1859, London, Gerald Duckworth, 1952).

Nightingale, Florence, *Death of Pastor Fliedner* (reprinted from *Evangelical Christendom*, 1864).

Nihill, Henry Daniel, *The Sisters of the Poor at St. Michael's, Shoreditch, and their Work* (London, private circulation, 1870).

Nihill, Henry Daniel, *The Sisters of St. Mary at the Cross. Sisters of the Poor and their Work* (London, Kegan Paul, 1887).

[North London Deaconesses' Institution], *The Second Annual Report and Balance Sheet* (London, 1863).

[Nurse's Manual, The], *The Nurse's Manual; or, Instructions for the sick chamber, together with some hints for the avoidance of colds and other diseases incident upon neglect or intemperance* (Cambridge, 1836).

Nutting, M. Adelaide and Dock, Lavinia L., *A History of Nursing* (New York and London, G. P. Pitman's Sons, 1907).

O'Brien, William Braithwaite, *A Cowley Father's Letters* (London, Todd, 1962).

Ollard, Sidney Leslie, *The Anglo-Catholic Revival* (London and Oxford, A. R. Mowbray, 1925).

Ollard, Sidney L. and Cross, Frank Leslie, *The Anglo-Catholic Revival in Outline*, Oxford Movement Centenary Series (London, S.P.C.K., 1933).

Ollard, Sidney Leslie, *A Short History of the Oxford Movement* (London, Faith Press Reprints 1963).

[Order of the Holy Paraclete], *Fulfilled in Joy. The Order of the Holy Paraclete, Whitby, and its Foundress, Mother Margaret by a Foundation Member* (London, Hodder and Stoughton, 1964).

Packard, Kenneth Gordon, *Brother Edward, Priest and Evangelist* (London, Geoffrey Bles, 1955).

[Parochial Order], *The Dawn Breaking* by the author of 'A Suggestion for the Times' (London, Skeffington, 1896).

[Parochial Order], *The Parochial, or Third Order (Anglican)* (Oxford and London, A. R. Mowbray, 1901).

Pavey, Agnes E., *The Story of the Growth of Nursing* (London, Faber and Faber, 1953).

Perry, William, *Alexander Penrose Forbes, Bishop of Brechin, the Scottish Pusey* (London, S.P.C.K., 1939).

Phillips, Charles Stanley, and others, *Walter Howard Frere, Bishop of Truro* (London, Faber and Faber, 1947).

Pinchard, Arnold Theophilus Biddulph (ed.), *The Religious Life* (London, S.P.C.K., 1934).

Potter, George, *Father Potter of Peckham*—autobiography (London, Hodder and Stoughton, 1955).

Povey, J. M. (Sister Mary Agnes), *Nunnery Life in the Church of England; or, Seventeen Years with Father Ignatius* (London, Hodder and Stoughton, 1890).

Poynter, F. N. L., *The Evolution of Hospitals in Britain* (London, Pitman Medical, 1964).

Prestige, George Leonard, *Pusey* (London, Philip Allan, 1933).

Prestige, George Leonard, *The Life of Charles Gore* (London, Heinemann, 1935).

Purcell, Edmund Sheridan, *Life and Letters of Ambrose Phillips De Lisle* (London, Macmillan, 1900).

[Religious, A.], *Monks and Nuns in Modern Days, By a Religious* (London, Church Literature Association, 1935).

Robins, Margaret W., *Mother Cecile of Grahamstown, South Africa* (London, Wells Gardner, Barton, 1911).

Robinson, Cecilia, *The Ministry of Deaconesses* (London, Methuen, 1914).

Romanes, Ethel, *Charlotte Mary Yonge: An Appreciation* (London and Oxford, A. R. Mowbray, 1908).

Romanes, Ethel, *The Story of an English Sister* (London, Longmans, Green, 1918).

Russell, George William Erskine, *The Household of Faith* (London Hodder and Stoughton, 1902).

Russell, George William Erskine, *Leaders of the Church, 1800–1900* (Oxford and London, A. R. Mowbray, 1905).

Russell, George William Erskine, *Dr. Pusey* (Oxford and London A. R. Mowbray, 1907).

Russell, George William Erskine, *Arthur Stanton: A Memoir* (London Longmans, 1917).

Sanders, Charles R., *Coleridge and the Broad Church Movement* (incl. Thomas Arnold) (Durham, N. Carolina, Duke University Press, 1942).

[Sellon, Priscilla Lydia], *Memos Relating to the Society of the Holy Trinity . . .* (London, Terry, 1907).

[Servants of Christ the King, The], *The Servants of Christ the King*, 1960 (*see also* Lloyd, R.).

[Servants of Christ the King, The], *In Company Together*, 1960.

Seymer, Lucy, *Florence Nightingale's Nurses. The Nightingale Training School 1860–1960* (London, Pitman Medical, 1960).

Shepherd, William Richard, *The Benedictines of Caldey Island* (Caldey, The Abbey, 1907).

Shipley, Orby (ed.), *The Church and the World: Essays on Questions of the Day*, first series (London, Longmans, Green, Reader and Dyer, 1866). 'Religious Confraternities'; 'Vows'.

Shipley, Orby (ed.), *The Church and the World: Essays on Questions of the Day*, second series (London, Longmans, Green, Reader and Dyer, 1867). 'Sisterhood Life'.

Shore, John, Baron Teignmouth, *A Letter to the Rev. Christopher Wordsworth . . .* (London, J. Hatchard, 1810).

Shorthouse, J. Henry, *John Inglesant* (London, Macmillan, 1909).

Simmons, Jack, *Southey* (London, Collins, 1945).

Sikes, Thomas of Guisborough, *An Address to Lord Teignmouth . . . Occasioned by his address to the Clergy . . .* (London, F. C. and J. Rivington, 1805).

Sikes, Thomas of Guisborough, *Second Letter to Lord Teignmouth, Occasioned by His Lordship's letter to The Rev. Christopher Wordsworth . . .* (London, J. Hatchard, 1810).

Simpson, William John Sparrow, *The History of the Anglo-Catholic Revival from 1845* (London, Allen and Unwin, 1932).

[Sisterhoods], *Sisterhoods Considered. With remarks upon the Bishop of Brechin's plea for Sisterhoods* (London, Rivingtons, 1850).

[Sisters of Charity], *Sisters of Charity and some visits with them* (London, Joseph Masters, 1855).

Smyth, Charles, *The Church and the Nation* (London, Hodder and Stoughton, 1962).

[Society of St Francis], *The First Twenty-Five Years* (Cerne Abbas, 1947).

[Society of St Francis], *S.S.F.* (Cerne Abbas, 1963).

[Society of St John the Evangelist], *Papers by Mission Priests of the S.S.J.E.* no. 3, Vocation (Oxford, S.S.J.E., 1899).

[Society of the Holy Cross], *An Address to Catholics from the Brethren of the Society of the Holy Cross, May 1869* (London, W. Knott, 1869).

[Society of the Sacred Mission], *Principles* (Kelham, 1909).

[Society of the Sacred Mission], *Kelham. A Statement* (Kelham, 1930).

[Society of the Sisters of Bethany], *The Society of the Sisters of Bethany, 1866–1966* (Bournemouth, 1966).

Southey, Robert, *Sir Thomas More: or, Colloquies on the progress and prospects of Society* (London, 1829).

Stanley, M., *Hospitals and Sisterhoods* (London, John Murray, 1854).

Stephens, W. R. W., *The Life and Letters of Walter Farquhar Hook* (London, Richard Bentley, 1878).

Stevens, Thomas Primmitt, *Father Adderley* (London, T. Werner Laurie, 1943).

Street, Arthur Edmund, *Memoir of George Edmund Street* (London and Edinburgh, John Murray, 1888).

Sykes, Norman, *The English Religious Tradition* (London, S.C.M. Press, 1953).

Tarrant, W. G., *Florence Nightingale as a Religious Thinker* (London, British and Foreign Unitarian Association, 1914).

Tooley, Sarah A., *The Life of Florence Nightingale* (London, S. H. Bousfield, 1904).

Towle, Eleanor A., *John Mason Neale* (London, Longmans, 1906).

Tracy, Alfred Francis Algernon Hanbury (ed.), *Faith and Progress—sermons Preached at the Jubilee of St Barnabas, Pimlico, A.D. 1900* (London, Longmans, 1900).

Trench, Maria, *The Story of Dr. Pusey's Life* (London, Longmans, 1900).

[True Institution of Sisterhood], *The True Institution of Sisterhood: Or, A Message and its Messengers. By L.N.R.*

Voll, Dieter, *Catholic Evangelicalism* (London, Faith Press, 1963).

Wakeling, George, *The Oxford Church Movement* (London, Swan Sonnenschein, 1895).

Walker, Charles, *Three Months in an English Monastery* (London, Murray, 1864).

Wand, John William Charles, *The Second Reform* (London, Faith Press, 1953).

Ward, Maisie, *Father Maturin. A Memoir* (London, Longmans, Green, 1920).

Ward, Maisie, *Young Mr. Newman* (London, Steed and Ward, 1948).

Warner, Robert Townsend, *Marian Rebecca Hughes* (Oxford, printed at the University Press by John Johnson, 1933).

Whibley, Charles, *Lord John Manners and His Friends* (London, W. Blackwood and Sons, 1925).

Wilberforce, Reginald G., *Bishop Wilberforce* (Oxford and London, A. R. Mowbray, 1905).

Williams, Norman Powell and Harris, Charles, *Northern Catholicism. Centenary Studies in the Oxford and Parallel Movements* (London, 1933).

Williams, Thomas Jay, *Priscilla Lydia Sellon* (London, S.P.C.K., 1950).

Williams, Thomas Jay and Campbell, Allan Walter, *The Park Village Sisterhood* (London, S.P.C.K., 1965).

Woodgate, Mildred Violet, *Father Benson, Founder of the Cowley Fathers* (London, Geoffrey Bles, 1953).

Woodgate, Mildred Violet, *Father Congreve of Cowley* (London, S.P.C.K., 1956).

Woodham-Smith, Cecil, *Florence Nightingale* (London and Glasgow, Collins (Fontana), 1964).

Woodward, Ernest Llewellyn, *The Age of Reform, 1815–1870* (Oxford, Clarendon Press, 1938).

Wordsworth, Christopher, *On Sisterhoods and Vows*—second edition, with a Reply to Canon Carter (Lincoln, 1879).

Pusey House Pamphlet Collection:
works on Anglican orders

323 Some account of St Mary's Home for Penitents, at Wantage,
     Berkshire: with an appeal . . . by the Chaplain. (Oxford, John
     Henry Parker, 1852, 29 pp.)

1086 A letter to the Right Hon. Sir John Coleridge, Visitor of the
      House of Mercy, Ditchingham, by the Ven. Hugh W. Jermyn,
      M.A. (dated 'Nettlecombe Rectory, Taunton, July 23rd, 1866')
      11 pp.)

1103 Tracts by the Brethren of the English Order of S. Benedict:
      No. 6 Monasteries in the Church of England, An appeal for the
      Claydon Monks. (Claydon, The Benedictine Brothers, 1863,
      18 pp.)

1732 A vindication, from the Bible and Book of Common Prayer, of
      the Society of the Holy Cross and of those clergy who teach
      confession as the doctrine of the Church of England . . . by a
      priest ordained by one of their order [Bishops of Established
      Church]. (London, Church Printing Company, 1877, 48 pp.)

2107 Sisterhoods on their trial or Protestantism, which? A sermon
      preached at S. Martin's Church, Liverpool . . . 1864, on which
      day a blessing was invoked on S. Martin's Home, and two
      sisters were admitted as probationers . . . by Cecil Wray, M.A.,
      Oxon. (London, G. J. Palmer, 1864, 23 pp.)

2643 Plea for a Missionary Brotherhood in India. A letter addressed
      to the Regius Professor of Pastoral Theology in Oxford, by the
      Rev. G. F. Willis, M.A., Vice-Principal of Cuddesdon Theo-
      logical College. (Oxford and London, James Parker, 1879,
      16 pp.)

3414 An appeal for the House of Mercy, Clewer (dated Lent 1856).
      By Thomas T. Carter. (London, Joseph Master, 1856, 4 pp.)

3415 'My dear Friend, You ask for some result of our "First Five
      Years" work at the House of Mercy . . .' Circular letter from
      T. T. Carter, Clewer, January 1856.

3416 A plea for Religious Societies in parishes, by a clergyman.
      (Oxford and London, John Henry and James Parker, 1857,
      19 pp.)

4756 The first five years of the House of Mercy, Clewer, by the
      Rev. T. T. Carter. (Second edition, London, Joseph Masters,
      185?, 20 pp.)

4622   Exposition of the Beatitudes, as applied to those about to embrace the Religious Life. The Evangelist Library. Edited by the [Cowley] Mission Priests of S. John the Evangelist. (London, J. T. Hayes, n.d., 39 pp.)

5060   A history of St. John's House (Norfolk Street, Strand) with a full account of the circumstances which led to the withdrawal therefrom of the entire Sisterhood and a refutation of the charges made against the Sisters . . . by R. Few (the survivor of its two originators in 1848). (London, W. Skeffington, 1884, 63 pp.)

6241   Revival of Monastic Institutions and their bearing upon society considered with reference to the present condition of the Anglican Church, by the Rev. Diedrich Wackerbarth. (Colchester, W. Totham, 1839, 52 pp.)

6242   An appeal for the formation of a Church Penitentiary, by the Rev. John Armstrong, B.A. (London, John Henry Parker, 1849, 15 pp.)

6243   An essay on Sisterhoods in the English Church, by the Rev. W. E. Sellon [brother of Mother Lydia]. (London, Joseph Masters, 1849, 31 pp.)

6244   Report of the inquiry instituted by the Right Reverend the Lord Bishop of Exeter, as visitor of the Orphans Home, established by the Sisters of Mercy, at Morice Town, Devonport, into the truth of certain statements published in the *Devonport Telegraph*, February 10th, 1849. (Plymouth, Roger Lidstone, 1849, 79 pp. +iv.)

6245   Charity under persecution: A sermon on behalf of the Sisters of Mercy and the orphan's Home, at Devonport, preached in the Church of S. Martin in the Fields, Liverpool, on the second Sunday in Lent, 1849, by the Rev. John Martin, M.A. (London, Joseph Masters, 1849, 18 pp.)

6246   A few words to some of the women of the Church of God in England, by Lydia, the Mother Superior of the Sisters of Mercy of Devonport and Plymouth. (Third edition, London, J. Masters, 1850, 24 pp.)

6247   A plea for Sisterhoods, by the Right Rev. A. P. Forbes, D.C.L., Bishop of Brechin. (Second edition, London, Joseph Masters, 1850, 24 pp.)

6248   A plea for the rights and liberties of Religious Women, with reference to the Bill proposed by Mr. Lacey, by Bishop Ullathorne. (London, Thomas Richardson and Son, 1851, 24 pp.)

6249   A plea for the rights and liberties of women imprisoned for life under the power of priests, in answer to Bishop Ullathorne, by Henry Drummond. (London, T. Bosworth, 1851, 65 pp.)

6250 Miss Sellon and the 'Sisters of Mercy': An exposure of the constitution, rules, religious views, and practical working of their society; obtained through a 'Sister' who has recently seceded, by the Rev. James Spurrell, A.M. (London, Thomas Hatchard, 1852, 41 pp.)

6251 Reply to a tract by the Rev. J. Spurrell . . . containing certain charges concerning the Society of the Sisters of Mercy of Devonport and Plymouth, by the Superior of the Society. (London, Joseph Masters, 1852, 28 pp.)

6252 A rejoinder to the reply of the Superior of the Society of the Sisters of Mercy of Devonport and Plymouth to a pamphlet entitled *Miss Sellon and the 'Sisters of Mercy'*, by the Rev. James Spurrell, A.M. By the same. (London, Thomas Hatchard, 1852, 78 pp.)

6253 Miss Sellon, and the Sisters of Mercy. Further Statement of the Rules, Constitution, and working, of the society called 'The Sisters of Mercy'. Together with an exact review of Miss Sellon's reply, by Diana A. G. Campbell, a novice lately seceded. (London, T. Hatchard, 1852, 36 pp.)

6254 Two letters to the Rev. Edward Coleridge, Eton College, by P. Lydia Sellon and Catherine E., S.M., dated January 14th, 1852, with an appeal for funds by Coleridge. (16 pp.)

6255 A letter to Miss Sellon, Superior of the Society of Sisters of Mercy, at Plymouth, by Henry, Lord Bishop of Exeter. (London, John Murray, 1852, 20 pp.)

6256 Miss Sellon and the Sisters of Mercy. A contradiction of the alleged acts of cruelty exercised by Miss Sellon, and a refutation of certain statements put forth in the tracts of the Rev. Mr. Spurrell, Miss Campbell, and others. With an appendix containing an address from the Sisters of Mercy to the Mother Superior, with her reply, by Commander Sellon, R.N. (Second edition, London, Joseph Masters, 1852, 43 pp.)

6257 Sisters of Mercy, Sisters of Misery: or Miss Sellon in the family; with some remarks on 'A reply to the Rev. James Spurrell'; 'Two letters to the Rev. Edward Coleridge', &c. &c., by the Rev. W. M. Colles, A.B. (Third edition, London, T. Hatchard, 1852, 24 pp.)

6258 Private Confession, Penance, and Absolution, Authoritatively taught in the Church of England. An address published in consequence of some statements contained in a pamphlet written by the Rev. James Spurrell, A.M., . . . also a letter to the Rev. M. Hobart Seymour in reply to some remarks made by him in a lecture on nunneries, by George Rundle Prynne, B.A. (Second edition, London, Joseph Masters, 1852, 28 pp.)

6259   Is it well to institute sisterhoods in the Church of England for the care of female penitents?, by the Rev. Thomas Thellusson Carter, Rector of Clewer, Berks. (Second edition, revised, London, Rivington, n.d., 15 pp.)

6260   The Nunnery Question. A report of the great Catholic meeting held at St Martin's Hall, Long Acre, March 21 1854 . . . (London, Burns and Lambert, 1854, 72 pp.)

6261   Mercy for the fallen. Two sermons in aid of the House of Mercy, Clewer, by the Rev. T. T. Carter, M.A. (London, Joseph Masters, 1856, 30 pp.)

6262   The Rev. J. M. Neale and the Institute of St. Margaret's, East Grinstead. Statement of the Rev. J. Scobell, [Rural Dean of Lewes] . . . &c. (London, Nisbet, 1857, 21 pp.)

6263   A postscript in reply to the Rev. J. Scobell's statement. (London, J. Masters, 1857, pp. 52–9.)

6264   The Lewes Riot, its causes and consequences. A letter to the Lord Bishop of Chichester, by the Rev. J. M. Neale, M.A. (London, Joseph Masters, 1857, 47 pp.)

6265   A letter to the Rev. John M. Neale, by the Rev. John Scobell, M.A. (London, Nisbet, 1857, 24 pp.)

6267   The first ten years of the House of Mercy, Clewer, by the Rev. T. T. Carter, M.A. (London, Joseph Masters, 1861, 40 pp.)

6268   Women's Work. A speech delivered in the Lower House of Convocation on Tuesday, July 9, 1861, by Richard Seymour, M.A. (London, Rivingtons, 1862, 24 pp.)

6269   The Two Ways of Christian Life, by A.S.C. (London, Joseph Masters, 1862, 25 pp.)

6270   Religious Communities of Women in the Early and Medieval Church, by Richard Frederick Littledale, M.A., LL.D. (Second edition, London, Joseph Masters, 1864, 42 pp.)

6271   Fair play for Brother Ignatius. A letter to the Right Reverend the Lord Bishop of London, by the Rev. Edward Stuart. (Second edition, London, Joseph Masters, 1864, 14 pp.)

6272   All Saints' Clergy House, Margaret Street, W. Private and Confidential. Exchange between E. Hoskins and Archbishop of Canterbury on Brotherhoods. (September 1866, 2 pp.)

6273   'Sisterhood' Nurses. A letter addressed to the Governors of St. George's Hospital, by the Rev. William Niven, B.D. (Second edition, London, Hatchard, 1866, 34 pp.)

6274   Reply to the Rev. W. Niven's Letter on Sisterhood Nurses, by Lord Josceline Percy. (London, Rivingtons, 1866, 16 pp.)

6275   The Great Want of the Church. (London, William Skeffington, 1868, 28 pp.)

6276 'We are able to give Dr. Pusey's paper verbatim' [on Sister-
      hoods] 16 in coll.

7402 Are 'Vows of celibacy in Early Life' inconsistent with the Word
      of God? or some remarks on the Lord Bishop of Lincoln's
      letter to the Ven. Sir George Prevost, Bart. entitled 'Sister-
      hoods and Vows' [8032], by the Rev. T. T. Carter. (London,
      Rivingtons, 1878, 24 pp.)

7627 On Guilds, or Brotherhoods, as supplying the Discipline of the
      Church, by William J. Irons, D.D. (London, J. T. Hayes, n.d.,
      24 pp.)

7823 The Religious Life Portrayed for the use of Sisters of Mercy.
      Translated from the French, with Introduction by The Rev.
      R. M. Benson. (London, J. T. Hayes, n.d., 63 pp.)

7837 Manual of the Religious Order of Repentance. Part 1. For the
      use of Brethren living in the world. (London, Joseph Masters,
      n.d., 61 pp.)

7848 A visit to East Grinstead. (London, Joseph Masters, 1865,
      12 pp.)

7852 A 'Sister's' Love: A sermon preached at St. Martin's Church,
      Liverpool . . . the Sunday after the death of Sister Charlotte, by
      Cecil Wray. (London, Rivingtons, 1866, 16 pp.)

8032 On Sisterhoods and Vows. A letter to the Ven. Sir George
      Prevost, Bart, by Christopher Wordsworth, D.D., Bishop of
      Lincoln. (London, Rivingtons, 1878, 27 pp.)

8438 Community of the Holy Cross: short account of its rise and
      history, by Elizabeth, Mother Superior. (n.d.)

8439 Special Appeal on behalf of The Sisters of the Holy Cross and
      their School and orphanage. (n.d.)

8807 The 'Sisters of the Church', and their work, by S.C. (London,
      Judd and Co., 1875, 16 pp.)

8900 Brotherhoods: or Plain Words, dedicated without their per-
      mission to his fellow 'Religious', and the leading men clerical
      and lay, of the Catholic Revival, by Brother Cecil, S.S.J.
      (London, The Church Press Company, 1869, 22 pp.)

9632 A statement of the late proceedings of the Lord Bishop of
      Chichester against the warden of Sackville College, East Grin-
      stead. (London, Joseph Masters, 1853, 26 pp.)

9634 Church Deaconesses. The Revival of the office of Deaconess
      considered; with Practical Suggestions; etc., by the Rev. R. J.
      Hayne, M.A. (London, John Henry and James Parker, 1859,
      16 pp.)

9958 Tracts on the Doctrine and Discipline of the Church, published
      by the Confraternity of the Holy Cross. No. 2. Monks and Nuns.
      (London, G. J. Palmer, n.d., 18 pp.)

10153 Father Ignatius and the Prayer Book. Reprinted from the *Manchester Courier*. (n.d.)

10183 The marvellous escape of 'Sister Lucy', and her awful disclosures respecting New Hall Convent, Boreham, Essex. (Fifth edition, London, Protestant Evangelical Mission, n.d., 24 pp.)

10551 On the establishment of an Oratory in London, by the Rev. Orby Shipley, M.A. (Third edition, London, Joseph Masters, 1871, 52 pp.)

11522 Education by Nuns: its failure and injurious tendencies. (London, Protestant Alliance, 1890, 8 pp.)

11968 An Awful Exposure of the Awful Disclosures of those two lying females Rebecca Reed and Maria Monk. Preface by John Bremner, R.C. Clergyman, Paisley, 15th April, 1836. (8 pp.)

11979 The Spiritual Life, a sermon preached on the Feast of St. Michael and All Angels, 1875, by the Reverend Father Harper, S.J., on the occasion of opening the chapel at the Convent of Poor Clares, Laurence Street, York. (London, Burns and Oates, n.d., 23 pp.)

12000 The Nunnery Question; or cases mentioned in the late debate on the inspection of nunneries. With authorities, and an outline of the Bill . . . by the Honorary Secretary of the Protestant Alliance, June 1853. (Third edition, London, 16 pp.)

12299 Protestant Alliance Tract No. LXI. Anglican Sisterhoods, sgnd. Charles Bird, Secretary. (London, Protestant Alliance, n.d., 4 pp.)

12511 Circumstances connected with the debate in the House of Commons on the Monastic and Conventional Institutions Inquiry Bill. July 2, 1873. (London, George Slater, n.d., 24 pp.)

12553 Revival of Conventual Institutions No. II. (Testimonies continued) pp. 255-60, n.d. [Article from unknown periodical.]

12554 Protestant Sisters of Charity; a letter addressed to the Lord Bishop of London, developing a plan for improving the arrangements at present existing for administering Medical advice and visiting the Sick Poor. (London, Charles Knight, 1826, 38 pp.)

12781 A Sister's Work: a sermon preached in substance at All Saints', Margaret Street, . . . 1869, by H. P. Liddon, M.A. (London, Rivingtons, 1869, 32 pp.)

12789 The Fast at the river Ahava. A sermon preached on the occasion of the opening of the New Chapel, S. Margaret's, East Grinstead, on S. Margaret's Day, 1883, by the Rev. L. Alison, M.A. chaplain of the community. (Cambridge, J. Palmer, 1883, 16 pp.)

12899 The Orphan's Home, for the orphan daughters of British seamen and soldiers, Morice-town, Devonport, under the patronage of the Lord Bishop of Exeter. Opened A.D. 1848. Reprinted from the *Guardian*. (London, William Odhams, 1849, 24 pp.)

12905 Nunneries. A lecture delivered in the Assembly Rooms, Bath, on Wednesday, April 21, 1852, by the Rev. Hobart Seymour, M.A. (London, Seeley's, n.d., 57 pp.)

12997 Brotherhoods. (An article from 'Church Work'—the monthly paper of the Guild of S. Alban), pp. 193–5, n.d. [Jan. 1859].

13575 Epistle of Ignatius, the Monk, to his disciples in the Lord Jesus . . . written from the Benedictine Monastery of the Church of England, in Norwich, in the Year of Salvation, 1865. (London, G. J. Palmer, 1865, 24 pp.)

13591 A proposal for the establishment of a Female Penitentiary in Norfolk or Suffolk, in connexion with the Church Penitentiary Association. (Norwich, Charles Muskett, 1853, 24 pp.)

13637 Convents. A Review of two lectures on this subject, by the Rev. M. Hobart Seymour . . . by His Eminence Cardinal Wiseman, Archbishop of Westminster, 1852. (London, Thomas Richardson and Son, n.d., 63 pp.)

13924 The Catholic Church of England and what she Teaches. A lecture by Father Ignatius . . . delivered in the Corn Exchange, Manchester . . . (Manchester, John Heywood, 1864, 40 pp.)

13985 Monks and Nuns. A lecture in reply to two lectures of 'Father Ignatius, O.S.B.' . . . by the Rev. W. A. Darby. (Manchester, John Heywood, 1864, 48 pp.)

14101 Ignatius, Monk of the Order of S. Benedict . . . to the Reverend Father Darby, Catholic Priest of the Diocese of Manchester. (Manchester, John Heywood, n.d., 32 pp.)

70887 House of Mercy, Clewer, near Windsor Eton, E. P. Williams printer, n.d., 24 pp. [contains letter to Bish. of Ox. dated 1850] [Prospectus by T. T. Carter].

70976 An account for the year 1852, of St. Mary's home for Penitents, at Wantage, Berkshire, and an appeal for assistance . . . by the Chaplain. (Oxford, John Henry Parker, 1853, 30 pp.)

71022 Report for the year 1853, of St. Mary's Home for Penitents, at Wantage, Berkshire; and a renewed appeal for its enlargement, by the Chaplain. (Oxford and London, John Henry Parker, 1854, 12 pp.)

71146 St. Mary's House for Penitents, Wantage, Berkshire: its first nine years; . . . with a few remarks on the work of Refuges as distinct from Penitentiaries, by the Chaplain. (Oxford, John Henry and James Parker, 1859, 44 pp.)

71164 A reply to the postscript of the Rev. John M. Neale . . . by the Rev. John Scobell, M.A. (London, Nisbet, 1858, 24 pp.)

71403 Sisterhoods in Asylums, by W. A. F. Browne, F.R.C.S.E., F.R.R.S.E., &c., Commissioner in Lunacy, Scotland. (London, J. E. Adland, 1866, 25 pp.)

71474 A statement of the object of the Order of Repentance, and of the qualifications and duties of the brethren. (London, Charles Cull, 1868, 12 pp.)

71591 Convent Inquiry. Religious Disabilities. Letter from Charles N. Newdegate, Esq., M.P., read at the meeting on Tuesday, April 9, 1872, at the Cutlers' Hall, Sheffield. (London, Cornelius Buck, 1872, 15 pp.)

71592 An Order of Rites, for the Assumption of the Religious habit, and for making a profession. Venice: 1612. Translated from the Latin. (Oxford, 1872, 42 pp.)

71823 Augusta: or, the refuted slanders of thirty years ago on the late Miss Sellon and her Sisters, once more refuted . . . by Mary Anne H. Nicholl. (London, Remington, 1878, 32 pp.)

71883 A Speech delivered in the Sheldonian Theatre, Oxford, on Monday, May 10, 1880, by Sir Richard Temple . . . in furtherance of the Oxford Mission to Calcutta. (Oxford, James Parker, n.d., 8 pp.)

72013 Vocation or the call of the Divine Master to a Sister's life, by the Rev. Charles C. Grafton. (New York, E. and J. B. Young, 1886, 8 pp.) [Advert for book published under this title and extract from chapter II.]

72064 Letters &c., from the Rev. E. B. Pusey, D.D. in *The Convent Magazine*, August 1888, pp. 265–7. (Oxford, Convent of The Annunciation, 1888.)

72207 The history of Ascot Priory and Memorials of Dr. Pusey. By the author of *Charles Lowder*. (London, 'The Churchwoman' (reprint), 1897, 24 pp.)

72216 The History of a Religious Idea, by Herbert Kelly, Director of the Society of the Sacred Mission. (London, Simpkin, Marshall, Hamilton, Kent, 1898, 182 pp.)

72216 A Society of the Sacred Mission. Nov. 1899. (A Pamphlet explaining the aims and organization of the S.S.M., contained in Pamphlet 72216.)

72269 Community of St. Peter. Founded A.D. 1861. Associate's Rule. St. Peter's Home and Sisterhood, Kilburn, 1900.

73738 Office of Installation of the Superior of a Religious House. With Episcopal Sanction. (n.d., 7 pp.)

73743 Thoughts on Christian Brotherhoods. (n.d., 4 pp.)

73267 Chronicle of Convocation. 1878 Report on Sisterhoods. (Viz Convocation Reports 19th Century.)

72484 Several reasons for establishing an Order of Christian Brothers for the Christian education of children, and especially for teaching them in parish schools, by George A. White, Baltimore in Maryland. (n.d., 34 pp.)

72777 University studies; how to be promoted on Christian principles. An address read before the Brotherhood of the Holy Trinity, at the General Chapter, June 1859. H. P. Liddon. (Oxford, privately, 1859, 22 pp.)

72782 Two addresses by the Rev. H. P. Liddon, M.A., read before the Brotherhood of the Holy Trinity at the General Chapter, June 1859, May 1861. (Oxford, privately, n.d., 34 pp.)

72848 The Fourteenth Year of St. Mary's Home for Penitents, at Wantage, Berkshire; with an appeal . . . by the Chaplain. (Oxford and London, J. H. and J. Parker, 1864, 13 pp.)

72865 The principles of Brotherhood. An address read before the Annual Chapter of the Brotherhood of the Holy Trinity, June 14, 1865, by R. M. Benson. (n.d., 19 pp.)

73607 Retrospect, being an address to the members of the Con- fraternity of the Most Holy Trinity by the Rev. W. R. Churton at the Annual Chapter, June 9, 1896. (Cambridge, J. Palmer, n.d., 35 pp.)

73713 Nature and objects of the Society of the Holy Cross. (n.d., 4 pp.)

73778 Community of S. John Baptist, Clewer. Nature and Objects. (n.d., 12 pp.)

73906 The Cowley Evangelist. March–May 1891. (pp. 33–80.)

74137 Sermon by Dr. Pusey. The Feast of the Holy Angels. (unpub., n.d., 3 pp.)

74225 Ascot Hospital for Convalescents and Incurables. (n.d., 4 pp.)

Name Index

Abbey, C. J. 114, 134–5
Abel-Smith, B. 281, 287
Acland, T. D. 171
Adderley, J. G. 310
Aiken, G. M. 166
Ainslie, Prebendary A. C. 200
Aitkin, Mr 304
Albert of Pisa 96
Alison, L. 328
Allchin, A. M. 109–10, 124, 133, 136, 145, 152, 154, 162, 168, 175–6, 178, 183–8, 195, 201–3, 211, 225–6, 246, 267–8, 310
Ambrose of Milan, St 24
Anderson, E. G. 276
Andrew, Father (see *Hardy, H. E.*)
Andrewes, L. 150, 162–4
Anson, P. F. 21, 29–30, 56–60, 76, 83, 103, 162, 168, 186–7, 193, 225, 227, 234, 249–50, 267–9, 310
Antony of Egypt, St 20, 24, 51
Aquinas, St Thomas 177
Armstrong, J. 172, 324
Arnold, T. 141, 179, 183, 310
Ashwell, A. R. 188, 226, 268, 310
Athanasius, St 24
Attwater, D. 157, 185, 193, 225, 310
Augustine of Hippo, St 24, 27, 46, 113, 150
Ayckbowm, E. 209, 211, 235, 310

Baker, J. E. 311
Baldwin, M. 38, 42, 58, 83
Balleine, G. R. 118, 124, 135–7
Baring-Gould, S. 155, 185, 228–9, 266, 305, 311
Barnes, A. S. 41–2
Basil 'the Great', St 24
Baxter, R. 136
Benedict VIII, Pope 91
Benedict XIV, Pope 63
Benedict of Nursia, St 8, 16–17, 21, 25, 27, 31, 35–41, 44–6, 53–4, 57, 60, 66, 90–5, 101–2, 152
Benham, W. 294, 309, 314
Bennett, A. H. 214–15, 226, 270, 273, 293, 298, 311

Bennett, F. 311
Bennett, W. J. E. 299, 308, 311
Benson, A. C. 226, 311
Benson, E. W. 166, 200, 209–11, 235, 311
Benson, R. H. 166, 317
Benson, R. M. 10, 136, 175–6, 192, 197, 208, 223–4, 227, 238–9, 251–3, 257, 261, 264, 267, 269–70, 311, 322, 327, 331
Berlière, U. 90, 101
Bernard of Clairvaux, St 3, 35, 40, 55, 78, 93–4
Bertouche, B. de 311
Bigg, C. 269, 311
Binns, L. E. Elliott 109, 124, 133, 135–6, 311
Biot, F. 158, 186, 243, 256–7, 268, 311
Blomfield, C. J. 172, 192, 217, 220–1, 299
Blunt, R. F. L. 203
Body, G. 106, 202–3, 255, 260
Bona, Cardinal 51
Bouyer, L. 57
Bowden, J. W. 244
Bramhall, J. 134, 163–4
Brandreth, H. R. T. 311–12
Bremner, J. 328
Brewer, E. D. C. 132
Bridges, R. S. 312
Brilioth, Y. T. 134, 137–8, 150, 184, 309, 312
Briscoe, J. F. 312
Brodrick, J. 57
Browne, E. G. K. 312
Browne, E. H. 149, 200, 276
Browne, W. A. F. 330
Bucher, F. 57
Bull, P. B. 206–7, 225, 256, 262, 269, 312
Burne, K. E. 166, 187, 312
Burnet, G. 164, 186
Butler, A. J. 226–7, 312
Butler, Dom. C. 30, 49, 56, 59, 61, 94–5, 102–3
Butler, W. J. 167, 200, 219, 221–2, 226, 245–6, 272, 277, 283, 306, 312, 323, 329, 331

Subject Index